RECKONINGS *and* RECONSTRUCTIONS

Southern Photography
from the Do Good Fund

edited by **Jeffrey Richmond-Moll**

essays by **Jasmine Amussen, Rosalind Bentley, W. Ralph Eubanks, Grace Elizabeth Hale, Lauren Henkin, Jeffrey Richmond-Moll, RaMell Ross, Alan F. Rothschild Jr.,** *and* **Jeff Whetstone**

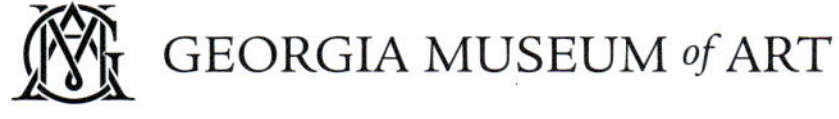 GEORGIA MUSEUM *of* ART | 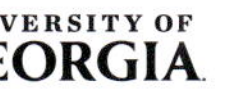 UNIVERSITY OF GEORGIA 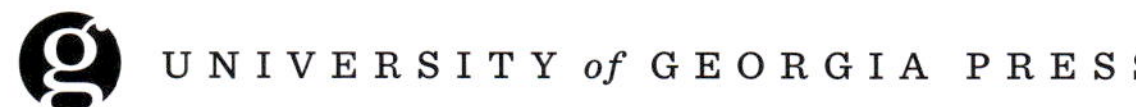 UNIVERSITY *of* GEORGIA PRESS

Published by the Georgia Museum of Art, University of Georgia, and the University of Georgia Press.
All rights reserved. No part of this book may be reproduced without the written consent of the publishers.
W. Ralph Eubanks retains the copyright to his essay.

Printed in Canada in an edition of 1500 by Friesens.
Design: Noelle Shuck
Department of Publications: Hillary Brown
Freelance editor: Lauren Walker
Museum interns: Reif Evans, Josie Lipton, Kaitlyn Page, Mae Ronaldo, Frances Redwine,
Ciel Rodriguez, Mikayla Tribble

Library of Congress Cataloging-in-Publication Data
Names: Do Good Fund, Inc., author. | Richmond-Moll, Jeffrey, editor. |
Amussen, Jasmine, writer of supplementary textual content. | Bentley,
Rosalind, writer of supplementary textual content. | Eubanks, W. Ralph,
1957- writer of supplementary textual content. | Hale, Grace Elizabeth,
writer of supplementary textual content. | Henkin, Lauren, 1974- writer
of supplementary textual content. | Ross, RaMell, writer of
supplementary textual content. | Rothschild, Alan F., 1960- writer of
supplementary textual content. | Whetstone, Jeff, 1968- writer of
supplementary textual content. | Georgia Museum of Art, editor.
Title: Reckonings and reconstructions : Southern photography from the Do
Good Fund / edited by Jeffrey Richmond-Moll ; essays by Jasmine Amussen,
Rosalind Bentley, W. Ralph Eubanks, Grace Elizabeth Hale, Lauren Henkin,
Jeffrey Richmond-Moll, RaMell Ross, Alan F. Rothschild Jr., and Jeff
Whetstone.
Description: Athens, GA : Georgia Museum of Art, University of Georgia :
University of Georgia Press, [2022] | Summary: "This exhibition and
accompanying catalogue are the first large-scale survey of the Do Good
Fund's remarkable and sweeping collection of photography made in the
South from the 1950s to the present. Since its founding in 2012, the Do
Good Fund has built a museum-quality collection of photography that
charts a visual narrative of the ever-changing American South. The
collection includes images by more than 25 Guggenheim Fellows, five
Magnum Photographers and two Henri Cartier-Bresson Award winners as well
as images by lesser-known or emerging photographers from the region. In
part a survey of the art and artists within Do Good's holdings, the
exhibition is also and more crucially a scholarly investigation of
southern photography since World War II"-- Provided by publisher.
Identifiers: LCCN 2022026962 | ISBN 9781946657145 (hardback)
Subjects: LCSH: Photography, Artistic--Exhibitions. | Photography--Southern
States--Exhibitions. | Do Good Fund, Inc.--Photograph
collections--Exhibitions. | Southern States--Social life and
customs--Exhibitions.
Classification: LCC TR645.A842 G4434 2022 | DDC
779/.99750074758473--dc23/eng/20220718
LC record available at https://lccn.loc.gov/2022026962
978-1-9466-5714-5.

TABLE OF CONTENTS

5
Foreword
William Underwood Eiland

6
Collector's Note
Alan F. Rothschild Jr.

10
Reckonings and Reconstructions
Jeffrey Richmond-Moll

18
Fables of the Reconstruction
W. Ralph Eubanks

24
A Woman is a Nation
Jasmine Amussen

30
Southern Rites: Religion, Ritual, and Communal Identity in Southern Photography
Jeffrey Richmond-Moll

42
The Plant Hardiness Zone
Jeff Whetstone

48
For the Nourishment of our Bodies
Rosalind Bentley

54
Slangless
RaMell Ross

60
Seeing the Athens Scene: Photography and Alternative Culture
Grace Elizabeth Hale

66
On Sacred Terrain
Lauren Henkin

72
Plates

With texts by Shelby Lee Adams, Rob Amberg, Rachel Boillot, Rosie Brock, William Christenberry, Dennis Darling, Carolyn Drake, Matt Eich, Jill Frank, Preston Gannaway, William K. Greiner, Alex Harris, Kevin Kline, Paul Kwilecki, Molly Lamb, Baldwin Lee, Deborah Luster, Elizabeth Matheson, Andrea Morales, Gordon Parks, Tamara Reynolds, Jerry Siegel, Rylan Steele, Mark Steinmetz, Brooke C. White, and Susan Worsham

236
List of Plates

242
Author Biographies

SPONSORS

The Wyeth Foundation for American Art

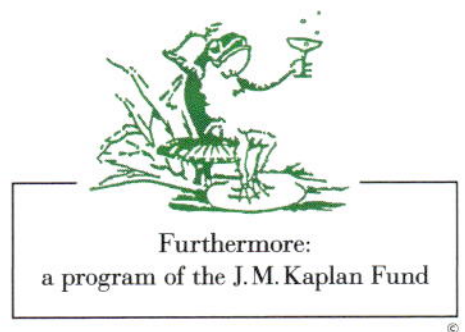

The Bradley Hale Fund for Southern Studies

The W. Newton Morris Charitable Foundation

The Friends of the Georgia Museum of Art

VENUES

Georgia Museum of Art, University of Georgia
October 8, 2022–January 8, 2023

Chrysler Museum of Art
August 11, 2023–January 7, 2024

Lowe Art Museum, University of Miami
February 8–May 18, 2024

Figge Art Museum
June 15–September 8, 2024

FOREWORD

MUCH DEBATE IN CRITICAL WRITING ABOUT PHOTOGRAPHY has centered on its truthfulness, whether the captured subject is transformed by the image-making into a sort of visual artifice. These works from the Do Good Fund may inspire similar discussion, but, regardless of the chatter, these pictures—and I purposefully use that word—are, as Do Good founder Alan Rothschild remarks, "about" something or someone, as in offering context, narrative, and a goad to imagination and to empathy. Southerners, and I am one, will find similar familiarities and consonances with these photographs as I do. They are invitations to embroidered truth.

We thank Alan Rothschild for this opportunity to do good things through reflection on images of the people, the places, the myths, *and* the realities of the South from these talented and articulate photographers. Alan was chair of our Board of Advisors at the Georgia Museum of Art, and we knew well his enthusiasm for the fine arts, where he firmly and decidedly places photography as a medium for delivering and inspiring veracity. Our funders have offered essential help with this project and we thank vociferously the Wyeth Foundation for American Art, the Furthermore Foundation, and the Bradley Hale Fund for Southern Studies at the University of Georgia Press, as well as the museum's Friends and the W. Newton Morris Charitable Foundation.

We are particularly glad that the exhibition's partners—the Chrysler Museum of Art, the Lowe Art Museum, and the Figge Art Museum—will bring the good news of the Do Good Fund to their communities for enjoyment, for analysis, and perhaps for debate. If anything, the project reveals the South not as a monolithic, homogeneous realm of lock-step cultural thought, but a region of various, divergent, and heterogeneous awareness and artistry, in short, a region where documents, reports, dispatches, and pictures from a polyphonic land use varied voices to tell stories of resistance and redemption, legend and (perhaps its antonym) truth.

— *William Underwood Eiland*
Director, Georgia Museum of Art, University of Georgia

COLLECTOR'S NOTE

TEN YEARS AGO, THE DO GOOD FUND acquired its first image, *Garlic*, by East Texas photographer Keith Carter (fig. 1). A few months later, four Columbus State University art students organized the fund's inaugural exhibition of twenty-five photographs—nearly the entire collection at the time—in a vacant storefront in our hometown of Columbus, Georgia. Do Good's collection now numbers nearly 800 pieces, and these photographs have been included in dozens of exhibitions in seven states.

During its first decade, Do Good's singular focus has been to build a museum-quality, public collection of photographs taken in the American South since World War II, by both well-known and emerging photographers. While the fund currently holds the work of twenty-five Guggenheim Fellows and five Magnum photographers, we are equally proud of the images by early and mid-career photographers in the collection. This democratic approach to acquiring photographs is also consistent with Do Good's mission to make the work widely accessible through collaborations with regional museums, nonprofit galleries, and nontraditional venues.

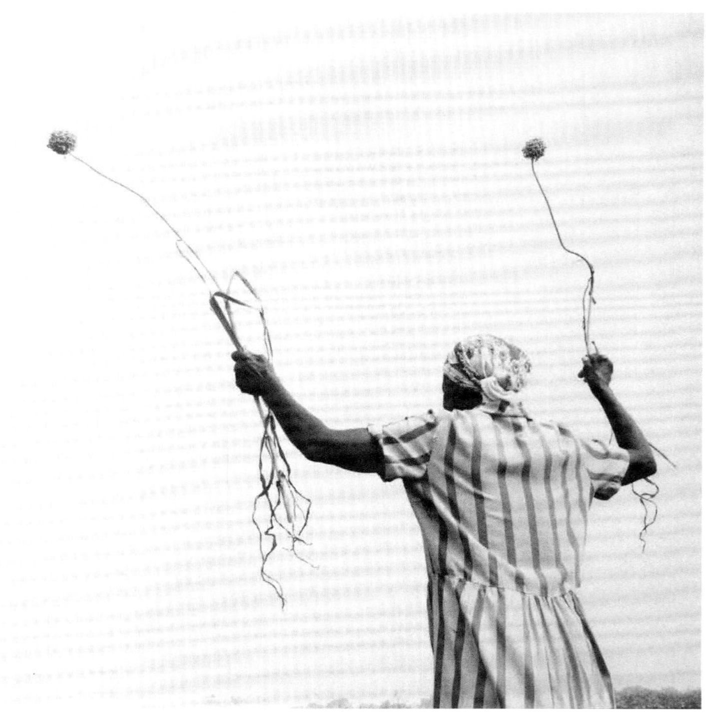

FIG. 1. Keith Carter, *Garlic*, 1991 (plate 20)

My personal interest in southern photography is rooted in a high school southern literature class that introduced me to Walker Evans's photographs in *Let Us Now Praise Famous Men*. Growing up in Columbus in the 1960s and 1970s, I did not have to go far to see scenes like those Evans documented in Hale County, Alabama, a generation earlier. While Atlanta, Charlotte, and the fast-growing southern coastal communities created a visual consciousness of the contemporary South in the 1970s and 1980s, the landscape Evans depicted in his iconic photographs still occupied much of the region, as his former student Baldwin Lee documented in his own photographic travels five decades later.

While pursuing a history degree at the University of Virginia, I found that a single Mathew Brady studio image of the Battle of Gettysburg or Evans's Great Depression–era portraits of Alabama tenant farmers told me more about the history of those events than chapters of a textbook. To me, each of these photographs truly was the equivalent of a thousand words. I also discovered that, as a white Georgian born six years after *Brown v. Board of Education*, the South's recent history was much more complicated than my prior education or life experience had revealed. As the individual images and stories in the Do Good collection bring to light, it is a place of bewildering contrasts, with great environmental beauty and degradation and vast economic opportunity and systemic oppression existing side by side throughout the region.

At its core, the Do Good Fund is a collection of visual stories of the contemporary American South. These stories are told by an increasingly diverse group of photographic storytellers, men and women, persons of color, from varying regions, cultural backgrounds, and sexual orientations. They tell us about life and death, work and play, in urban, rural, and suburban settings, from the Piney Woods of East Texas to coal-mining communities in West Virginia to the clear springs and sandy beaches of Florida.

In my mind, most of the images in the collection are *about*, rather than just *of*, something. What attracted me to Carter's *Garlic* was more than just the magic moment he captured of the woman swinging two freshly harvested garlic plants overhead. It was also the style of her dress and fragment of landscape at the bottom margin of the picture, both clues to a larger story just beyond the frame.

My hope is that the images in the collection will be viewed not only as worthy examples of the photographic craft, but also as windows through which to discover more about ourselves and the place where we live. This is important, because as Eudora Welty said, "one place comprehended can make us understand other places better."

— Alan F. Rothschild Jr.
Founder, Do Good Fund

ESSAYS

RECKONINGS AND RECONSTRUCTIONS

Jeffrey Richmond–Moll

IN THE AMERICAN SOUTH, THE LAND REMEMBERS. It remembers for us and in spite of us. Photographers of the region often train their lenses upon the land precisely because of its power as a repository for memory, confronting us with what we have long forgotten or ignored. Here, their pictures say, is a space to engage with a past that is at once enigmatic and inescapable, though often steeped in trauma and seemingly always enduring growing pains toward healing and reconstruction. In a photograph from his recent series *What Has Been Will Be Again* (fig. 1), Jared Ragland points our gaze downward onto the earth where the Alabama state capitol building once stood, the ground glistening with glittery detritus in tragic irony. On this spot, apocryphal accounts say, Creek chief Yoholo-Micco lamented the dispossession and genocide of Indigenous peoples with a kind of romantic resignation: "I come here, brothers, to see the great house of Alabama and the men who make laws and say farewell in brotherly kindness before I go to the far west." This is soil that was stolen. This is the soil where we have buried suffering and that southern photographers have tilled to expose that pain. And, in glimmering moments, this is the soil where seeds, planted over centuries of toil, might one day burst forth into fruits of renewal and reconciliation. As nature groans for restoration, photographers have sought to lay bare resilient bonds of community, bold acts of joy, and moments of breathless exuberance.

Reckonings and Reconstructions offers the opportunity to traverse these landscapes richly contoured by tension and contradiction. This book and the accompanying exhibition are the first large-scale survey of southern photography from the Do Good Fund's sweeping photographic holdings. Established in 2012, Do Good has built a museum-quality collection of photography that charts a visual narrative of the ever-changing American South. In recent years, the fund has prioritized acquisitions of photographs by women artists and artists of color, and fostered the professional growth of young photographers through a purchase prize and an artist-in-residence program, which supported Ragland's recently completed series last year. As the fund continues to collect and support working photographers, this catalogue represents a snapshot in time, featuring 125 photographs by 73 artists from the collection, diverse in gender, race, ethnicity, and region.[1]

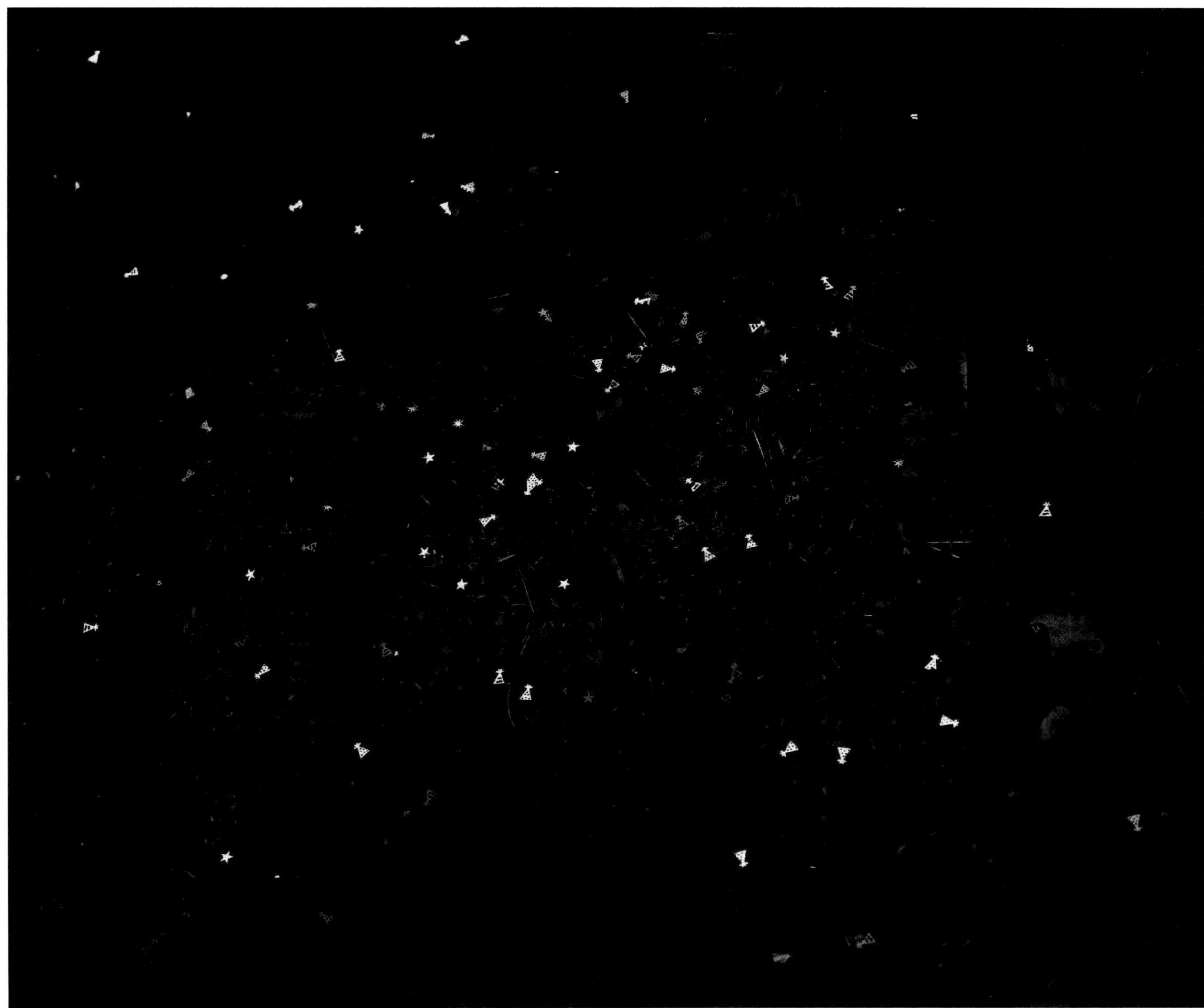

FIG. 1. Jared Ragland (b. 1977), *Tuscaloosa, Tuscaloosa County, Alabama. Glitter scattered on ruins of the former Alabama state capitol building,* 2021. Archival pigment print, 21 × 24 ½ inches. The Do Good Fund, Inc., 2022–7.

While in part a survey of the Do Good's collection, this catalogue is also, and more crucially, a scholarly investigation of southern photography since World War II. Here, "southern photography" is also a term held loosely—a porous classification evolving over generations and across the popular imagination. For photographers and critics alike, the landscape has offered a visual proving ground for defining what and where "the South" might be. These artists often disregard traditional geopolitical boundaries like state borders or historical artifacts like the Mason–Dixon line. Instead, their work calls to mind more organic, less anthropocentric markers, such as what geographers and naturalists have termed the "kudzu line." This invasive vine, whose creeping shoots and tendrils crawl across the book's cover, was introduced to the South in the early twentieth century as a soil stabilizer across deforested swaths of Georgia, Alabama, and Mississippi. Yet the so-called "Miracle vine," which was thought capable of resurrecting a "washed-out anemic gullied" landscape ravaged by the monocultures of the slavery and post-Reconstruction economy, would become an archetype for invasive species in the United States as nature retaliated against human mismanagement.[2] The kudzu line—this creeping vine-like boundary, seemingly always advancing—also suggests that, on a warming planet of unseasonable weather and shifting migration patterns, the South is constantly encroaching on the North. Perhaps it offers a metaphor for our growing understanding of the complicity throughout US history of northern politicians and entrepreneurs in purportedly "southern" problems like chattel slavery.

Rather than demarcating a "South," this project is guided by two key concepts, as the southernisms in its title suggest. The photographs assembled here are reckonings. They contend with the past, they tally and give an account, they surmise, and they assert that change must come. Photographs from Kristine Potter's *Dark Waters* series—acquired by Do Good too late to appear in the show—underscore the "feedback loop" between nature and southern folklore, particularly within the region's tradition of murder ballads. "Many of those songs recount the murder of a woman at the hands of a man, whose body is left submerged in water," Potter observes. By pointing to unrepented histories of violence against women in the region that are often hiding in plain sight, photographs like *Deep River (where Naomi was drowned)* (fig. 2) seek to lift female victims from their violent fates and resurrect their lives.[3]

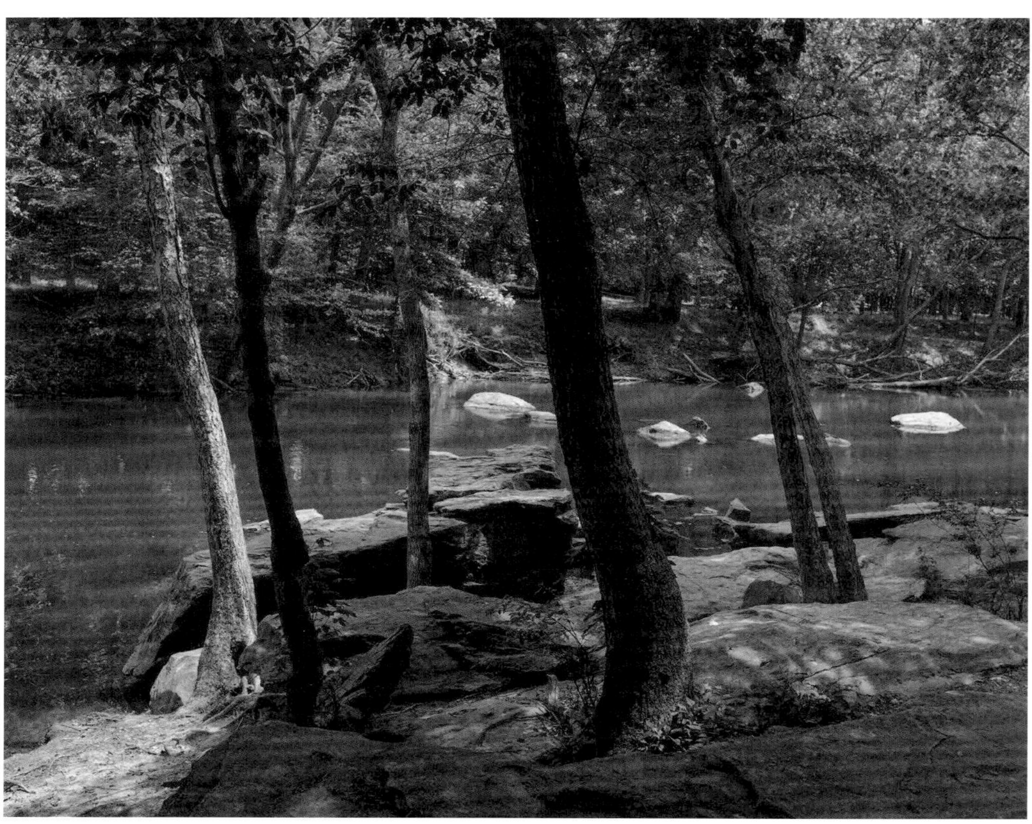

FIG. 2. Kristine Potter (b. 1977), *Deep River (where Naomi was drowned)*, 2019. Gelatin silver print, 20 × 25 inches. The Do Good Fund, Inc., 2021–22.

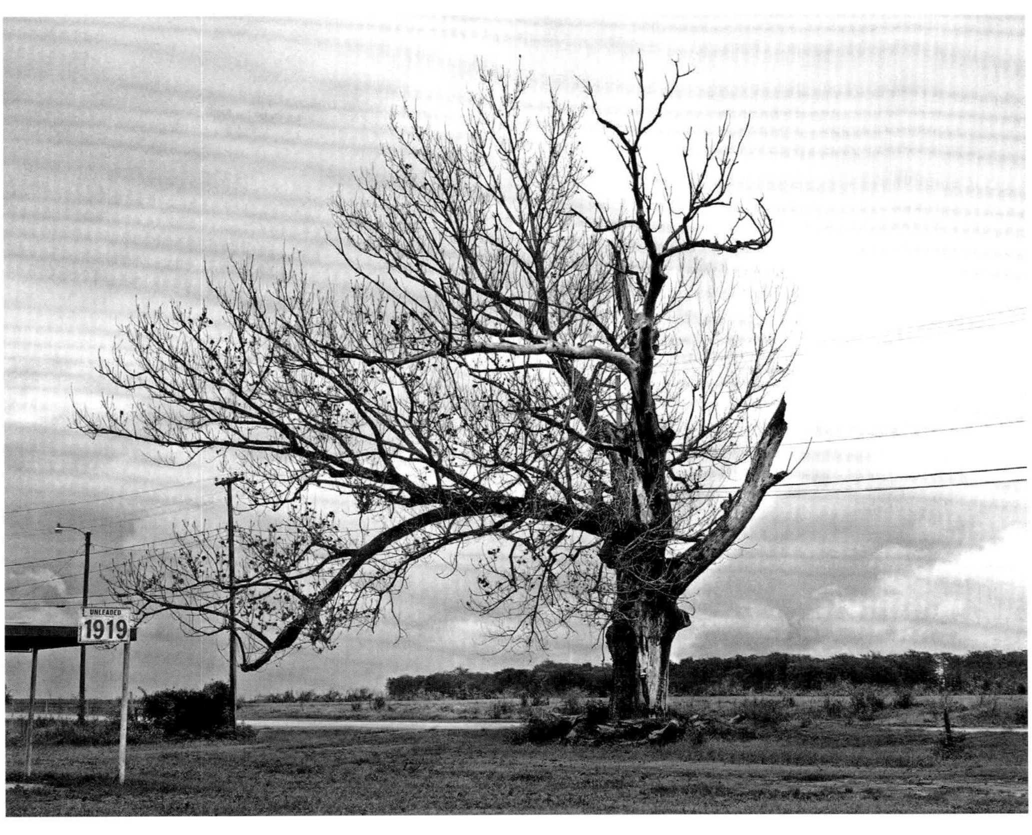

FIG. 3. Trent Bozeman (b. 1992), *Hanging Tree*, 2021. Inkjet print, 16 × 20 inches. The Do Good Fund, Inc., 2021–88.

The photographs in this exhibition are also reconstructions. They note the failed efforts to reconstruct this region throughout US history, they mount a renewed campaign of restoration and repair, and they imagine a world as it ought to be. Trent Bozeman's work—also a late addition to Do Good's collection—acknowledges the possibilities for photography to build communities. Produced in the small Arkansas Delta town of Elaine, where he founded a summer photography program for children, *Hanging Tree* (fig. 3) alludes to the deadliest race massacre in Arkansas history. In 1919, white mobs, aided by federal troops, murdered hundreds of Black sharecroppers from the community. Split in two—half scarred and splintered, half alive with outstretched boughs—Bozeman's tree symbolizes both memories of a violent past and the possibility of regeneration. Here, as with any process of reconstruction, regrowth unfolds without neglecting history, laying bare its scars. The sign for unleaded gas, priced at $1.919, also precludes any possibility of forgetting, just as the various trees the community has planted over the decades in honor of the massacre's victims become a place on which to hang both memory and hope.

Over the past decade, survey exhibitions of southern photography have focused almost exclusively on the work of twenty-first-century photographers—or on images of "the newest New South," as stated in one recent catalogue.[4] What rings ever more clearly at this moment in our nation's history is that we cannot understand the present realities and identities of the American South—be they legacies of racial injustice, the indelible marks of the Confederacy on the built environment, or the impact of ecological recklessness—without a thorough grounding in the region's past, including its photographic traditions. We also aim to reach beyond the American South, acknowledging that southernness is a shared sensibility rather than a consistent culture rooted in a specific geography. Consequently, visions of southern culture vary widely based on the locations and compositions of the people imagining the region.

In the spirit of recent exhibitions like *Southern Accent: Seeking the American South in Contemporary Art*, this project approaches the South as an open-ended question, investigating southern realities and mythologies in thematic fashion.[5] Specifically, the exhibition unfolds across six central themes: land, labor, law and protest, food, ritual, and kinship. These themes are inherently expansive and internally paradoxical. In this way, the project raises key questions that identify and problematize fixed ideas of an "American South" and "southern photography." For the purposes of the book, I have preferred to interweave these themes more fluidly and organically across the essays and artist commentaries that follow.

In "Land," a range of photographs articulates the fragile interface between nature and culture in the South. Paul Kwilecki's loggers (plate 62) suggest a kinship between these workers and the landscape while alluding to the extractive drive historically associated with the economy of slavery in the region. Meanwhile, on the seemingly innocuous space of a playground (plate 59), Stacy Kranitz points to the ravages of settlement and sprawl, as well as the disproportionate impact of environmental degradation on marginalized communities—or what Rob Nixon describes as the slow, often invisible ecological violence wrought upon disempowered populations around the world.[6] Imperceptible in the photograph, the insidious and otherwise unseen environmental threats become clear through its title.

In "Labor," we find photographers reckoning with long, deeply painful histories of enslaved and incarcerated labor in the region, as in Elizabeth Matheson's *Slave Quarters* (plate 83). Others, like Debbie Fleming Caffery (plate 16), string together histories of quotidian labor, creativity, and caretaking, suggesting that small acts of stewardship and creation can collectively resist long-standing forms of oppression and erasure. Such photographs also upset the problematic power dynamics of the camera, which has historically exacerbated otherness and more deeply entrenched exploitative systems.

In "Law and Protest," we see how photographs have intervened in both existing legal structures and acts of resistance from the civil rights era to Black Lives Matter. Gordon Parks's *Outside Looking In* (plate 94) illuminates how "the myth of Blackness aged into fact and grew into laws [and] evolved from there to become tacit."[7] These photographs reveal how the pernicious inequalities of southern identities became codified and concretized in law. Images from Sheila Pree Bright's *#1960Now* series (plates 11 and 12) highlight the tensions of enforcing such laws in the South and underscore the long road toward restitution and reconstruction.

In "Food," photographers conjure the rich traditions of southern foodways and cuisine, which have fostered some of the most coherent notions of regional identity. And yet, as Baldwin Lee's *Beans* reveals (plate 72), food justice has played a key role in southern photography. These and other photographs emphasize the cultural identities that intertwine with histories of agriculture and cuisine and the disparities between abundance and lack that define southern food systems. Carolyn Drake's *Mexican Grocery* (plate 28) also shows how foodways can map complex patterns of migration in the long history of the South, from the African diaspora across the Middle Passage to the industries dependent on Central and South American labor and beyond.

In "Ritual," we find photographs that capture southern community and identity through civic ceremonies and religious rites. Here, perhaps most clearly, we discover how southernness is "an emotional idea" that requires constant performance and reinscription.[8] In William Christenberry's *China Grove* (plate 22), institutional religion appears embedded in—even inextricable from—the red clay of the region. In Andrea Morales's *Southern Heritage Classic Parade* (plate 87), we see a dynamic example of how communities use rituals to fashion themselves and preserve or revive shared traditions.

Finally, in "Kinship" we witness how photography as a medium has signaled exclusion and estrangement, yet also relationship and belonging in the American South. In Lawson Little's *Georgia* (plate 78), a Black woman holds a small framed photograph; she is likely the domestic worker pictured alongside her white employer in the miniature picture. The camera has long privileged some communities and marginalized others, yet here we see a surprisingly tender picture of interracial, interclass affinity. Peyton Fulford's entwined figures (plate 40) also assert unity, constructing alternative relational structures that resist separation of "kin" by race, blood relation, and other entrenched markers of identity.

These six themes link disparate works in Do Good's collection and capture southern history, culture, and identity in all their complexity and contradictions. Through its installation, where clusters of objects variously construct and deconstruct each thematic category, the exhibition reckons with the idea of southernness as a coherent category. In so doing, *Reckonings and Reconstructions* resists notions of the South as a retrograde region. Instead, it presents the enigmatic, ever-changing qualities of the place and its people—a place where despair and hope, terror and beauty, pain and joy, and indignity and dignity coexist and commingle; a place seeking reconciliation and restoration captured by photographers with an ethical vision for a "Better South."

Following a series of essays on these themes, this catalogue features brief perspectives from twenty-six photographers on their work. Modeled after Do Good's ongoing "Small Talks" project, these accounts provide a critical yet otherwise unknown context behind each picture and reveal unique insights into an artist's process and the moment of inspiration and creation. Collectively, these texts convey the multivocal quality of narrating the American South that we discover throughout the photographs in the Do Good Fund.

This book would not have been possible without these many voices, including Do Good founder Alan Rothschild, whose vision and forethought in building the collection made possible the rich perspectives gathered here on the ever-changing American South. His photographic memory (pun intended) and his unwavering support of the exhibition, along with the masterful organizational skills of Do Good staff members Eliza Daffin, Jessica Hughes, and Hallie Fivecoat, were invaluable to its success. I extend my deepest thanks to the many photographers in this exhibition, especially those who contributed brilliantly to the texts in this catalogue, and to the seven essayists, who brought immense insight and profound delight to these pictures.

At the Georgia Museum of Art, I am thankful for director William Underwood Eiland, who has long believed in this project; curatorial assistant Kathryn Hill's heroic organizational efforts and keen insights from the project's nascent stages, as well as her research assistance alongside intern Ciel Rodriguez; the brilliant graphic design of Noelle Shuck and the elegant cover treatment by intern Mae Ronaldo, the constant assistance of director of communications Hillary Brown and intern Josie Lipton, and the deft editorial hand of freelance editor Lauren Walker; the nimble coordination of complex shipping and tour details by associate registrar Amber Barnhardt and deputy director Annelies Mondi; and the brilliant exhibition designs of Todd Rivers and Elizabeth Howe Marable, along with Larry Forte and Robert Russell. Across the University of Georgia campus, Nicholas Allen and his colleagues at the Willson Center for Humanities and Arts have been friends and advocates of the exhibition from the beginning; and the leadership and marketing team at the University of Georgia Press, especially director Lisa Bayer, have committed steadfastly to the realization and promotion of this book.

Finally, this book is dedicated to my children, Beck and Willa, who are now growing up as adopted southerners, where life is slower, community is crucial, and traffic is a foreign concept. I reckon that one day, maybe one day soon, they will be part of the healing and renewal that their world needs and that the pictures in this book yearn to make known.

NOTES

1 In the months between the finalization of this exhibition's checklist and the production of this catalogue, the Do Good Fund acquired sixty-three prints by Burk Uzzle from the MUUS Collection, a commissioned series of twenty-three photographs by Jared Ragland, and works by Trent Bozeman, Ashleigh Coleman, Kristine Potter, and Jeff Whetstone, among others.

2 Channing Cope, "Miracles Worked on Eroded Lands," *Atlanta Constitution*, January 21, 1948. See also Derek H. Alderman, "Channing Cope and the Making of a Miracle Vine," *Geographical Review* 94, no. 2 (April 2004): 157–77. A 2011 report by the U.S. Forest Service indicates that kudzu's pervasiveness has been long overstated and that the image of this invasive pest has overshadowed larger causes of habitat loss in the South, including overfarming and suburban sprawl. Kudzu, in other words, has become a "green plague" precisely because of its visibility along southern roadsides. Richard Solomon, "Kudzu is So Much More Than the 'Vine That Ate the South,'" Slate, August 28, 2021, https://slate.com/news-and-politics/2021/08/kudzu-south-japan-metaphor.html.

3 Kristine Potter, quoted in "Kristine Potter: The Landscape Echoes," *Juxtapoz Magazine*, June 18, 2020, https://www.juxtapoz.com/news/magazine/kristine-potter-the-landscape-echoes/.

4 Mark Sloan and Mark Long, eds., *Southbound: Photographs of and about the New South* [exhibition catalogue] (Charleston, SC: Halsey Institute of Contemporary Art, College of Charleston, 2018), 9. These include the Ogden Museum of Southern Art's *New Southern Photographers* (2018–19), the Halsey Institute for Contemporary Art's *Southbound* (2018–21), and the High Museum of Art's *Picturing the South: 25 Years* (2021). These exhibitions have also investigated southern culture primarily through the work of individual photographers.

5 Trevor Schoonmaker, "Southern Accent: The Sound of Seeing," in Miranda Isabel Lash and Trevor Schoonmaker, eds., *Southern Accent: Seeking the American South in Contemporary Art* [exhibition catalogue] (Durham, NC: Nasher Museum of Art at Duke University, 2016), 57.

6 Rob Nixon, *Slow Violence and the Environmentalism of the Poor* (Cambridge, MA: Harvard University Press, 2013).

7 RaMell Ross, quoted in Richard McCabe, "Liberated Documentarian," Bitter Southerner, October 28, 2021, https://bittersoutherner.com/feature/2021/liberated-documentarian.

8 William Faulkner, *Intruder in the Dust* (1948; New York: Vintage, 1991), 149–50. In Faulkner's novel, the author uses the phrase "emotional idea" to describe the southern protagonist's perception of the North. But the term can apply equally to internal and external constructions of southern identity.

FABLES OF THE RECONSTRUCTION

W. Ralph Eubanks

THE AMERICAN SOUTH IS A PLACE FROM WHICH MUCH HAS
been conjured and out of which much has been distilled. That is why the South
is not simply a place. It is also an idea, one that continues to be a part of cultural discourse in the United States as we debate and redefine the meaning of
American history, particularly the legacy of the enslavement of Black Americans.
Consequently, photography of the South carries a real and imagined burden, both
for the photographer and the audience. The place and the idea of the place affect
not only the viewer of the image but also the person behind the camera.

Well into the twenty-first century, the South continues to be a large blank screen
onto which many, both outside and inside the region, project ideas that define
our very notions of the place. Sometimes these projections reflect a mythical and
mysterious narrative not rooted in the region's daily realities. Given our country's
pervading myths and fables about the South, it is little wonder that images of this
place carry cultural power. Knowing that a particular landscape in a photograph
originated in a southern place or space—or was created by a southern artist—can
skew our way of seeing, perhaps because the category of "southern photography"
has long existed as a segregated artistic space.

Images of the South sometimes echo the region's elegiac yet tortured and contested past even when they capture the imprisoning reality of the present. With the
preponderance of certain visual tropes—particularly the Southern Gothic—it is
easy to forget that the South's visual narrative is varied. During the Great Depression, photographers on federal government commissions so closely documented
the South that its image sometimes seems frozen in time. When I visit some
of those same places today, it seems as if time has only melted along the edges.
Hence, a photograph of a southern road is not just a view of dusty well-traveled
soil; it is also an image onto which history, memory, and meaning have long been
imprinted. Although photographs are remarkably dependent upon context, we
often think of them as analogues of reality. Still, preconceived ideas and stereo-
types of the place affect the nation's way of seeing the South as much as they
influence the way artists capture its reality in a photograph.

In examining southern photography, we must look at photographs as a way of
untangling the points of intersection captured in an image, both visually and
historically. That is especially true when considering a collection like the one
assembled by the Do Good Fund, which is simultaneously inclusive of and
at odds with the region's segregated cultural memory. As Susan Sontag once
proclaimed, "Photograph collections can be used to make a substitute world."[1]

I have always taken her assertion to mean that one can construct a whole new world by taking numerous photographic points of view and organizing them into new ways of seeing.

Since images of the South are sometimes viewed through preconceived ideas of place and space, I have chosen to examine a selection of these pictures in an unconventional way. Specifically, I have gathered selected prints from the Do Good Fund's collection into a series of triptychs, through which I aim to explore multiple layers of southern photography. These images inspire the viewer to see a connection between this region below the Mason–Dixon Line and the rest of the country that lies above that archaic, artificial border. Ultimately, I hope these photographic triptychs subvert the foreignness we often associate with the South and transform what we see in images of this place.

If these pictures have a soundtrack, it would be R.E.M.'s 1985 album *Fables of the Reconstruction*, which played on repeat as I laid these images on the floor and walls of my studio to see what spoke to me. "The walls are built up stone by stone," Michael Stipe sings in "Driver 8," a phrase I kept coming back to as I contemplated each photograph in this collection. For me, the scenes of the South captured in this collection flow like images from the window of the Southern Crescent railcar that "Driver 8" describes. Thinking of images connected "stone by stone" also made me realize that each photograph has its own story, but when grouped—selectively and imaginatively—the pictures tell a complex narrative of the South, much like the songs that make up R.E.M.'s most southern album.

The term "triptych" originates from the Greek *triptykhos*, meaning "three-layered" or "three folds." That is a fitting way to look at southern photography since the American South is a richly layered region. By adopting the convention of a triptych of southern images, we can perceive the region's visual narrative with a richer and wider field of vision, and thus begin to see what is particularly southern about a photograph as well as what is uniquely American about it. In tying three images together, I aim to conjoin the mythic South, the historical South, and the familiar South into something that could only be captured through the broader American project. I hope the viewer will begin to see how these photographs explore the varied iconography of the South and the ways its people and landscapes are linked to ideas, places, and spaces outside the region. This way of organizing the photographs is not intended to inspire adoration of a specific idea of the South, as did the Southern Agrarians in their famous 1930 manifesto *I'll Take My Stand: The South and the Agrarian Tradition*. Rather than demand devotion, these triptychs encourage the viewer to meditate on the region with greater depth.

Seeing these images as triptychs also evokes Roland Barthes's photographic paradox, in which two competing messages—documentary evidence (denotation) and the rhetoric of the image (connotation)—make the images readable.[2] In considering the competing messages among the various "panels" in each triptych, I believe we can begin to expand our understanding of the South.

Can photography help extend our understanding of the South and see the region in a broader American context? Yes, but what we see in an image often depends on what we already know. Take for instance, Eli Reed's *Children at Play, Tunica (Sugar Ditch), Mississippi* (fig. 1). The uninformed viewer might not know that the photograph was taken in what was then the poorest county in the nation—the "Sugar Ditch" refers to the ravine of raw sewage that once ran through a neighborhood in Tunica. Without such context, we might view the image as capturing the fun and whimsy of two boys at play with no thought of the poverty and racial segregation that landed them in that specific setting. And while this photo was made in that mythical Mississippi space known as the Delta, replace the dirt road with asphalt and it could be a depiction of the urban poor, North or South.

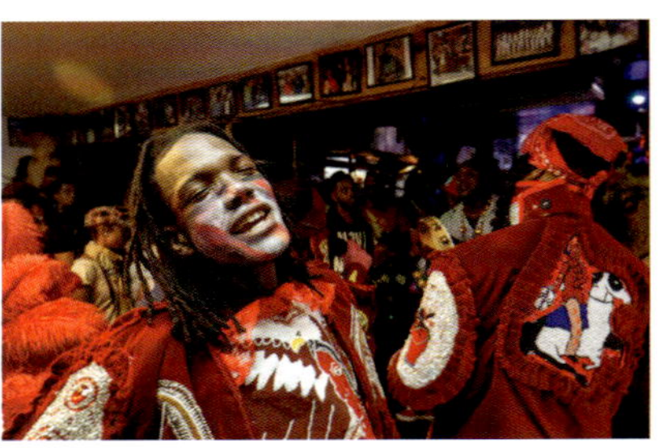 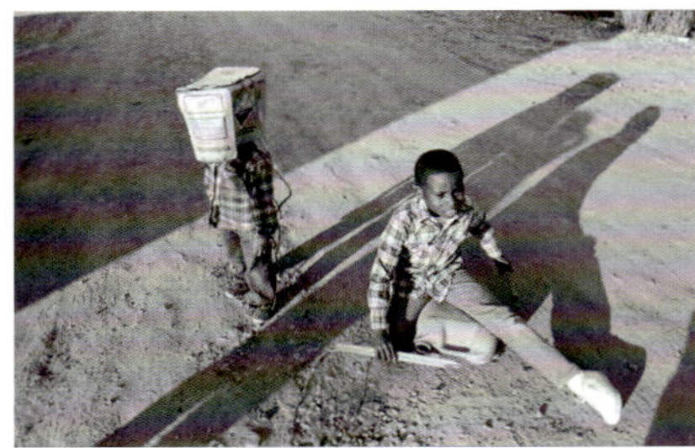 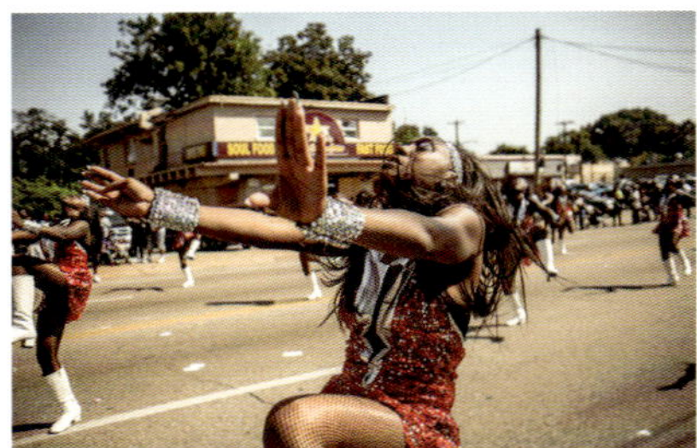

FIG. 1. (left) L. Kasimu Harris, *Come Tuesday (Sportsman's Corner)*, 2018 (plate 53)

(center) Eli Reed, *Children at Play, Tunica (Sugar Ditch), Mississippi*, 1986 (plate 97)

(right) Andrea Morales, *Southern Heritage Classic Parade*, 2017 (plate 87)

The other two images in this imagined triptych—L. Kasimu Harris's *Come Tuesday* and Andrea Morales's *Southern Heritage Classic Parade*—capture their subjects in moments of unbridled joy. *Come Tuesday* is part of Harris's series of photographs of vanishing Black bars and taverns in his native New Orleans. In these spaces, Harris writes, "tradition is paramount—and I fear what will become of my city if these traditions are lost."[3] Similarly, Morales captures a parade in Memphis's Orange Mound neighborhood, a place that was once a plantation where the majorette's ancestors could have been enslaved. It is also a photograph that could have been taken in my Mississippi hometown in 1967, in the days of segregation when Black schools gave parades just for Black folks, removing the burden of Jim Crow from the streets of a town for a brief moment on a crisp fall afternoon. Combined, these three photographs depict Black joy and pain, together with a fear of erasure that is felt across the country as the demographics of neighborhoods shift along racial and class lines. And *Children at Play* reminds us of not just the issue of poverty in the South's distant and recent past, but also of the issue of income inequality that continues to haunt our nation.

We might flank Matt Eich's *Firehose baptism, Newport News, Virginia* with two similarly framed photographs from Gordon Parks's *Segregation* series: *Outside Looking In, Mobile, Alabama* and *Mr. and Mrs. Thornton, Mobile, Alabama* (fig. 2). In September 1956, *Life* magazine titled Parks's story "The Restraints: Open and Hidden," an equally apt title for Eich's series of images. *Firehose baptism* is part of the *Invisible Yoke* project, the yoke being the unseen weight of memory we all carry. Like a religious triptych, this one merges the mythic and the mystical with the mundane and the profane. These three images also make the burden of collective memory clearer and reveal a connection with the open and hidden restraints that exist today.

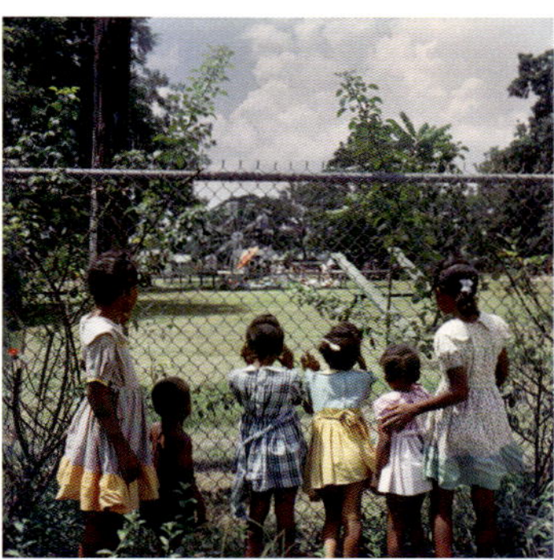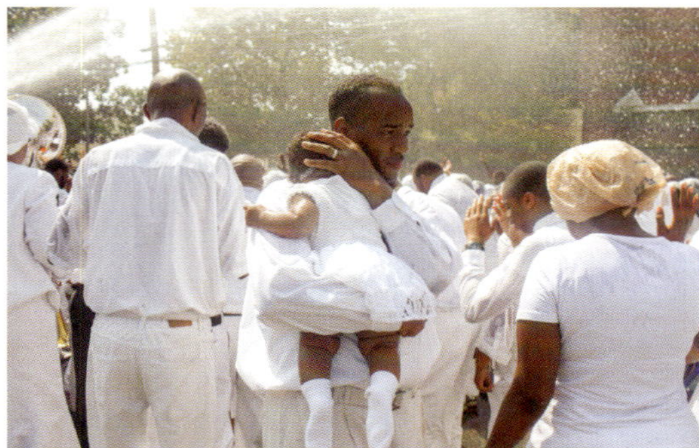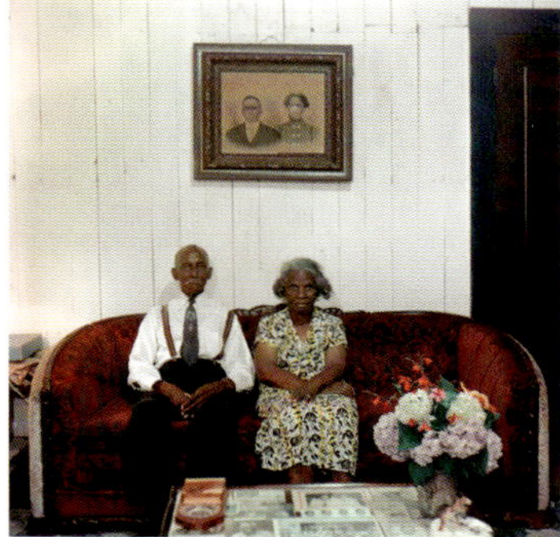

FIG. 2. (left) Gordon Parks, *Outside Looking In, Mobile, Alabama*, 1956 (plate 94)

(center) Matt Eich, *Firehose baptism, Newport News, Virginia*, 2013 (plate 33)

(right) Gordon Parks, *Mr. and Mrs. Thornton, Mobile, Alabama*, 1956 (plate 93)

FIG. 3. Gordon Parks, *Untitled, Shady Grove, Alabama*, 1956. Archival pigment print. Courtesy of and copyright the Gordon Parks Foundation.

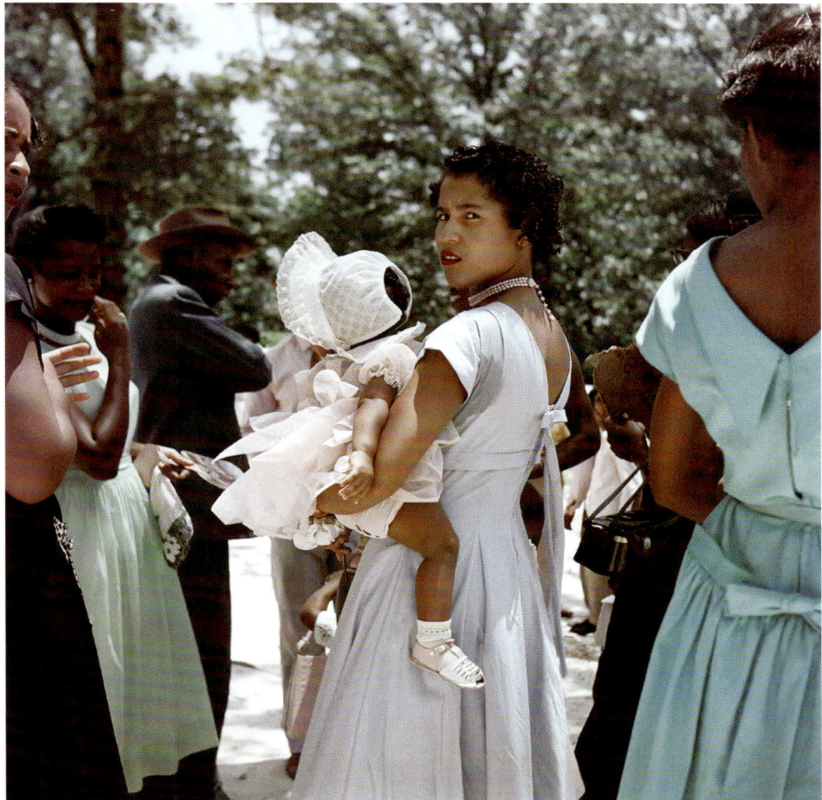

Another one of Parks's photographs could take the place of *Mr. and Mrs. Thornton* in this triptych. In his 1956 work *Untitled, Shady Grove, Alabama* (fig. 3), a woman holds a young child in a pink dress and white bonnet much in the same way as the man shielding the girl's head in Eich's photograph. Both images also share a certain timelessness. In this new triptych, I see the children standing at the fence on the left, with Eich's image in the center and Parks's untitled image on the right. This grouping encourages us to contemplate both the visual coherence of these images and the ways in which the American past collides with the American present.

In his 1958 essay "The Search for Southern Identity," historian C. Vann Woodward proclaimed that a "Bulldozer Revolution" had "already leveled many of the old monuments of regional distinctiveness." He further predicted it could eventually erase "the very consciousness of a distinctive tradition along with the will to sustain it."[4] Woodward's idea emerges photographically in the works of Alex Christopher Williams, Jeff Rich, and Mark Steinmetz (fig. 4).

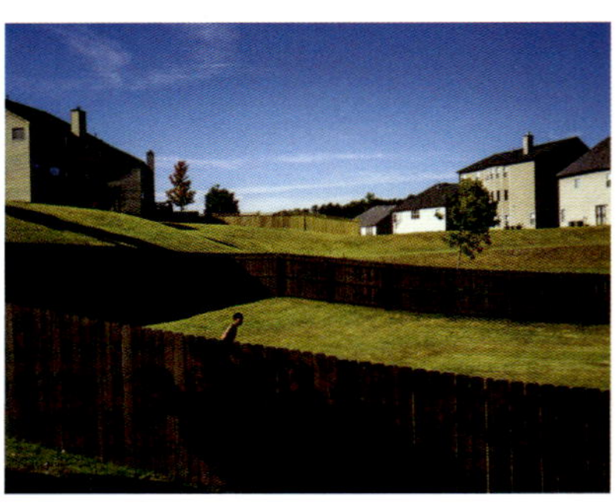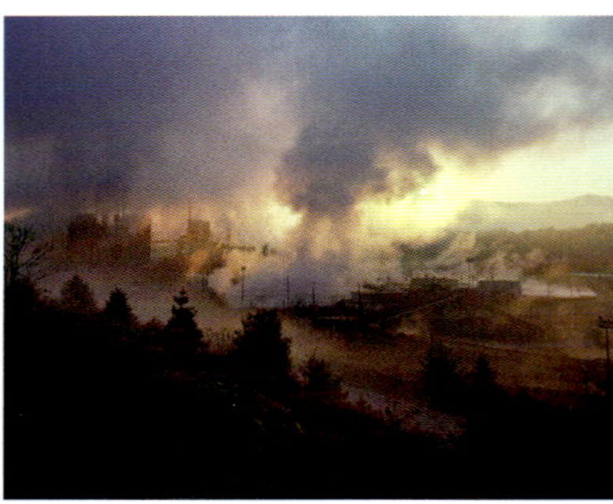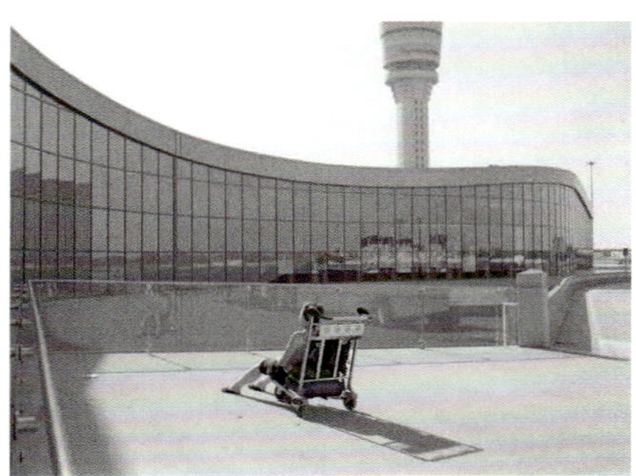

FIG. 4. (left) Alex Christopher Williams, *Untitled*, 2016 (plate 122)

(center) Jeff Rich, *Blue Ridge Paper Mill, The Pigeon River, Canton, North Carolina*, 2008 (plate 101)

(right) Mark Steinmetz, *Atlanta Airport*, 2016 (plate 115)

In an untitled image of a maze of suburban fences, Alex Christopher Williams captures the results of the bulldozer revolution that Woodward feared. While we think of the suburbs as a white space, behind the fence stands a young person of color, echoing the way southern suburbs have become the home of the region's expanding Black middle class as well as a haven for recent immigrants from Latin America and Asia. Mark Steinmetz's *Atlanta Airport* represents the new monuments of the South as it brings to mind the apocryphal statement "when you die, whether you are going to Heaven or Hell, you have to change planes in Atlanta." Jeff Rich's *Blue Ridge Paper Mill* sits at center of this triptych, exposing the darker side of the suburbanization and industrialization of the South. The photograph also suggests how the South has suffered from exploitation by American industry and reminds us of the critical need for attention to the national issue of environmental justice. The sea of smoke and fog envelops nearby homes, quite obviously affecting the quality of life for those who live in the factory's shadow.

In a final triptych (fig. 5), Debbie Fleming Caffery's moving image of two rugged dark hands seems to represent the ways people in the South have continued to pour their labor into southern soil, despite the bulldozer revolution. Michael Stipe reminds us that the kudzu-covered South is still with us, with vines and branches casting shadows way out of place. Similarly, Maude Schuyler Clay's *Delta Hunters*, with its solitary bare tree behind the gun-wielding hunters, captures what remains of the traditions of the rural South.

Like the ways southern place is represented in its literature, southern photography also exemplifies how the region is held in memory. Viewers often seek some notion of truth or reality in a photograph, since it is considered a medium that provides evidence and holds moral imperatives. Yet while a photograph can be a way of remembering, as W. G. Sebald notes in his novel *Austerlitz*, the process of developing an image can be linked to forgetting: "In my photographic work I was always especially entranced, said Austerlitz, by the moment when the shadows of

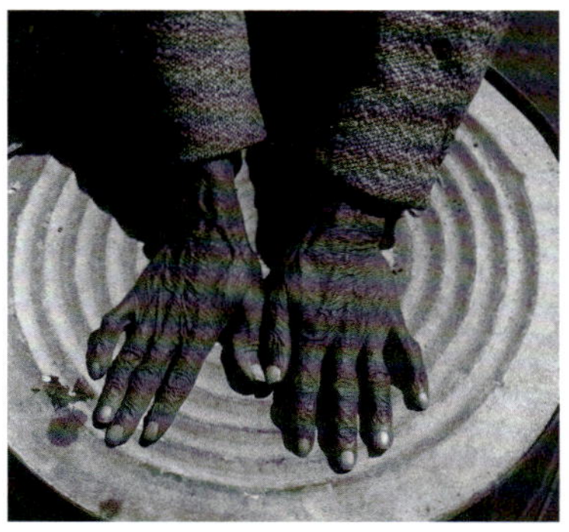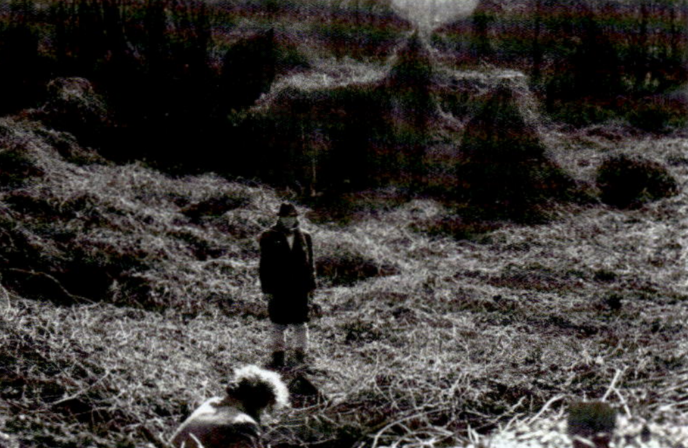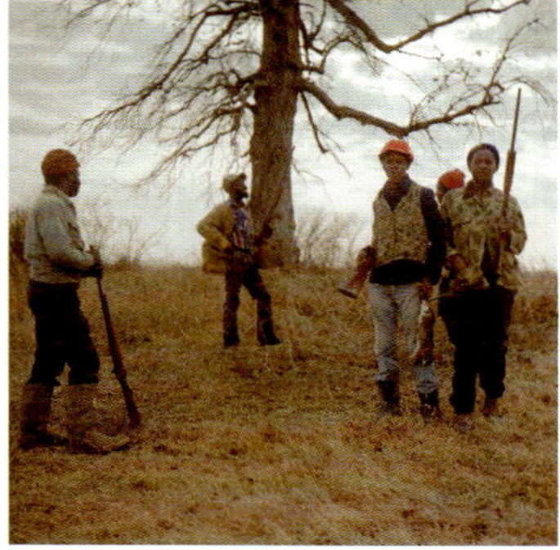

FIG. 5. (left) Debbie Fleming Caffery, *Harry's Hands*, 1984 (plate 16)

(center) Michael Stipe, *Lynda, Jeremy, kudzu field, Athens*, 1982 (plate 116)

(right) Maude Schuyler Clay, *Delta Hunters*, 1984 (plate 23)

reality, so to speak, emerge out of nothing on the exposed paper, as memories do in the middle of the night, darkening again if you try to cling to them, just like a photographic print left in the developing bath too long."[5] Just as the process of developing a photograph depends on the right medium, sometimes the truth and ideas emerge only when an image is juxtaposed with other photographs. Using a solitary image to represent a particular visual idea of the South means that only one dimension of southern place comes into focus and other ideas of place are forgotten. Regarding images of the South, it is important that all the shadows of the reality of the region be exposed. An image can entrance us if we begin to see it as part of a broad narrative of the southern past and present.

That broad narrative of the South is also linked to what is uniquely American about how its people and places have transformed and evolved. Southern photography today is more than just fables; it is a reconstruction and reimagining of those fables alongside new ideas and ways of seeing. Understanding southern place and landscape and its connection to American history and memory can be transformative. Photography helps to reveal these connections.

NOTES

1   Susan Sontag, "Photography Unlimited," *New York Review of Books*, June 23, 1977, 25–32.

2   Roland Barthes, *Image, Music, Text*, trans. Stephen Heath (London: Fontana, 1977), 19.

3   L. Kasimu Harris, "A Shot Before Last Call: Capturing New Orleans's Vanishing Black Bars," *New York Times*, February 24, 2020.

4   C. Vann Woodward, "The Search for Southern Identity," 1958; repr. in *The Burden of Southern History*, 3rd ed. (Baton Rouge: Louisiana State University Press, 1993), 6–7.

5   W. G. Sebald, *Austerlitz*, trans. Anthea Bell (New York: Random House, 2001), 109.

A WOMAN IS A NATION

Jasmine Amussen

WHILE WRITING THIS ESSAY, THERE WAS A SUDDEN DEATH in my birthplace of Eureka Springs, Arkansas. A small town—I tell people it's easier, faster, and more cost effective to visit my nephew in Alaska—nestled in a holler in the Ozark Mountains, between Crystal Bridges Museum of American Art and the global headquarters of the Ku Klux Klan. Since leaving almost twenty years ago, I have visited sporadically for births and deaths. My sisters and I were all born at home, delivered by the same midwife. My midwife's only daughter was born a week before I was and was there when I arrived. It was for her father's passing I came, to be surrounded by the women again doing the labor of birthing and dying. I like coming here for those bodily processes. They feel more real here, somehow. Has anyone ever died in California? Or did they just not take their vitamins?

In the opening of William Faulkner's novel *As I Lay Dying* (1930), the matriarch Addie Bundren watches her eldest son Cash build her simple wooden coffin outside her deathbed window (fig. 1). She does not find this morbid or disgusting. Her gaze is steady and without repulsion, without fear. Addie lays her literal and metaphysical weight upon her family's shoulders, which they accept. She has created the world in which her family lives, and her death forces their world to grow larger as they carry her body across Mississippi. I always wondered why our southern literature was willing to show women with such an unflinching gaze, in their deaths and their labors and their strengths and weaknesses. But, aside from the documentation of slavery, this view of women isn't shown as much in photography. There is an aphorism that goes something like "A man is a person, a woman is a nation." Looking at the images of women in the exhibition *Reckonings and Reconstructions: Southern Photography from the Do Good Fund*, I was struck by the nations that women were building through their labor, the lessons they were teaching their children, and the South they were creating, brick by brick, image by image.

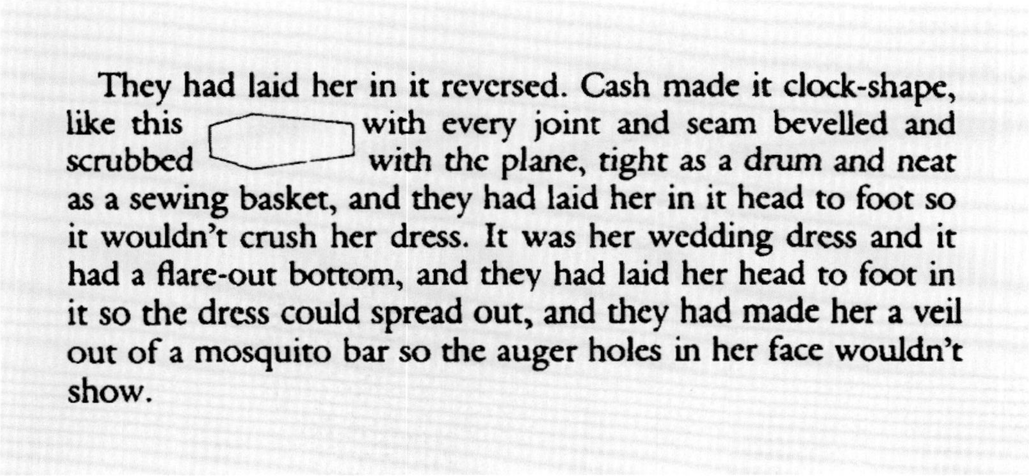

They had laid her in it reversed. Cash made it clock-shape, like this ⬡ with every joint and seam bevelled and scrubbed with the plane, tight as a drum and neat as a sewing basket, and they had laid her in it head to foot so it wouldn't crush her dress. It was her wedding dress and it had a flare-out bottom, and they had laid her head to foot in it so the dress could spread out, and they had made her a veil out of a mosquito bar so the auger holes in her face wouldn't show.

FIG. 1. Excerpt from *As I Lay Dying* by William Faulkner, © 1930 and © renewed 1958 by William Faulkner. Used by permission of Random House, an imprint and division of Penguin Random House LLC. All rights reserved.

One could argue that there are differences between a photograph made for documentary purposes, a photograph made for personal reasons, and a photograph made on a lark. Whatever the reason, whatever the motivation, most southern photographers are men, and many images of women in this exhibition are made by men. What I am interested in is the gaze leveled upon these photographs, which is unusual. While images of lonely, decaying manses have long been the foundation of what we call southern photography—all the way from Clarence John Laughlin in the 1930s and 1940s to the cottage industry of today's gelatin and silver-plate images of aching trees and desolate vistas—there is another view, one of honesty and pride and simplicity without the saccharine (and, frankly, offensive) pallor of nostalgia.

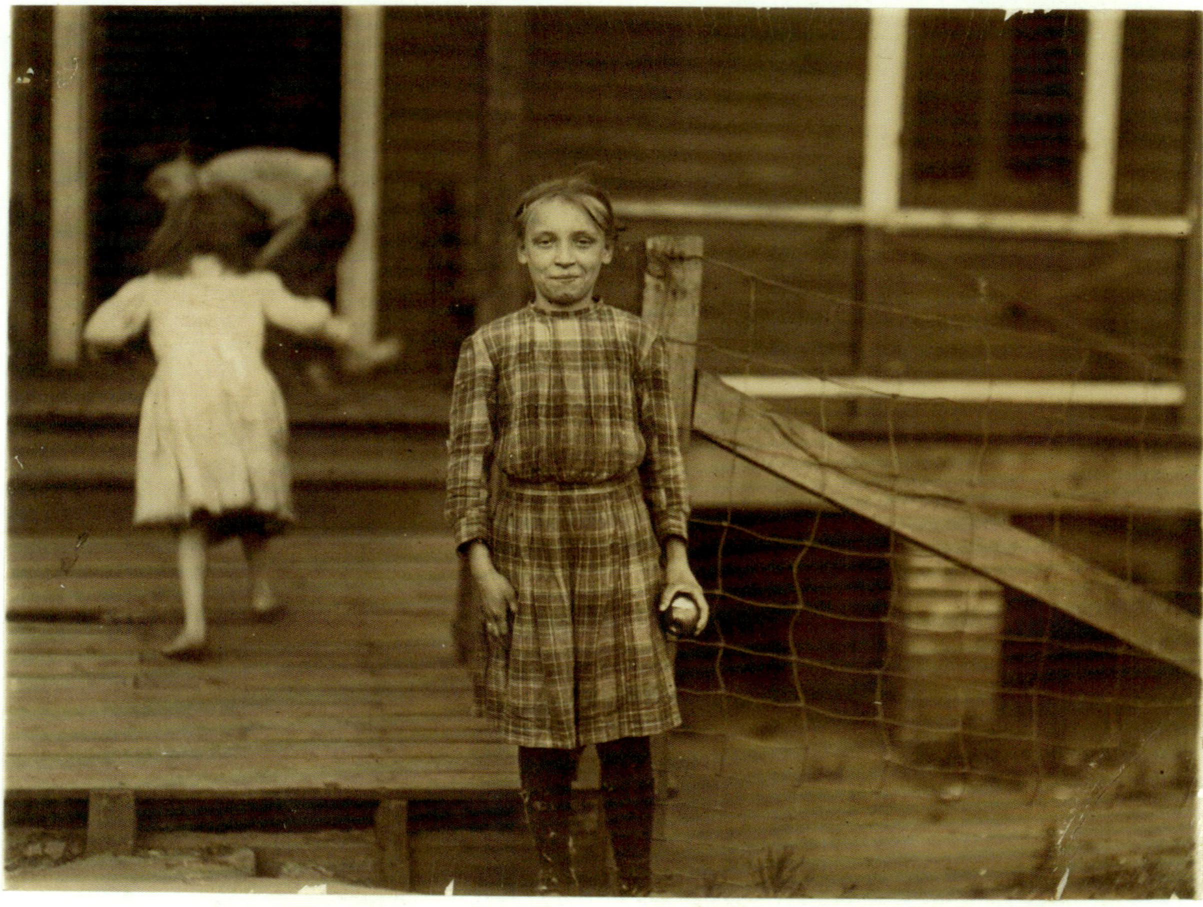

At the turn of the twentieth century, the National Child Labor Committee set out to "promote the rights, awareness, dignity, well-being, and education of children and youth as they relate to work and working."[1] The committee hired photographer Lewis W. Hine to travel the US, photographing children and young people in fields, factories, and homes (fig. 2). Rules varied from state to state, but the general consensus was that there was never a child under the age of ten working in any farm or establishment. In 1909, just as today, we knew that to be false. The work of the land and the work of southern people residing on that land has always been that of the immediate family as well as the family created by fiat.

Created sixty years after the portrait of the slyly smiling Minnie Lee and her apple, Paul Kwilecki's photograph of a two-family home near Attapulgus in Decatur County, Georgia, depicts a world that Addie Bundren and Minnie Lee would recognize. Not because of the poverty, but the steadiness, the evenness of the gaze (fig. 3). A figure who could be a mother, a grandmother, or an older sister is tending to laundry and younger family members in the background. In the foreground, a woman who appears pregnant is tending to the hair of a young girl. She sees the camera, she sees through the camera. She's annoyed by the repetitive nature of the chore being done, but, even more than that, she won't let the photographer go unremarked upon, unnoticed. What are you doing? What

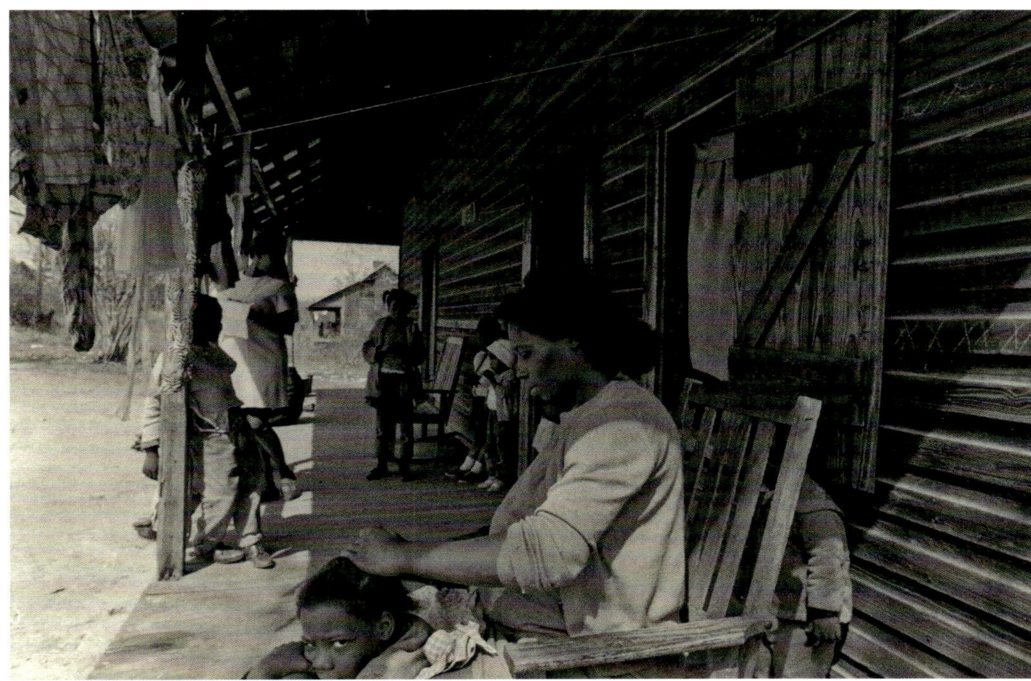

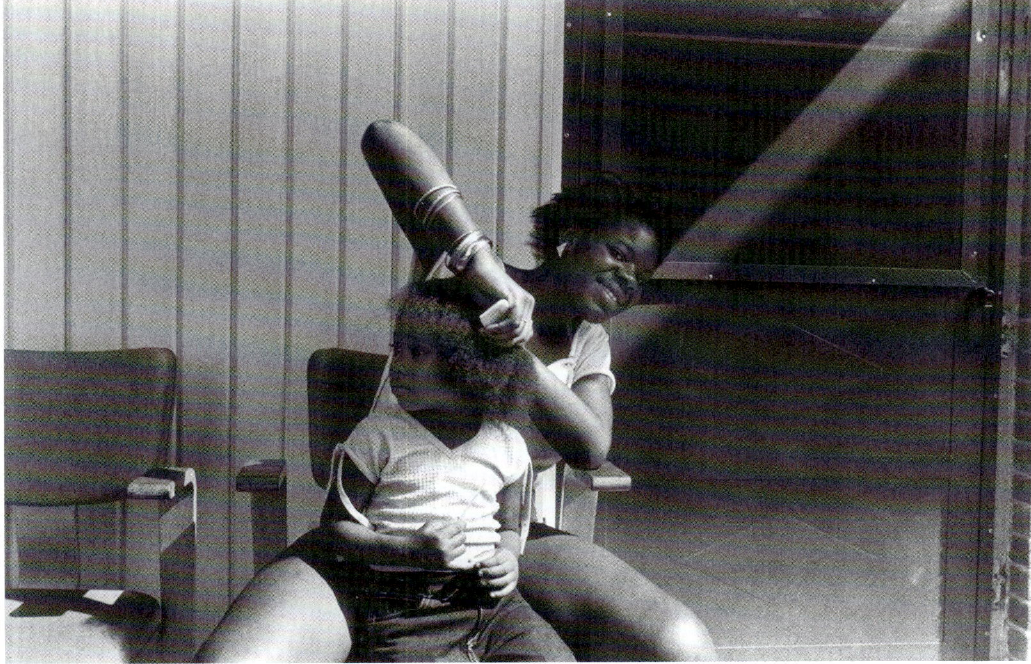

FIG. 3. Paul Kwilecki, *Two-family tobacco tenant house*, 1964 (plate 60)

FIG. 4. Dawoud Bey (b. 1953), *Combing Hair, Syracuse, New York*, 1986. Gelatin silver print. High Museum of Art, Gift of Eric Ceputis and David W. Williams, 2017.449. © Dawoud Bey. Courtesy of Stephen Daiter Gallery, Chicago.

is the point of what you are doing? Another photographer would have attempted to make something cute or charming out of her glare. But this is her world. She takes the measure of what she sees and finds it wanting. While the tobacco industry that employed this family continues to fall, the grooming of Black women's hair is a nearly ten-billion-dollar industry that continues to grow year after year (fig. 4). This photograph, while depicting a domestic scene, suggests preparations for the labor outside the home. The girl's hair must be done to be kept out of the way for when she goes to work.

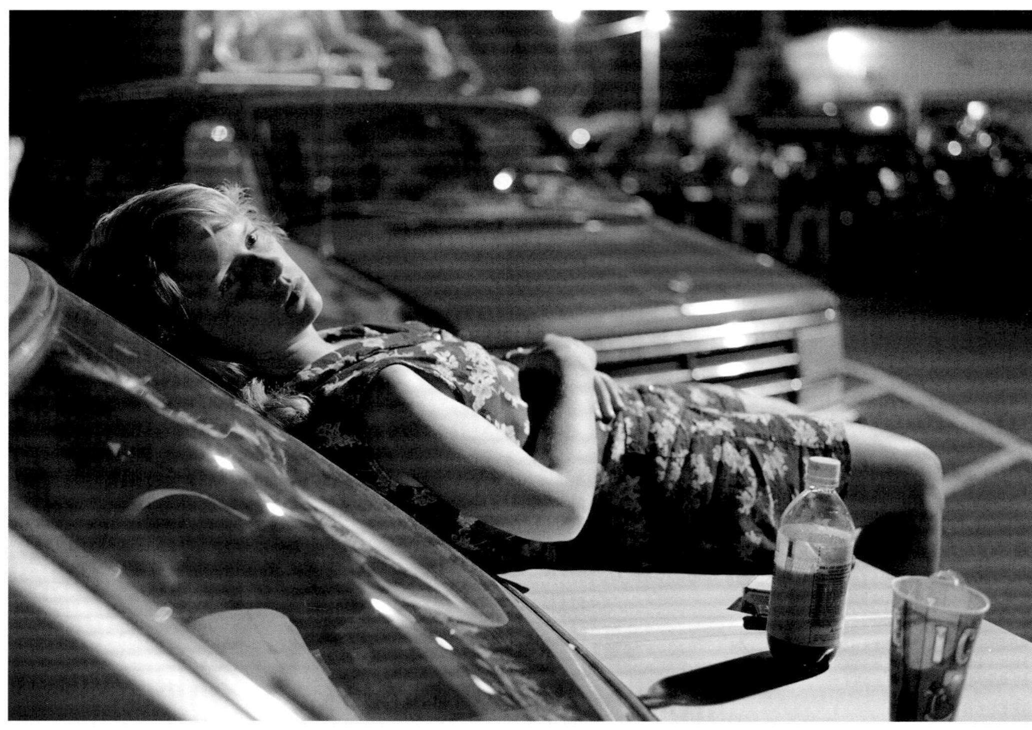

FIG. 5. Mark Steinmetz, *Athens, Georgia*, 1996 (plate 114)

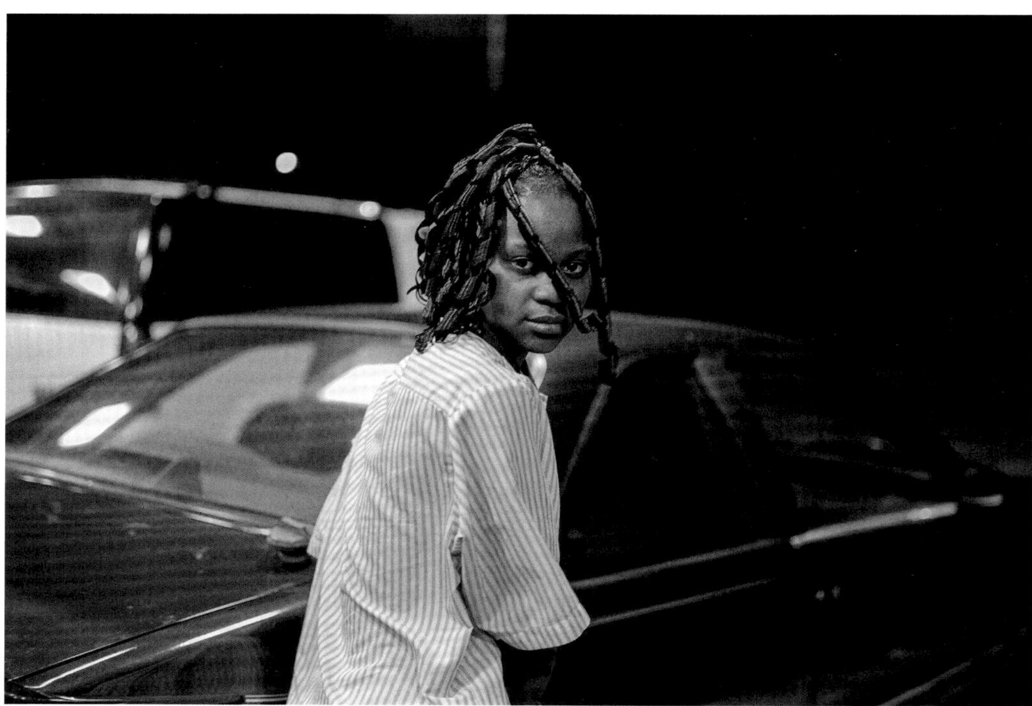

FIG. 6. Mark Steinmetz, *Off Route 316, Barrow County, Georgia*, 1994 (plate 112)

The socialization of children is a form of labor that straddles the domestic and exterior spheres. The things imparted at home are reflected in the choices made outside. The choice of church, the level of education, potential spouses, and the type of future children can be expected to grow into are all determined by women. Images such as Dennis Darling's *Family at Klan Rally* (plate 25) are the ones people are accustomed to seeing, just like the aching trees and slave quarters. But, the assumptions—racist, country, whatever—miss what makes this photo so fascinating. If we can say that everyone in this photograph belongs to the same family, the discrepancies are interesting. The young boy in the foreground has uncombed hair, his pants are held up with elastic, and he is shirtless. The arm of the boy next to him is also bare, suggesting that he is shirtless, too. The picture was captured in 1974, and yet the protagonist of this scene is dressed just as she would have been in 1944, 1954, 1964. The women are neatly combed, dresses pressed. What work are these girls and women supposed to be doing at a Klan rally? The social work of advancing the view of the nation. The most important work a woman can do.

Darby English, writing in *Artforum* about Kara Walker's exhibition at Kunstmuseum Basel, states, "If it's hard to report an experience of Walker's art in wholes, that's because hers is an art of parts, an assemblage of mediums, scales, characters and tones. They emerge continuously, fade in and out of one another, overtake or are overtaken, dip in and out of the real."[2] While English is writing about the way "fantasies complicate facts," this is also the problem we face when describing the South. It's slippery, evasive, and just like Walker's work, it's obsessively about slavery. Unlike Walker, however, it's desperate to pretend slavery exists in some other self-contained past, one without any lingering effects. Labor, extraction, rare-earth elements—all of the worst things about the capitalist exploitation of people are on bald display in the South. The broken nonwhite bodies in crop fields of blood, the poor white bodies dying an agonizing slow death as their lungs turn black with coal. Some images in *Reckonings and Reconstructions* feature elderly men at the end of a workday, alone in a post office or a dress shop. Young mine-working men are also shown alone. And the photographs of built structures are defined by the absence of people. The narrative of the southern experience of labor is dark, alienating, and punishing. The march of right-to-work laws, union busting, cheap resources, and cheap labor add to the isolation—if no one lives here, works here, does anyone have to live with the consequences? But the images of women, they are never alone. They are never shown in any ways but ways of power, of witness (figs. 5 and 6). The South is the place where this nation was built, maintained, and where it will succeed or fail. And the women will decide.

NOTES

1   Brian Greenberg and Linda S. Watts, *Social History of the United States* (Santa Barbara, CA: ABC-CLIO, 2009), 236.

2   Darby English, review of *A Black Hole is Everything a Star Longs to Be*, Kunstmuseum Basel, June 5–September 26, 2021, in *Artforum* 60, no. 4 (December 2021), https://www.artforum.com/print/202110/darby-english-on-kara-walker-87227.

SOUTHERN RITES: RELIGION, RITUAL, AND COMMUNAL IDENTITY IN SOUTHERN PHOTOGRAPHY

Jeffrey Richmond-Moll

RELIGION AND RITUAL HAVE LONG BEEN INSEPARABLE FROM southern cultural identity, though not always in the ways we might think. As anthropologist Victor Turner observed, rituals perform a sense of communal unity and reinscribe both alliances and distinctions among individuals. This is the "invisible yoke" that suffuses Matt Eich's photographic series of the same name, binding together the communities of his native southeastern Virginia. Yet, because rituals are often temporary, societies depend on these rites for the continued performance and ongoing re-presentation of group identity. In other words, for communities to imagine themselves as real, they use rituals to continually materialize their identity in lived reality and to feel it in their bodies.[1] This essay uses photography to consider southern rituals—whether religious, civic, or social—as diverse modes of creating and preserving communal identity.

To be sure, institutional religion is embedded deeply in the landscape of this region. William Christenberry's *China Grove Church, Hale County, Alabama* (plate 22) pictures a small white chapel tucked into the bend of a rural dirt road. Rooted in red clay among a sea of trees, rural Protestantism appears inextricable from the South's ecological fabric and enmeshed within the numinous realm of southern memory, which Christenberry's work so often explores. Meanwhile, Rylan Steele's *Ave Maria* series upsets these autochthonous understandings of evangelicalism and the southern landscape. In one photograph (plate 111), the arched roof of a cathedral rises above the housetops of this Catholic planned community in southern Florida, built by Tom Monaghan, the founder of the

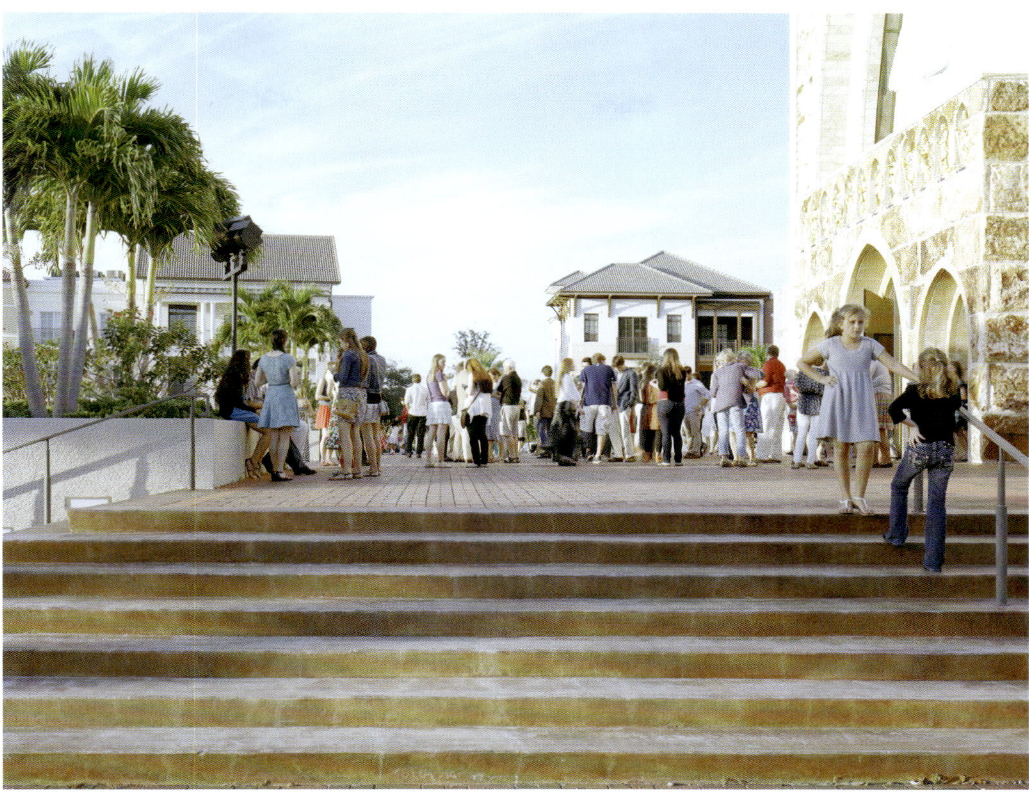

FIG. 1. Rylan Steele (b. 1980), *Oratory Gathering*, 2014. Archival pigment print, 15 × 19 1/2 inches. The Do Good Fund, Inc., 2014-47. Copyright the artist.

Domino's Pizza empire. If the Old South arose under the hegemony of evangelical Protestantism—never monolithic, as scholars of religion now note, but characterized by "a widely diffused concatenation of beliefs, practices, impulses, and extensions without a center"—the massive demographic shifts of the New South have brought the end of the Bible Belt as it has often been understood.[2] At Ave Maria, where the ubiquity of "the Church" collides with the rise of sprawling master-planned cities, Florida swamps transform into fantasies of heavenly community. Religion literally undergirds and unifies the architectural fabric and environmental engineering of an entire town (fig. 1).

In the book accompanying Steele's *Ave Maria* series, poet Nora Wendl interweaves her text with the utopian language of literary critic Lewis Mumford: "It is our utopias that make the world tolerable to us."[3] By combining poetry (more often associated with lyricism and the imaginary) with photography (often understood as factual), Steele's book subverts the technology of the camera as a tool of rationality and documentary fact. By questioning this concept of photography as fact, and by defying the longstanding strategies that photographers have used to document religion in the South, Steele also challenges our often one-dimensional ideas about southern religiosity. After all, as art historian Robert Cozzolino observes, the supernatural cannot be precisely defined and rigidly contained; it is "liminal" in its natural state, "welcoming fluidity, ambiguity, and the blurring of boundaries."[4]

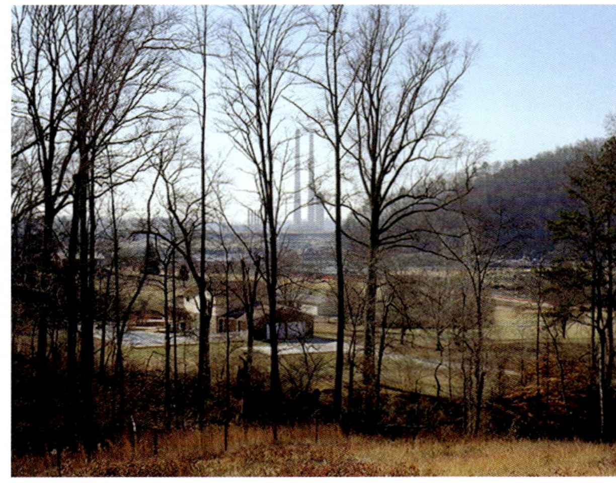

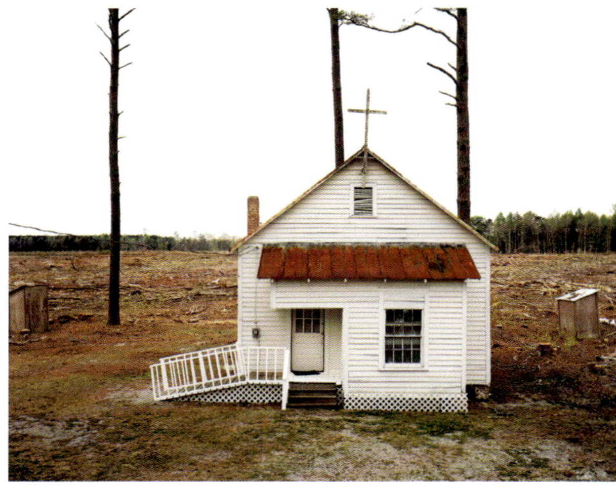

FIG. 2. Jeff Rich (b. 1977), *Coal Fly Ash Spill, Kingston Fossil Plant, Emory River, Harriman, Tennessee*, 2009. Archival inkjet print, 20 × 25 inches. The Do Good Fund, Inc., 2020–9. © Jeff Rich.

FIG. 3. Burk Uzzle (b. 1938), *Clear Cut Church, North Carolina*, 2006. Inkjet print, 20 × 24 inches. The Do Good Fund, Inc., 2020–58. © University of North Carolina at Chapel Hill, Photograph by Burk Uzzle.

Never fixed or stable, the religious identity of the American South has continuously evolved. In 1785, Thomas Jefferson contrasted citizens of the northern colonies, who were "superstitious and hypocritical in their religion," with those of the South: "fiery, voluptuary, indolent, unsteady, independent, . . . without attachment or pretensions to any religion but that of the heart."[5] What makes Jefferson's statement so startling today is the extent to which Americans have come to associate the South with fervent religious dogmatism; how ingrained H. L. Mencken's century-old vision has become of a culturally and intellectually sterile region governed by "Baptist and Methodist barbarism"; and how entangled religion and politics have seemed in the Bible Belt.[6] Without doubt, these narratives have prejudiced outsider perspectives of the region. What the photographs in the Do Good Fund's collection help us to see, however, is the historical contingency of these perceptions and the need to challenge common assumptions about southernness and religion.

Like Steele's looming cathedral, as eerily ever-present as the power plants in Jeff Rich's images of industrial disaster sites (fig. 2), southern churches do not always sit comfortably in the landscape. In photographs by Burk Uzzle, for example, these buildings cling uneasily to their small plots of land. In *Clear Cut Church, North Carolina* (fig. 3), we witness the vulnerability of a small chapel—and, by extension, its church-going rural community—to the radical ecological transformations wrought upon southern terrain. If such sanctuaries help make spaces sacred through naming, boundary-keeping, and ritual, Uzzle also demonstrates the tensions and fragile divisions among nature, culture, and spirituality in our modern day.

Titus Brooks Heagins's photographs of the changing neighborhood of East Durham, North Carolina, likewise demonstrate how new communities have transformed southern religious identity. *Marivi's Quinceañera* (plate 54) depicts the rite of passage when a fifteen-year-old girl transitions from childhood into womanhood. Quinceañeras often begin with a Spanish-Catholic Mass, and Heagins shows Marivi processing down the aisle of Durham's Immaculate Conception Church. This congregation has sought to merge the affluent white community of this gentrifying section of the city with the Spanish-speaking residents who also call it home, including many immigrants from El Salvador. In fact, Marivi's "Quince" is likely the Salvadorean version of the ceremony, also called *la fiesta rosa*, with her pink gown and accessories signifying the age of innocence that these young women are leaving behind. Heagins's photographs convey the regality and common humanity of these and other marginalized communities—groups for whom such rituals enable the importation and continuation of ancestral identity even amid geopolitical displacement.

Across the South, devotion and revelation also spill out of churches and revival tents, down streets and forest paths, filling visionary art environments like Reverend John D. Ruth's Drive-Through Bible Park in Woodville, Georgia (plate 80). Photographer, folklorist, and curator Roger Manley devoted his career to documenting the landscapes of self-taught artists, many of them self-styled prophets and members of the clergy. As southerners often joked, "Ministers needed to know how to paint a sermon as well as preach one."[7] In 1985, Manley photographed Rev. Ruth at the fifth stop in his "Chronological Bible Poem," a sweeping history of the Judeo-Christian history from Egypt to the United States.[8] Proudly standing beside his painted signs and sculptures with a pen and notebook in hand, Ruth's pose befits a modern-day gospel-writer, whose life's work layers the personal and historical, the individual and universal.

Equally solemn and formal in pose is Shelby Lee Adams's *Blind Serpent Handler* (plate 2), whose highly traditional frontality is ironically undercut by a leopard-print clip-on tie, a low-hanging clothesline, and the detritus of a smashed can and overturned toy car. Adams does not ignore the sensationalism of snake handling—a practice that originated in Appalachia in 1910 when a Tennessee preacher named George W. Hensley sought to apply a contested series of verses in Mark 16 by calling on the faithful to take up serpents as a display of the Holy Spirit.[9] Rather than purely objective documentary, however, Adams sees his portraits as "a long autobiographical exploration of creativity, imagination, vision, repulsion, and salvation."[10] By leaning on the popular conflation of the snake handler with the Appalachian and southern "other," Adams considers his own position as a native southerner and in relation to stereotypical ideas of the region, particularly as those ideas have been perpetuated through photography. As Paul Kwilecki once cautioned, photographs violate the continuity of life, and we must not be carried away by the exoticism of intense piety and unfamiliar ceremonies. Instead, Kwilecki continued, we must remind ourselves: "Prayer meetings and church services overlap shopping and the people in church are jurors at the courthouse. Sunday's picknickers are machine operators on Monday."[11]

As Kwilecki and Adams would also agree, documentary photography is never free from the personal agenda of the photographer. In the case of Adams's blind man, we should consider his blindness as not simply a commentary on his unswerving obedience to his religion. (Is this "blind faith," or is he one of the faithful whom Jesus described to a doubting Thomas, "Blessed are those who have not seen and have believed"?) It was also Adams's blind grandmother who taught him to be an artist, "to observe closely the world around me" and "develop my own visual sensibilities so acutely that I could see for her."[12] In *Blind Serpent Handler*, Adams asks: How does photography perform communal identity, both for the photographer and for the sitter? And, in the media's ritualistic production of Appalachian charismatic Christianity, how does popular culture disingenuously perform identity on the American South's behalf?

Outsiders have used photographs to prescribe southern religious identity as far back as the 1930s, when Farm Security Administration (FSA) photographers traversed the region looking for what they considered "truly religious" in contemporary America. In seemingly benign church portraits, which depict the architecture of southern religion with no people present, artists such as Walker Evans sought an authentic sacredness undefiled by the pettiness of humanity. To Evans, true religion was characterized by a purer, more generalized sense of spirituality reflected in a purity of light and architectural geometry—a "material spirituality, embedded in form" that lacked any reference to everyday ritual and doctrine.[13] Yet, as Don Norris's latter-day church portraits suggest (fig. 4), these are not merely vernacular structures. Such buildings are carefully designed and lovingly preserved physical expressions of spiritual commitment, which often emulate fashionable and handsome styles even in the remotest of southern locales.[14]

The collective caretaking of a church building is itself an affirmation of community, as William Ferris has shown. Growing up along Highway 61 southeast of Vicksburg, Mississippi, Ferris attended Rose Hill Church alongside a predominantly Black congregation, where he learned to sing hymns and spirituals. His photographs of Rose Hill (plates 34 and 35) were his attempt to record a largely oral spiritual tradition: "I realized there were no hymnals in the church and

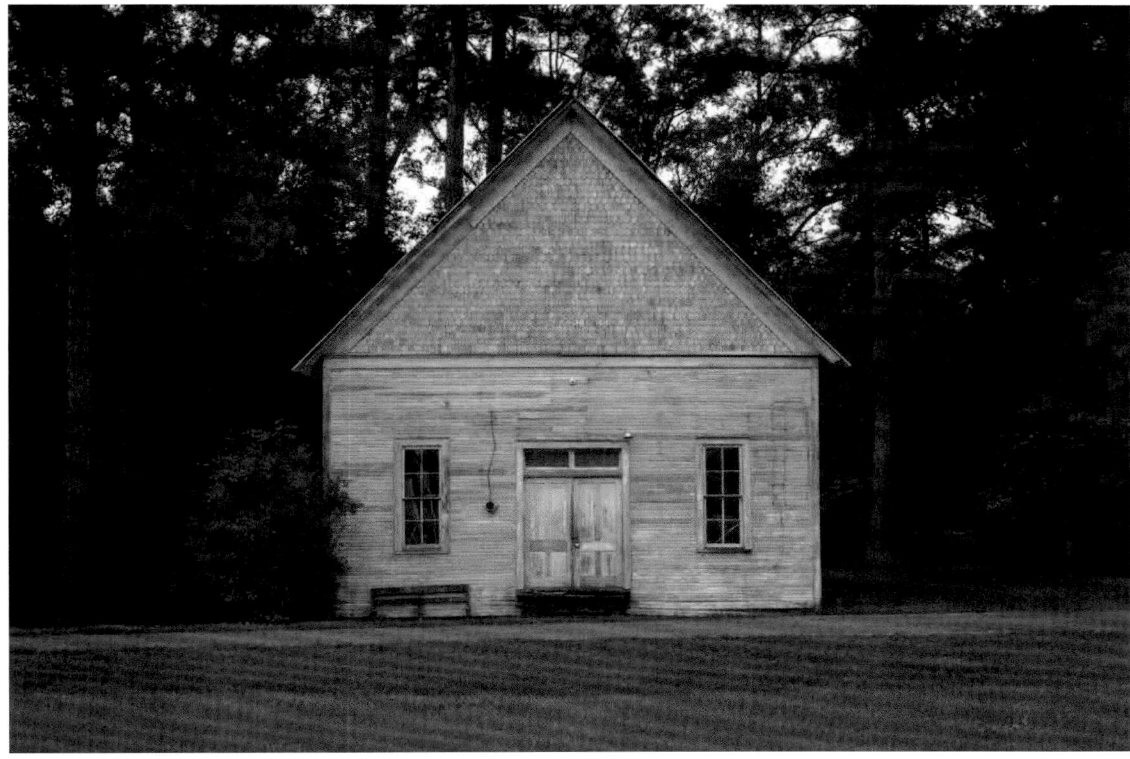

FIG. 4. Don Norris (b. 1940), *Hathorn Methodist Church (ca. 1902), Hathorn, Mississippi*, 2009. Digital pigment print on heavy rag paper, 11 × 17 inches. The Do Good Fund, Inc., 2015–46. © Don Norris.

when those families were no longer there, the music would disappear."[15] But the pictures also underscore the significance of church properties to Black autonomy and self-advocacy. In the Jim Crow South, the church was one of the rare institutions that African American communities controlled and legally owned outright.[16] Hence the astounding number of attacks against rural Black church buildings by pro-segregation white southerners, who saw the Black church as a threat to their status quo and a force for racial equality.

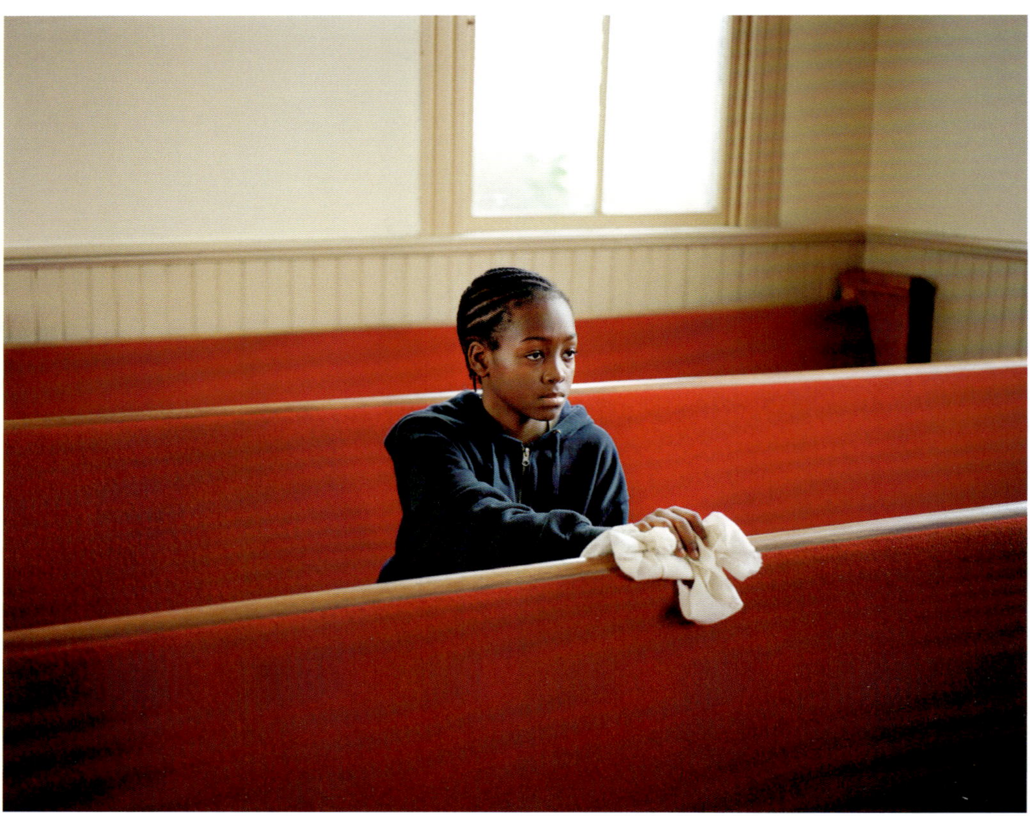

FIG. 5. Susan Worsham (b. 1969), *Jamel Cleaning His Church, VA*, 2011. Archival pigment print, 20 × 25 inches. The Do Good Fund, Inc., 2014–10. © Susan Worsham.

Photographs of church interiors and exteriors are therefore political, cultural, and economic assertions of Black agency and resistance to legacies of disenfranchisement and dispossession. These buildings are artifacts of Black craftsmanship, constructed by earlier generations of lumberers, carpenters, and laborers. In *Jamel Cleaning His Church* (fig. 5), where a young boy pauses as he tenderly polishes rows of pews, Susan Worsham captures the communal responsibility and ongoing work of caretaking that is incumbent upon younger generations. Through the stewardship of people like Jamel and through the repetition of their rituals, the Black church links present-day congregants to their ancestors and ensures their collective existence for the future. In short, as Grace Hale observes, "Churches are an essential place where people make and mark history."[17]

River baptisms offered another means of connecting a believer and their congregation to the long line of saints that preceded them (fig. 6). In her study of FSA photographs of American religion, Colleen McDannell notes that, in the South, baptism was a communal rite more important than the Lord's Supper. In

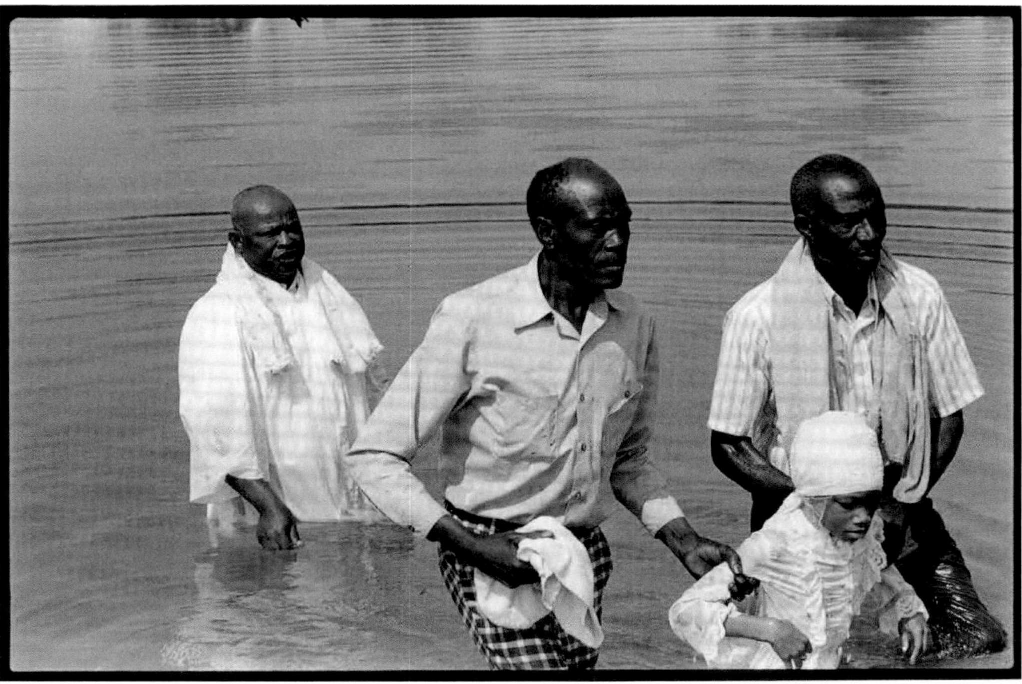

FIG. 6. Paul Kwilecki (1928–2009), *Rev. Mitchell and Lisa Spear at a Mt. Zuma baptism in the Flint River*, 1977. Gelatin silver print, 11 × 14 inches. The Do Good Fund, Inc., 2017-28. © The Paul Kwilecki Family.

these pictures from the Depression era, it is often difficult to separate the nature of individual conversion from a church's will to a common identity and experience.[18] Photographs like Alex Harris's *Ocean Baptism, Currituck County, North Carolina* (plate 51) reiterate this communal endeavor, which finds parallels in the participatory, relational enterprise of photography itself. "Documentarians learn about the world by participating in it," Harris writes. "They immerse themselves in particular communities in hopes of getting to know individuals, people viewed not as subjects, but as colleagues, as teachers, as friends to whom one appeals for information and help."[19] Like Shelby Lee Adams, whose photograph of a serpent handler is also a search for himself, perhaps Harris finds in this immersion baptism a metaphor for his own "immersive" photographic practice. To extend the metaphor, southern evangelicalism insists on the importance of publicly describing personal religious experience, in part as a way to gain more converts. Hence, words like "witness" and "testify" are central to the southern religious vocabulary.[20] If photography is essentially an act of bearing witness, these photographs participate in the ways that religion binds a community together.

Ritual simultaneously acknowledges and resists the ephemeral. Through ritual, communities summon the truths that give them meaning, re-minding and re-membering in ways that overcome human forgetfulness and root identity in both the brain and bones. Especially for communities facing marginalization and erasure, ritual is also a form of defiance. In Colby Deal's *Ethereal* (plate 26), staged in the Third Ward of Houston, Texas, an otherworldly apparition seems to arrest time and decay. Romantic and nostalgic, Deal's white-clad woman on a crumbling porch is a display of "beauty in defiance," linking the spirits of this ward's past with the bodies inhabiting its present even as traditions disappear and communal memory is erased.[21] Deal flyposted blown-up photographs like *Ethereal* on buildings across the Third Ward, reminding viewers of the external forces changing and gentrifying these communities. As the prints deteriorate, their fragmented images haunt the neighborhood like spectral echoes of a vanishing past.

Other photographs in the Do Good Fund's collection demonstrate how rituals offer a means of communal resistance and social justice. Matt Eich's *Firehose baptism* (plate 33) shows the boisterous fanfare and thick mist of a United House of Prayer event in Newport News, Virginia. In this mass baptism scene, where opened hydrants rain down on the crowd, we ought not lose sight of the radical social implications of the water's source. The firehose—the infamous instrument of suppression during the civil rights movement, when police officers unleashed physical violence on peaceful protesters—is refashioned into a means of redemption and transcendence.

Funerary rituals have similarly helped communities corral collective power in the face of systemic inequality. As artist Derek Fordjour remarks, in the Black funerary tradition after the Civil War, the new technology of embalming fluid allowed mourning families to preserve a physical sense of life among the dead. Black funeral directors became the center of their communities for the ways that they could help arrest bodily decay and resist the trauma of so much premature death.[22] One thinks of those moments of collective grief and anguished efforts to reverse the transience of the human frame in Baldwin Lee's *Augusta, GA*.[23] With this open casket, we feel the tragedy of childhood death and the crushing weight of the health and economic inequities that ravage marginalized communities. Meanwhile, in Jane Robbins Kerr's dynamic photograph, Betty the "Hallelujah Lady" welcomes guests to the funeral of the photographer's friend Ella Mae James (plate 57). Betty's exuberant movement and exalting shouts remind her community that, in the face of loss, we still shout Hallelujah—"praise the Lord." Like in Deal's *Ethereal*, the supernatural fights off the ephemeral.

Rituals are perhaps most powerful in the American South for the way they generate collective memories at risk of being forgotten or erased. Sometimes groups use this power of ritual to make social memory visible and intelligible to pernicious ends, perhaps most infamously in what historian Arthur Remillard calls the "civil religion" of the Confederacy and "The Lost Cause."[24] The elaborate rites of white supremacist memory in the South at the turn of the twentieth century commemorated an "inexhaustible Confederate dead," and thereby conjured "an equally limitless southern (white) memory." At prominent sites in the heart of southern towns such as Willis Park in Bainbridge, Georgia (fig. 7), organizations like the United Daughters of the Confederacy visualized these myths in statues and memorials, claiming "cultural authority over virtually all representations of the region's past."[25]

As the Black Masking Indian parades in New Orleans demonstrate, ritual also can forge community identity and revival in places where the dominant society has continually suppressed or effaced other communal histories. Formed during an era of Black persecution, these "proudly separate" parades link their contemporary participants to early-nineteenth-century enslaved Americans who escaped Louisiana plantations and formed new societies in the swamps,

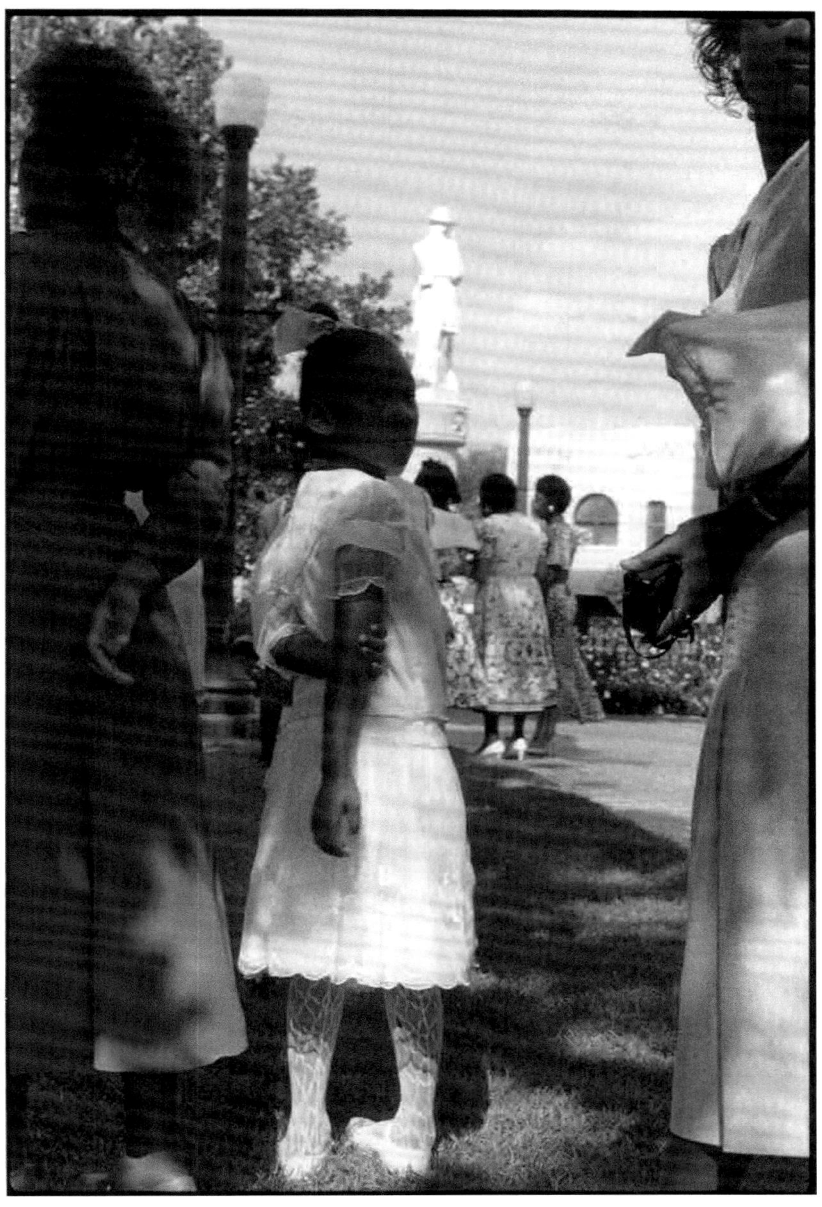

FIG. 7. Paul Kwilecki (1928–2009), *Wedding reception, Willis Park*, 1989. Gelatin silver print, 14 × 11 inches. The Do Good Fund, Inc., 2017–36. © The Paul Kwilecki Family.

often through the help of Indigenous communities.[26] Keith Calhoun's portrait of Darryl Montana, chief of the Black Masking Indian tribe the Yellow Pocahontas Hunters, shows Montana in full regalia (plate 17). With a headdress weighing roughly sixty pounds and a suit covered with West African–style beadwork that the Montana family produced over a full year in a communal sewing effort, Montana subverts the glorification of white culture that came to structure the city's early carnivals. These parades, filmmaker Sascha Just notes, "function as correctives to the dominant historical narrative that portrays New Orleans as heir to a white European history that largely neglects the African and Native American shared heritage of resistance."[27] This is especially true of Darryl Montana himself, whose great-great-uncle was a child of Indigenous and formerly enslaved parents and founded the first of these masking tribes, the Creole Wild West, in 1879.

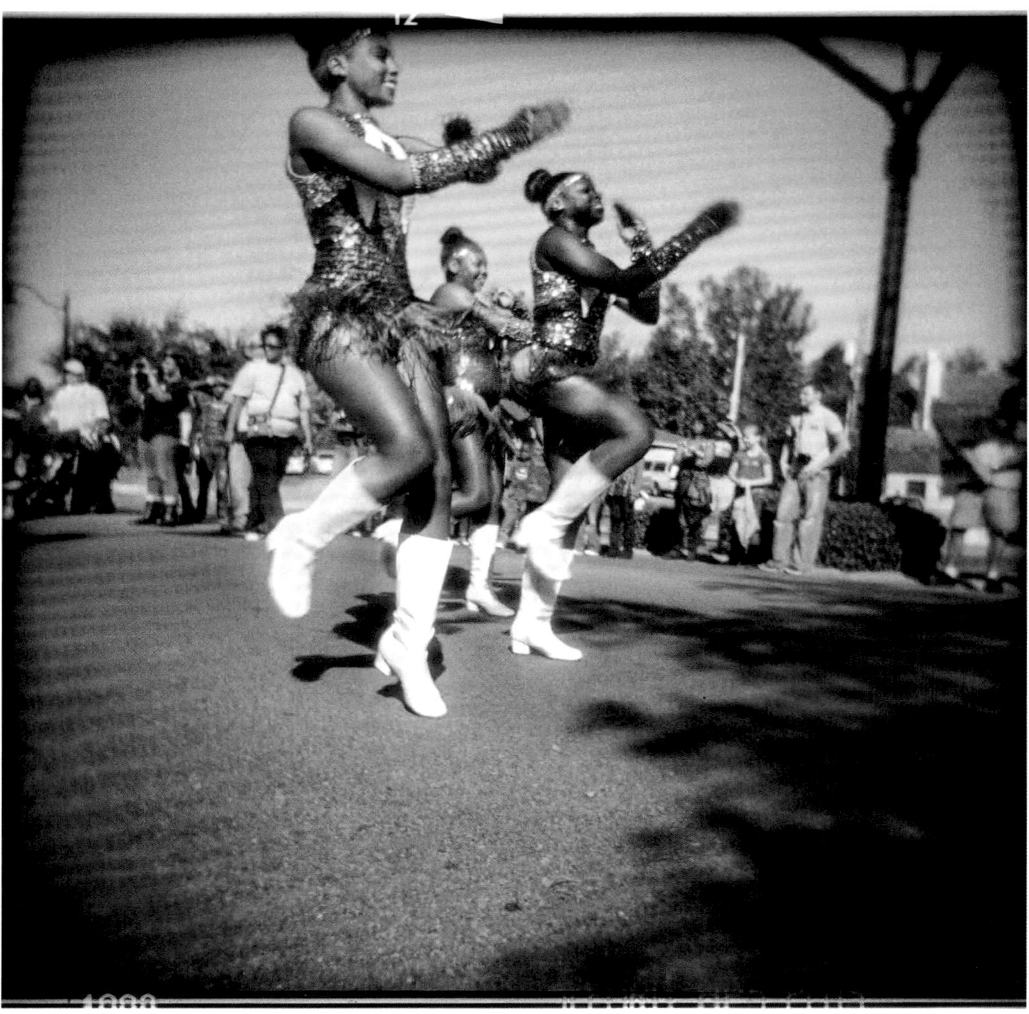

FIG. 8. Betty Press (b. 1942), *Highsteppers, Heritage Parade, Hattiesburg, Mississippi*, 2014. Gelatin silver print, 15 × 14 ⅞ inches. The Do Good Fund, Inc., 2016–56.

In taking on the labor and burdens of memory, culture-bearers like Montana join with their communities for the cause of reclamation and renewal. Andrea Morales's *Southern Heritage Classic Parade* (plate 87) and Betty Press's *Highsteppers* (fig. 8) offer additional examples of Black communities wresting the language of "southern heritage" from longstanding rituals of white supremacy. Morales's photograph shows the Elite Starz of Nashville marching down Park Avenue in Memphis's Orange Mound on the eve of the annual football game between rivals Jackson State University and Tennessee State University. Orange Mound was the first neighborhood in the city built by African Americans for African Americans, dating back to Elzey Eugene Meacham's purchase of the acreage from the former Deaderick plantation.[28] Morales's majorettes traverse a landscape reclaimed from the darkness and violence of chattel slavery for Black ownership, agency, and enterprise. Arms outstretched and faces raised skyward, the exuberant dancers seem to pause in a moment of transcendence. Orange Mound is hallowed ground, another kind of civil religious landscape, where the performers on the street and the spectators on porches, yards, and sidewalks join together in near-sacred communion and breathe in the air of freedom.

NOTES

1   Victor W. Turner, *The Ritual Process: Structure and Anti-Structure* (Ithaca, NY: Cornell University Press, 1969), 131–32. For an application of these ideas to southern culture more broadly, see R. Celeste Ray, ed., *Southern Heritage on Display: Public Ritual and Ethnic Diversity within Southern Regionalism* (Tuscaloosa: University of Alabama Press, 2011).

2   John Hayes, "Deconstructing the Bible Belt," in *Navigating Souths: Transdisciplinary Explorations of a U.S. Region*, ed. Michele Grigsby Coffey and Jodi Skipper (Athens: University of Georgia Press, 2017), 62, 65, and 69. See also Rylan Steele and Nora Wendl, *Ave Maria* (Savannah, GA: Aint-Bad, 2016).

3   Lewis Mumford, *The Story of Utopias* (New York: Boni and Liveright, 1922), 11.

4   Robert Cozzolino, "Introduction: America Is Haunted," in *Supernatural America: The Paranormal in American Art* (Chicago: University of Chicago Press, 2021), 12.

5   Thomas Jefferson to François Jean de Beauvoir, Marquis de Chastellux, September 2, 1785, in *The Papers of Thomas Jefferson*, vol. 8, *25 February–31 October 1785*, ed. Julian P. Boyd (Princeton, NJ: Princeton University Press, 1953), 468.

6   H. L. Mencken, *Prejudices, Second Series* (New York: Alfred A. Knopf, 1920), 136 and 137.

7   Colleen McDannell, *Picturing Faith: Photography and the Great Depression* (New Haven, CT: Yale University Press, 2004), 106.

8   Jonathan Williams, Roger Manley, and Guy Mendes, *Walks to the Paradise Garden: A Lowdown Southern Odyssey*, ed. Phillip March Jones (Lexington, KY: Institute 193, 2019), 52. Ruth's Bible Park no longer exists, but in 1988, Art Rosenbaum recorded Ruth giving a full tour of the park to fellow professor Richard Olsen and their students from the University of Georgia. "Video of Reverend John Ruth at Bible Park, Woodville, Georgia," April 26, 1988, Georgia Folklore Collection, Walter J. Brown Media Archives and Peabody Awards Collection, University of Georgia Libraries, Athens, Georgia.

9   Verses 17–18 of chapter 16 are not in some of the earliest manuscripts of the Gospel of Mark, and scholars debate their authenticity. Verse 18 reads, "They shall take up serpents; and if they drink any deadly thing, it shall not hurt them; they shall lay hands on the sick, and they shall recover" (King James Version).

10 Shelby Lee Adams and Lee Smith, *Appalachian Portraits* (Jackson: University Press of Mississippi, 1993), 11.

11 Paul Kwilecki, *Lowly Wise: Book One: Scenes of Religion In and Around Decatur County, Georgia* (Privately printed, 1992), 10 and 45.

12 Shelby Lee Adams, "The Picture Man," in *The Appalachians: America's First and Last Frontier*, ed. Mari-Lynn Evans, Holly George Warren, and Robert Santelli (New York: Random House, 2004), 200.

13 McDannell, 56–57.

14 Ibid., 89.

15 Michael Blair, "A Sense of Place: William Ferris Interviewed by Michael Blair," *BOMB Magazine*, March 27, 2019, https://bombmagazine.org/articles/william-ferris-interviewed/.

16 In 1933, the Episcopal minister Joseph W. Nicholson and Black pastor Benjamin E. Mays asserted, "The church was the first community or public organization that the Negro actually owned and completely controlled. And it is possibly true to this day that the Negro church is the most thoroughly owned and controlled public institution of the race." Nicholson and Mays, *The Negro's Church* (New York: Institute of Social and Religious Research, 1933), 269.

17 Grace Elizabeth Hale, "Signs of Return: Photography as History in the U.S. South," *Southern Cultures* 25, no. 1 (Spring 2019): 38.

18 McDannell, 100–1. McDannell particularly cites the baptism photographs of Marion Post Wolcott (1910–1990).

19 Alex Harris, introduction to *A World Unsuspected: Portraits of Southern Childhood*, ed. Alex Harris and Sheila Bosworth (Chapel Hill: University of North Carolina Press, published for the Center for Documentary Photography, Duke University, 1987), xvii.

20 Charles Reagan Wilson and David Wharton, *The Power of Belief: Spiritual Landscapes of the Rural South* (Staunton, VA: George F. Thompson, 2016), 19.

21 Colby Deal and Jade Chao, "Déjà Vu in Houston's Third Ward—Colby Deal," *Magnum Photos*, April 4, 2021, https://www.magnumphotos.com/theory-and-practice/deja-vu-houston-third-ward-colby-deal/.

22 Derek Fordjour, "A Celebration of Life (with an Interview by C. J. Bartunek)," *Georgia Review* 75, no. 3 (Fall 2021): 656–57.

23 Baldwin Lee, *Augusta, GA*, 1984. Archival pigment print, 16 × 20 inches. The Do Good Fund, Inc., 2016–30. Due to the sensitive subject matter pictured in this photograph, we have agreed not to reproduce the image in this essay.

24 For more on this topic, see Arthur Remillard, *Southern Civil Religions: Imagining the Good Society in the Post-Reconstruction Era* (Athens: University of Georgia Press, 2011).

25 W. Fitzhugh Brundage, ed., *Where These Memories Grow: History, Memory, and Southern Identity* (Chapel Hill: University of North Carolina Press, 2000), 2, 8, and 14.

26 Sue Beeton, "Mardi Gras Indians: Rituals of Resistance and Resilience in Changing Times," in *Rituals and Traditional Events in the Modern World*, ed. Jennifer Laing and Warwick Frost (London: Routledge, 2014), 189 and 192.

27 Sascha Just, "Big Chief: The Black Indian Tradition of New Orleans," in *Black Resistance in the Americas*, ed. D. A. Dunkley and Stephanie Shonekan (New York: Routledge, 2018), 127.

28 In 1890, widow Mattie Deaderick sold the property to Meacham, a white real estate developer. Ignoring her request not to sell land to Black people, Meacham developed the first subdivision specifically for African Americans. Residents purchased the lots from Meacham for $40 each but had to build their houses, churches, and other structures. This arrangement gave the community a sense of individual and communal ownership.

THE PLANT HARDINESS ZONE

Jeff Whetstone

YOU HAVE A SEED IN YOUR HAND. It has something to give you, something that you want: a decorative flower, a delicious vegetable, or a nourishing root. You wait for the right time of year, you dig a hole, you lay the seed in, cover it with soft dirt, and nurture it. You check on it and patiently watch it grow. You feed it and protect it as best you know how. And depending on the plant, you harvest it and repeat the process over and over.

Now let's look at the sowing of a seed from the perspective of the plant. Attract a human by its desire for aesthetics or for nourishment. Make it want you. Make it need you. Make it make a place for you. Make it decide to dig. If it does, it is invested in you. It will water you and protect you, and your roots can grow and connect with all the wisdom of the soil going back to the ancient seas. Feed your human, make it appreciate your beauty, and when it is time to begin again, call your animal back. It will know what to do with your seeds. They have been trained for millennia.

Plants have played us, especially in the South. Most of the United States Department of Agriculture's plant hardiness zones 7 and 8 (the American Southeast) have everything going for them from a plant's point of view: ample sun, a good amount of precipitation, shallow water tables, seasons that allow for rebirth, and a culture bound to flora.

If we consider the South as a place that plants made (after all, they were here half a billion years before us) and see this region through their desires, we can come closer to understanding how we can love a place that hurts us. We can reconcile how southerners can be tied forever to a place that sometimes seems to want to push us out; how we can miss dearly the place we left for our own good; or how we vow to never leave it, no matter what the cost. These are the sentiments of being owned by the land.

Revered evolutionary biologist W. D. Hamilton argued that if genes had desires, they would want to propagate over time and space to reach a sustainable equilibrium.[1] Of course, genes don't have brains, or desires. But, if we look at evolution through this model, the miracle of procreation is a force greater than the fitness of any individual. It uses both competition and collaboration within and among species. The dispersion of many species of plants depends on the desires of animals, including us. If we imagine the world we live in from that perspective, how have the landscape and culture of the South become so intertwined?

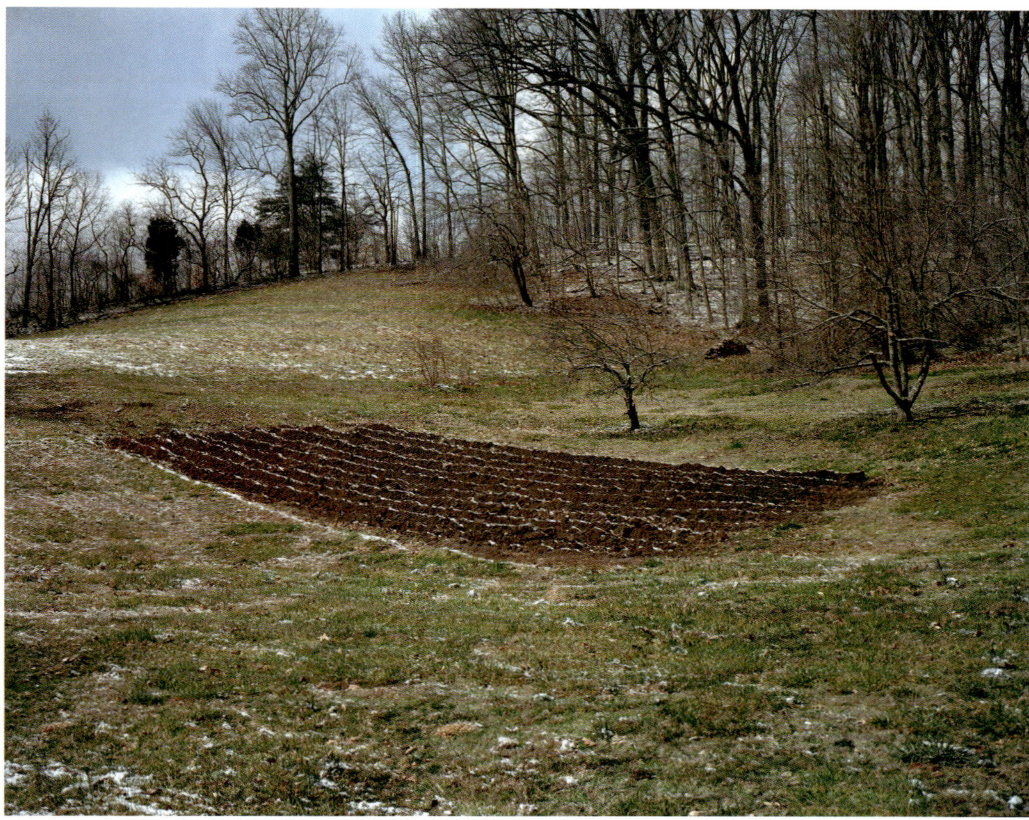

FIG. 1. Mike Smith (b. 1951), *Gray, Tennessee,* 1996. Archival pigment print, 20 × 24 inches. The Do Good Fund, Inc., 2014–33. Copyright the artist.

Consider Mike Smith's *Gray, Tennessee* as the beginning of a life cycle (fig. 1). Imagine that the patch of plowed land was inevitable, pre-ordained millions of years ago, when what we now call a sweet potato (or whatever crop will be sown in this humble space) was evolving toward a connection to human desire. The code inside each variety of sweet potato cell strives for the most fecund plant, and one strategy is to become the vegetable that animals desire the most. The sweet potato has become a human ally, surviving generation after generation under our care and protection. In Smith's picture, the plant has played on human labor and ingenuity to land on a hillside in Tennessee—sown, cared for, savored, and saved for the next season. The sweet potato itself made these furrows using a human body connected to a rototiller.

Georgia Rhodes's *Roadtrip* (plate 100) is a concise statement about desire and plants. The driver of that car has a heart like a bee. They drove directly into the most flamboyant and fecund plant we know. The goldenrod will play on your visual desires like a love song on the radio plays to your emotions. The goldenrod's yellow indicates summer is coming to a close. "Do now what you desire most," it declares, "because soon it will be Autumn, a time to work and prepare." That plant beaconed this road tripper. It knew what it was doing. It covered the romantic driver and the interior of their Honda Civic with its pollen so that it could pollinate new, never-met-before goldenrod faster than the wind, 500 miles down the road, spreading its intelligent genes into a new frontier.

RaMell Ross's *Interface* (plate 102) speaks of older, wiser plants. Why did these tupelos, poplars, and cypresses beckon people to build a ramp there? The serene and haunting tone of Ross's image may offer a clue. "Come," the plants say. "Look. Be Still. Be quiet. Listen to my birds." When we take in this solemn sight, exhale, and relax, the trees explain, "This is what we can do for you. We don't just make wood for your economy. We can give you a sacred moment. Don't you want that now? Then save us. Build yourself a place to revere the last of us. Remember this." The plants are using humanity's desire for sublime beauty and need for atonement as their own last defense.

As William Faulkner famously wrote, "The past is never dead. It's not even past." Except if there is kudzu in your yard. Then the past is devoured and digested. Wily kudzu may be the most strategic plant alive. It exploited American "ingenuity" and desire for the "exotic," for the "quick-fix," and the late-nineteenth-century obsession with the Orient to get on a boat in Japan and come to the South to save our vanishing topsoil. Kudzu found its glory in our southern sun and vast tracts of overgrazed, eroding land that couldn't support other plant competition. It lives now as one of the most enduring symbols of the region. It is almost impossible to imagine the South without kudzu, which is deemed invasive but welcomed here with open arms. In the summer it is the beautiful snake of a vine that gets us kicked out of Eden. In the winter it is a grotesque temple erected to our own shame. Kudzu is here to stay, reminding us of who we are. While it buries the past, like in Mark Steinmetz's *Athens, Georgia* (fig. 2), it also makes a monument of it, a grisly monument to loss. Kudzu symbolizes the South's fertility and our disgrace and satisfies the southerner's predilection for the dramatic and gothic.

The dark legacy of American capitalism, the horror of slavery and racism, the southern mythologies of beauty and purity, and the great global cultural rise of Black art may be all be tied to the diabolical genetic coding of two other invasive plants: tobacco and cotton. These plants played human greed and addiction like a puppet master.

Tobacco placates our mood while cultivating our addiction. When the first wave of colonizers transformed the sacred Indigenous plant into a cash crop, tobacco reached an evolutionary plateau. It inserted itself into world economies, from

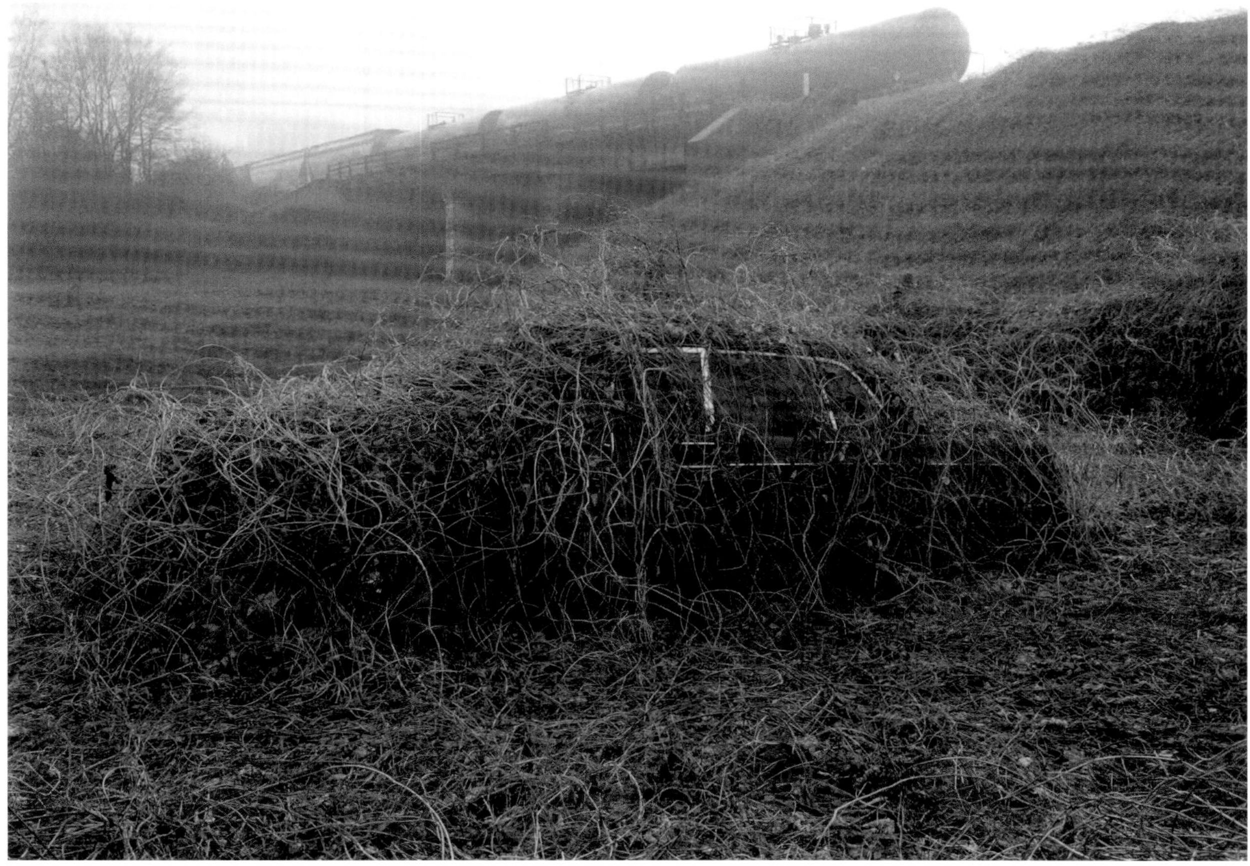

FIG. 2. Mark Steinmetz (b. 1961), *Athens, Georgia*, 1997. Gelatin silver print, 12 × 17 ½ inches. The Do Good Fund Inc., 2014–25. © Mark Steinmetz.

the holdings of multinational corporations to the pocketbooks of small farmers throughout the South, like those pictured in Rob Amberg's *Angie and Juanita Shelton Unloading Tobacco, Hopewell, Madison County, NC* (plate 4).

Cotton knew from seven thousand years before 1619, from seven thousand growing seasons, seven thousand generations of evolution, how to entwine the human species within its exposed flower of pure cellulose. Its flower is so strangely beautiful and so perfectly useful that it is hard to imagine human evolution without it. Once cotton inspired the haptic intelligence and exacting imagination of Egyptians and Mayans to build elaborate tools for spinning its fibers, this plant was ready to take over the world. Cotton found in the South perfect soil and greedy colonizers doped up on capitalism who would do and risk anything, even the soul of a nation, for profit. Ruddy Roye's *Shack Up Inn* (plate 104) directly ties contemporary state violence against Black people to the violence directed upon the enslaved by a nation under the spell of King Cotton. America remains hobbled and unatoned. But cotton came out pretty. In a relatively short evolutionary period, the cotton plant population went from being a wild bush sparsely scattered and isolated in fields that speckled scrubland to occupying 2.5 percent of the earth's arable land.

Perspective and vantage point are elemental to the medium of photography. The point of view of the photographer—how and where they are pointing the camera—informs us, sometimes subconsciously, of the artist's position on a particular subject. That point of view is sometimes referred to as "the gaze." Often considered a pejorative term, as in phrases like "the male gaze on the female body," or the "white gaze on the Black body," the gaze is the privilege of the artist's viewpoint.

Many contemporary cultural theorists advocate for a reading of portraiture that shifts interpretation from a focus on the photographer's position to the histories and futurities of the people whose lives are interrupted by what Ariella Azoulay calls an "event" of photography.[2] Furthermore, as Kaja Silverman argues, "The camera is less a machine . . . than a complex field of relations."[3] It is a vehicle that knits together a relationship between the eye behind the viewfinder, complete with its own intrinsic desires; the body in front of the lens, present with its own narratives; and the culture that feeds the need for photography. By inquiring about the histories, positions, and situations orbiting the event of a photograph, we find a more complete structure for how it can be interpreted.

I don't intend to equate oppressed people with plants. But what might the models of photographic inquiry suggested by Azoulay, Silverman, Tina Campt, and others offer when considering the evolutionary and cultural histories of flora?[4] Perhaps the photographs in the collection of the Do Good Fund can offer a deeper, more complete interpretation of the trajectories of the South. In a picture about a place, does knowing how a plant species connects to culture grant us greater understanding of the photograph? What is the plant's point of view toward the photographer? Of course, plants don't have eyes, just highly evolved light sensors; and they aren't sentient beings, though recent studies have proven them to be communicative and socially collaborative across multiple species.[5]

But imagining plants by using a model that grants them agency and by contraposing them with the gaze of an artist allows us to see how the South's natural history is intertwined with its cultural history. And how we humans are bound to both. Even in the Anthropocene, nature owns us completely.

NOTES

1   W. D. Hamilton, "The Genetical Evolution of Social Behavior," *Journal of Theoretical Biology* 7, no. 1 (1964): 1–16.

2   Ariella Azoulay, *The Civil Contract of Photography* (New York: Zone Books, 2008). In writing about photographs of the politically oppressed, Azoulay maintains that the event of a photograph extends in time, from the genesis of the situation in which the photograph was made to its dispersal and reading.

3   Kaja Silverman, *The Threshold of the Visible World* (New York: Routledge, 1996), 136.

4   See Tina Campt, *Listening to Images* (Durham, NC: Duke University Press, 2017).

5   Richard Powers's novel *The Overstory* (2018) is based on studies by Suzanne Simard that prove that plants exhibit interspecial signaling. The primary source publication is: Suzanne W. Simard, David A. Perry, Melanie D. Jones, David D. Myroid, Daniel M. Durall, and Randy Molina, "Net transfer of carbon between ectomycorrhizal tree species in the field," *Nature* 388, no. 6642 (August 1997): 579–82. See also Michael Pollan, "The Intelligent Plant," *New Yorker*, December 15, 2013, https://www.newyorker.com/magazine/2013/12/23/the-intelligent-plant.

FOR THE NOURISHMENT OF OUR BODIES

Rosalind Bentley

I AM PICKY ABOUT BACON BUT DO NOT STAND ON CEREMONY.

A prepackaged grocery store purchase is perfectly fine, though I do inspect the lean-to-fat ratio and thickness of the slices. From time to time, I'll buy $11-per-pound, pre-cut ribbons from the butcher's case but only after dithering between the applewood-smoked and pepper-crusted varieties. If I'm feeling flush and fancy, I may spend more for a small slab at a weekend farmers' market.

As for tomatoes, I'm not above eating them out of season if the craving for a BLT hits hard in January. I can afford an organic heirloom variety grown and shipped from a warmer clime to a produce bin in my neighborhood supermarket.

These choices are middle-class proclivities that are in their own way obscene. It is hard to look at this exhibition's photographs of food and the many ways it is procured, prepared, and served and not be reminded of the generational struggle that preceded me. A war on poverty and battle against segregation allowed me to be well fed. It is a privilege to be able to say I've never known a missed meal cramp, at least not by necessity (fig. 1).

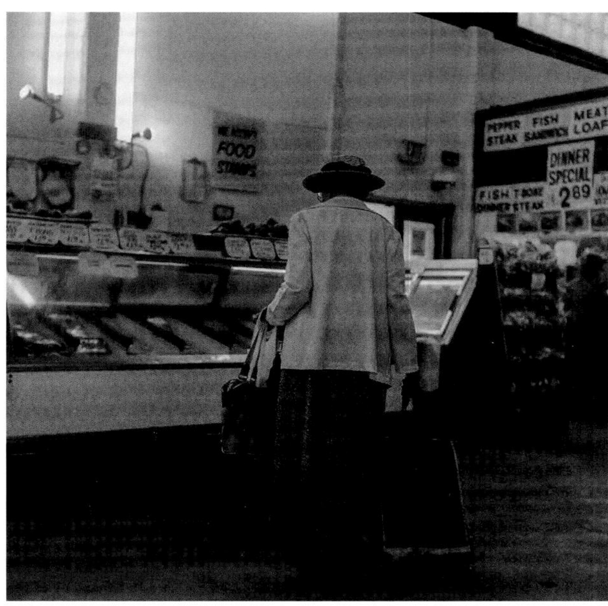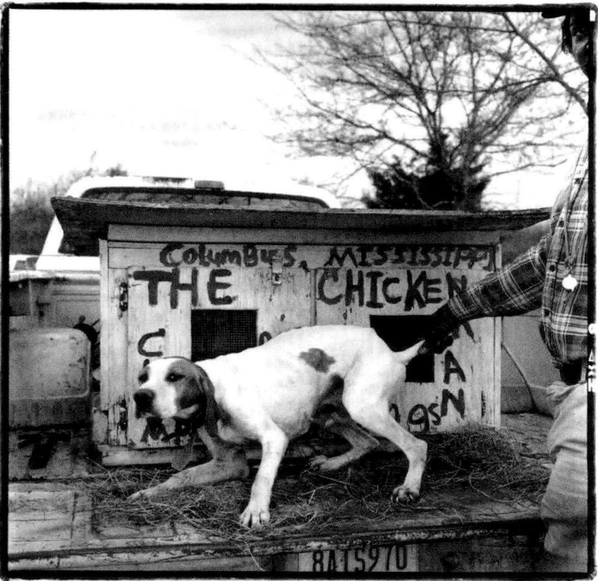

FIG. 1. Marilyn Suriani (b. 1951), *Auburn Market, Atlanta*, 1978. 24 × 24 inches. The Do Good Fund, Inc., 2014–55.

FIG. 2. Birney Imes (b. 1951), *The Chicken Man's Dog, Lowndes County, Mississippi*, 1990. Gelatin silver print, 10 × 10 inches. The Do Good Fund, Inc., 2015–55.

My South, our South, has always been a land of both abundance and lack, of plenty and paucity. It is a place of oysters Bienville and rare duck breast served from heirloom silver, of chicken gizzards and rice crowded atop old, chipped plates. Of wombs heavy with child and malnourished maternal hips too narrow for safe births. Of Junior League and bridge club luncheons nibbled over Battenberg lace tablecloths and of a meal eaten only because someone in the household went out and grew it, caught it, or shot it (fig. 2). The Do Good Fund's collection of food photography shouts and whispers these stories.

Photographer Jimmy Nicholson lives along the seams of land binding Florida, Georgia, and Alabama. The acreage is rich and fertile. Beginning in the late 1800s, Gadsden County, Florida, where Nicholson now lives, was awash with shade tobacco farms. They thrived in the fecund soil. Black workers tended the crop from seed to harvest. Sepia photographs of the era capture the exhaustion, poverty, and resignation of each Black body seared daily in sunny, green fields. By the 1970s, the north Florida tobacco industry collapsed, no competition for cheaper imported leaves. Farmers turned to tomatoes, and, in turn, to Black and brown bodies to tend them. Around that time, Nicholson visited the studio of photographer Richard Parks in Tallahassee's first indoor shopping center, the Northwood Mall, about two miles from my childhood home. Nicholson has said Parks's eye, his rendering of north Florida life in black and white, changed the way Nicholson produced his own images.

Nicholson's portrait of a dark-skinned farm worker balancing a bucket full of mature green tomatoes atop his head feels of the era when tobacco ruled (plate 92). The dirt road bisecting the fields. The head rag tied askew underneath his chin. The face set with resignation. The body bearing not what W. E. B. DuBois described as the "gift of sweat and brawn to beat back the wilderness, conquer the soil, and lay the foundations of this vast economic empire."[1] This body seems bowed by weariness.

Yet, the sweat-stained shirt is contemporary. The groaning pail is plastic. The hands are gloved. This is what getting fresh tomatoes to a supermarket, into a grocery bag, and onto a BLT looks like in 2020, when Nicholson took the picture in the fields of Gadsden County. Did this worker get paid fair wages? Did he get enough to eat? And if he had children, did his kids go to bed with full stomachs in the late hours after his picture was taken?

I tell my mother about this photo because she was reared on a farm about forty miles from where Nicholson captured the image. "You don't remember those fields?" she asks me. "We used to pass them all the time going back down home." Back down home, meaning our family's ancestral farm or what remains of it. And no, I barely remembered the scenes she so vividly recalled. "You could see the people out there working from the road."

She worked in fields as a child. The family was poor but never hungry because they had their own farm: fruits, vegetables, cows, chickens, pigs. (Maybe that's why the term farm-to-table has always made me chuckle. It's not new to those who grew up rural.) The smokehouse built before my mother was born stood into my adulthood. Cuts from slaughter were cured in that oak outbuilding. Nothing was wasted, from snout to tail (fig. 3).

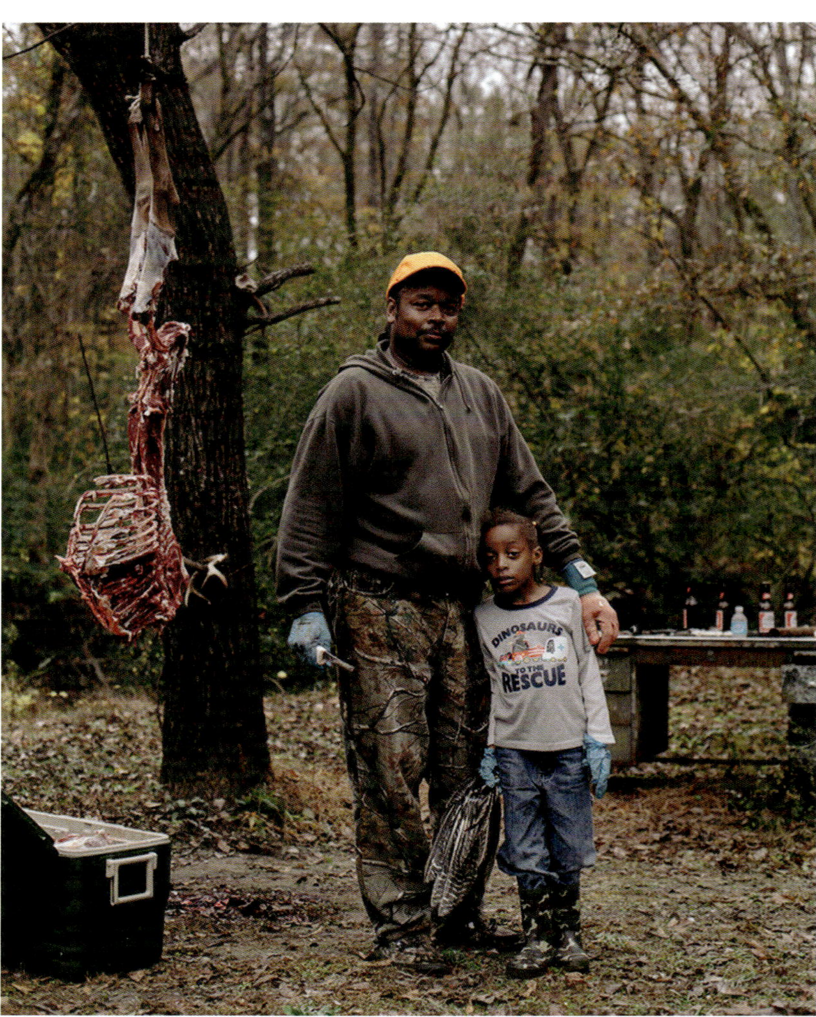

FIG. 3. Whitten Sabbatini (b. 1990), *Jeffrey & Jr. Skinning a Deer*, 2011–12. Archival pigment print, 30 × 24 inches. The Do Good Fund, Inc., 2013–14.

In Jeff Whetstone's photograph of a hog killing in eastern Kentucky, white hands remove entrails from a pig carcass in the early stages of butchery (plate 120). Black hands, both those of my family and their neighbors, did it on our farm. So I'm told. I never witnessed a hog killing. But the process, regardless of race, remains essentially the same and is executed with a universal goal: to make sure no one goes hungry.

Whetstone was an artist in residence at Appalshop around the time he took the photograph in Oscaloosa, Kentucky. It repels. The pig's large intestine is swollen with waste. It compels. Its skin is hairless, pale, and rubbery. Beneath the rind is fat to be rendered into lard. This is the promise of nourishment. Easter hams. New Year's Day ham hocks. Sunday chitterlings. Bacon.

What I know of hog killing on small, rural farms pretty much begins and ends with the fact that slaughter is typically done in winter. A plaid flannel shirt and the sleeve of a thick coat suggest it was cool when Whetstone took the black-and-white picture. How had the day begun? For that I asked two witnesses, separated from the Kentucky killing by two states, five decades, segregation, and race: my mother and her older cousin John Howard.

Step one. John Howard: "The hogs would be fed for weeks or months with corn and peanuts until they reached about 200 pounds. There were a couple ways to kill them: by gunshot or hammer. Then they would cut 'em so they would bleed out."

Step two. My mother: "They had a big enough pot you could put a hog in it. You had to build a fire under it and get the water scalding hot. . . . One man would catch the hind legs and another one catch the front, then put it in the kettle of water. When they pulled it out, you could run your hand over it and the hair would come off, then it would be white skin because all the hair had come off him."

Step three. John Howard: "Once they had him bled, scalded and shaved, then they'd hang him up then cut him from neck to tail and take out the innards. The large intestines were for chitlins and the small intestines for sausage casings."

Step four. My mother: "With the head they'd make hog head cheese."

Salt and smoke came next. Slab by slab, the oak smokery filled with meat.

If they still eat pork, people who lived that experience probably prefer their bacon thick. My mother does. Perhaps the men of Oscaloosa, Kentucky—captured by Whetstone in the midst of step three—do, too.

Small gestures make modest meals memorable. A tomato server, whether stainless steel or tarnished hand-me-down silver plate, laid next to slices of white bread and pristine rounds of Cherokee Purples from a backyard garden, conveys care, order, and pride. Maybe there won't be enough for everyone to have a second or third helping, but the first plateful can have an air of ceremony.

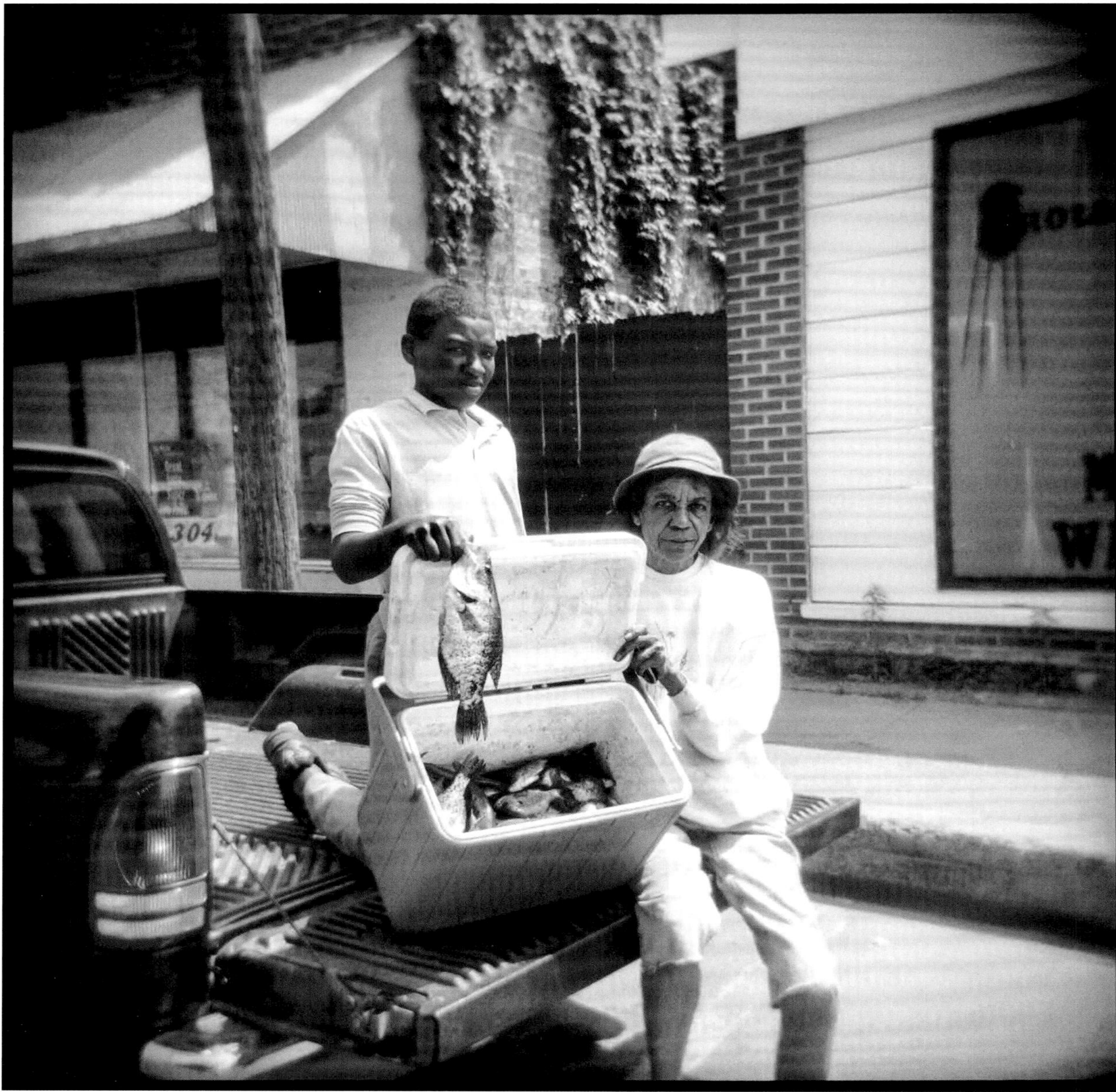

FIG. 4. Betty Press (b. 1942), *Fishing Trip, Rolling Fork, Mississippi*, 2010. Gelatin silver print, 15 × 14 ⅞ inches. The Do Good Fund, Inc., 2016–57.

This collection invites us to contemplate the overlap of scarcity and plenty. Take Carolyn Drake's photograph of a linen-draped table dressed with food of southern aspirational welcome (plate 29). Slices of pound cake, crumbly and buttery, form a ring like fallen dominoes atop a gleaming, silver-plated serving platter. Next to it, nosegays of pink roses match the pink edges of deviled eggs arranged on a deviled egg tray. We are called to imagine how long the peeled boiled eggs marinated in beet juice before proud hands split them, scooped out the yolks, mixed the yellow centers with mayonnaise (was it Duke's?), mustard, and sweet chunks of pickle relish, and then refilled each egg white before dusting them with paprika. Clearly, they were popular. Remnants of pale, ruby beet juice dot the tray's empty slots. Did the host spend their last dollars to make this a special occasion for a loved one? Did they pull out the best that they had even though, week to week, they barely get by?

In Betty Press's black-and-white photograph of the spoils of a fishing trip near
Rolling Fork, Mississippi (fig. 4), we imagine the fish fry that came later. The
ice chest in the back of the pickup truck is loaded with fresh catch, proudly dis-
played by two anglers. Who cleaned the fish? Who watched the fillets get coated
in cornmeal then dunked in bubbling oil? Was there potato salad and collard
greens? Who took foil-wrapped plates home to feed those who couldn't make it?
Did the meal fill them up?

Looking at the honey-toned cabinets in Lauren Henkin's portrait of a kitchen—
neat, spotless, with clean pots and pans in a drying rack next to the sink—I'm
reminded of the humble, dignified, working-class kitchens where I was nurtured
and fed three home-cooked meals a day (plate 56). A place where I was served
squash cooked in bacon fat rendered from thin slices, rice topped with tomatoes
reduced to sweet gravy. Henkin's photograph is titled *Whoever comes to me shall
not hunger, and whoever believes in me shall never thirst.*

I wonder if those kitchen cabinets are full. 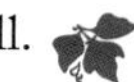

NOTES

1   W. E. B. DuBois, *The Souls of Black Folk* (Chicago: A. C. McClurg
    and Co., 1903), 262–63.

SLANGLESS

RaMell Ross

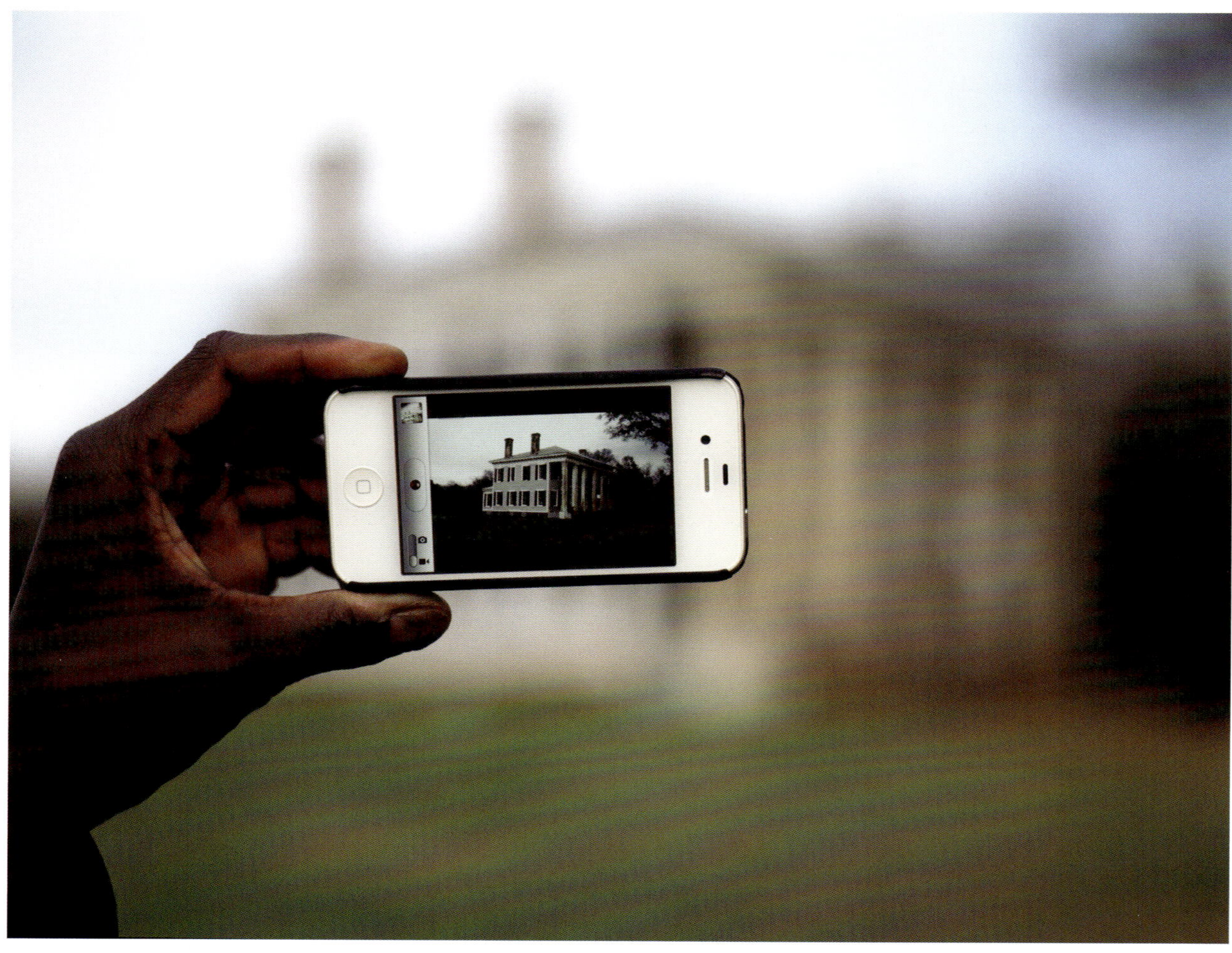

RaMell Ross, *iHome*, 2012 (plate 103)

THE CASE: To be a photograph of the American South. To be an image that regards the Historic South's impression. To be an index, a document, a testament, a moment, a facsimile, a reference, a distillation, a memory . . . of that physical and nonphysical region. To feel *of* the South, and southern, like an accent can. To ring the southern bell. Gonggg. To be like infrared, resonating below the Mason–Dixon line.

PERCEPTION: To be a picture of the American South. To be extrajudicial, and lean southern. To have the South in your bones. To be invisibly skeletal. To organize a scarecrow's affects and *feel* southern, like a southern meal. To be all the South can be. Or not be, what the South is not. To be portable like the South, the mythology's globally trafficked, non/fiction railroad. To be southern bound, directionally speaking. To be southern bound again, in heritage, glass, leather, or sauce. To be sketched by southern drawls, like echolocation (in a darkness satin, literary, and timeless). To be one of the cardinal directions of the Western world, logic. To not smell of the South but evoke a southern odor.

Like, Gaaawwdddd damn! You smell that?

to hint and hush in bits of yesterday

to be a frame of southern architecture and baptize the offspring of the old country's rationale

to be of bonkers democracy and make a stooge of silence

to propagate a multiverse in the minds of children

to have materialized a people's identity

to look me dead in the eye

To remake the South familiar, like a William Christenberry image, in the slangless, southern vim. To magnetize the road-trip romanticism of sentiment in old things. To be window and grave. And lap the shores of Atlantis. To be its own southern language and allegorically, give down the country. To be southern like the South's time, part ghost, part momentum.

To be America's domestic foreigner. To be the Cheshire Cat's grin.

CRITIQUE: To polish the South's veneers. And spark serotonin (as a defense mechanism against visibility). To be guilty by association, and the master of equanimity. To be inside, the inside of the text, without contemporaries or a bead of sweat. To be a photo-place of the American South.

to silence the veld's hymns

and bow out of moral guidance

to laugh, not cry, and laugh and laugh

then cry

to treat Blackness like portraiture

to treat Whiteness like light

to fetishize the icon, and know when it's high noon

to be rooted in the past as a shadow, while under the future

to hide in plain sight

and attract the thrift store art collector

to be full-stop lyrical and gild the canon

and overexpose the person in order to underexpose the person

with a sanitized South in kind

with the dirty South in mind

JUDGMENT: To be a photograph of the American South—i.e., sluggish outside of theme—i.e., prefer a formalist author—i.e., reward an arrested bed frame or an object's suspension or an abandoned, historized car, with dopamine. To be revue.

To point with a Christian choir and on one's tiptoes, to avoid making sounds. To look everywhere but down and in, and down, and in. To prefer genre monogamy and love the southern daze.

to prefer depiction to discovery, tradition to innovation, sharpness to intractability

to be an iceberg that is only photogenic above water

to be right-brain humanism left-brain landscape

to have an executive function talking about heaven and serpents and eschatology

to have never taken off one's clothes

to shroud an ongoing state of piloerection

to have forgotten the tan (a body like silk and a tongue tied longways)

to prefer aestheticizing flora and fauna (including humans!), with deadpan, euphemistic vibrancy

to consider the avant-garde-anything malintent

To be paradigmatic of absence and presence; presence in absence, absence in presence; of the southern photograph's matryoshka doll spiritual sociality. To get the southern picture and know only before the horizon, behind the time, from a tree saddle, with a sky beam to blind and guide the premonitions of the approaching now. To get the southern picture and turn the southern cheek. To be emotionally southern and think of therapy as kryptonite.

To be all the South can be, because of what it wasn't.

AIM: To be a photographic artifact of the southern United States. To be material memory, like a scratch and sniff. Or binary-coded memory, able to tip the literal scale. To be southern matter, in alchemy, value, or otherwise. To start from the bottom and now be here, and to always have family in the Black Belt. To have listened closely to the South, and derived legibility from its light. To be a free-willed photograph of the American South, rare and pure black, brown, soil and mud. And dance and jazz and riddle and electrocute and blow smoke with semiotics, despite the surface tension of an uphill battle and the iron core of the good ole boy's gravity.

To get the southern picture. And turn back the other cheek. To peer into time's Tetris and fortuitously trace the end of the rainbow to South Africa; and find then, at both ends, a protovisuality. To escape Aunt Jemima's syrup through the help of Polaris, and return, star studded, after ceaseless cosmic showers, to say:

pardon, pardon, pardon

me,

a rhizome from your suffrage

i got the picture

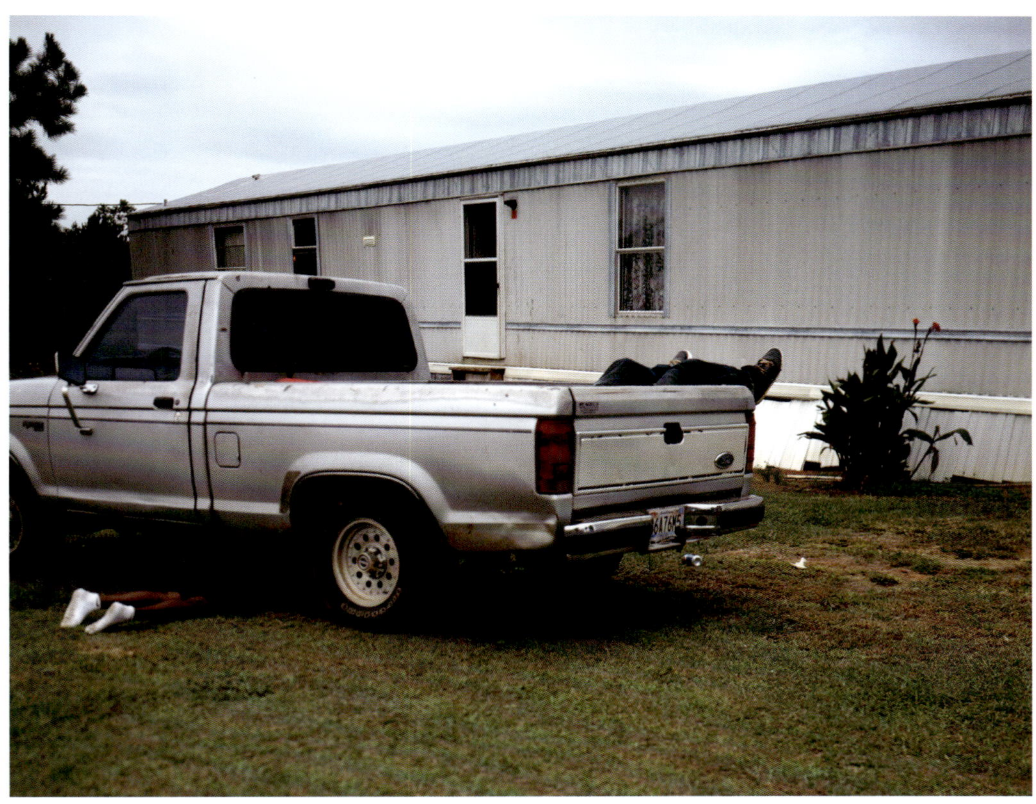

RaMell Ross (b. 1982), *Brothers Z*, 2012. Archival pigment print, 36 × 46 inches. Image courtesy the artist.

PERSONAL APPROACH: To be so hungry for self as to eat the picture of the South. And eat the Giving Tree, its strange fruit, every mailbox and road sign from Texas to Maryland, and even eat the honorable hand that fed, a mouth in a southern photo-genetic chewing motion. To use the excrement for a permanent installation in the archive of the Library of Congress. To then consider the installation fertilizer for a new body of southern images.

POSSIBILITY: To be a photograph of the American South and be liberated, having known death.

SEEING THE ATHENS SCENE: PHOTOGRAPHY AND ALTERNATIVE CULTURE

Grace Elizabeth Hale

THERE'S A SHADOW EXHIBITION IN MY MIND, photographs no one took or bothered to save: the first time Ricky Wilson and Keith Strickland dressed up in drag in their old house on Pulaski Street; Michael Stipe meeting Jeremy Ayers at a house party; Vanessa Briscoe "trying out" for the band that would become Pylon; the sweaty smash of the second and third 40 Watts; Vic Chesnutt writing "Speed Racer" in a battered notebook; Laura Carter marrying her girlfriend on the stage of the Uptown; and Jennifer Hartley in the loft of the original Grit. I want pictures of the Athens that gave the world not only the B-52s, R.E.M., Pylon, and so many other great bands but also the place that taught everyone who paid attention that they did not have to move to New York, that they could make their art and music with their friends, wherever they happened to be. I want bohemian Athens, queer Athens, alternative Athens—that fusion of people and place that taught so many of us that, if we really wanted to be alive, we had to make our own culture. I want Athens, the scene.

The Do Good Fund has collected a few photographs like the ones I have imagined, pictures that capture something of the look and feel of young people turning themselves and part of a sleepy southern college town into one of the essential birthplaces of that 1980s and 1990s mashup of counterculture and bohemia—indie culture. Like so many others who built this new Athens, Michael Stipe attended the University of Georgia's art school and thought of himself as an artist as well as a musician. In a black-and-white print from 1982 (fig. 1), Stipe depicts his sister Lynda Stipe and Jeremy Ayers, Athens's original bohemian and a figure who transformed almost everyone who got to know him, including Michael in the late 1970s and, in the mid-1980s, me.

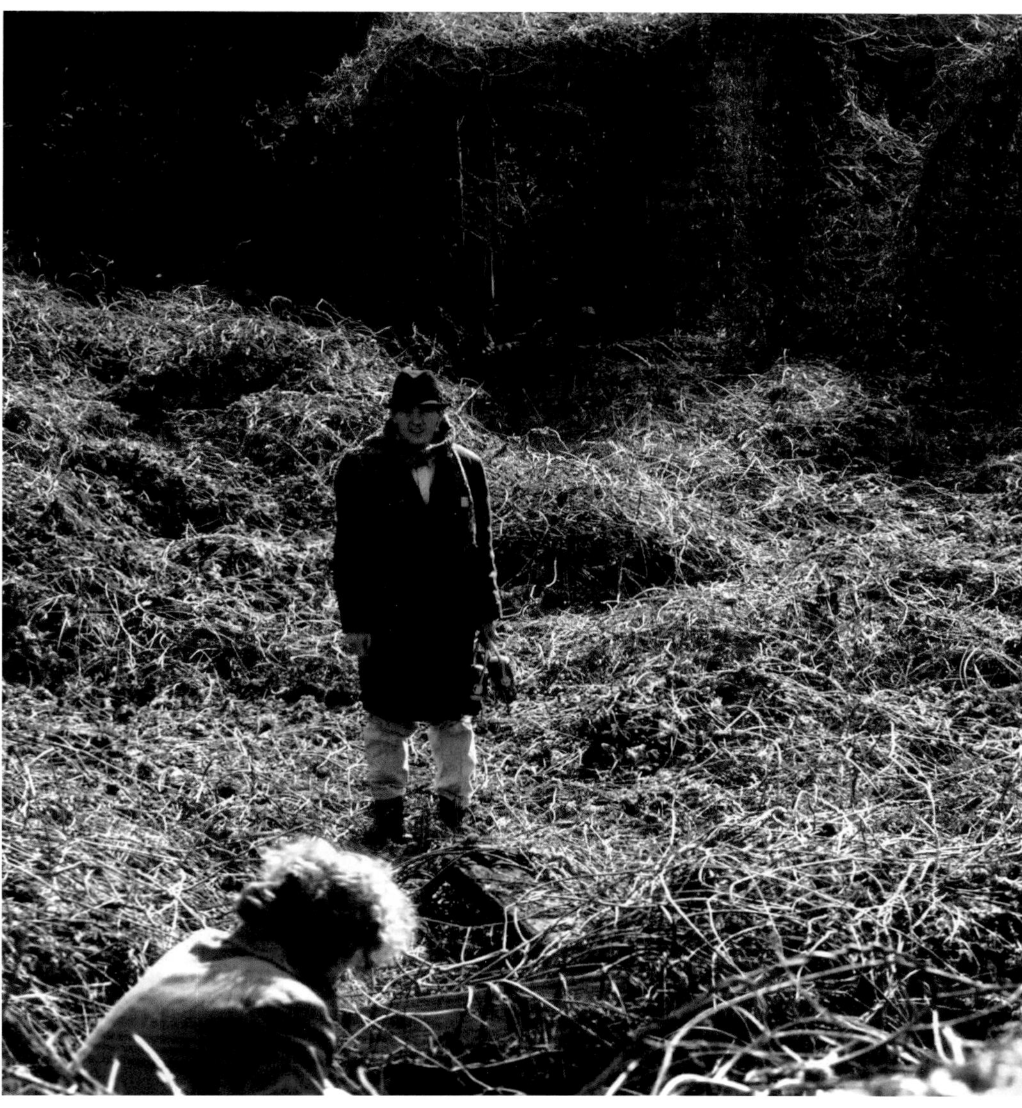

In Stipe's photograph, Lynda squats in the foreground with her back to the camera, cut off by the edge of the frame, as the sunlight melts her curls into a halo. Ayers stands deeper in the field, a trick of perspective that makes it look like his right boot is planted in her golden hair. Kudzu covers everything except the two figures and the ghostly trunks of a thick line of saplings at the far back, their days numbered, their fate as victims of the advancing vine already sealed. Ayers's fedora points to what is most interesting: a draped ruin in the center of the top third of the picture. Some kind of structure pulled apart and covered by the destructive weed seems to hover there, its doors splayed outward, its roof a tent of vines. You have to look closely to see the dark break in the pattern, the opening, possibly a portal to some other realm. Is Ayers asking Lynda, and maybe Michael, too, if they want to enter? Is he asking us? Is Stipe pointing the way? And isn't this the same place where another friend of Michael's, the artist and musician Carol Levy, took the photograph that appeared on the front of R.E.M.'s first album, *Murmur*? Stipe's kudzu creates a perfect metaphor for just how hard it can be to see the traces of the indie scene on the landscape of Athens.

This is one powerful reason there is not an Athens "look," a school of photography that announces through its formal qualities and its content that it belongs to "Athens." Instead, there are artists like Sandra Phipps in the 1980s and Carl Martin in the 1990s who photographed Athens musicians even as they also made other pictures. Sometimes, this work transcends its documentary origins. For example, Martin's series of prints of the singer-songwriter Vic Chesnutt in his wheelchair in the parking lot of the Bulldog Inn glow with an uncanny radiance (fig. 2), revealing something of Chesnutt's contradictory combination of vulnerability and stubbornness and his rootedness in the eccentricities of rural southern culture. There are also artists based in Athens, like former UGA photography professor Mark Steinmetz (fig. 3), who have achieved a measure of art world success but have not been a part of the scene and have mostly not attempted to photograph it. And finally, there are former UGA students like Pamela Pecchio who were a part of the scene and turned their friends into models for their art school assignments on their way to careers based mostly on images made elsewhere.

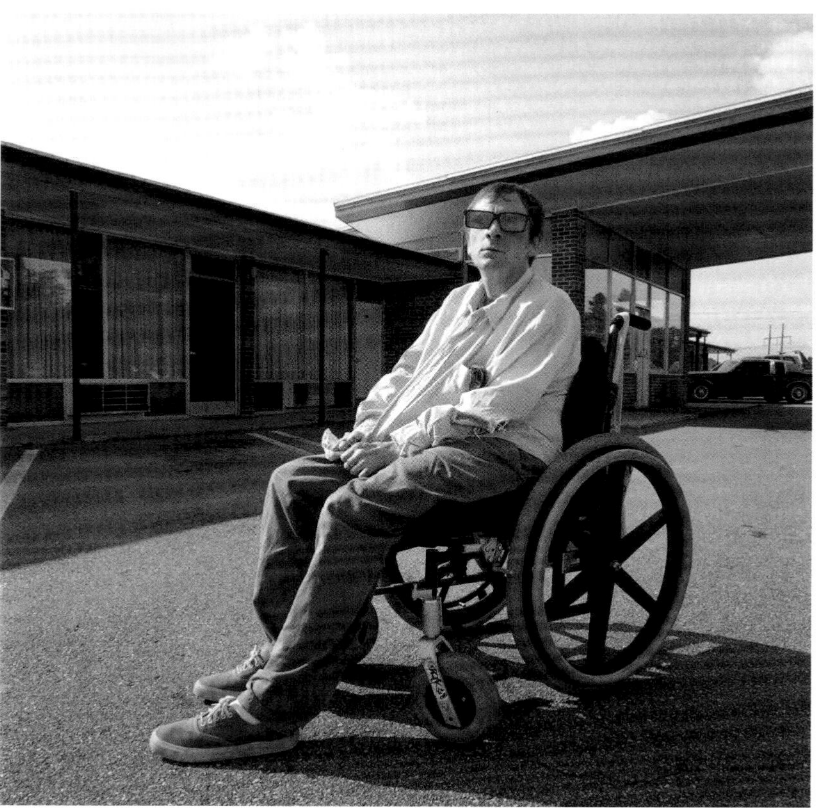

FIG. 2. Carl Martin (b. 1958), *Vic Chesnutt, Late Summer 1996, Athens, GA*, 1996. Gelatin silver print (from digital film scan). © Carl Martin.

But there's another reason, too, and it's not unique to photography. Despite the success of Athens-based musicians across nearly five decades, there has never been an Athens sound. Why should there be an Athens look? Instead, many of the creative people who live and work in this southern college town too far from the Atlanta airport and the interstates to get anywhere easily share one thing: an Athens attitude, a stubbornly independent way of working and an interest in finding inspiration in the materials at hand. Long before it spread throughout the indie culture that Athens people did so much to create,

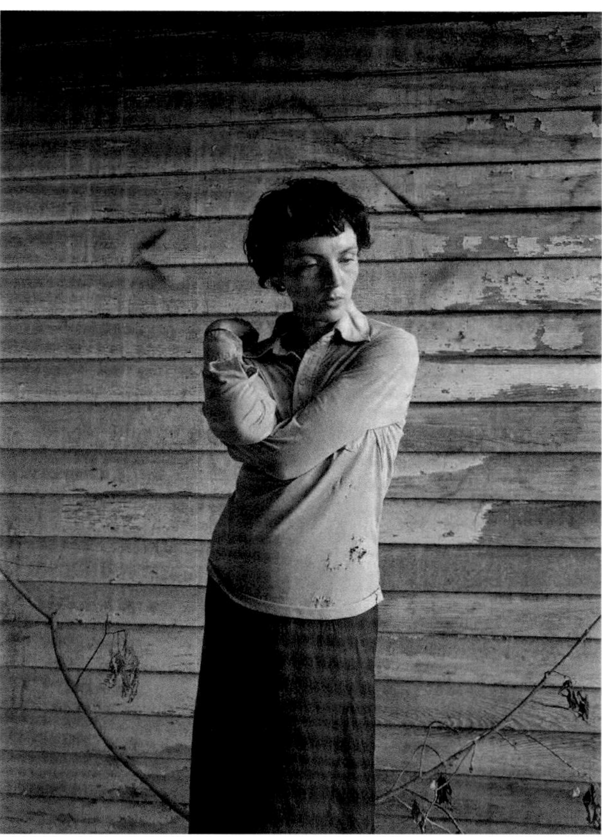

FIG. 3. Mark Steinmetz (b. 1961), *Margaretha, Athens, Georgia*, 1999. Gelatin silver print, 17 ⅛ × 11 ¹⁵⁄₁₆ inches. The Do Good Fund, Inc., 2018-44. © Mark Steinmetz.

63

do-it-yourself reigned. An ideology as well as a practice, DIY often applied to every aspect of creative labor, from the act of imagination and the physical work like printing or recording to the logistical work of circulating what you have made to willing buyers.

Athens people often tried to turn the fact of their isolation into a virtue. They made it a badge of honor to work outside and without much attention to the concerns of art or music as a business. But this obsession with autonomy worked better for the musicians than the artists. Rock music, even in its self-consciously underground rather than pop forms, is a popular art form. It is relatively cheap to make and reproduce and sell, and it has a mass audience (even if that concept means something different in an underground club than in a coliseum). Musicians depended on people who loved music but also on folks who just wanted to drink and dance and flirt. Visual artists, including photographers, depended on collectors, individuals, and institutions that bought work. Athens scene participants created a local network of music clubs, festivals, and recording studios. What they did not develop were galleries and museums working to cultivate collectors who could support the careers of local artists.

What we are left with then in the Do Good collection are some interesting photographs made in and near a college town called Athens. Pamela Pecchio studied with Steinmetz at UGA as an undergraduate, hung out at the 40 Watt, and worked at The Grit after it moved to Prince Avenue. Her 1997 photograph depicts her friend Mitchell's heavily tattooed left arm splayed across the

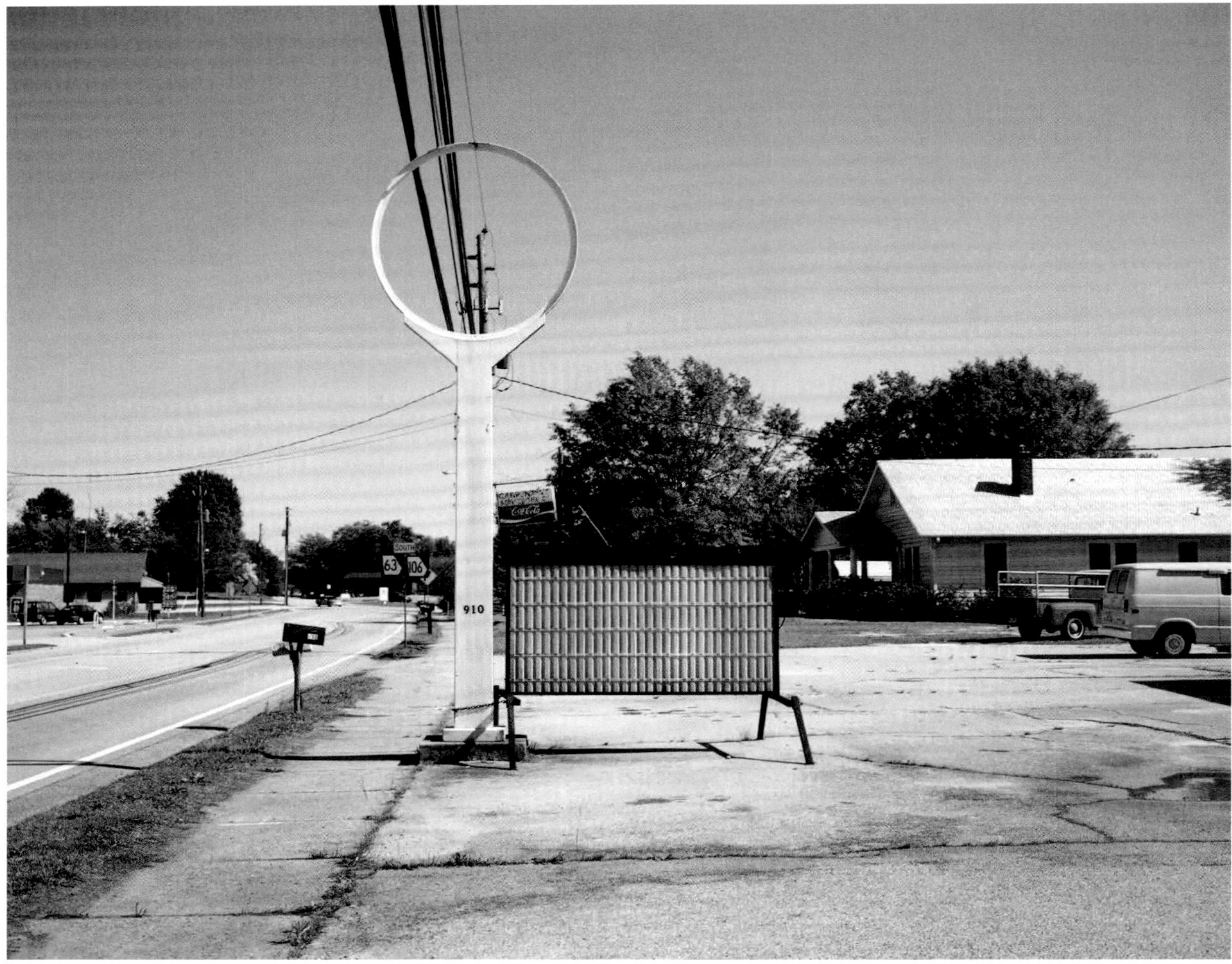

FIG. 4. Georgia Rhodes (b. 1988), *Untitled* from the series *Monologues*, 2012. Archival inkjet print, 20 × 25 inches. The Do Good Fund, Inc., 2016–43.
© Georgia Rhodes.

leather-wrapped steering wheel in the bright red interior of a meticulously restored midcentury car (plate 95). At first glance, it's a photo that offers a certain intimacy. You stare at Mitchell's flesh. Your eyes can trace the intricate patterns of his tattoos and the creases in his skin. If you want to, you can imagine the painful process, all the needle pricks required to create that sleeve thick with designs. And yet, peering into the depth of the image, the car's interior, Pecchio's composition brings your gaze up short. Instead of Mitchell's eyes or some fragment of his face that will seemingly provide access to his inner life, what appears is the back of his head, cut diagonally by a dark shadow that fills the right top corner of the frame. Instead of a window on the self, we get a self looking out a window. Pecchio's picture pulls you in only to push you away. It asserts the limits of knowing.

The photographer Carl Martin moved to Athens in the mid-1990s and still lives there. Between 1996 and 1998, he made the color photograph *Men in Car* as part of his *Downtowners* and *Toward Salvage* series (plate 82). In the image, the driver and two passengers sit in the grayish, oldish sedan parked at the curb in front of an electrical substation with its tangle of poles, wires, and pylons. The light comes in at a low angle, brightening the car and setting its rusty undercarriage aglow. There's an earnest feeling to this picture; a matter-of-factness about what seems to me like alchemy: the way light and form turn what should be an everyday scene of three working-class men either going to or coming from work into something momentous and even sacred.

Georgia Rhodes, who earned her master of fine arts degree at UGA, upends expectations by shooting her 2014 color photograph *Roadtrip*—a tangle of green leaves and yellow flowers growing through a broken window—from the interior of a junked car (plate 100). Even better is a 2012 untitled photograph from her *Monologues* series (fig. 4). A two-lane blacktop traces the left side of the image and runs toward an intersection in the background, a bit of a dying rural settlement north of Athens on the way to Toccoa. Powerlines strung both vertically and horizontally create a swooping grid, a partial template for an exercise in the rule of thirds. Along the road, old houses have been converted to businesses that no longer run, their lawns paved with patched cement, their signs blank. One of these signs, the kind of portable billboard once ubiquitous outside non-chain businesses and small southern churches, stands in all its horizontal blankness like a headstone without a name. All that is left of the other sign is a metal pole topped with a metal circle, empty of the round sheet painted with Texaco or some other gas station's logo. We're stranded here without a sign.

There is no Athens school of photography. There are simply artists who live and make work there, part of a creative community that exists because of the university and the scene. Their best pictures do what all great art does: they help us see.

ON SACRED TERRAIN

Lauren Henkin

WHAT MAKES THE EXPLORATION OF PLACE SO IMPORTANT?

We can look back throughout the history of photography and note the pivotal work of William Henry Jackson, Laura Gilpin, William Christenberry, Robert Frank, and Robert Adams as significant to our understanding of place. Their photographs go beyond documentation, creating unique dialects of visual language—offering what we had not seen before in sharp clarity. Gilpin, the great chronicler of the American Southwest, once described her pull to place in this way: "There is something infinitely appealing in this land which contains our oldest history, something which once known will linger in one's memory with a haunting tenacity."[1]

What motivates an often expensive and challenging pursuit of place can be driven by several factors. For some, it is curiosity; for others, a desire to share a personal narrative; and for still others, an effort to engage in a deep and prolonged investigation that lands somewhere between truth and tale. For so many photographers both past and present, the American South offers the opportunity to delve into all three. The Do Good Fund enables us to mine the depth and vastness of these investigations.

From Jeff Rich, we learn about the Mississippi River watershed and the impact of environmental regulation (or deregulation) on natural resources. *Blue Ridge Paper Mill* (plate 101) is a beautiful rendering of light and color, a photograph that in formal terms is reminiscent of the grand and majestic early landscapes of the American West. But, as viewers digest the densely rich hues and navigate the frame, we are left with the question of whether what we see in the distance is fog or smog. This uncertainty invites us to consider whether something toxic can also be profoundly beautiful.

Caitlin Peterson's project *The Seven Natural Wonders of Georgia* is a different kind of investigation, one in which our ownership of nature—or our perception of ownership, especially as tourists—mars the experience of the natural world. *Stone Mountain* (fig. 1) depicts an odd intersection of architecture, landscape, and people. We see a long plane of windows framing views of a rocky mountaintop traversed by sightseers. Still one of the most popular tourist sites in Georgia, the mountain is best known for the monumental Confederate memorial carved into its side, begun in 1915 but not completed until 1972. Peterson's image is at once disturbing and bizarre, suggesting that the experience of a manufactured "nature," especially a space meant for quiet reflection, is both inauthentic and absurd.

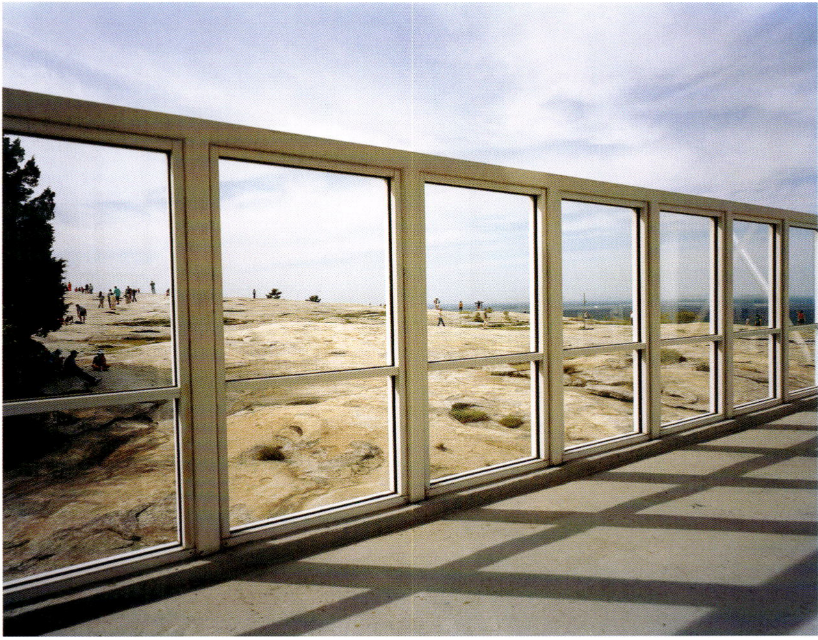

FIG. 1. Caitlin Peterson (b. 1991), *Stone Mountain*, 2012. Digital C-Print, 23 ½ × 29 ½ inches. The Do Good Fund, Inc., 2014–62. © Caitlin Peterson.

For many photographers, the South holds such intrigue, so much possibility. Being the subject of many great artists, it still beckons—and likely always will—as the ultimate test of photographic inquiry. And if that is so, then Hale County, Alabama, is the epicenter of that pursuit. Since the mid-1930s, when Walker Evans made some of his most famous photographs in Hale County, this place and surrounding communities have been the focus of pivotal works by other great photographers such as Gordon Parks and William Christenberry.

Every photographer I know has studied Evans's photographs of Hale County at some point in their career. When I began photographing, I remember poring over Evans's *American Photographs* (1938) with a kind of wonder and awe, transfixed by the clarity of vision and blunt visual language. I adopted his view of what makes a photograph: "it is the capture and projection of the delights of seeing; it is the defining of observation full and felt."[2] "Full and felt" I interpreted as the act of filling the frame with as much emotional punch as possible. As sharp as a scythe, it almost hurts to look at them.

In 1936, the same year Evans was working in Hale County, William Christenberry was born in Tuscaloosa. For Christenberry, Hale County was the playground of his youth, where he spent many summers with his grandparents. He would eventually follow the common advice given to writers—"write what you know"—and present Hale County in a completely different voice than Evans: fully clothed in seductive color and intimate dialogue.

Christenberry's photographs, made decades after Evans's, bring new life to our understanding of this place. In Evans's black and white, we understand form (fig. 2); in Christenberry's color, we understand a broader context of these structures, especially as American vernacular (plate 22). Trees are no longer backdrops from which sun-washed buildings radiate; they are now lead actors in unfolding narratives.

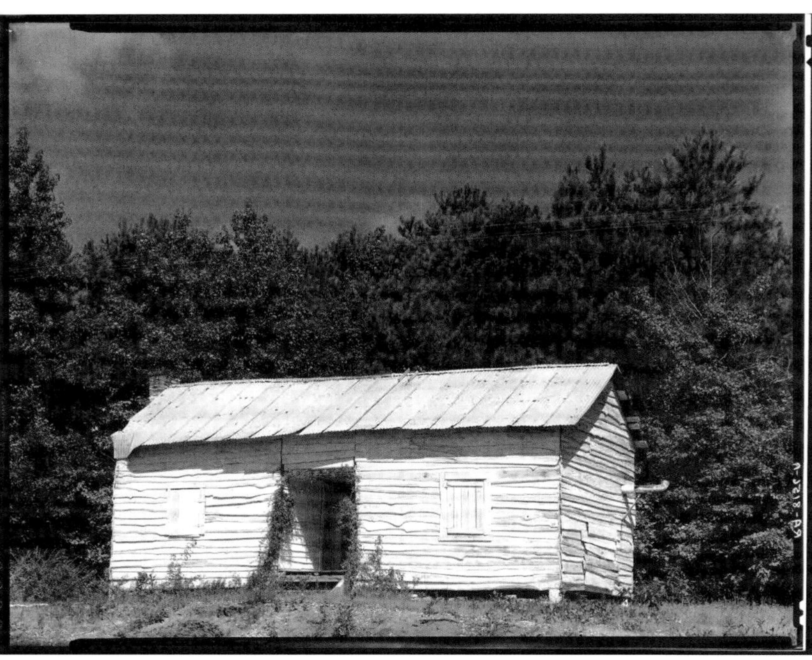

FIG. 2. Walker Evans (1903–1975), *Cabin, Hale County, Alabama*, 1936. Gelatin silver print, 7 ⅜ × 9 ½ inches. Library of Congress, Prints & Photographs Division, Farm Security Administration/Office of War Information Black-and-White Negatives.

These photographs fascinate me. Like the most beautifully rendered architectural elevations, fully frontal and without adornment, these quiet scenes lay bare their true selves—unvarnished, thorny, and saturated.

Like Evans's, Christenberry's photographs evoke the constant push and pull between survival and loss. The overpowering domination of nature, which endeavors to reclaim what was once hers, conveys the life that endures beyond abandonment. The vanquished building reminds us that what is fabricated can so rarely sustain itself beyond a single human lifespan. As Jeff Rosenheim writes, "Such is the idiosyncratic nature of photography: what begins as an image of survival becomes the opposite, an image of loss."[3] Christenberry's photographs are a great testament to the perpetual tension within this medium—that the camera's articulation of a fraction of a second can so cleverly express the passing of time.

When thinking about the history of photography and the genealogy of great photographers, we can draw a clear connection from Evans to Christenberry. Evans, who became Christenberry's mentor and friend, said of the younger artist's photographs, "They seem to write a new little social and architectural history about one regional America (the deep South). In addition to that, each one is a poem."[4] Christenberry's family knew many of the subjects in Evans's images, and Evans's *Let Us Now Praise Famous Men* would become an inspiration for Christenberry's work in Alabama. In 1973, Evans accompanied Christenberry on a trip to Hale County; it was Evans's only trip back since photographing there in the 1930s.[5]

But we can go further back, to the images that served as guides for Evans's photographs in Alabama. Just before he began work for the Department of Agriculture's Resettlement Administration, Evans delved into Mathew Brady's gripping pictures of the Civil War. Brady's work had just started being featured in exhibitions and publications, possibly connecting the catastrophic events of the Civil War and the Great Depression. Rosenheim writes of Brady's influence on Evans, "His study of the thousands of war photographs suggested to the artist both a worthy subject on which to focus—the social facts of the Depression—and an approach to that subject that was direct and uncompromising."[6]

Rosenheim surmises that Evans's exploration of a cemetery in the National Military Park in Vicksburg, Mississippi, which memorialized one of the most important battles of the Civil War, was an act of retracing Brady's steps. In the photographs, Evans focuses on the monuments in what Rosenheim says is "as close as Evans could get to photographing the men Brady had portrayed seventy years earlier."[7] I would propose an alternative conclusion. Evans made those photographs not to get close to subjects of Brady's photographs, but, instead, to be closer to Brady himself.

Two photographs, both in the Metropolitan Museum of Art's collection, are of particular significance. One is a photograph that Evans made, presumably of Mathew Brady's home (fig. 3); the second was made by Christenberry of Evans's home (fig. 4). Both are exterior views pointing toward the front door. They feel like intimate notations, reminders of the photographers' respect for each of their predecessors.

FIG. 3. (left) Walker Evans (1903–1975), *[Colonial Revival House with Statuary on Lawn, Birthplace of Mathew Brady?, Golden's Bridge, New York]*, 1934. Film negative, 8 × 10 inches. The Metropolitan Museum of Art, 1994.258.47. © Walker Evans Archive, The Metropolitan Museum of Art.

FIG. 4. (right) William Christenberry (1936–2016), *Front Door of Walker Evans's House, Old Lyme, Connecticut*, 1972. Chromogenic print, 5 ⅛ × 3 ⁷⁄₁₆ inches. Courtesy of the Estate of William Christenberry. © Christenberry, LLC.

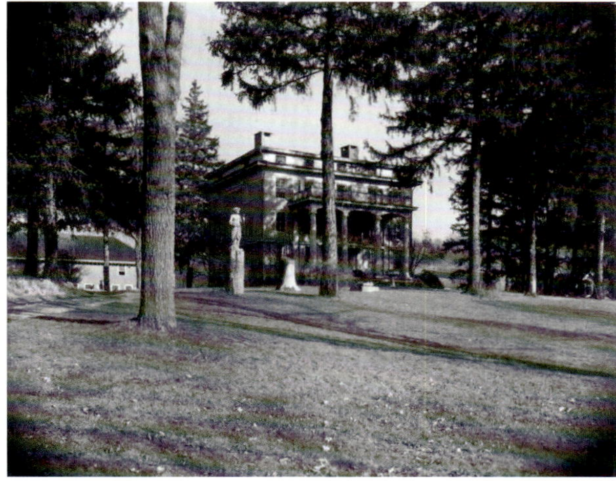

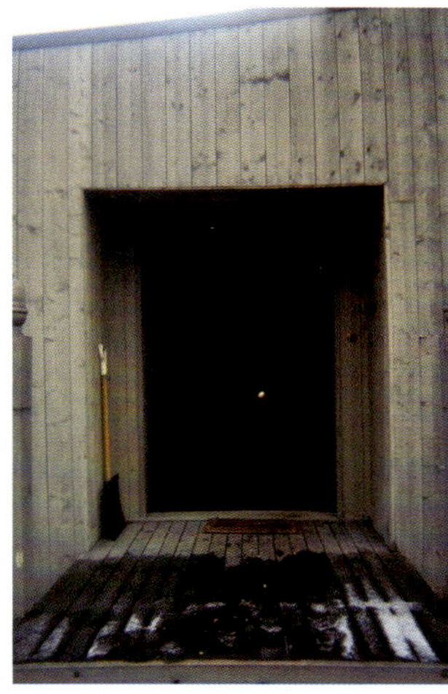

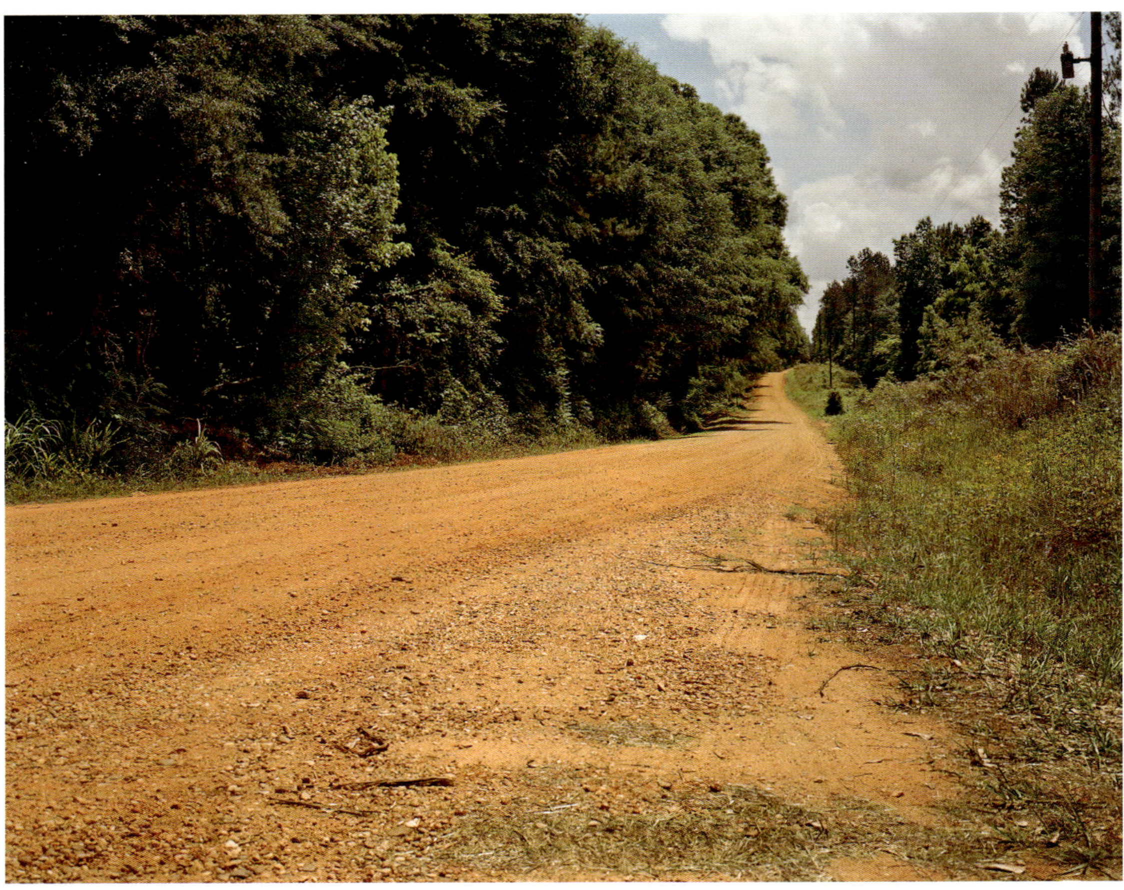

At times, an artist can feel the tug of the past, an indefinable urge to trace the history of one's medium—to feel the same light, to challenge one's eyes to see something new, or to inscribe the shared terrain as did those that came before you. It is one of the most exciting and challenging prospects for an artist—to continue a conversation when everything important seems to have been said already.

I myself had that opportunity in 2015 as the inaugural Do Good Fund artist in residence. I spent a month in Hale County, indulging in one of the greatest gifts an artist can receive: unscripted time to wander and wonder. Everything I saw felt unexpected: chartreuse hues of green from an unusually wet spring; rich clay-like reds in the soil from hematite, an iron oxide compound native to the South; and striking cerulean blues that prompt childhood memories of long summer days spent roaming. It was this palette of primary colors that struck me the most about Alabama. Every moment was tinged with mystery. I remember within the span of five miles I saw a beautiful field of grasses quieted by the weight of a humid day; a car burning on the side of a two-lane road, without evidence of how the fire started or how it might end; a bland house made extraordinary by the warmth of the horizontal light at sunset. I attended church services while I was there, a completely new experience for me. One of the pastors kept repeating in a steady rhythmic pace, "The life of the flesh is in the blood." It felt like an appropriate title to give this photograph (fig. 5). There seemed to be so much life in that bloodied soil.

Hale County, small in area and population, carries a weight of photographic history disproportionate to its size. It is not solely important because of the photographs that have been made there. Its greatest role may be as a permanent genealogical marker from which young photographers can trace their lineage and claim their rightful place within a community of artists. Within its boundaries are the trees, that ground, those buildings. They are not just subjects but prompts to create a new visual language, ready to be spoken for the first time by future seers.

NOTES

1   Laura Gilpin, *The Pueblos: A Camera Chronicle* (New York: Hastings House, 1941), 7 and 23.

2   "Walker Evans," Collection, J. Paul Getty Museum, accessed February 8, 2022, https://www.getty.edu/art/collection/artists/1599/walker-evans-american-1903-1975/.

3   Jeff Rosenheim, "'The Cruel Radiance of What Is': Walker Evans and the South," in *Walker Evans*, ed. Maria Morris Hambourg [exhibition catalogue] (New York: Metropolitan Museum of Art in association with Princeton University Press, 2000), 60.

4   Quoted in Benjamin Forgey, "Christenberry: Growing Up But Not Away," *Washington Post*, April 24, 1983.

5   Matt Schudel, "William Christenberry, artist of a crumbling, memory-haunted South, dies at 80," *Washington Post*, November 29, 2016; and James Agee and Walker Evans, *Let Us Now Praise Famous Men* (Boston: Houghton Mifflin, 1941).

6   Rosenheim, 74–75 and 77.

7   Ibid., 82.

PLATES

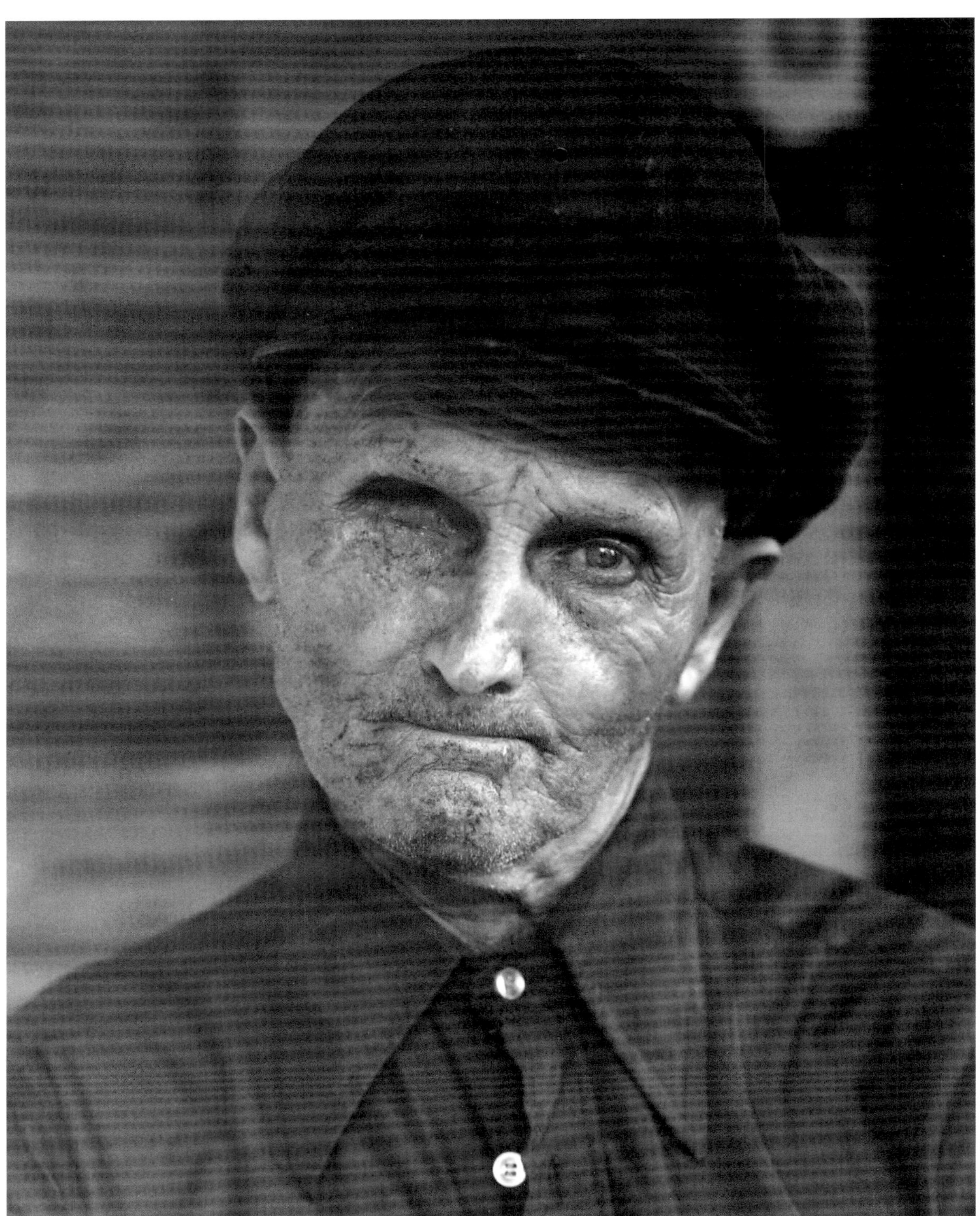

MY GRANDMOTHER, WHOM I ADORED, SLOWLY WENT BLIND

while I was growing up and I often walked and guided her around on her farm. So, when I meet and photograph anyone new who is blind, I talk through everything I'm doing while working to make their photograph. This serpent handler's name was Ray; I knew him previously and was familiar with his religion.

The Pentecostal Holiness Serpent Handlers with Signs Practiced is a dedicated religious sect located throughout the southern Appalachian Mountains. They believe the serpent is the symbol of the Devil on earth and the Holy Ghost anoints members with the gift to take up serpents to show sinners and the world God's power over Satan. One can take up serpents on their own faith but that can be more perilous.

On this day, I asked Ray to wait to open the serpent box containing a rattlesnake until I had set my 4 × 5 camera on a tripod and positioned my lights. He couldn't wait for me to get everything in position and do test Polaroids. Instead, he felt the "anointing" and "took up" the serpent. Knowing anything could happen and I could miss the best moment, I started making pictures. Despite my intentions, the glare reflected off his glasses and in the window in the background. Later, after developing the film and printing, I felt the lighting actually gave the image a contemporary look. When giving Ray and his family prints months later we discussed what to title Ray's picture. I asked what they thought about naming the image *Blind Serpent Handler*, and we agreed that it would demonstrate their faith more strongly by using the word "blind."

— *Shelby Lee Adams*

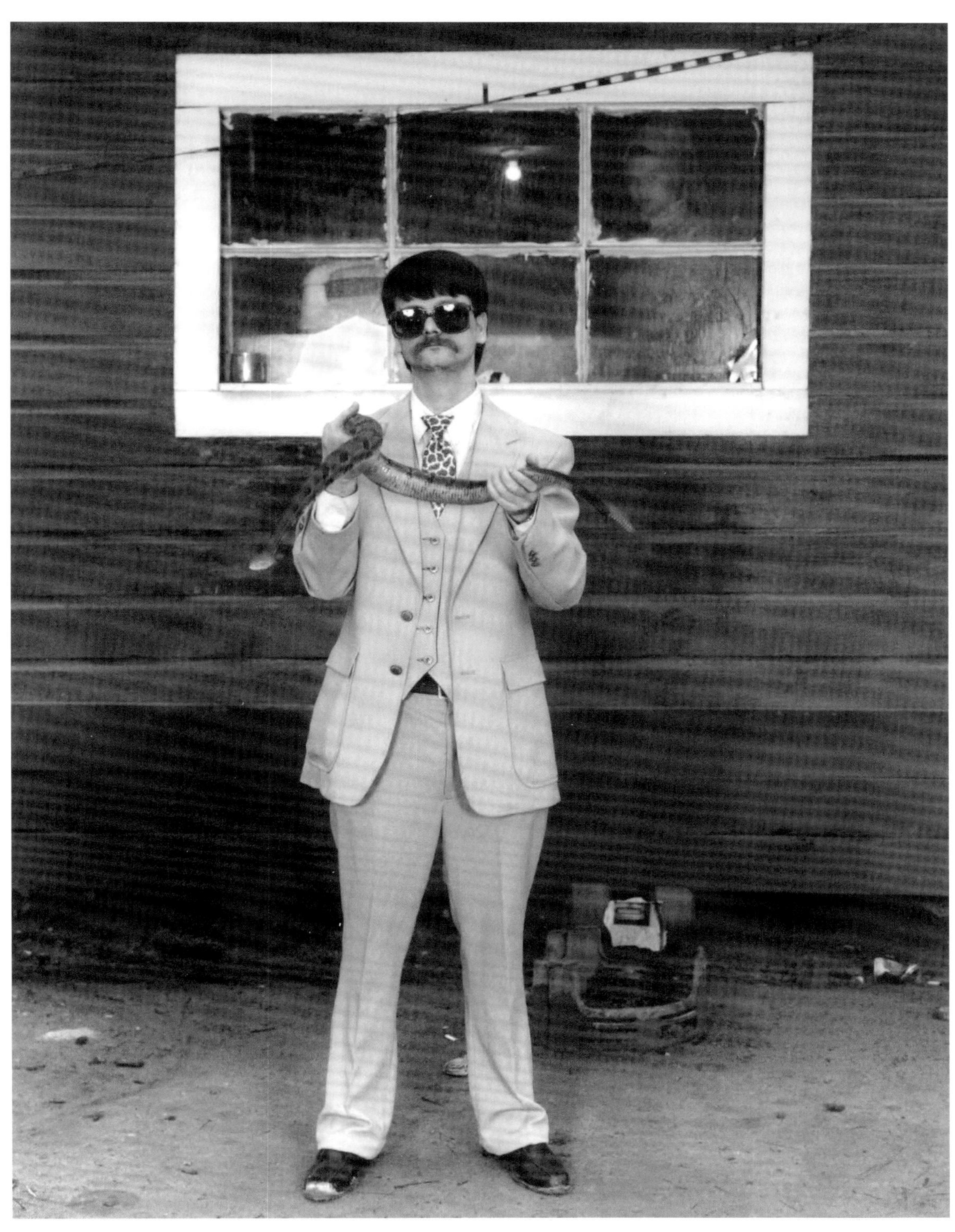

PLATE 2
Shelby Lee Adams, *Blind Serpent Handler*, 1987

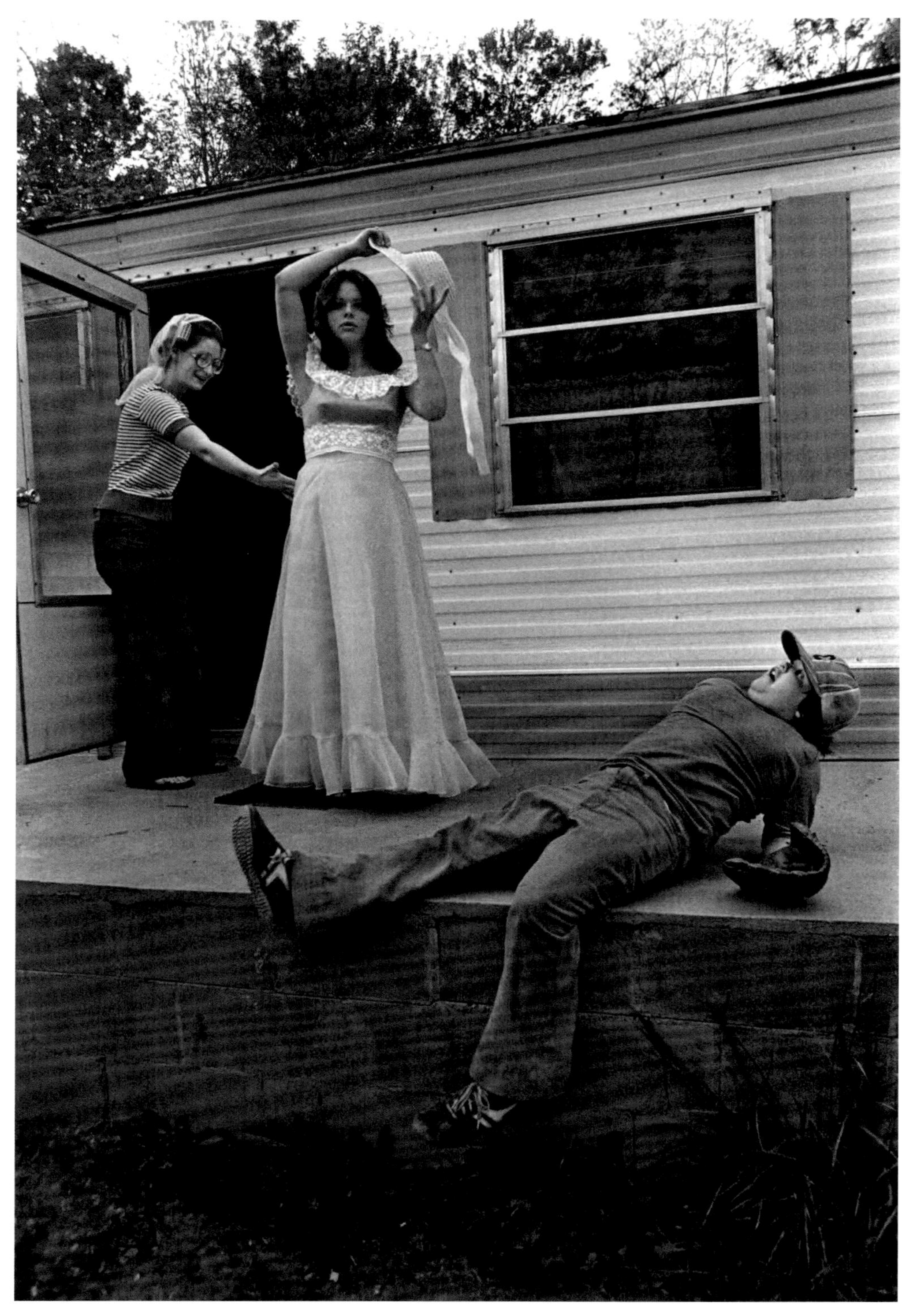

PLATE 3
Rob Amberg, *Vicky Ray on Prom Night, Sodom, Madison County, NC*, 1977

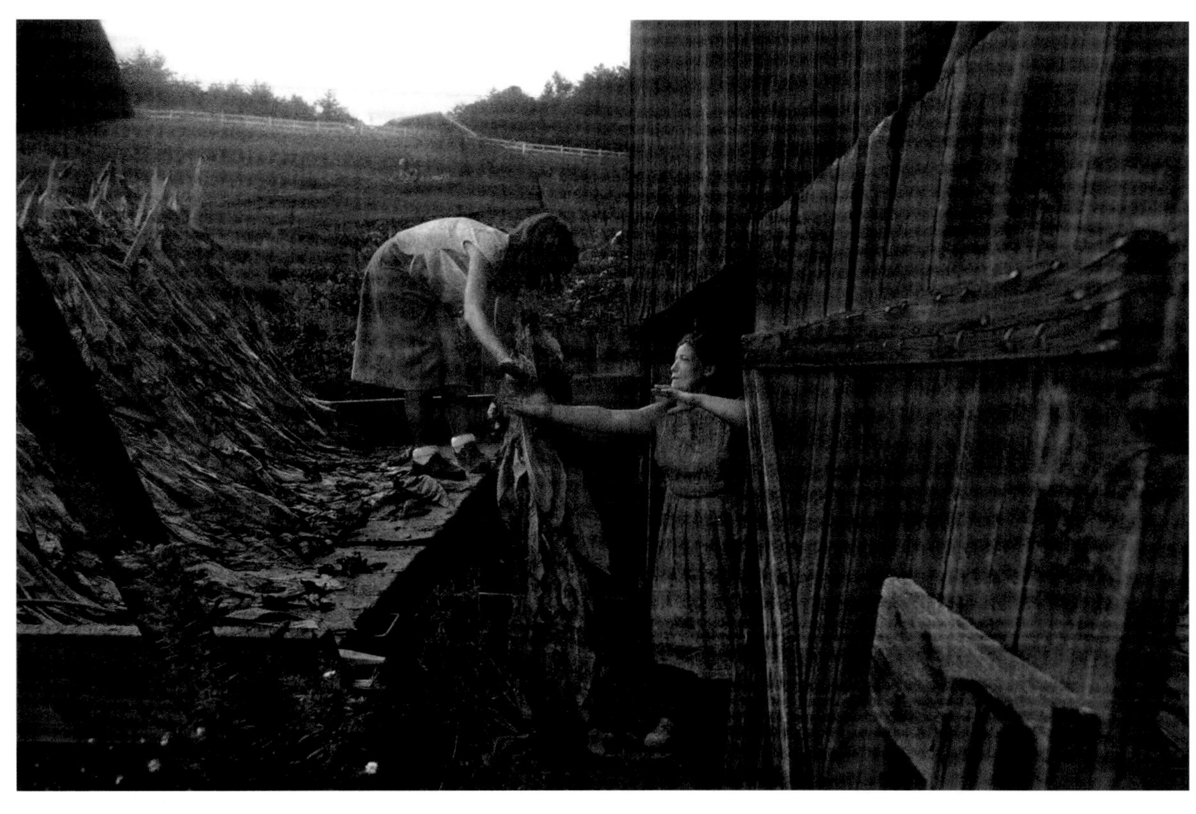

PLATE 4
Rob Amberg, *Angie and Juanita Shelton Unloading Tobacco, Hopewell, Madison County, NC*, 1983

IN 1987 WHEN I MADE THIS PHOTOGRAPH, I was working as staff photographer and director of communication for the Rural Advancement Fund (RAF), a nonprofit, farm advocacy organization working in the two Carolinas. One of my duties was to document the farm crisis in rural America that had forced thousands of family farmers into bankruptcy and off their farms. My involvement with photography had grown out of my social action work in the 1960s, and I viewed photography as a tool for social change. My work with RAF provided an opportunity to act on that belief.

I had traveled to Bishopville, South Carolina, to spend time with a farmer who was struggling to stay in business. My visits with farm families usually took the form of me hanging out for a period of days. I was interested in the day-to-day life on these farms and in their communities, sensing that in the ordinary we found the universal. In the course of my stay in rural South Carolina, we went to a farm estate auction where the farmer hoped to pick up equipment for an affordable price.

I wandered around the grounds making photographs of faces in the crowd and items on the sale tables, nothing very exciting. But, when the auctioneer held up the painting of the farm's original farmhouse, instinct took over and I sat down in front of him and exposed a half dozen negatives.

For me this image tells an obvious story—an object being sold at auction—factual evidence that offers something recognizable and believable. But knowing this was an item being sold as part of the dissolution of the farm gave it a different meaning. Not only was the painting of the farmhouse being sold, along with the farm itself, but the *image* of the farm—its way of life, its history, and its day-to-day—was being sold, too. It is this hidden meaning, one less specific and more universal, that speaks to a culture being dissolved, which gives this photograph its power and resiliency.

— Rob Amberg

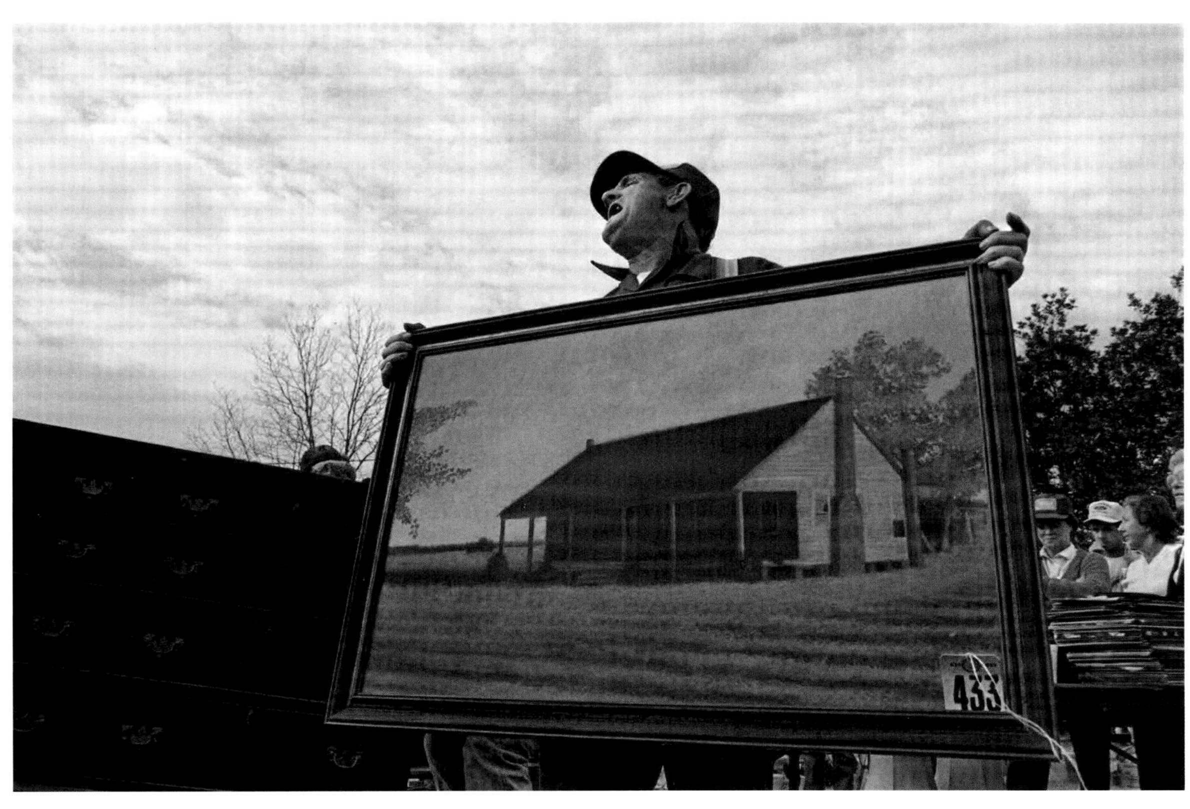

PLATE 5
Rob Amberg, *Estate Auction, Bishopville, SC*, 1987

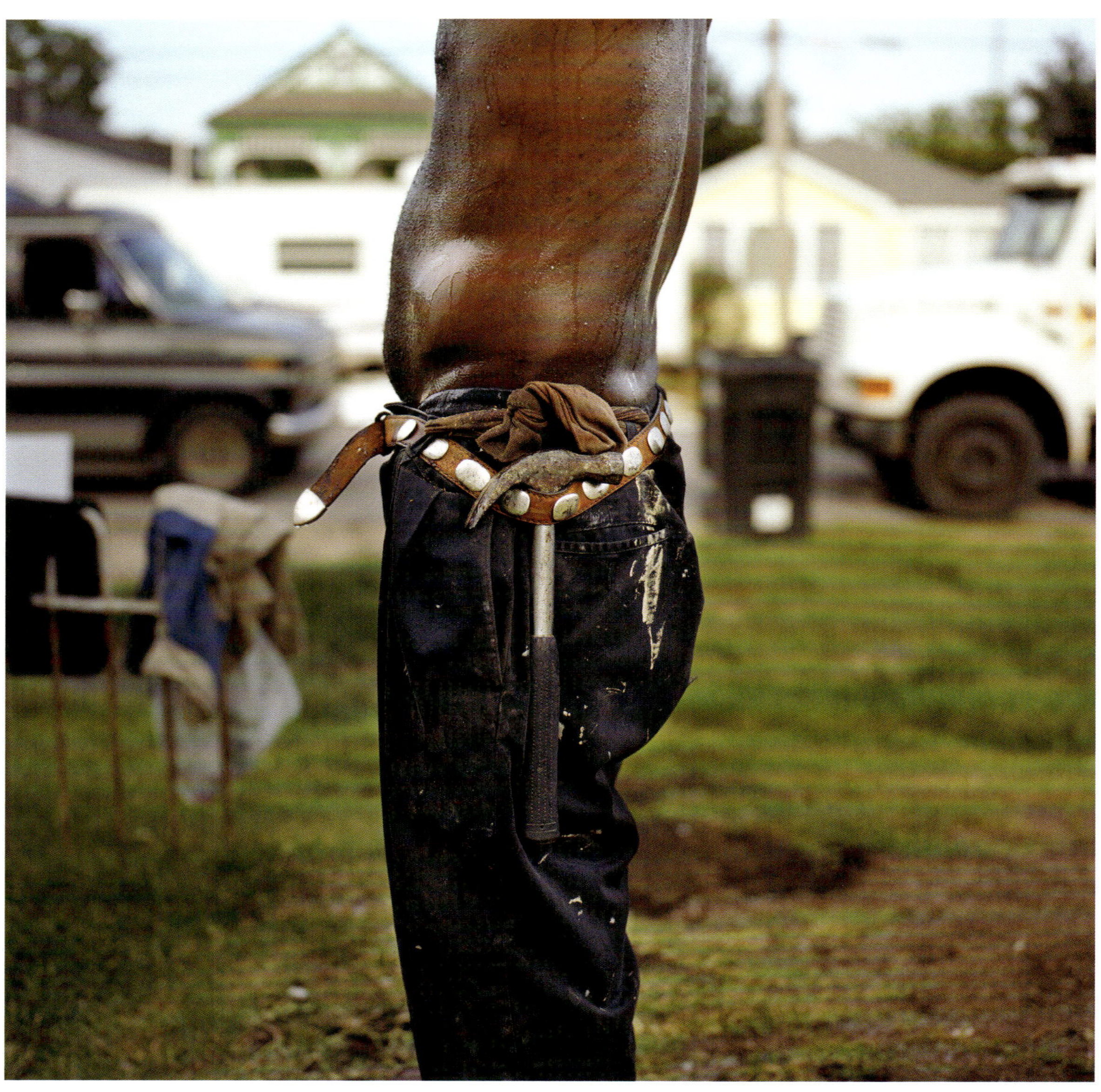

PLATE 6
Dave Anderson, *Toolbelt*, 2007

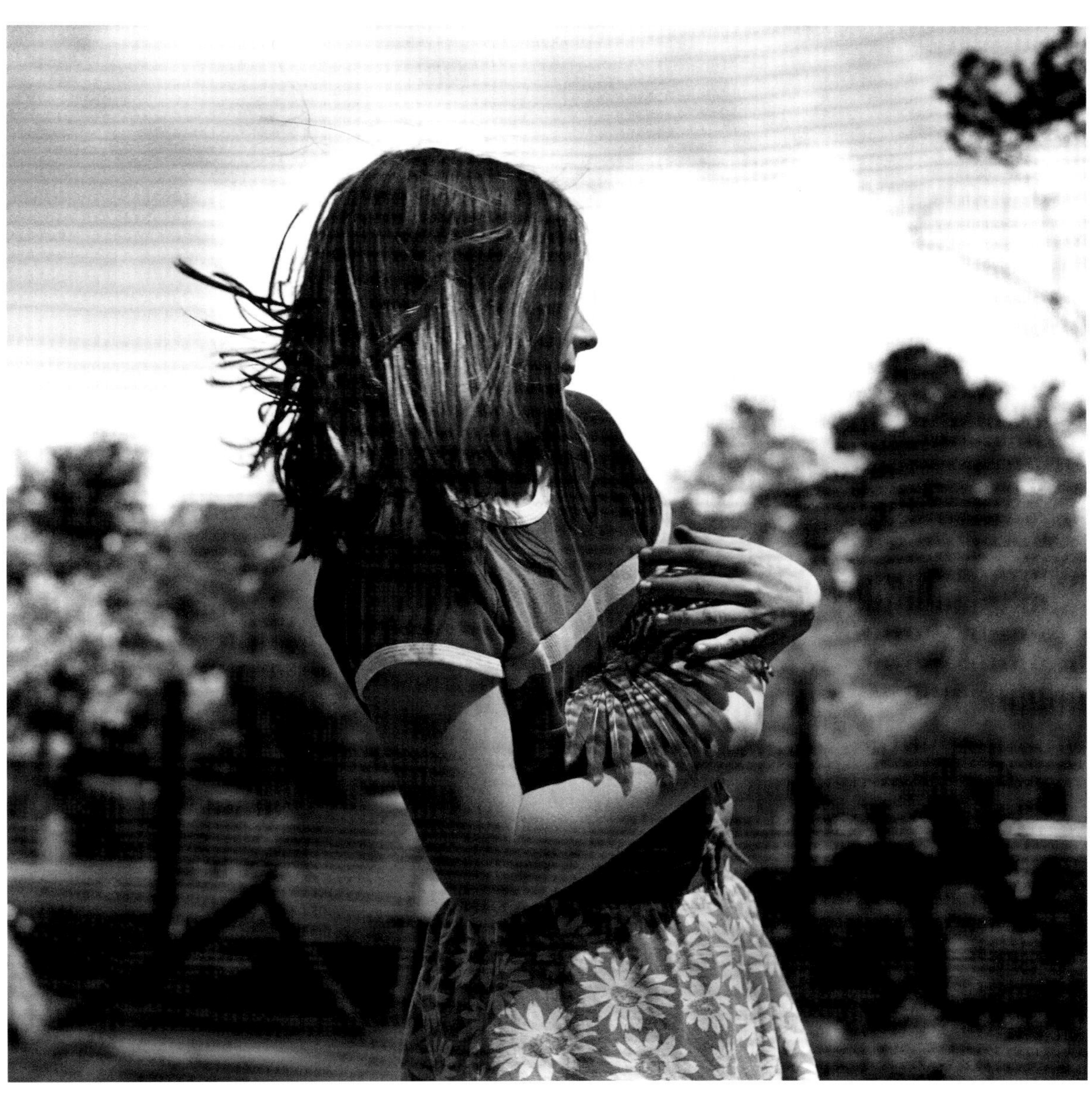

PLATE 7
Dave Anderson, *Breeze*, 2004

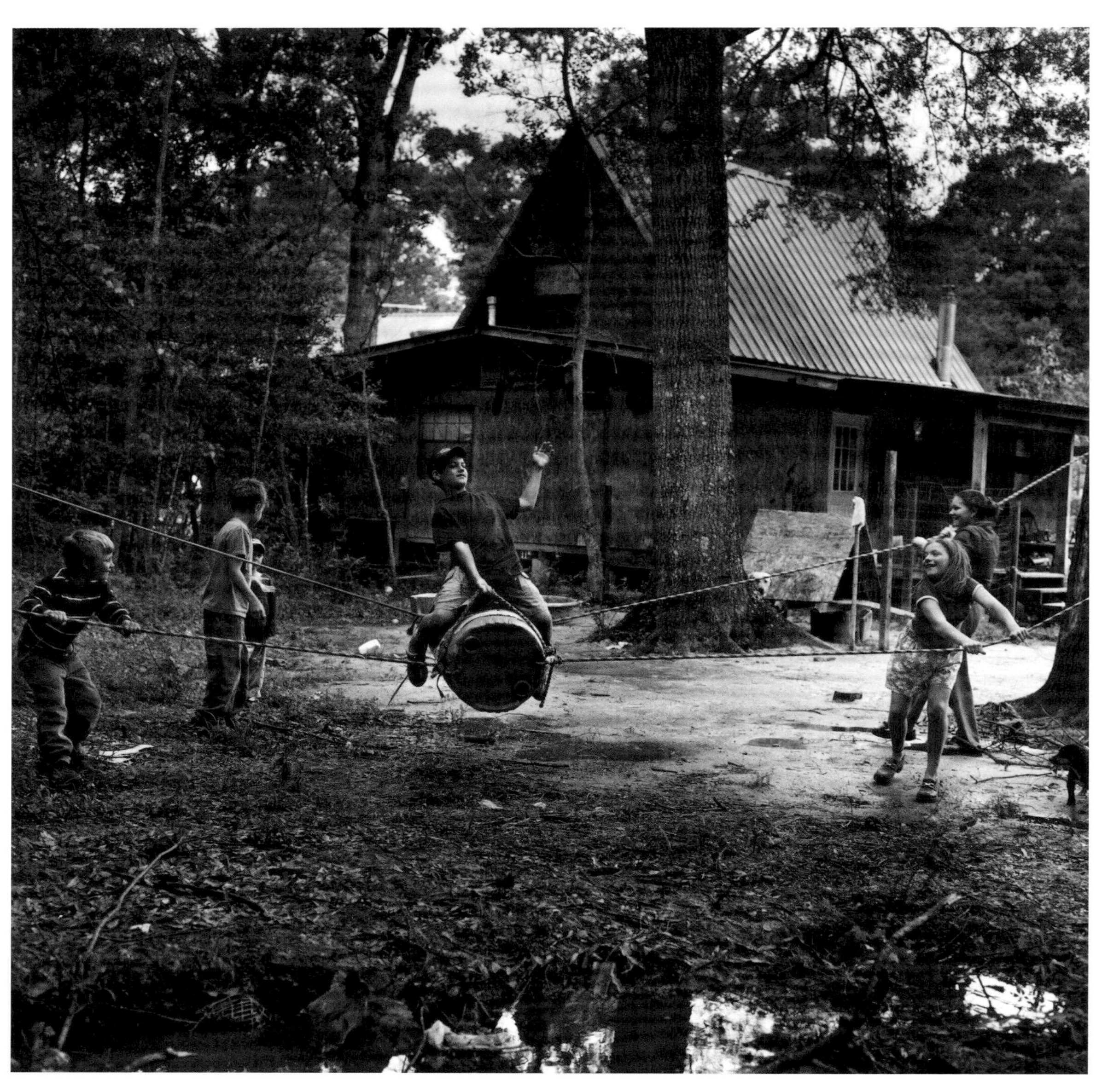

Dave Anderson, *Jug Riding*, 2004

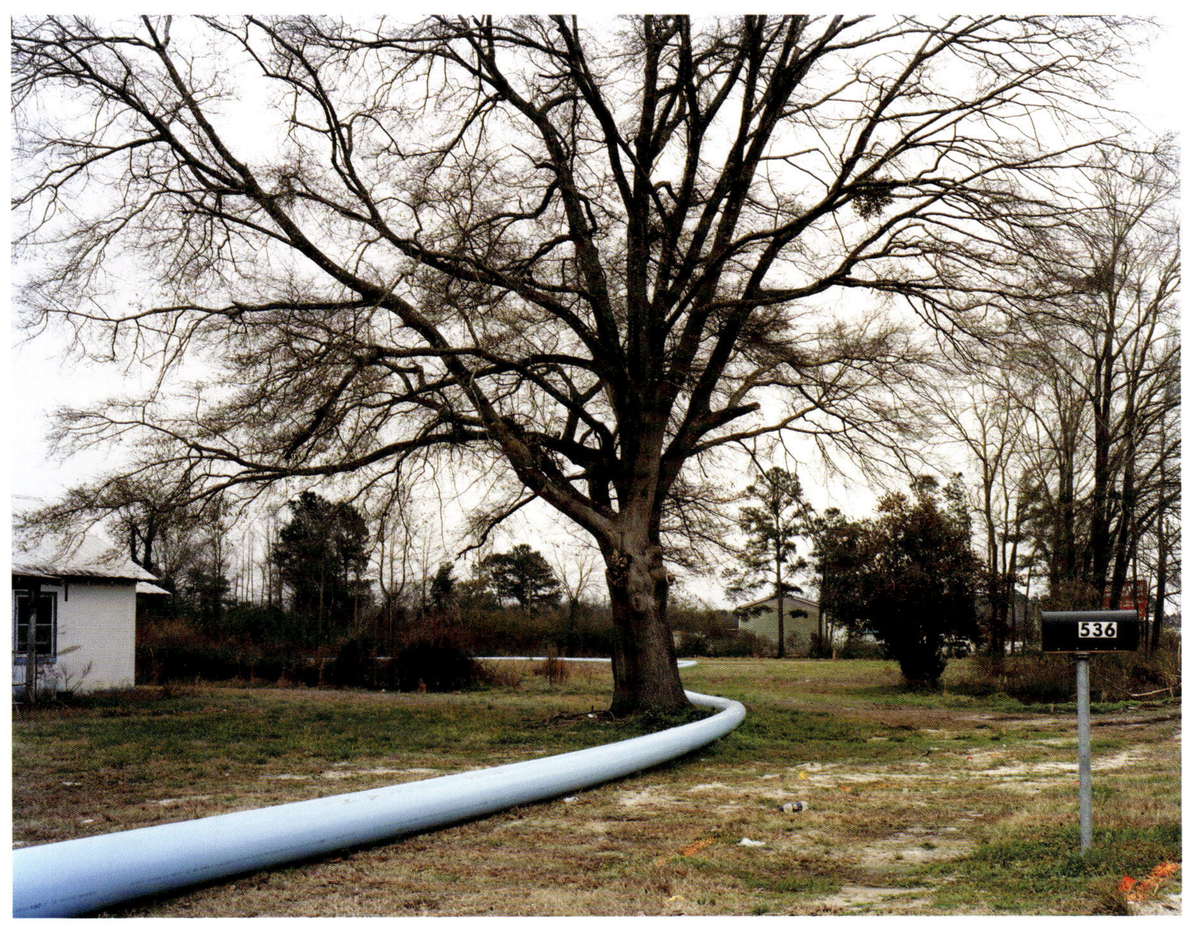

PLATE 9
Rachel Boillot, *28464, Marty's Place, Teachey, NC*, 2014

THE STORY HERE IS ALL IN THAT RED HOE.

Ida was not expecting me that Saturday morning. Nor were *any* of the local
residents gathered bright and early outside the post office. I had gotten to a
point in my travels where I was relying on word of mouth more than any pre-
liminary research. And the day before, a man in Vance told me about the town
of Sherard. He said something to the tune of, "So long as the building stands,
that is the yellowest post office in the state of Mississippi," adding that it might
not stand long. The nearby Farrell P.O. had already closed, and Sherard would
likely be next. That turned out to be true.

Anyway, I pull up and there's a whole group of people outside the P.O., which
made me a little nervous. I was clearly interrupting something, all eyes sudden-
ly on me. I still had New York plates and everything. It turned out a snake was
right there by the front door, and Ida is *deathly* afraid of them. So the whole
town was on her front steps to help out. I ended up helping dispose of it, too.
I felt like I had to prove myself! Honestly, I think that's why this picture exists.

The experience was an important lesson for me, really. The truth is that a
portrait is always about the relationship you, the photographer, have with the
person on the other side of the lens. And while I wouldn't go so far as to say
Ida trusted me after that, she let me in just enough. I felt really grateful for
that. Because, to me, this picture is about Ida's domain—which, while it existed,
mattered. I think she saw that I knew that. That I respected the yellowest post
office in Mississippi—no ideas but in things, right? And that I respected her,
too: Ida in her domain.

— Rachel Boillot

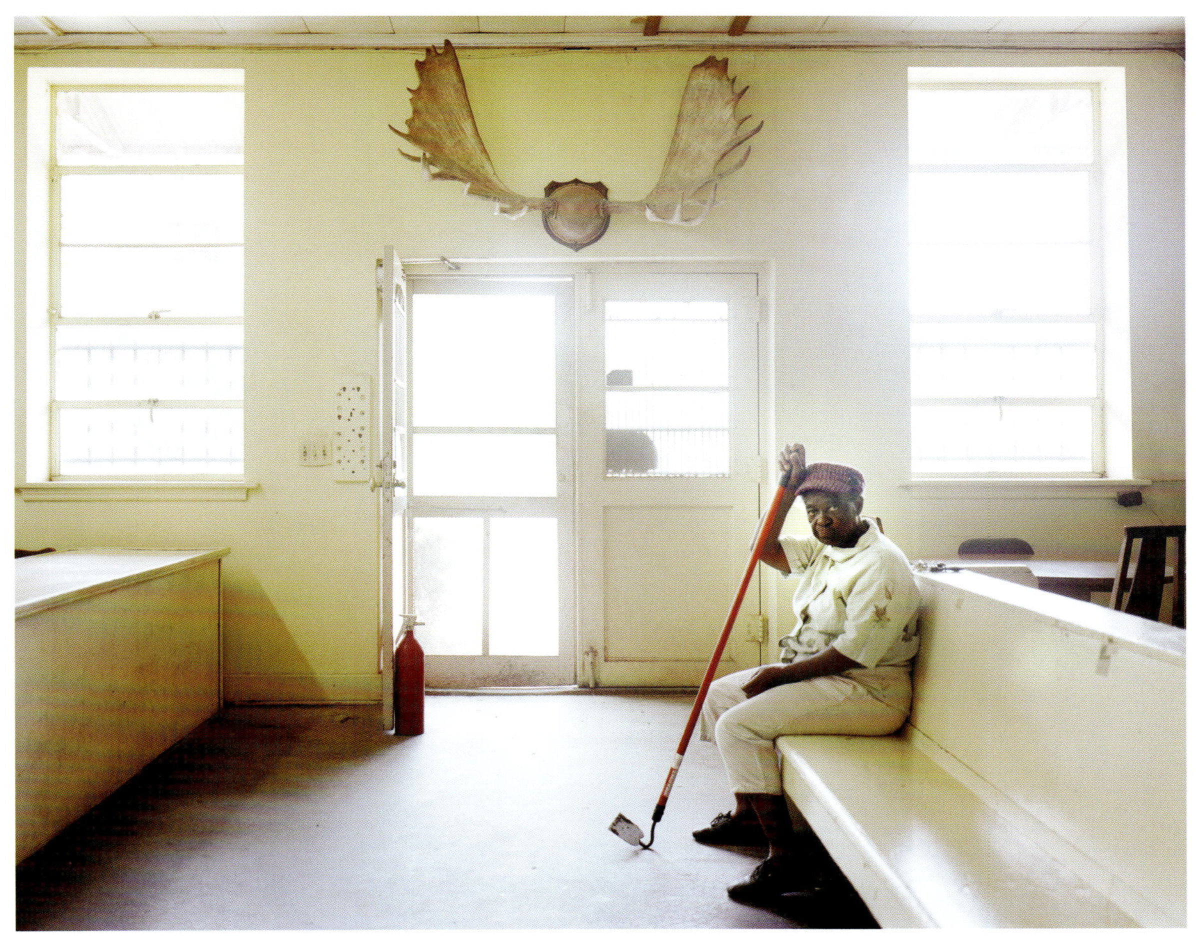

PLATE 10
Rachel Boillot, *Postmistress Ida, Sherard, MS*, 2013

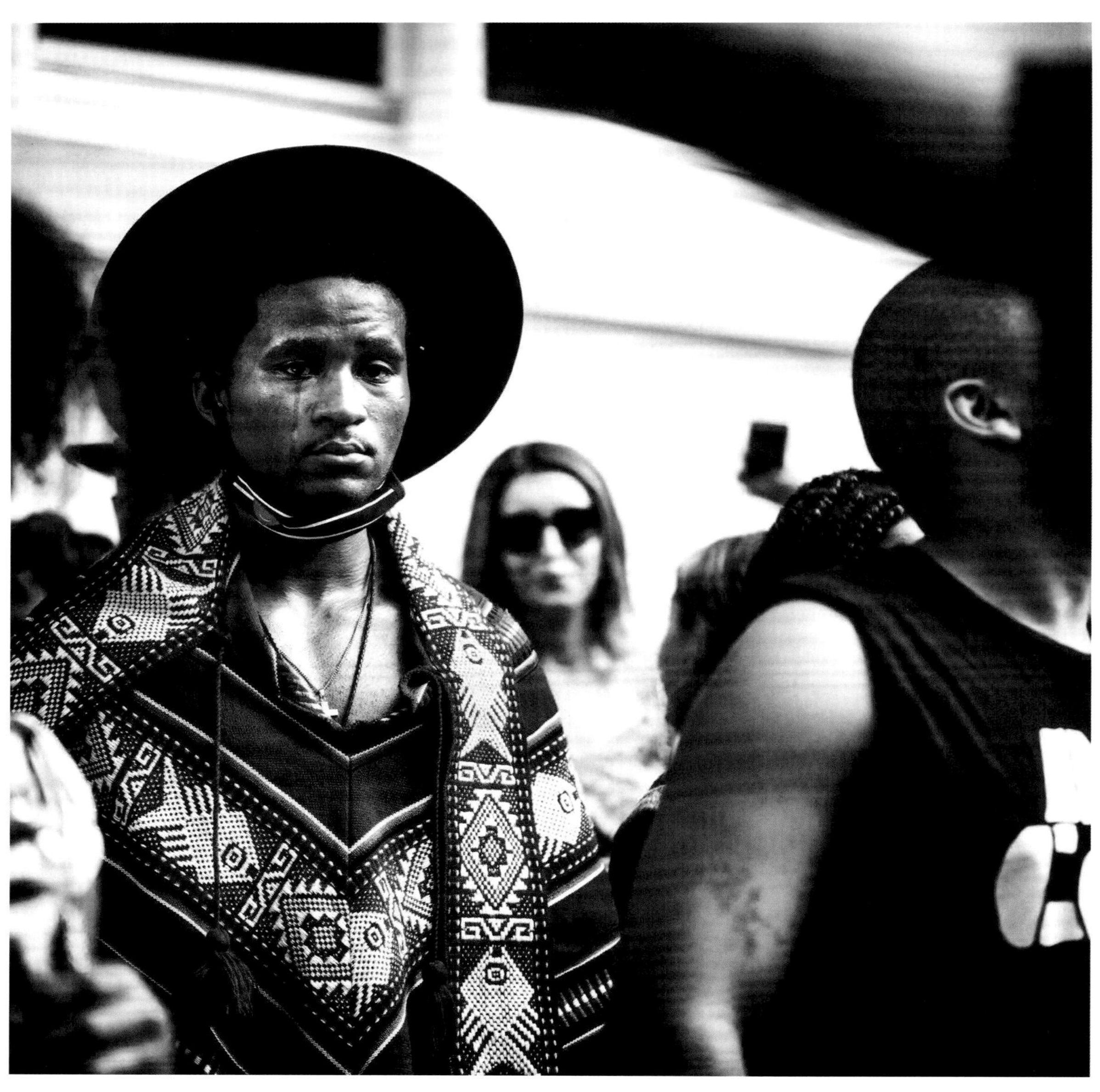

PLATE 11
Sheila Pree Bright, *#SayHerName*, 2016

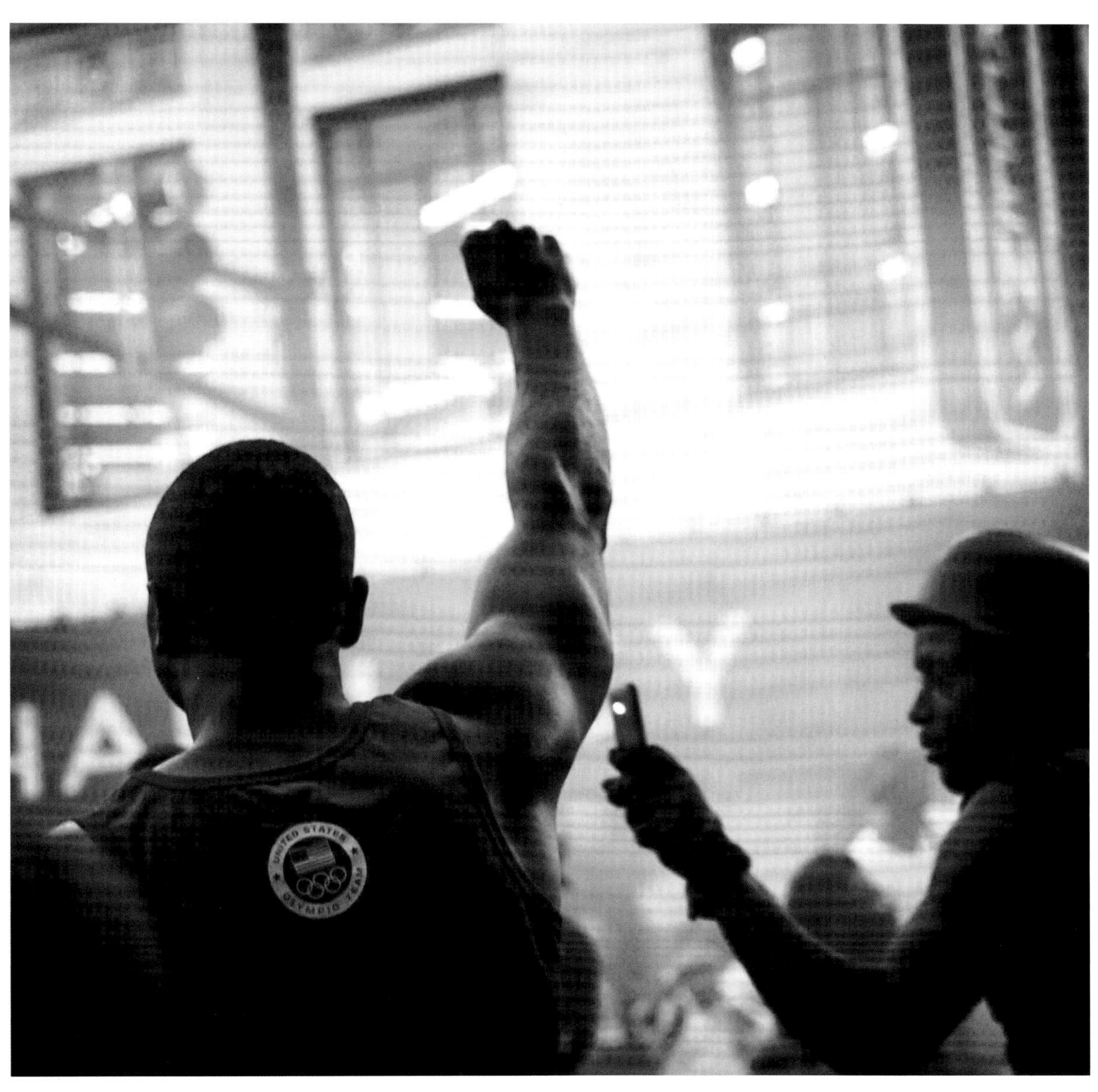

PLATE 12
Sheila Pree Bright, *#ATLisReady*, 2016

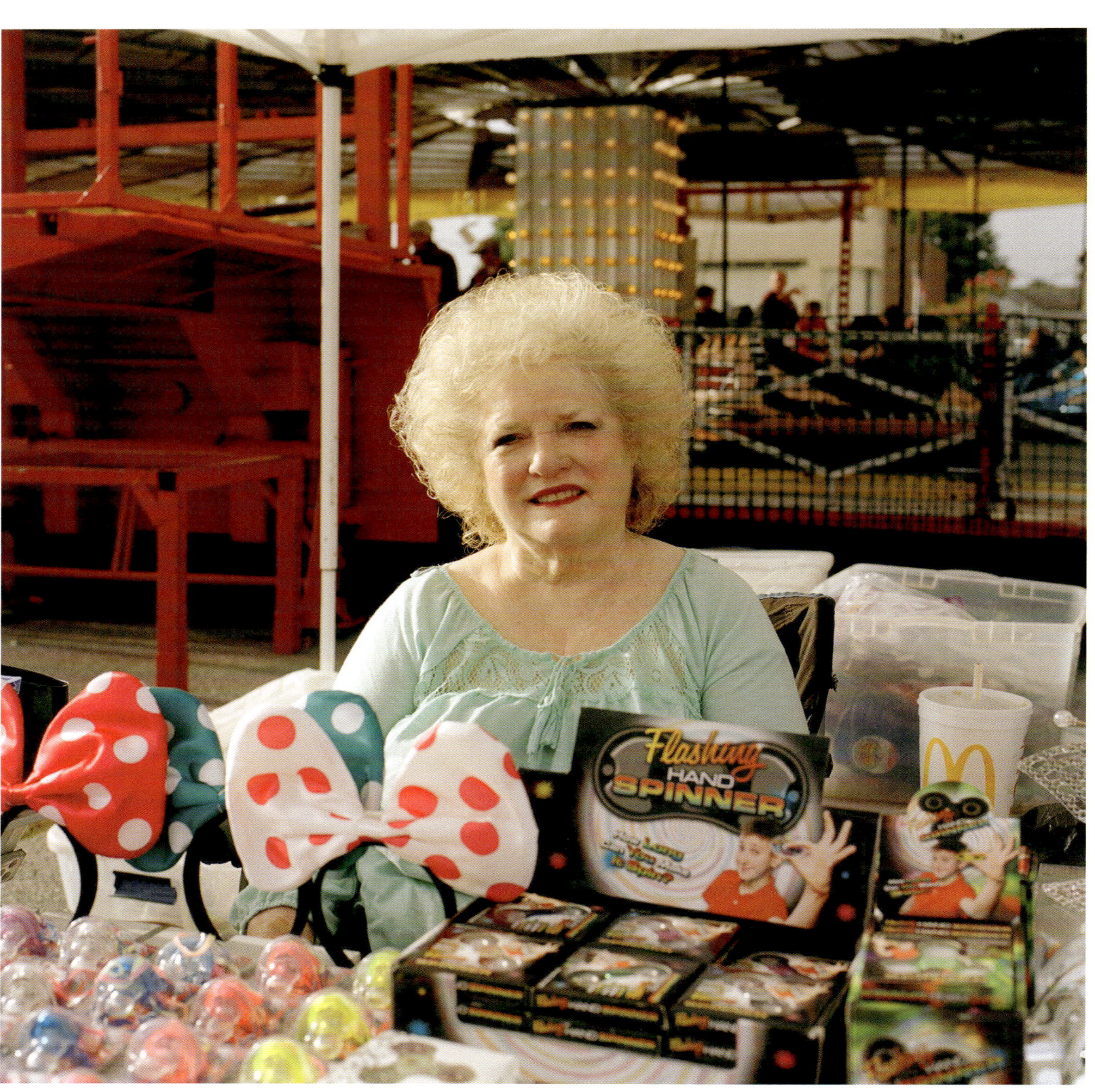
Flashing
HAND
SPINNER

PLATE 13
Rosie Brock, *Woman at Fair*, 2017

I MADE *ROSE BUSH PORTRAIT* during my first semester of graduate school, a time when I was feeling frustrated with my work and process. I had just relocated to the South to pursue my master of fine arts degree at the University of Georgia, and found myself in a destabilizing transition period. I frequently drove around in search of photographic subjects, but the results were usually unremarkable.

A few months into the semester on a long weekend, I decided to travel to East Tennessee to attend an annual storytelling convention. I spotted the subject of the photograph on my way to the second day of the event as he was walking down the street. His incredibly bright white hair reflected the sunlight. Feeling beckoned by this stranger's presence, I quickly turned my car around and pulled into the closest gas station. A few moments later he sauntered up, seemingly unaware of me. I hurriedly asked to photograph him, explaining that I was enthralled by his appearance.

The gas station was next to a McDonald's and a red rose bush separated the two parking lots. After settling beside the bush, he told me that his name was Mikey McCool. He was born on August 8 and felt a particular affinity with his zodiac sign, Leo (the lion). We continued to speak as I subtly directed his facial expressions and poses. Our conversation about his hair led him to share about his childhood and family. His hair, Mikey said, was due to albinism, inherited from his mother. He then told me that when he was eight years old he had witnessed his mother's rape and murder. Afterwards, his half siblings were sent to live with their dad and he hadn't seen them since.

After months of photographic failure, Mikey's presence and our interaction felt not only revitalizing, but nearly ordained. He seemed almost like an angelic spirit that I had been lucky enough to encounter. In the months after meeting Mikey, I began to consider how a photograph can represent a spiritual or mythical entity, which is a concept that continues to guide my practice.

— Rosie Brock

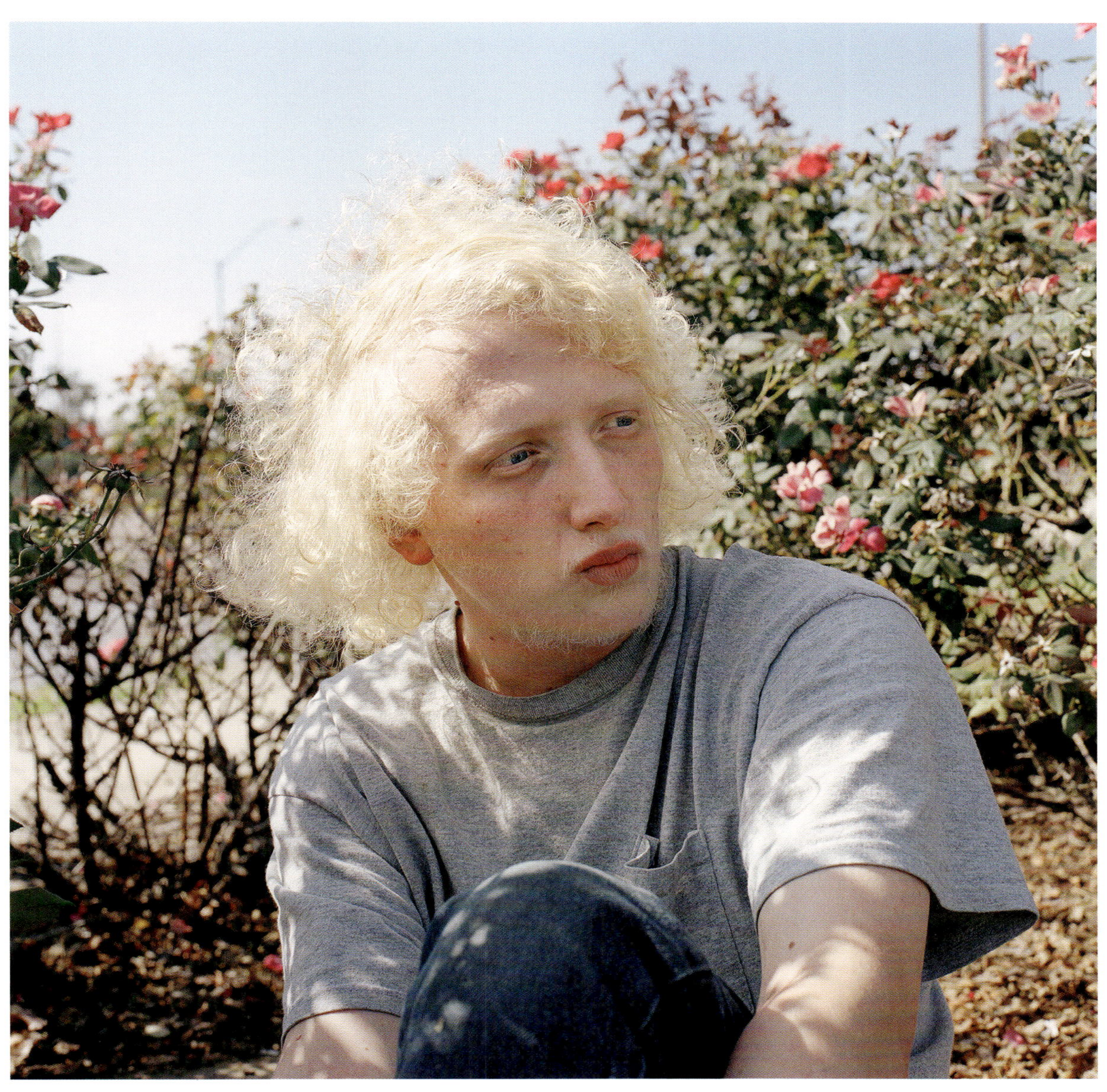

PLATE 14
Rosie Brock, *Rose Bush Portrait*, 2019

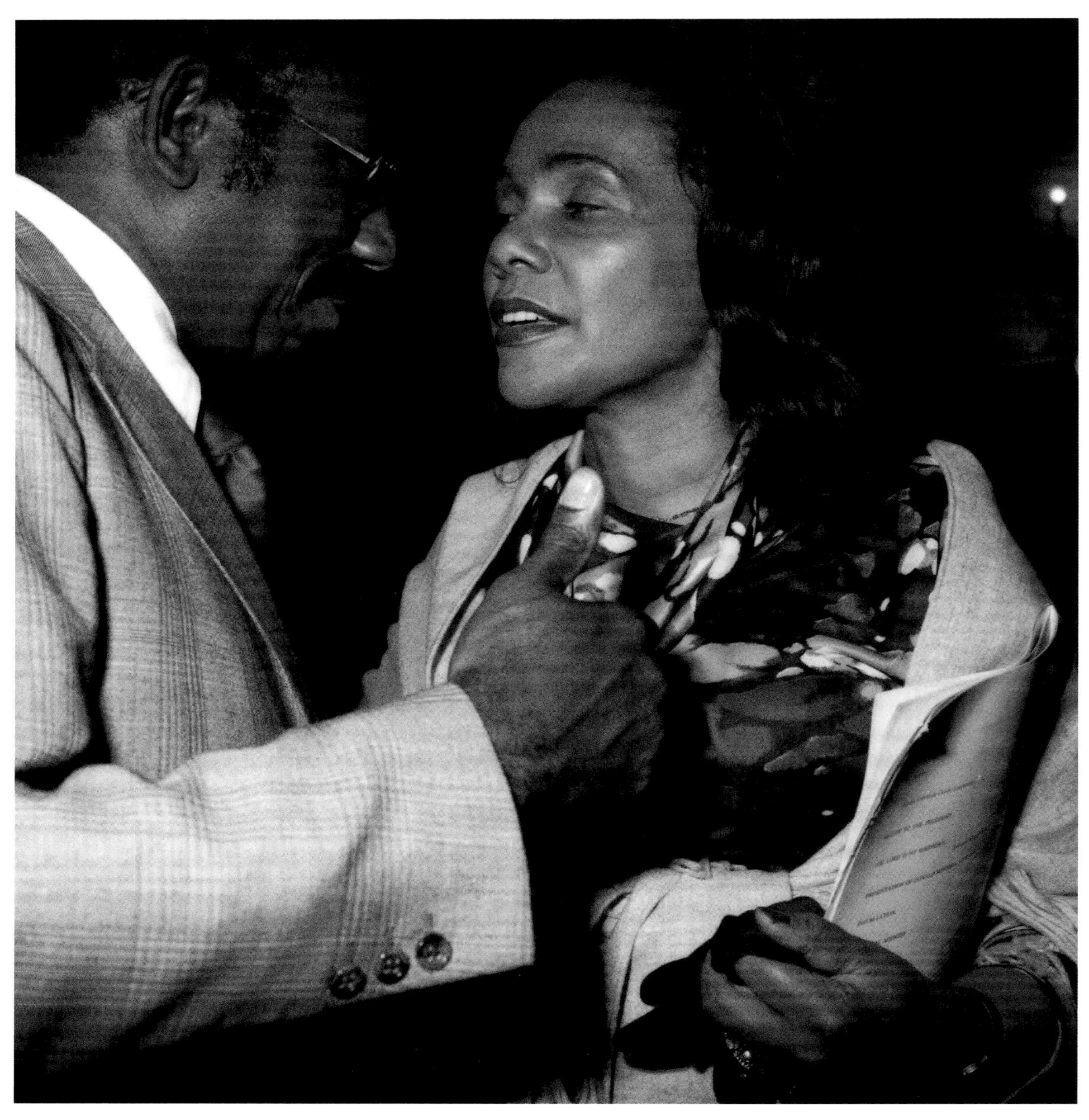

PLATE 15
Lucinda Bunnen, *Herman Russell and Coretta Scott King, at Spelman College*, 1977

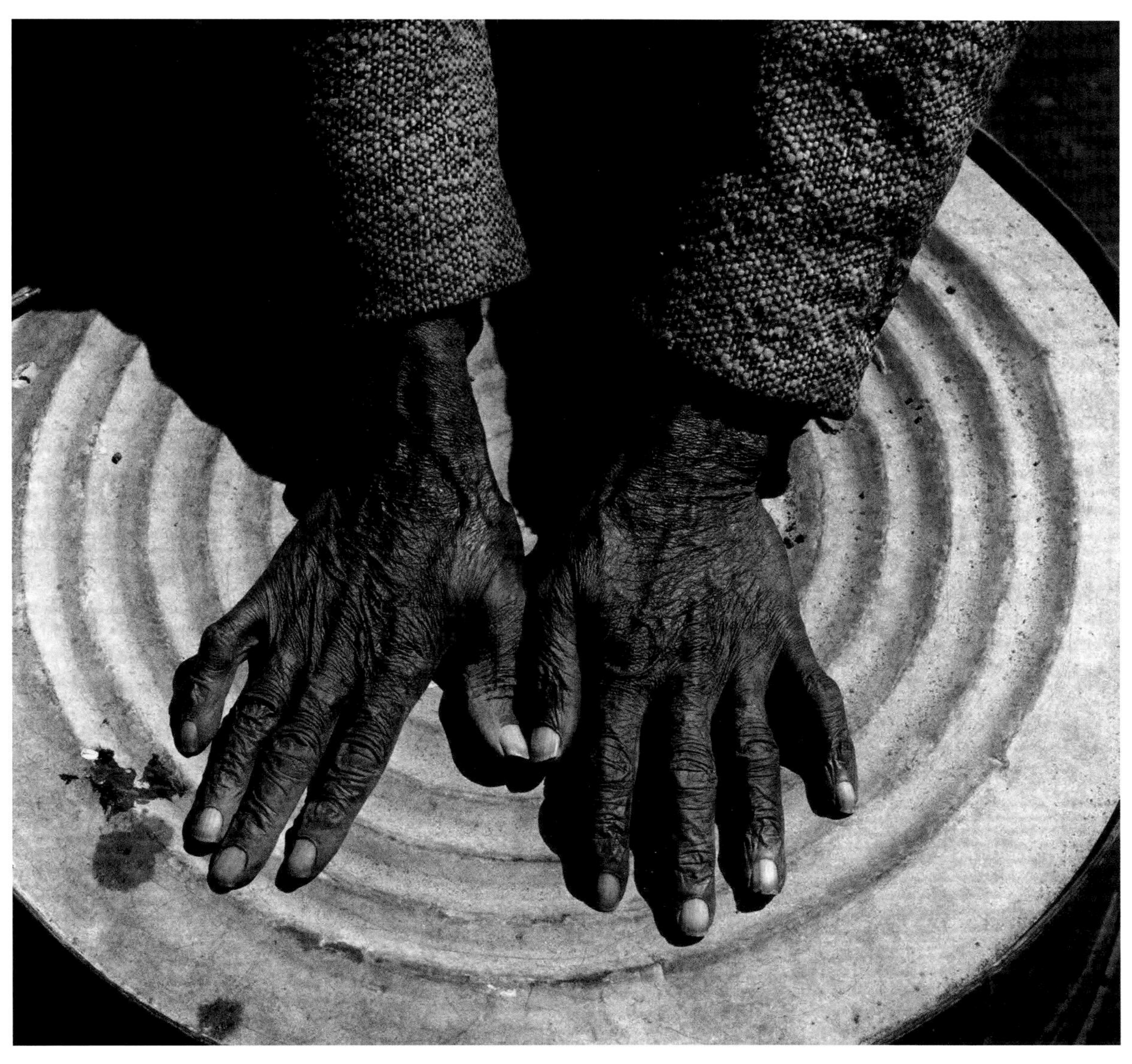

PLATE 16
Debbie Fleming Caffery, *Harry's Hands*, 1984

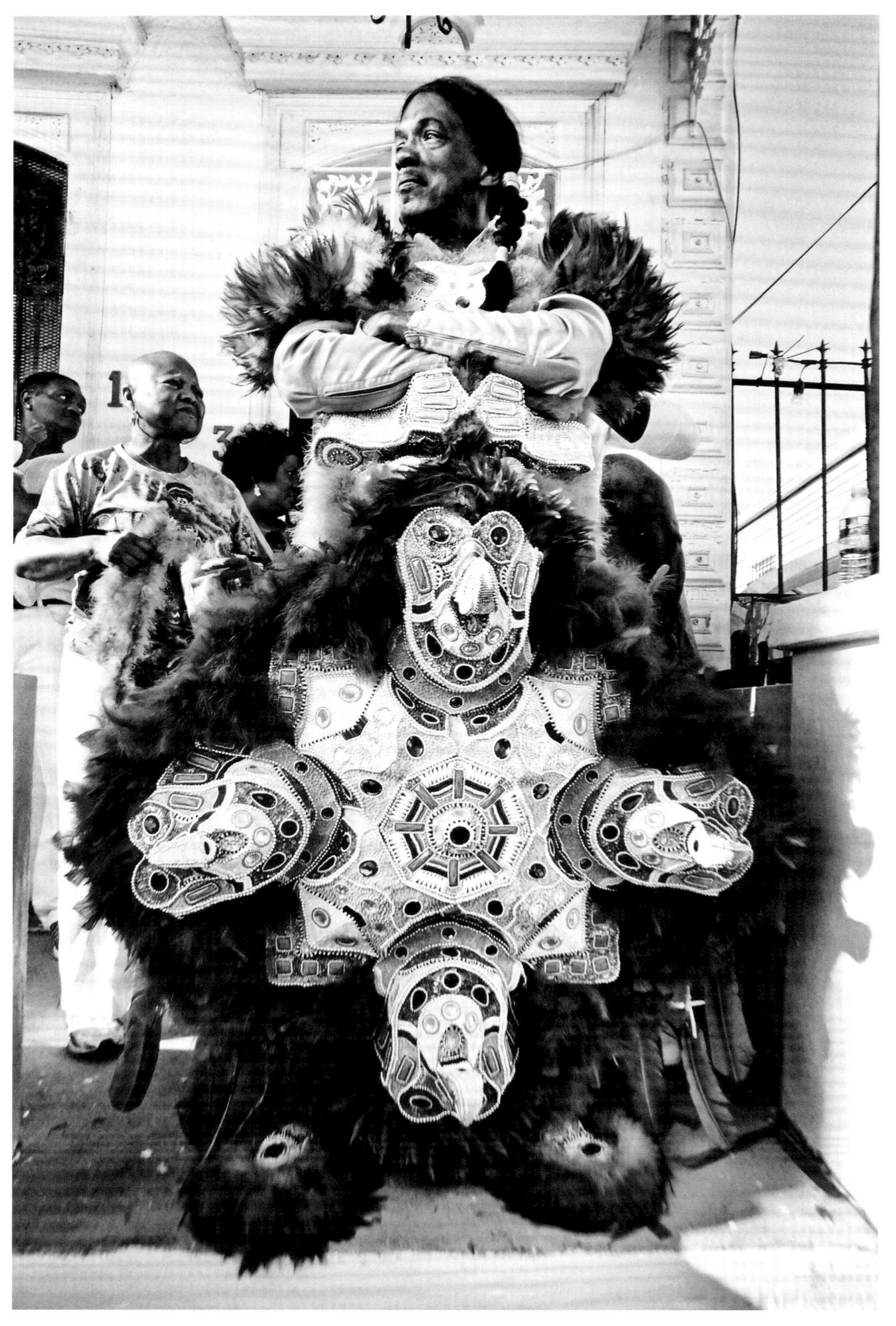

PLATE 17
Keith Calhoun, *I'm the One They Talk About, Big Chief Darryl Montana, the Yellow Pocahontas*, 2016

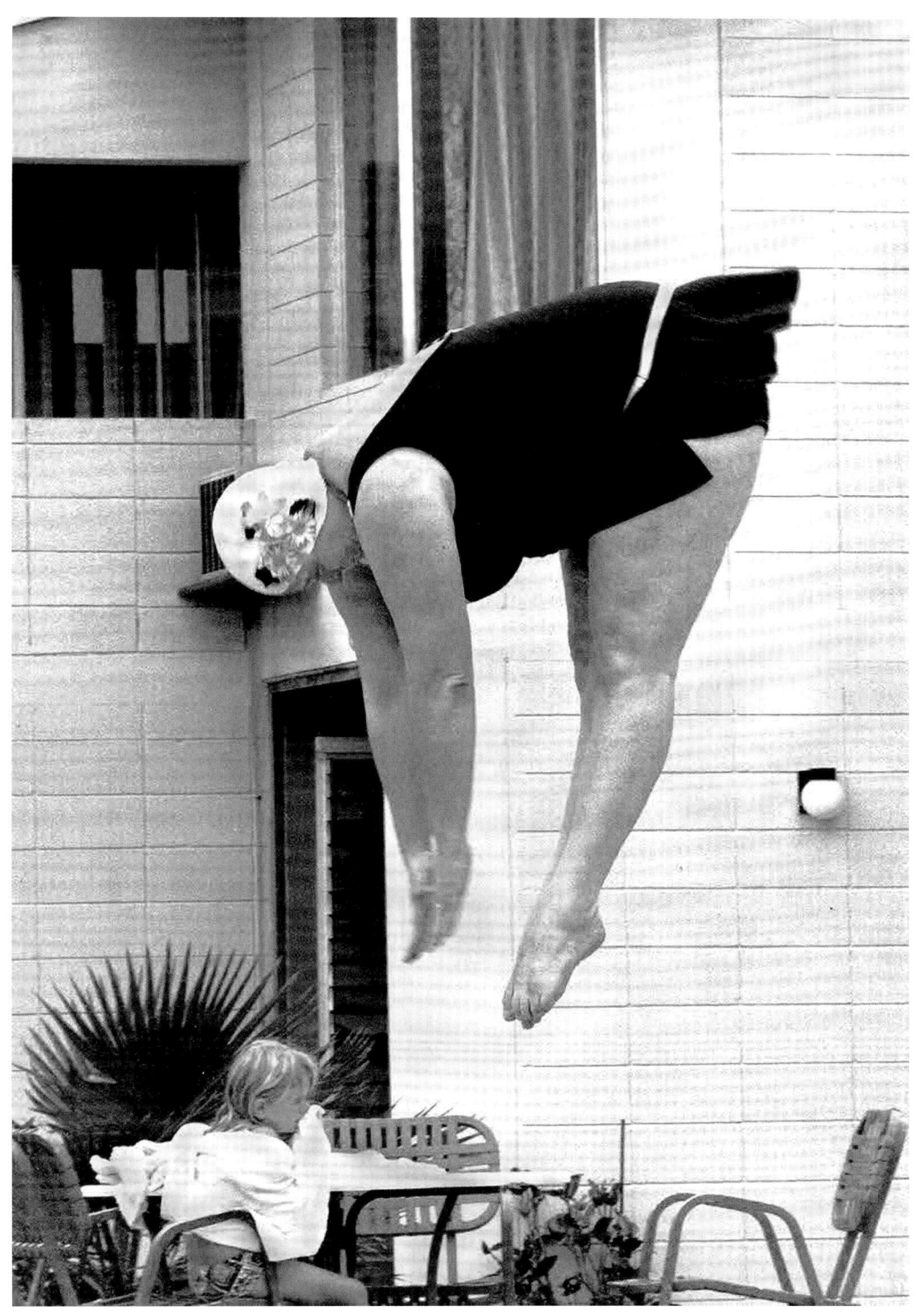

PLATE 18
Michael Carlebach, *Key West*, 1971

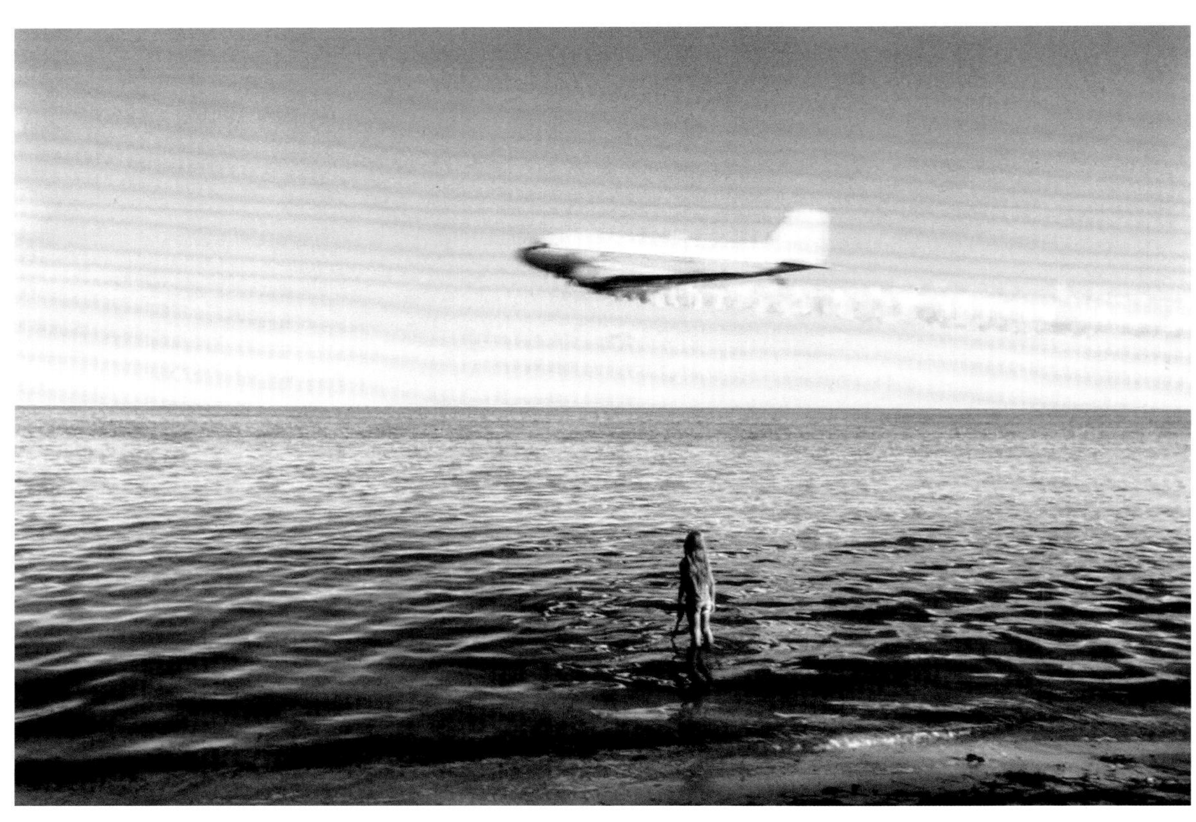

PLATE 19
Michael Carlebach, *Mosquito spray plane, North Key Largo, Florida*, 1980

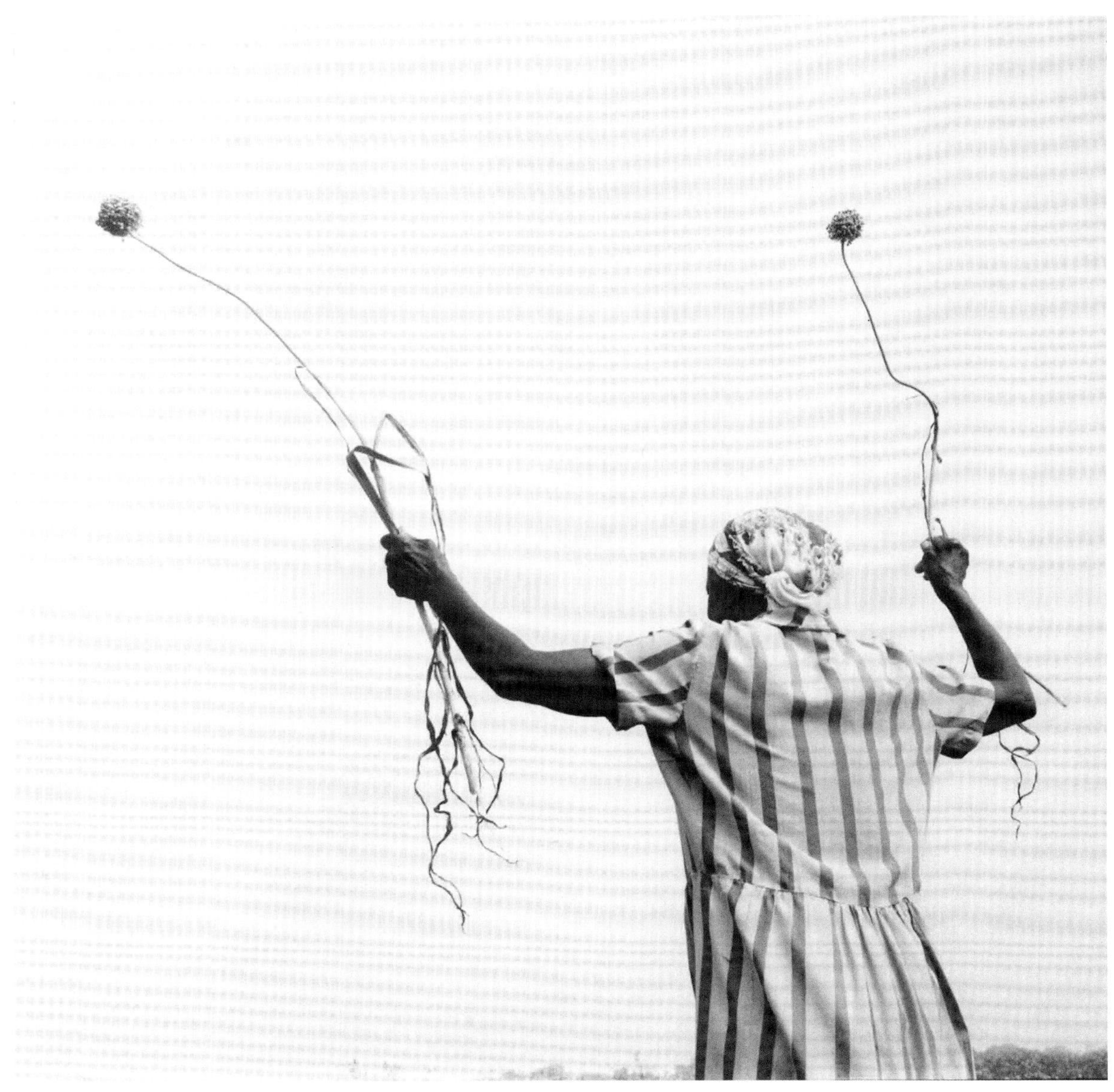

PLATE 20
Keith Carter, *Garlic*, 1991

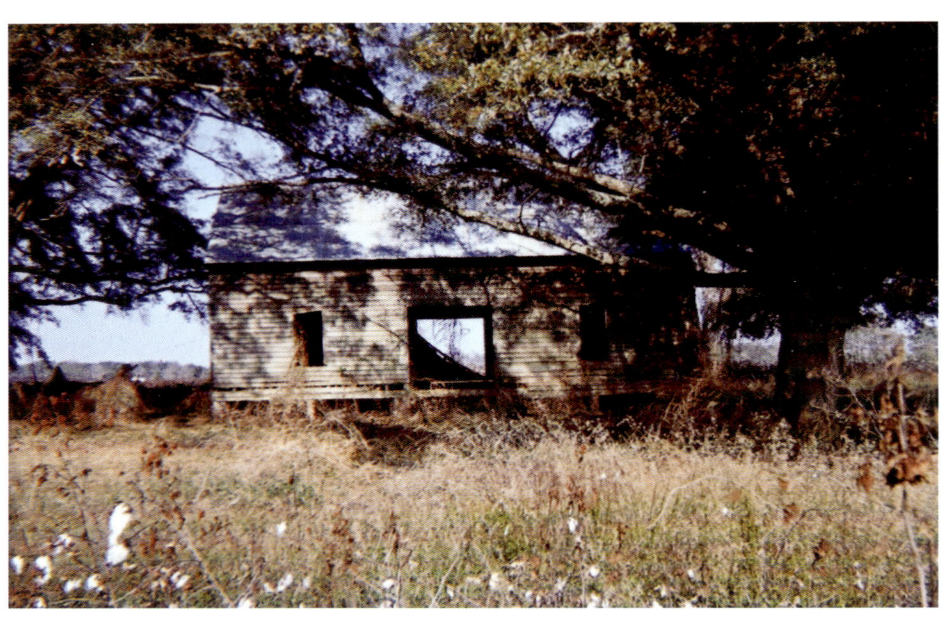

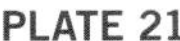

William Christenberry, *Abandoned House in Field (View III), Near Montgomery, Alabama*, 1971

IF I REMEMBER CORRECTLY, it was in the spring of 1977 that Lee
Friedlander and I were at an outdoor café in Washington when he mentioned
that he'd be interested in seeing what I could do with a large-format camera.
Another friend, Caldecot Chubb, had an 8 × 10–inch Deardorff view camera,
a beautiful piece of equipment. Cotty brought it down from New York that
summer, gave me a few rudimentary tips on how to use it, and left it with me
to take on my annual trip down south. I really didn't know anything about it
technically. It is amazing that I got any exposures right. Nick Nixon, who was
one of the first of my artist friends to see the proof prints of that first trip in
1977, looked at them and said, "My goodness, Christenberry, you use that big
camera just like you do the Brownie—straight ahead, tilt down." I didn't know
anything about all these swings and tilts (and I still don't). . . .

There are some subjects that particularly lend themselves to the big camera.
One of my favorite pictures is called *China Grove Church*. I think I made it in
1979. This to me is a good example of how the large camera can function to do
something that I had wanted to do for a long time, and that is to capture the
feeling of aloneness of a beautiful church down a country road. I'm not saying I
couldn't have done it with the small camera but to my mind, this one did it.[1]

— William Christenberry

---

1   From William Christenberry, "The Large Format Camera," in *William Christenberry: Working from Memory, Collected Stories*, ed. Susanne Lange (Göttingen, Germany: Steidl Publishers, 2008), 29–30.

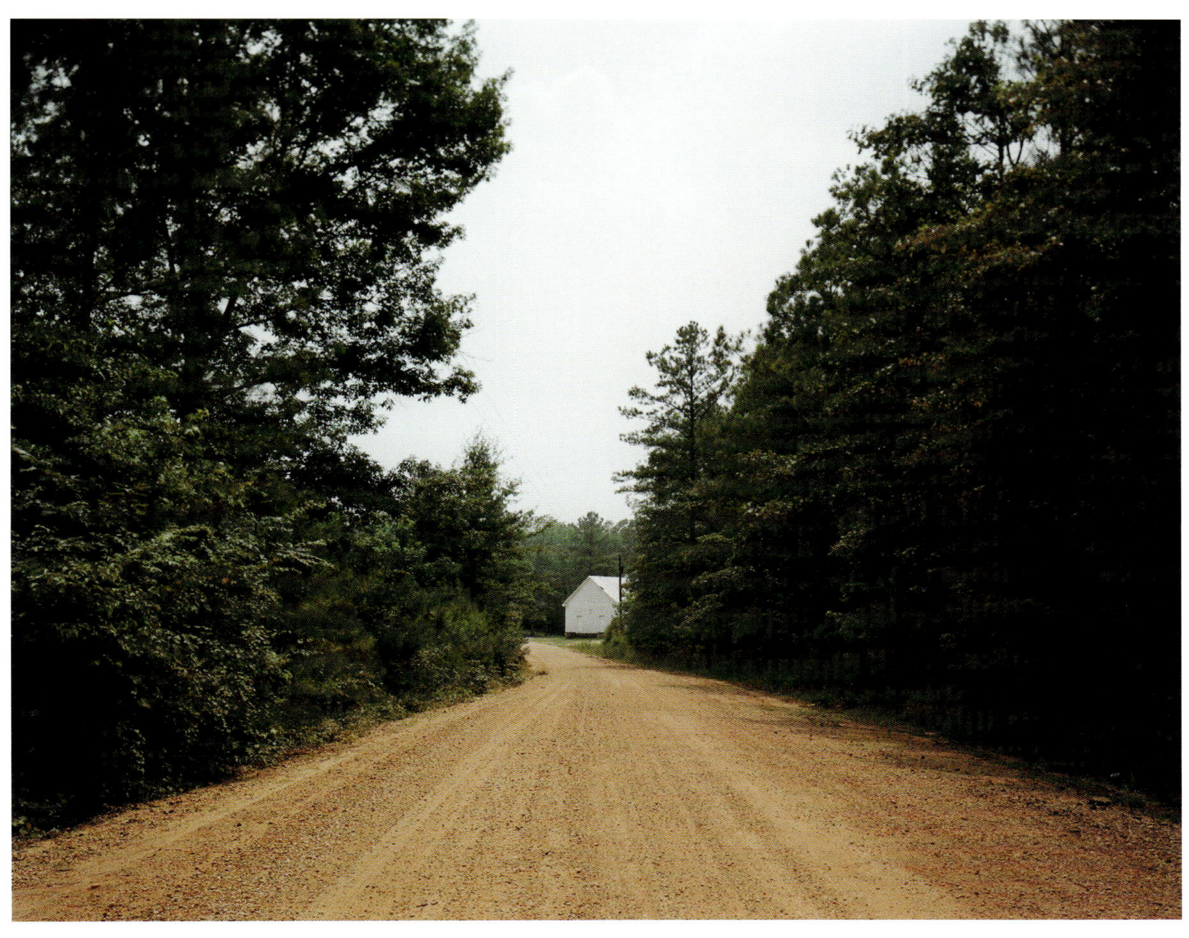

PLATE 22
William Christenberry, *China Grove Church, Hale County, Alabama*, 1979

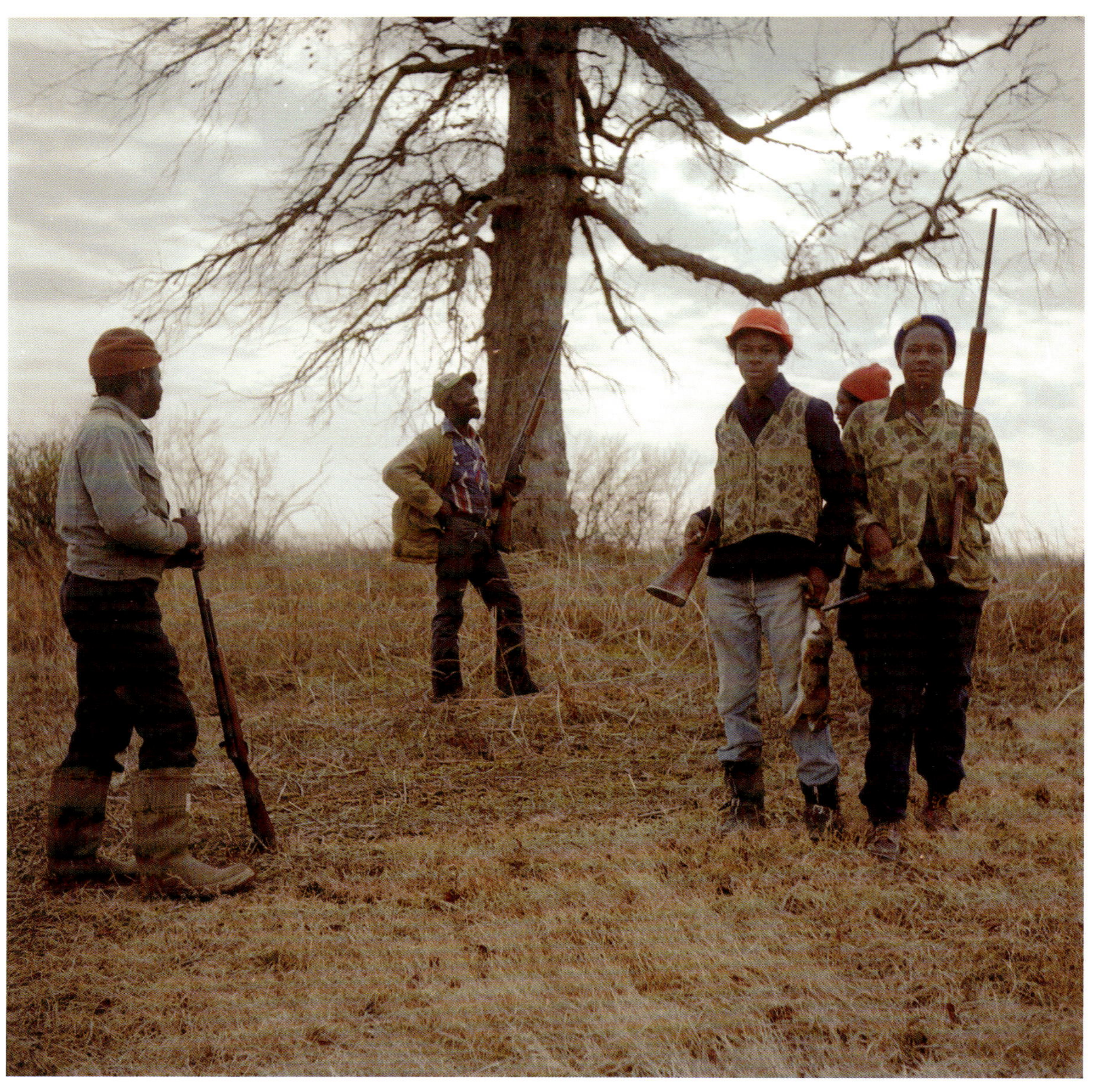

PLATE 23
Maude Schuyler Clay, *Delta Hunters*, 1984

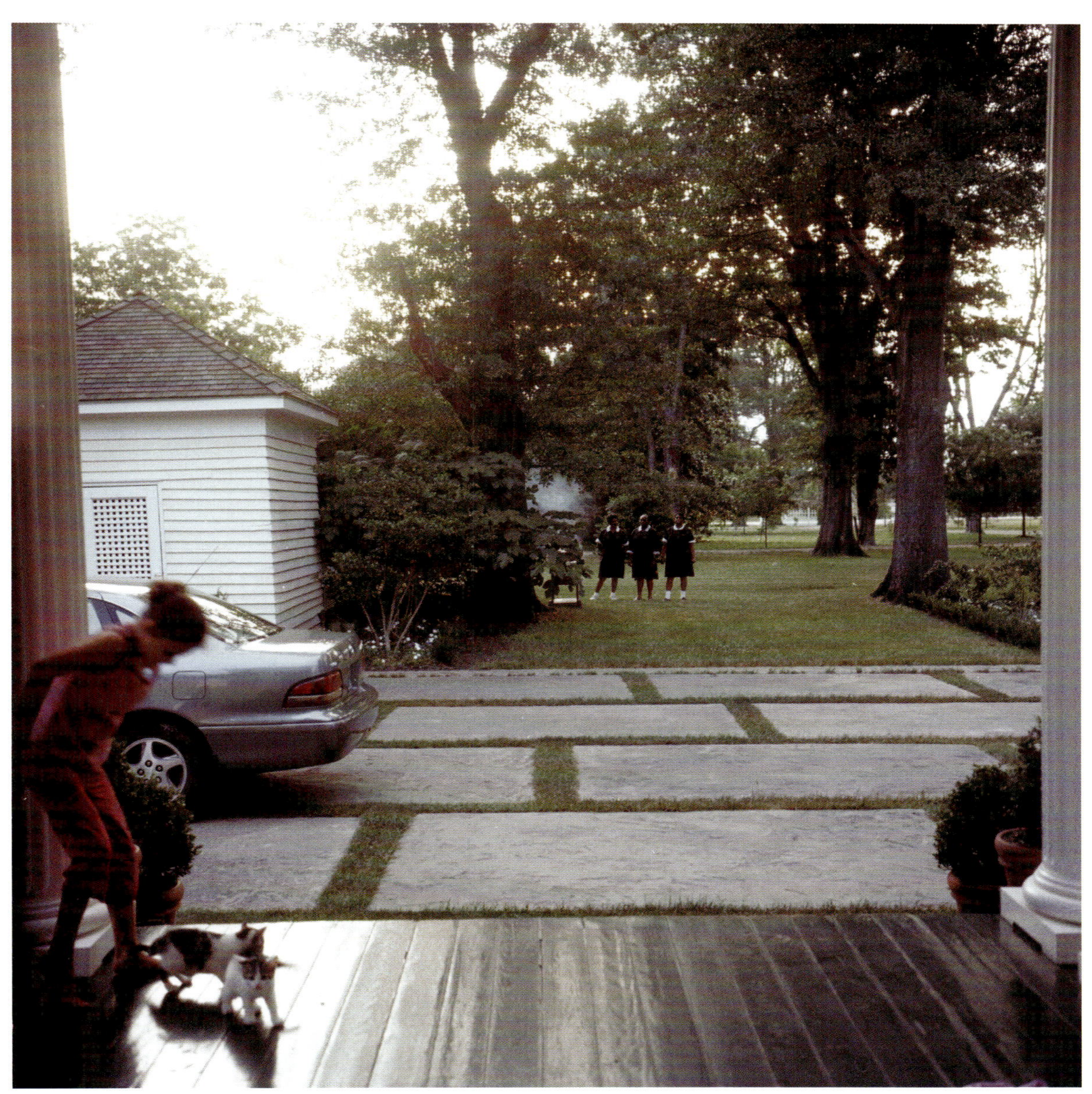

PLATE 24
Maude Schuyler Clay, *Sophie with Kittens, Sumner, Mississippi*, 2002

IN 1973, AFTER FINISHING MY MFA at the School of the Art
Institute of Chicago, I moved back south. For my thesis, I had photographed two different groups: Chicago's motorcycle gangs and members of
the American Nazi party. I now wanted to photograph the Klan. I contacted a young man not much older than me. He had recently been made the
Imperial Wizard of the Louisiana-based Klan. He invited me to his home
in Baton Rouge, Louisiana, and we talked. His name was David Duke.
After visiting and showing him my portfolio, he invited me to a Klan rally
in Walker, Louisiana, the following weekend. It was to be the first of many
rallies that I would attend. The photograph in this particular exhibit was
taken at a daytime rally in South Carolina. Afternoon rallies tended to be
family affairs similar to old-fashioned church picnics. Fellowship, food, and
a side of preaching. Night rallies were more serious affairs—crosses lit and
adults only. In 1976, I attended a rally in Plains, Georgia. Just before dusk,
a local man, offended that the Klan was demonstrating in his hometown,
drove his car into the Klan's makeshift speaker platform and then out into
the crowd. Dozens of people were injured. I was taken to the hospital in
critical condition. The Klan sent me get-well wishes. The following year, I
attended a few more rallies, but soon moved on to different interests. Offi-
cially, things in the Klan were changing. Vanishing were the white robes and
the hoods. Their replacements: military black uniforms and riot helmets. I
was on borrowed time. I moved on.

— Dennis Darling

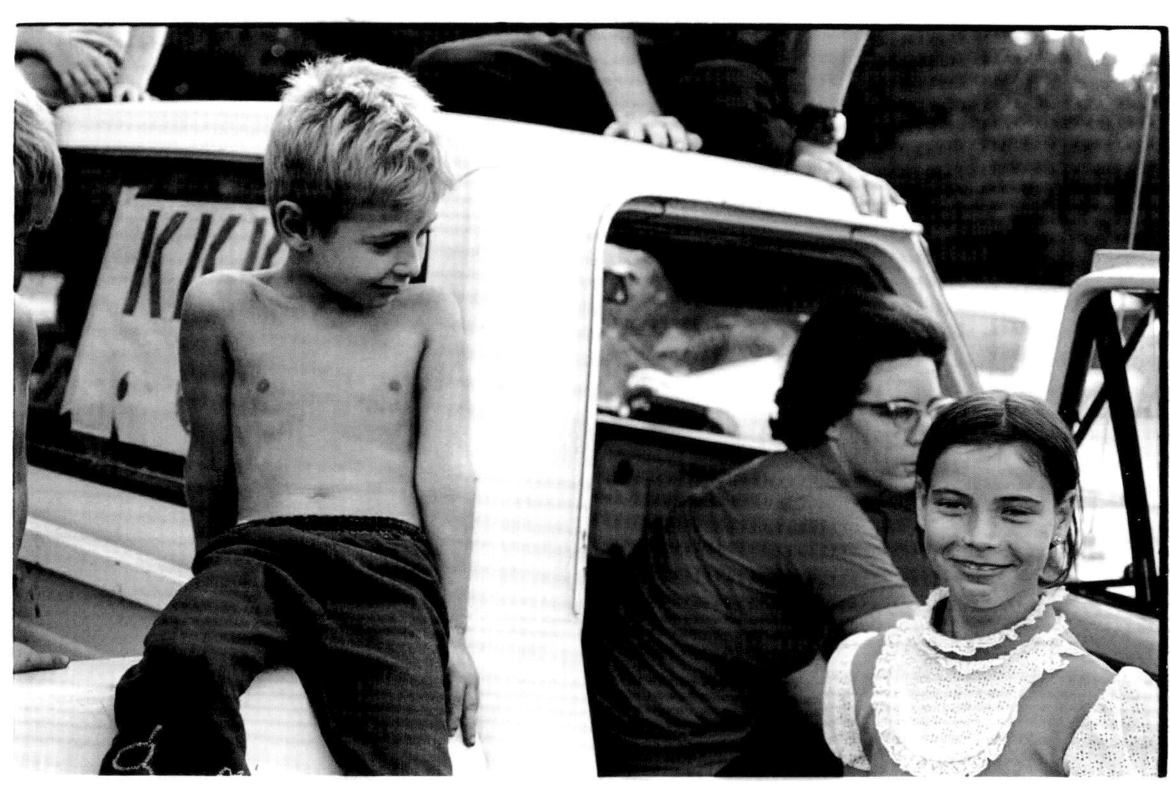

PLATE 25
Dennis Darling, *Family at Klan Rally, South Carolina*, 1974

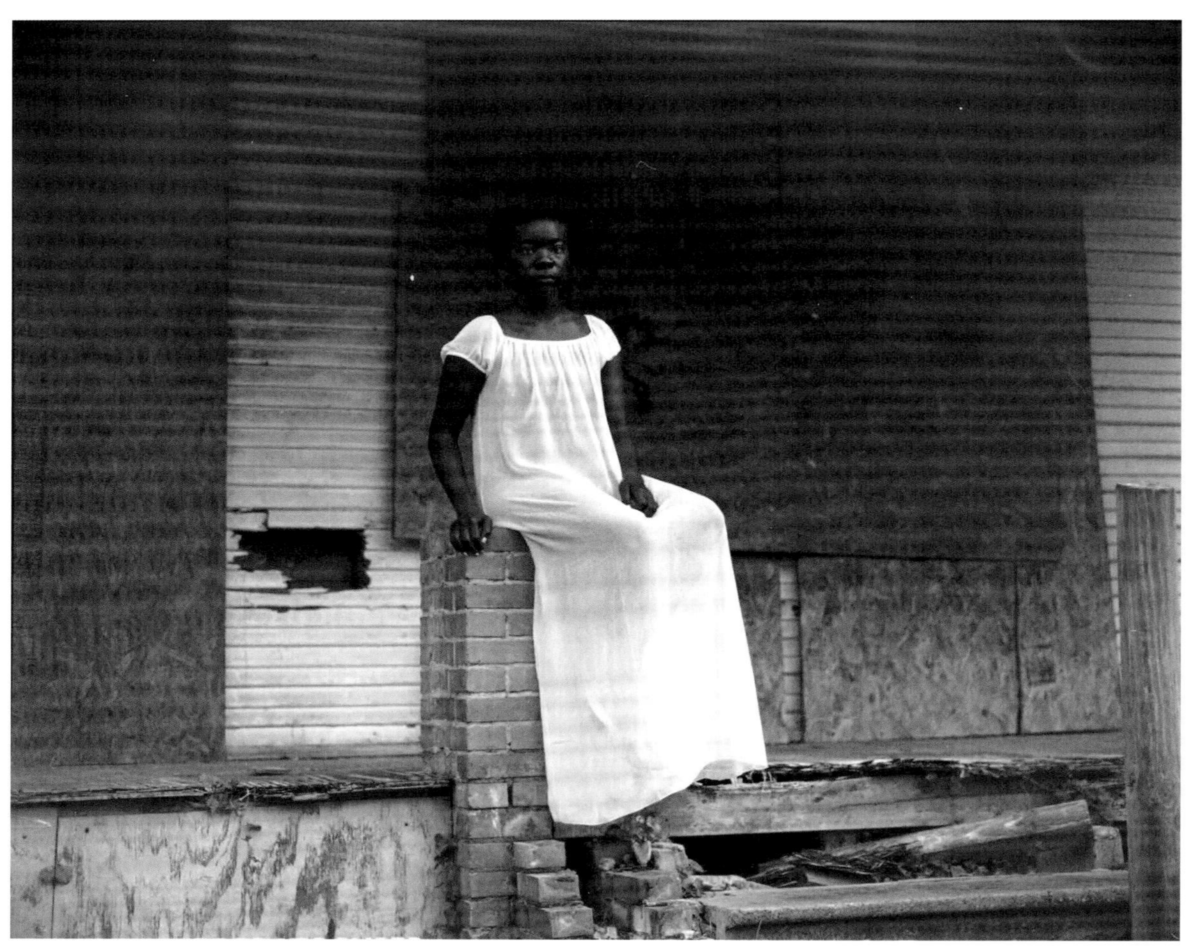

PLATE 26
Colby Deal, *Ethereal*, 2017

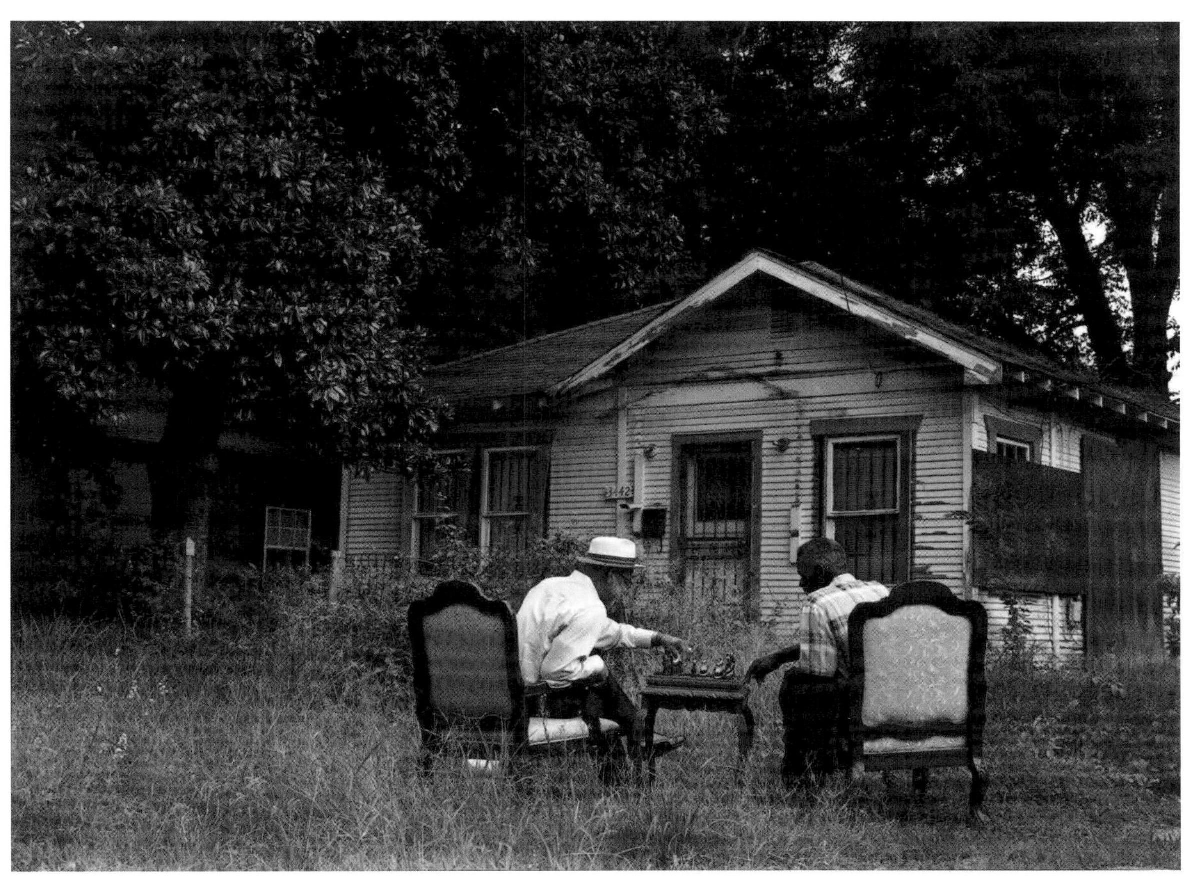

PLATE 27
Colby Deal, *Pressure Chess*, 2017

I WAS HIRED TO VISIT A SMALL TOWN IN ALABAMA to make
photos for a news story about how the influx of Mexican and Guatema-
lan workers in the chicken industry was transforming the community. On
assignments like this I had only a couple days to visit a lot of places. I joined
family dinners and church services, visited a school, chicken farms and
chicken factories, and explored the changing storefronts on the town's main
street. I remember walking into this grocery store and turning toward the
wall and simply thinking, "That's beautiful." That is what initially motivated
me to go out to the car and lug in the tripod to take a picture. In a sense,
there are three levels of framing at play in the image: the religious icons are
hung in ornate golden frames, which are then framed by the painted flowers,
and finally, in my image, all of that is framed again by rows of grocery store
products and carts. Each moment of framing was undertaken by different
people, with different intentions, at different moments in time.

— Carolyn Drake

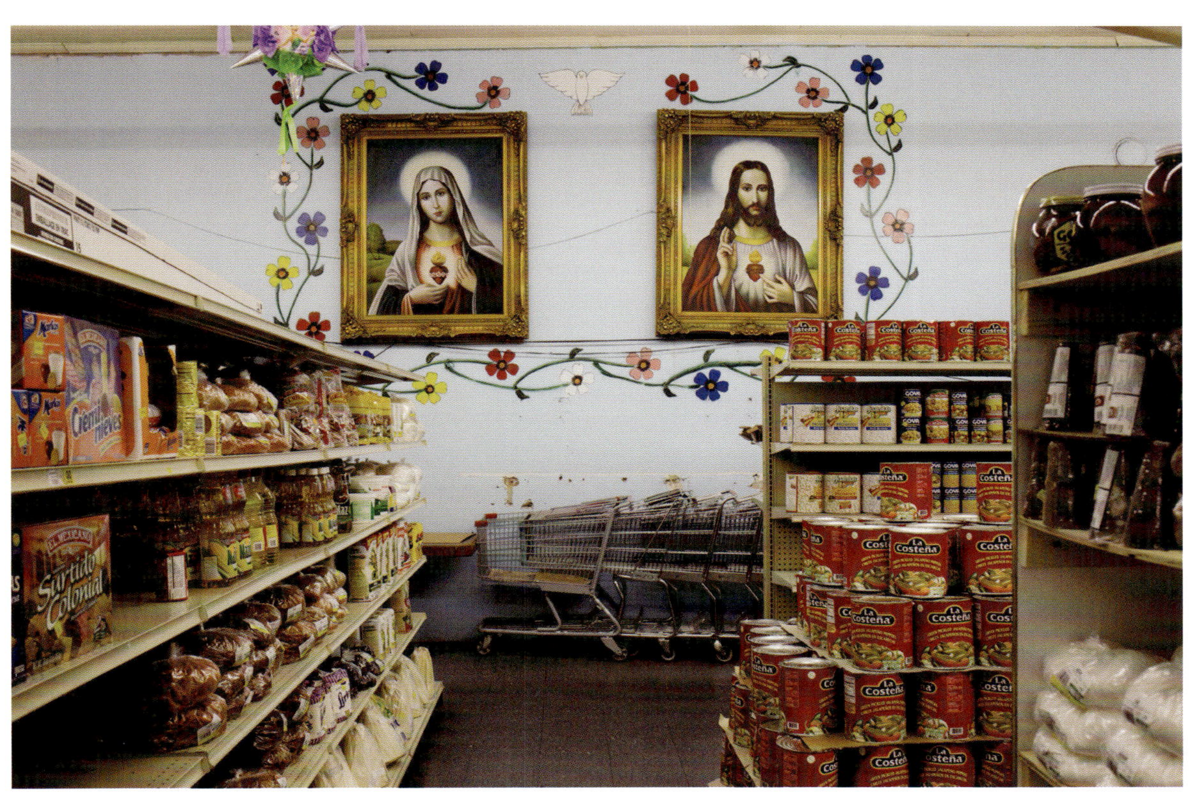

PLATE 28
Carolyn Drake, *Mexican Grocery, Albertville, AL*, 2013

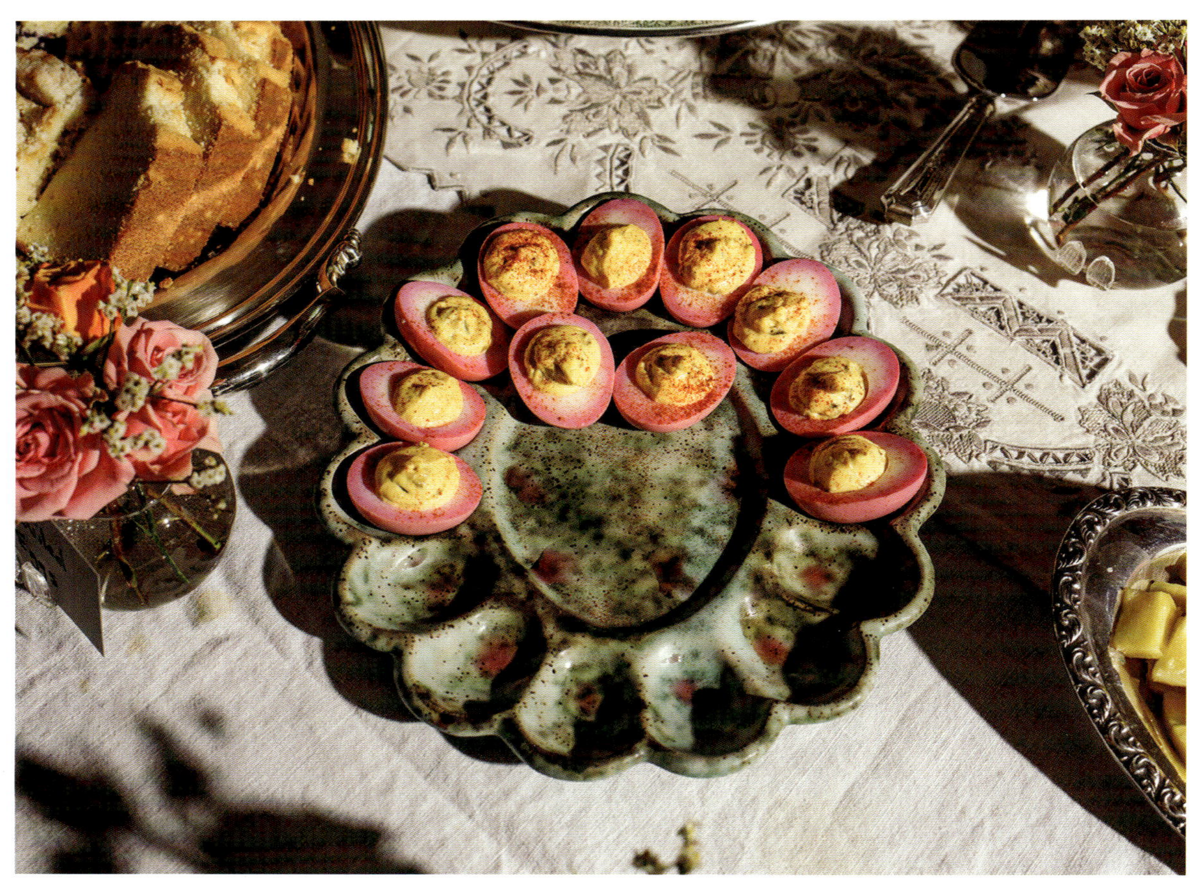

PLATE 29
Carolyn Drake, *Deviled Eggs*, 2017

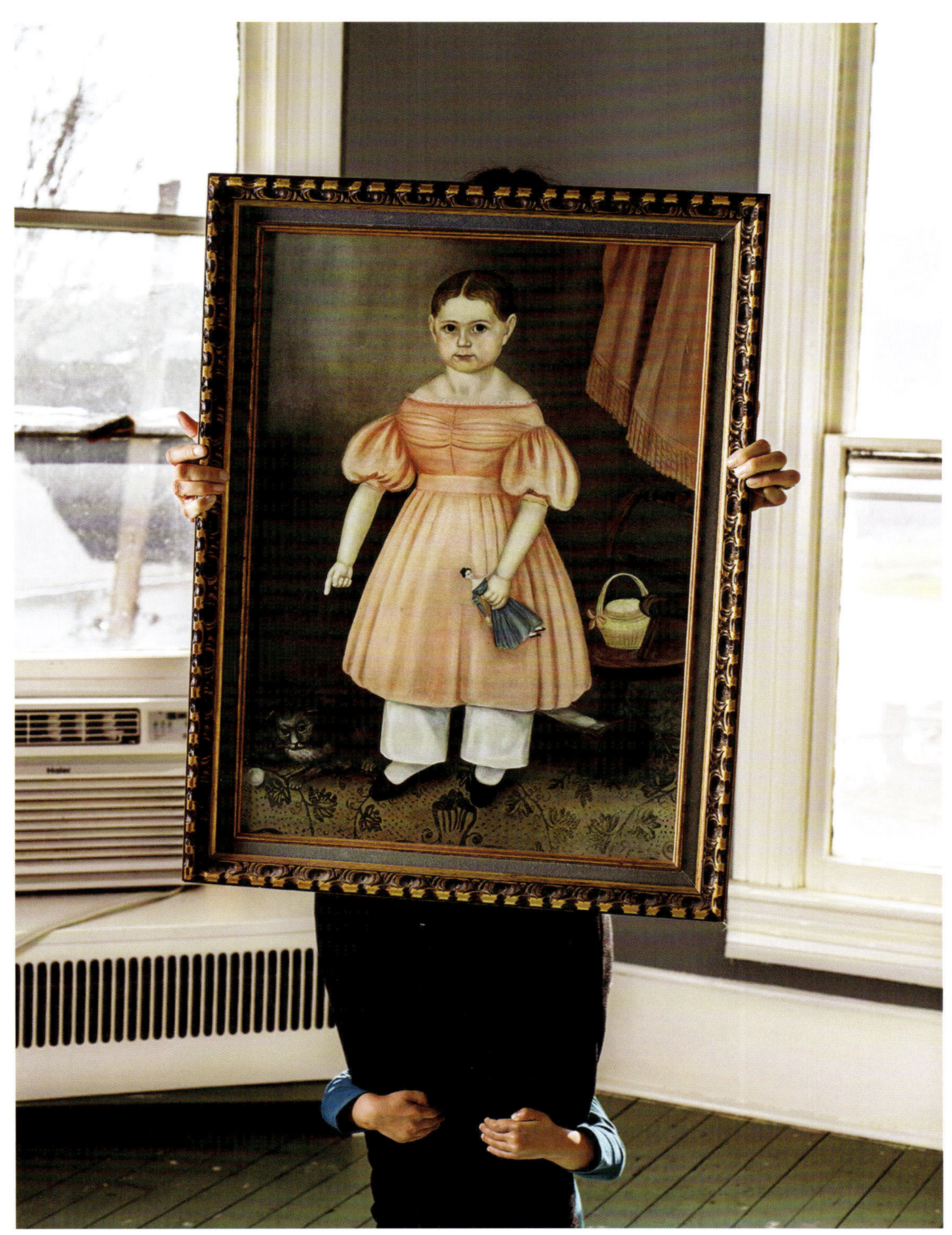

PLATE 30
Carolyn Drake, *Megan and Hazel Sue*, 2018

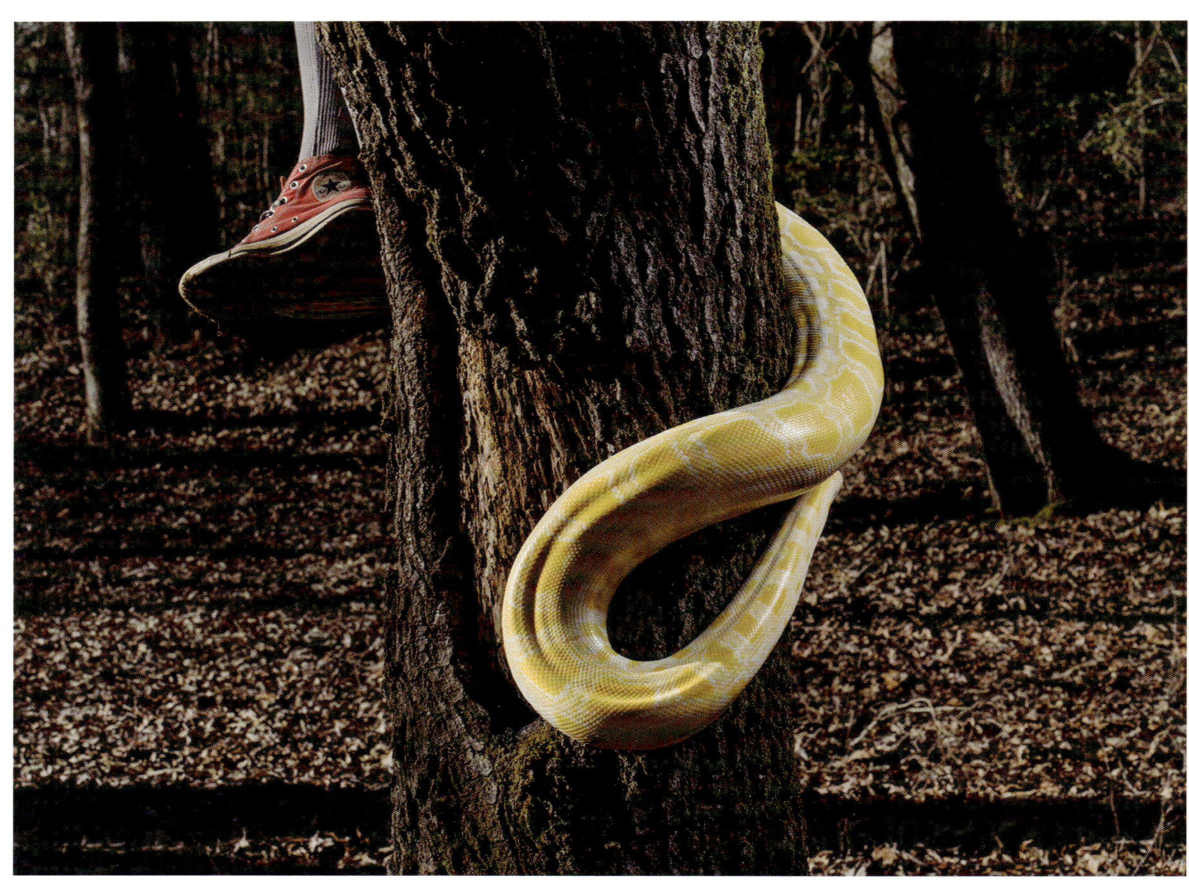

Carolyn Drake, *Elise with Snake*, 2019

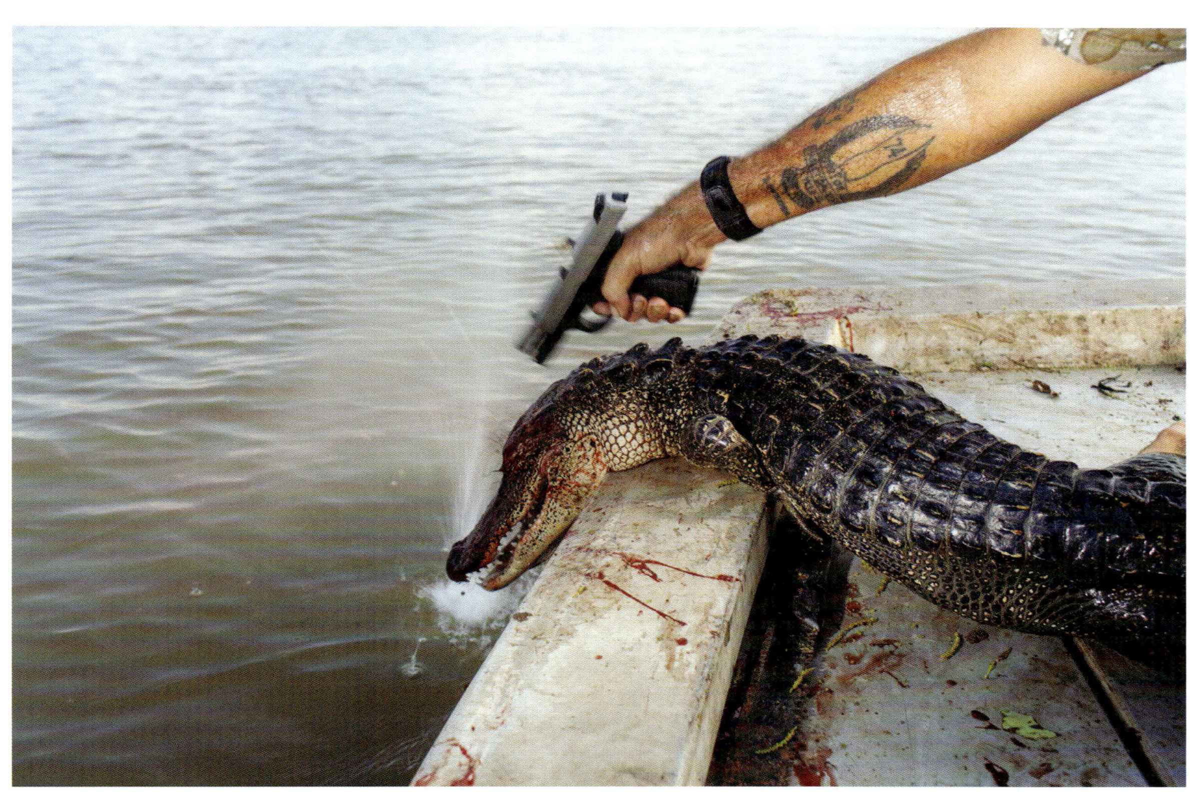

PLATE 32

Matt Eich, *Double-Tap, Shell Island, Louisiana*, 2009

ASPECTS OF MY CHILDHOOD ALWAYS MANAGE TO WORM
their way into my photographs. This image is drawn from the *Invisible Yoke* series, which considers how collective memory shapes our identities as Americans. I grew up in rural southeastern Virginia as the oldest of four children in a conservative home. As a child, I saw images of river baptisms, people dressed in all white undergoing this ritual of submission, purification, and rebirth. I'd also seen some images of the United House of Prayer (UHOP) firehose baptisms, which tour the East Coast.

For two years I'd focused on creating a museum exhibition of the *Seven Cities*, the third volume of the *Invisible Yoke*, which was set in the Hampton Roads region of Virginia where I was raised and was then raising my own children. Two weeks before the exhibition's opening, a friend alerted me that UHOP had planned a firehose baptism stop in Newport News. The event was scheduled for midday when the sun was harsh and overhead. I arrived to find quite a scene. As a total outsider to this community, I tried to move lightly and unobtrusively, but I still caught more than a few critical glances questioning my presence. A brass band brought the crowd to life and folks swayed, danced, prayed, and sang along. The preacher, Sweet Daddy Bailey, sat on a covered stage, as young women fanned him with palm fronds. Firehoses were attached to hydrants at each end of the street and began spraying water straight up in the air, raining down a heavy mist on the white-clad crowd that soaked us through. I kept my cameras wrapped in plastic bags but had to stop to dry them off several times.

A young man carrying a baby girl in a white dress moved through the crowd, tenderly pressing her to his chest. He is turned away from the rest of the crowd, simultaneously of and apart from it. His protective body language made me think of holding my own young daughter and the inherent contradictions of bringing someone into the world while trying to protect them from it. Of the hundreds of photographs I made that afternoon this one has stayed with me the longest.

— Matt Eich

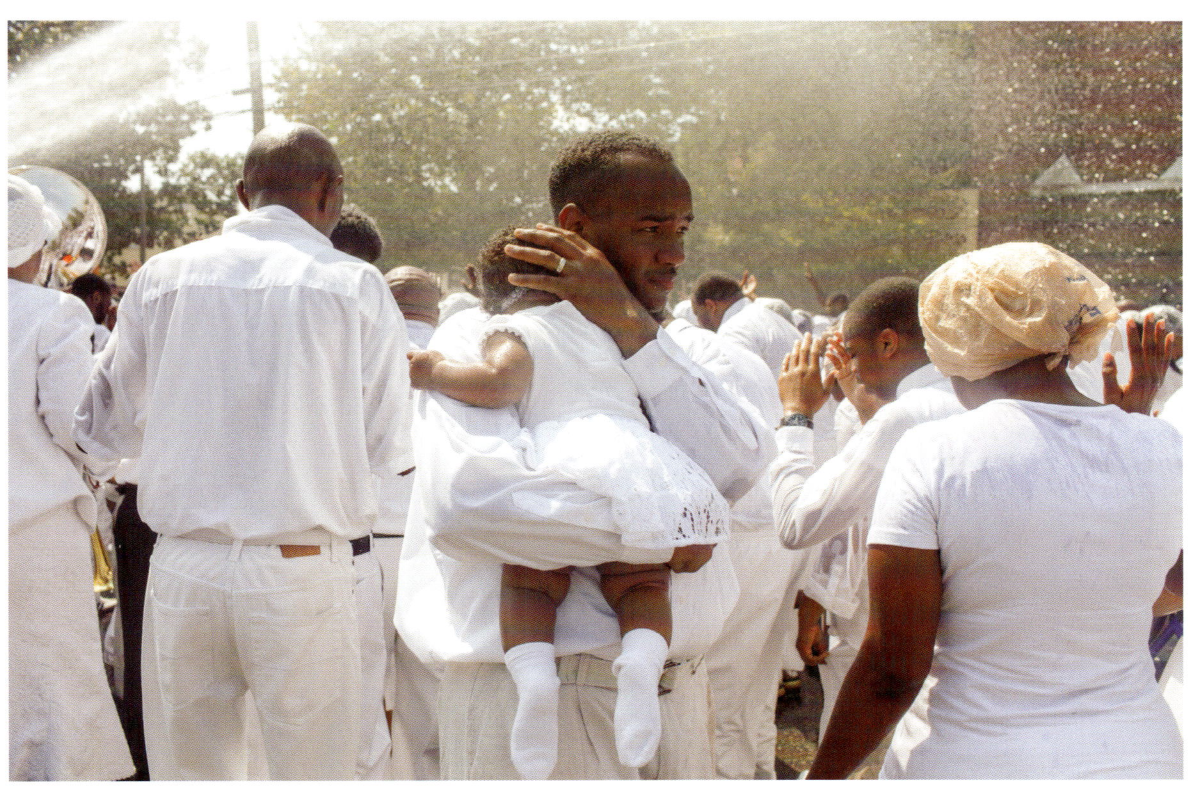

PLATE 33
Matt Eich, *Firehose baptism, Newport News, Virginia*, 2013

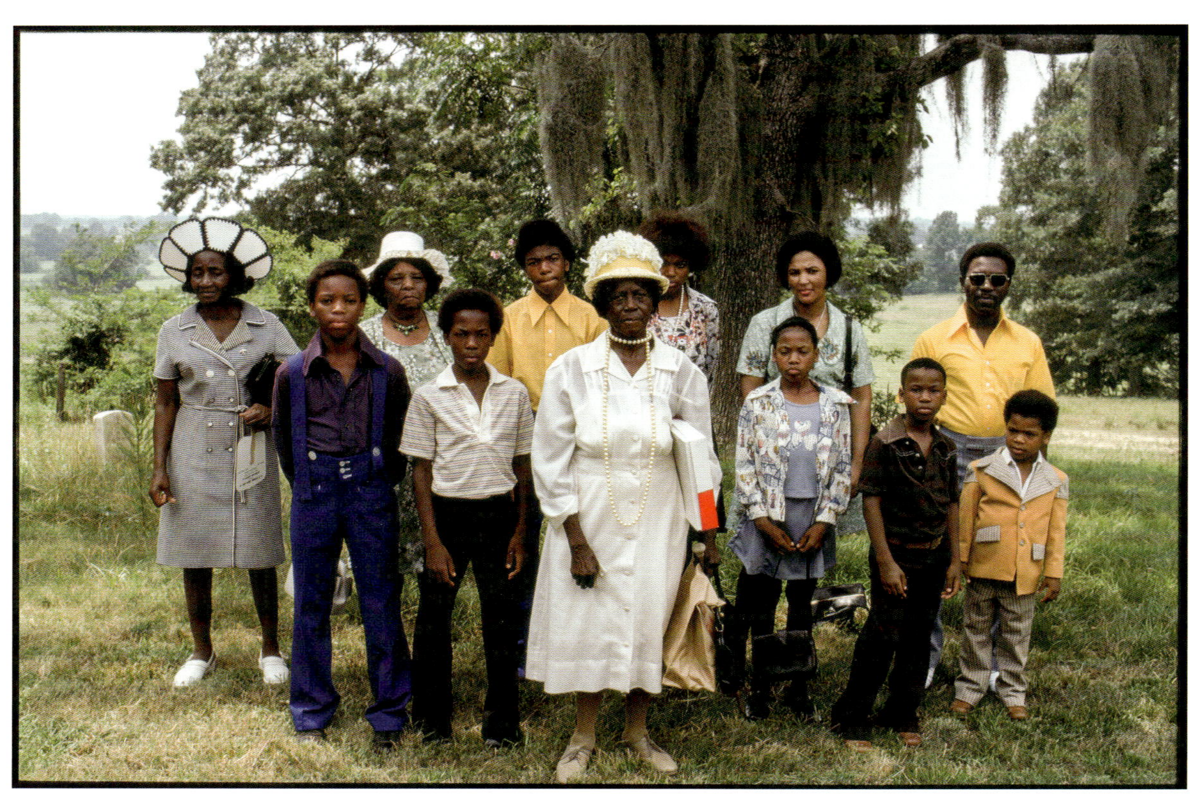

William Ferris, *Rose Hill Church, Fisher Ferry Road, Warren County, Mississippi*, 1975

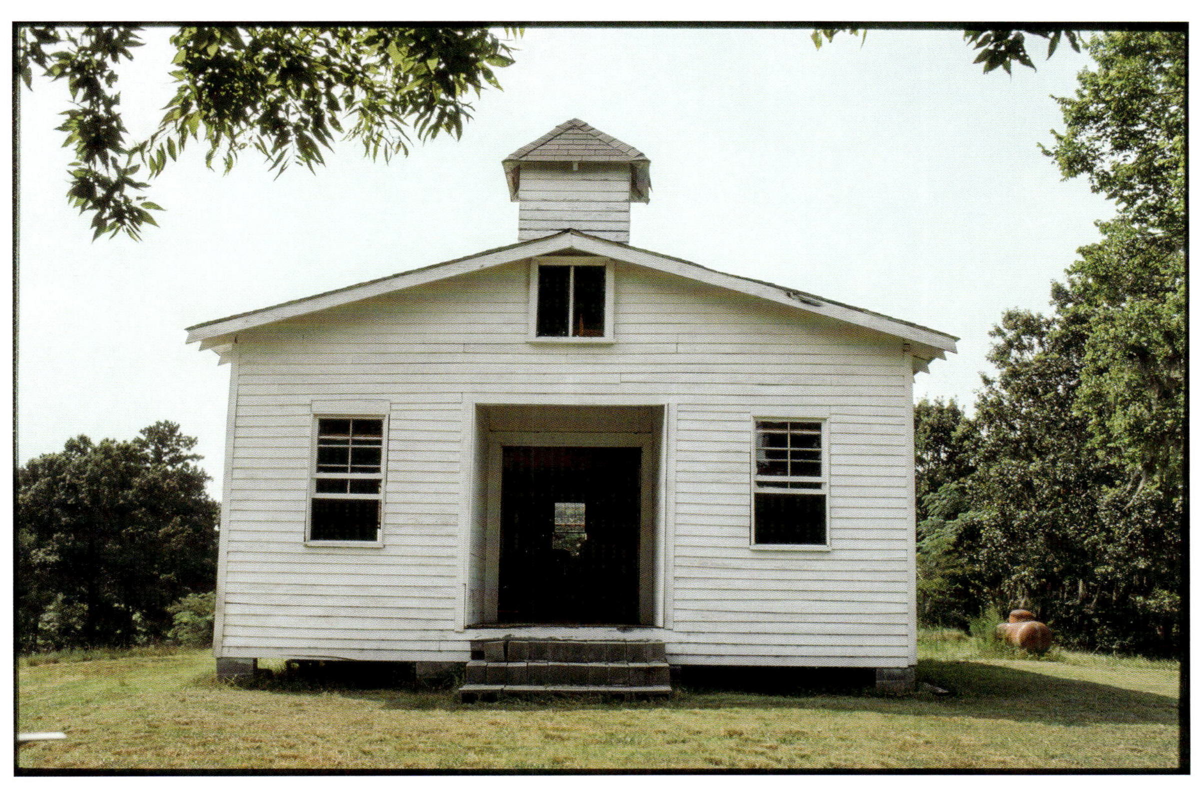

William Ferris, *Rose Hill Church, Fisher Ferry Road, Warren County, Mississippi*, 1975

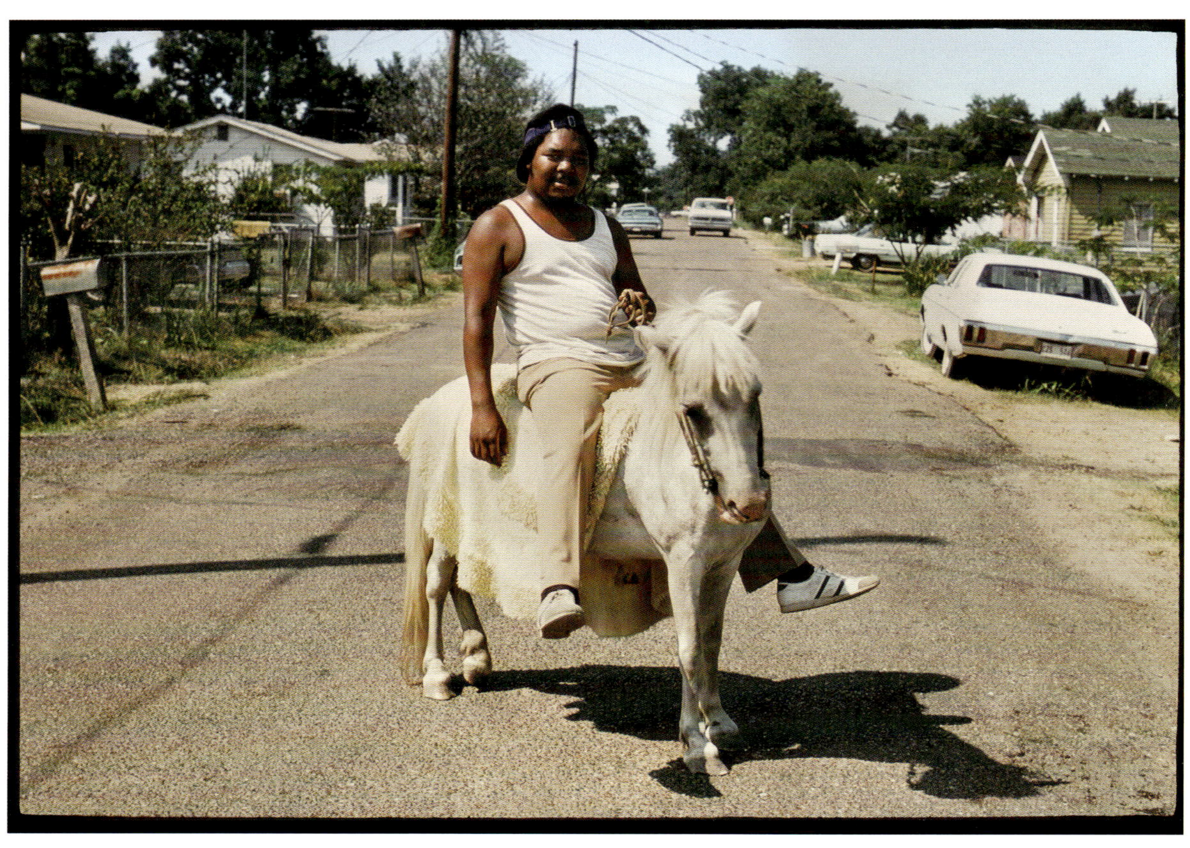

William Ferris, *Unidentified rider and pony, Yazoo City, Mississippi*, 1975

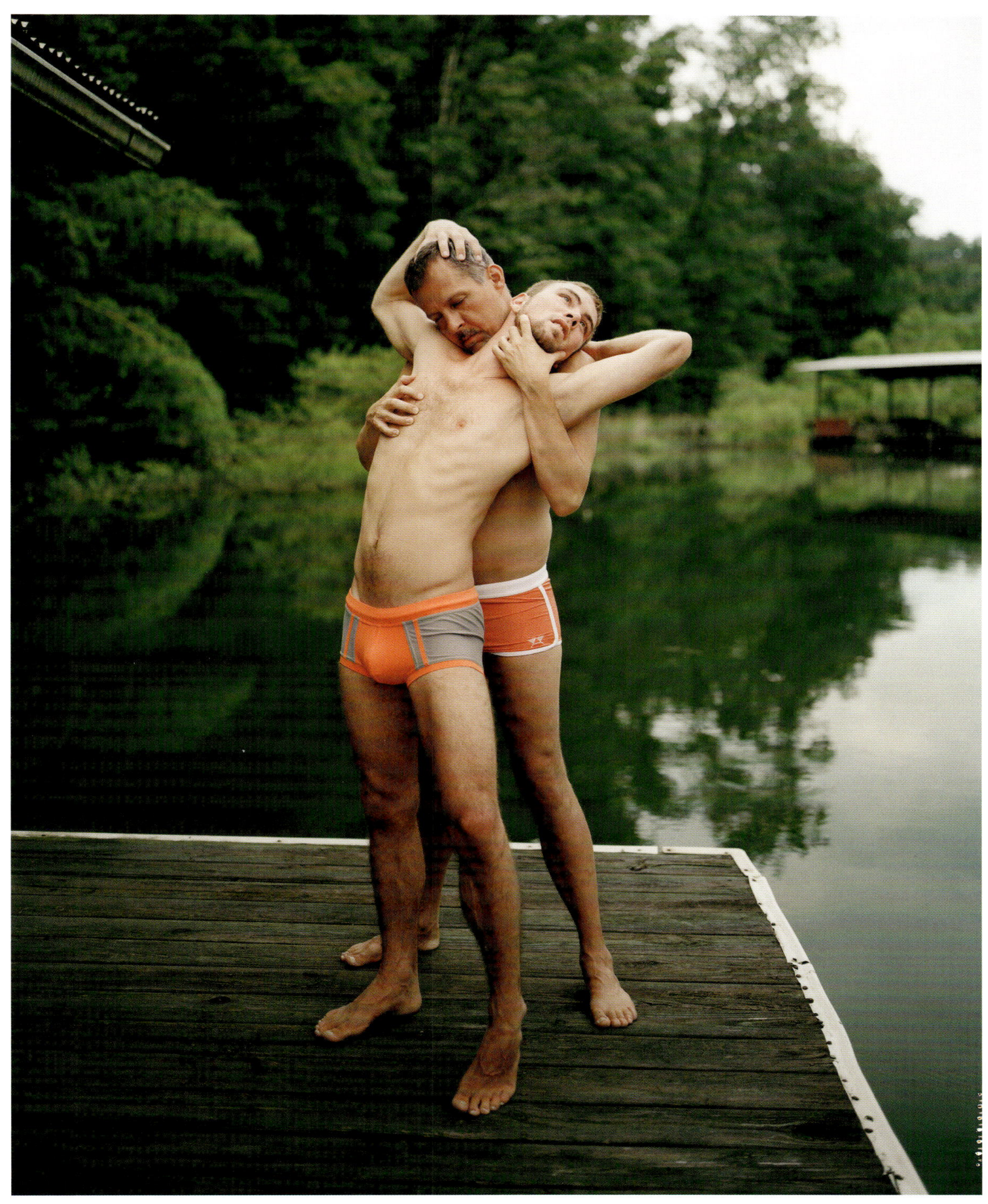

Jill Frank, *Couple on Dock*, 2013

IN MY PICTURES, I TRY TO FORMALIZE, DISTILL, serialize, and monumentalize casual social behaviors. This work unfolds in the real world, with real people who want to be photographed. Often when I am asked to explain an image, I feel conflicted. I rarely know the people in my pictures. I only know what appears to be happening, not what is actually happening. I like the tension of not knowing what is a performance and what is authentic. I like making pictures that respond to the world of appearances.

Over the course of three years I visited a student-housing enclave in Athens, Georgia, to make photographs. On my first visit, I happened upon a quiet cluster of multicolored houses and learned that the "yellow house on the corner would be having a huge house party" that night. Rather than photograph the party, I decided to show up the next morning very early to document its aftermath. Because I work with a large-format camera, I often have to wait for the right picture—and it is often in waiting that life becomes more complicated. With limited 4 × 5 film, I photographed the people who trickled out in the morning light against the multicolored siding. I made two exposures of each person and later I became fascinated with the two negatives, which revealed tiny shifts in expression and emotion between each exposure. These are two of the people who stayed the night at the party. People often ask why the young red-haired woman was crying, or if that is actually a hickey on the young man's neck. It is not up to me to say. They didn't give me their stories to tell; they only gave me permission to make a photograph.

— Jill Frank

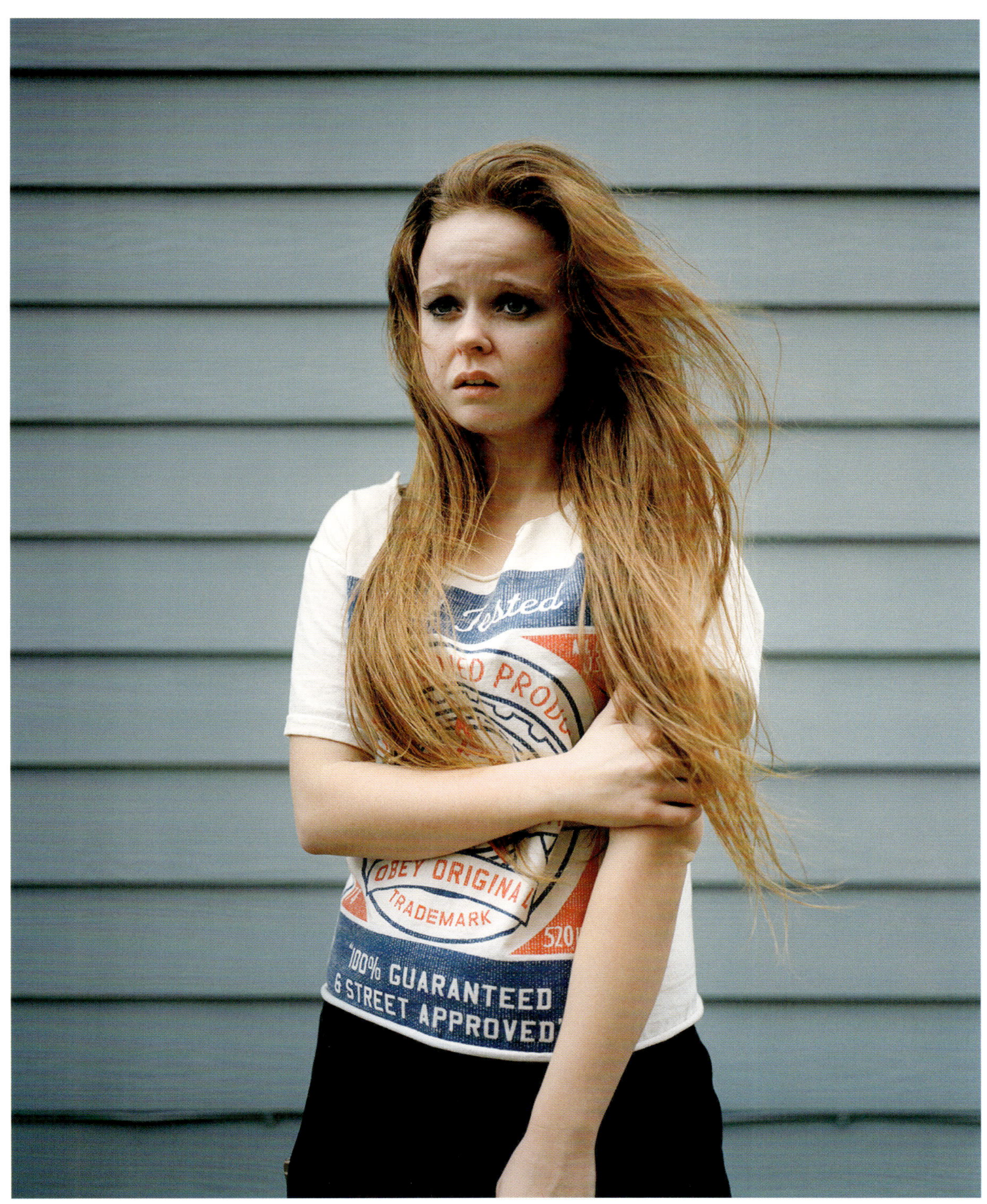

PLATE 38
Jill Frank, *everyone who woke up at the yellow house 1*, 2016

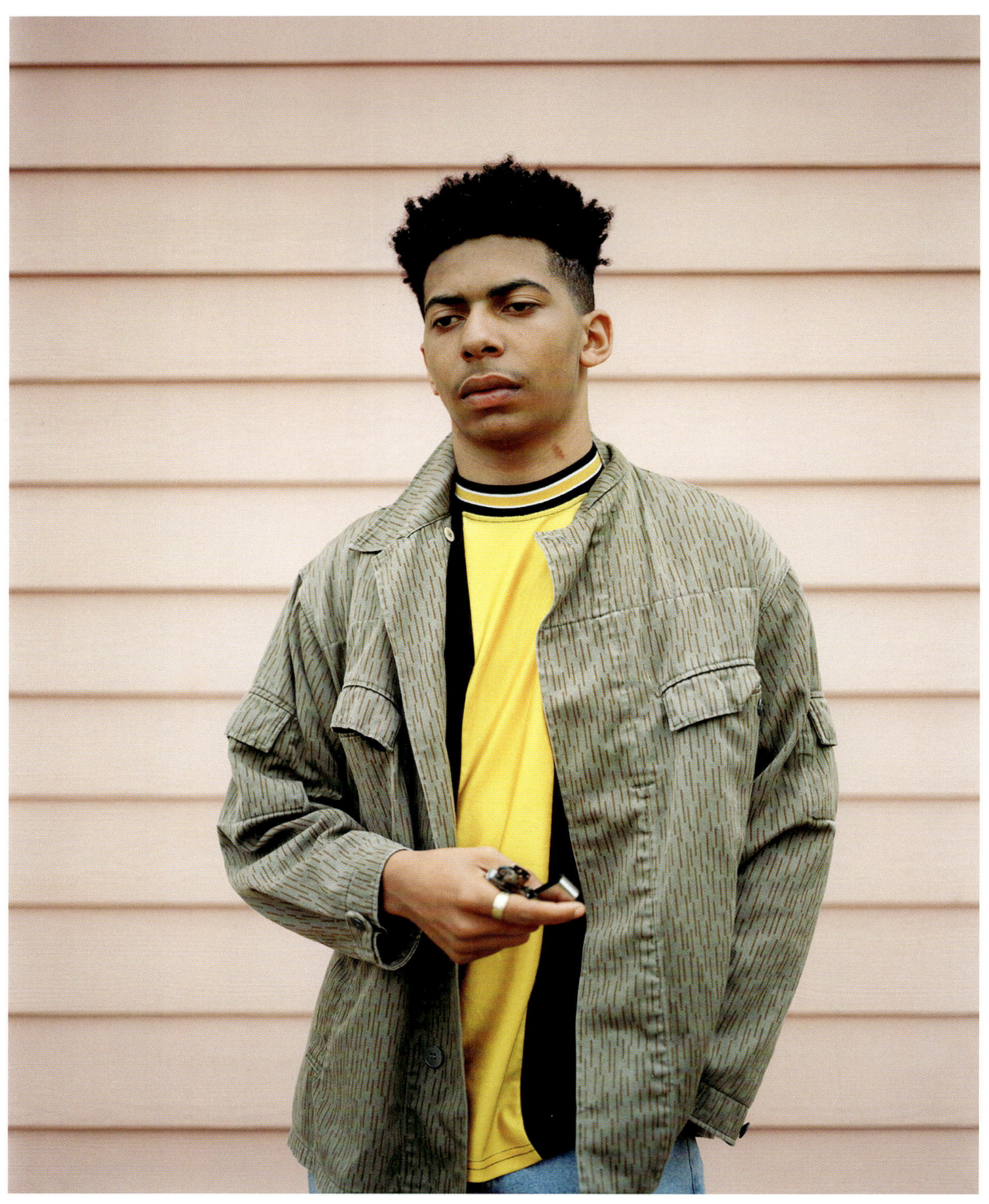

PLATE 39
Jill Frank, *everyone who woke up at the yellow house 3*, 2016

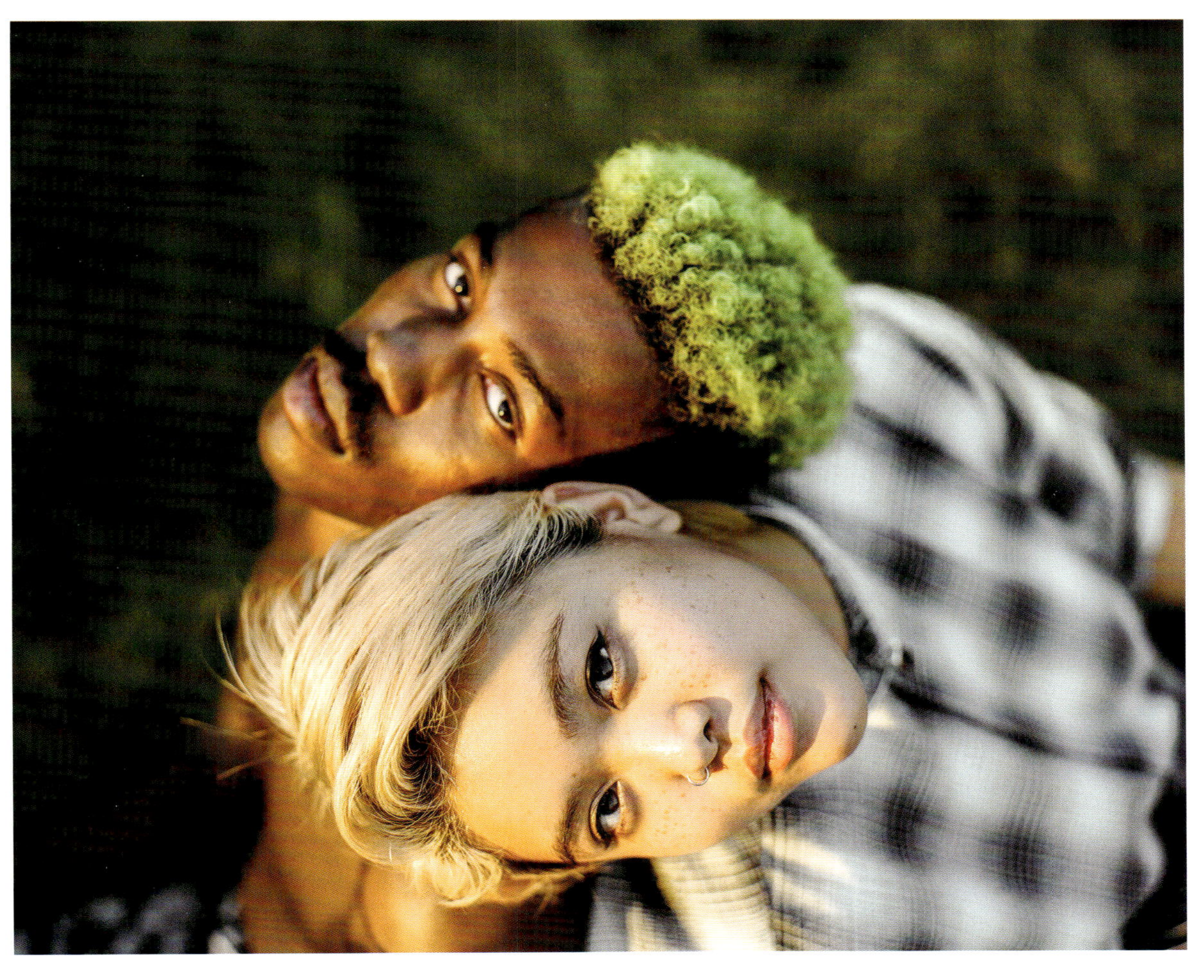

PLATE 40
Peyton Fulford, *Becoming One (Annie and Trevor)*, 2016

OCEAN VIEW AVENUE IS THE MAIN THOROUGHFARE that
runs east to west and defines this neighborhood in Norfolk, Virginia. I must
have gone up and down that road a thousand times over the course of my
five years living there and making this body of work.

Early in my career, I worked as a newspaper photographer. On slow news
days, I was often sent out to look for feature photos to help fill the paper.
It may not be the safest way to travel, but I love driving around without a
specific destination, my head turning from left to right, scanning the sides
of the road until something catches my eye. Many of the photographs in
Between the Devil and the Deep Blue Sea were made this way.

I try not to think too much while I'm photographing. Instead, I rely on
intuition and serendipity. One day, late in the project, I was driving around
as the sun was starting to set and I noticed a man who had set up a temporary watermelon stand on the side of the road. I had never seen him before.
He had a great face and I knew I could make a good picture. But when I
pulled over and asked him if I could photograph him, he politely declined.
People around here are typically game, but I just couldn't convince him.
Disappointed, I gave up and started walking away. As I was leaving, I made
a quick picture of his roadside setup: a halved watermelon propped up on
a plastic bag and a rusty metal folding chair. I thought I had missed the
opportunity, but during the editing process, this photograph stood out.

I have always loved roadside attractions, and value their place in America's
cultural history. Watermelons are also undeniably linked to the mythology
of the South. But for me, this is an image that reflects the changing neighborhood I was trying to capture: nondescript apartment buildings along a
busy suburban road and one farmer's livelihood.

— Preston Gannaway

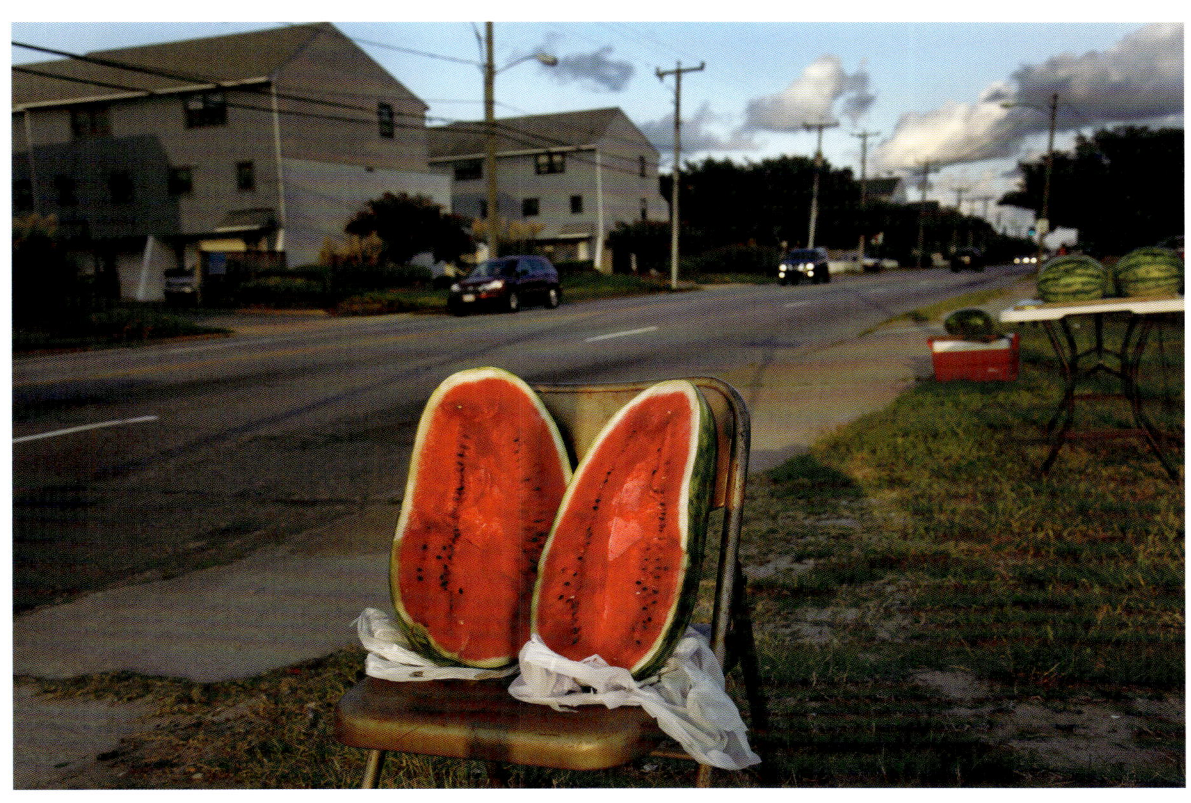

PLATE 41
Preston Gannaway, *Watermelons*, 2013

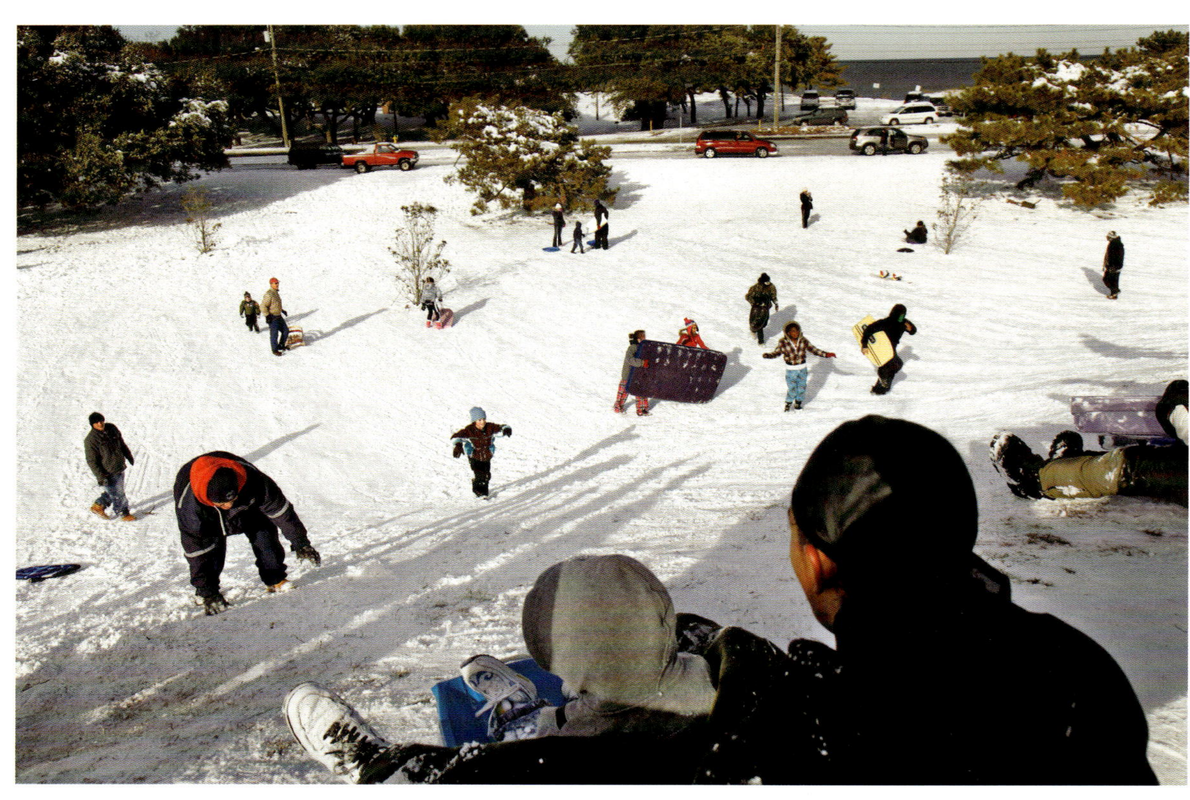

Preston Gannaway, *Sledding*, 2010

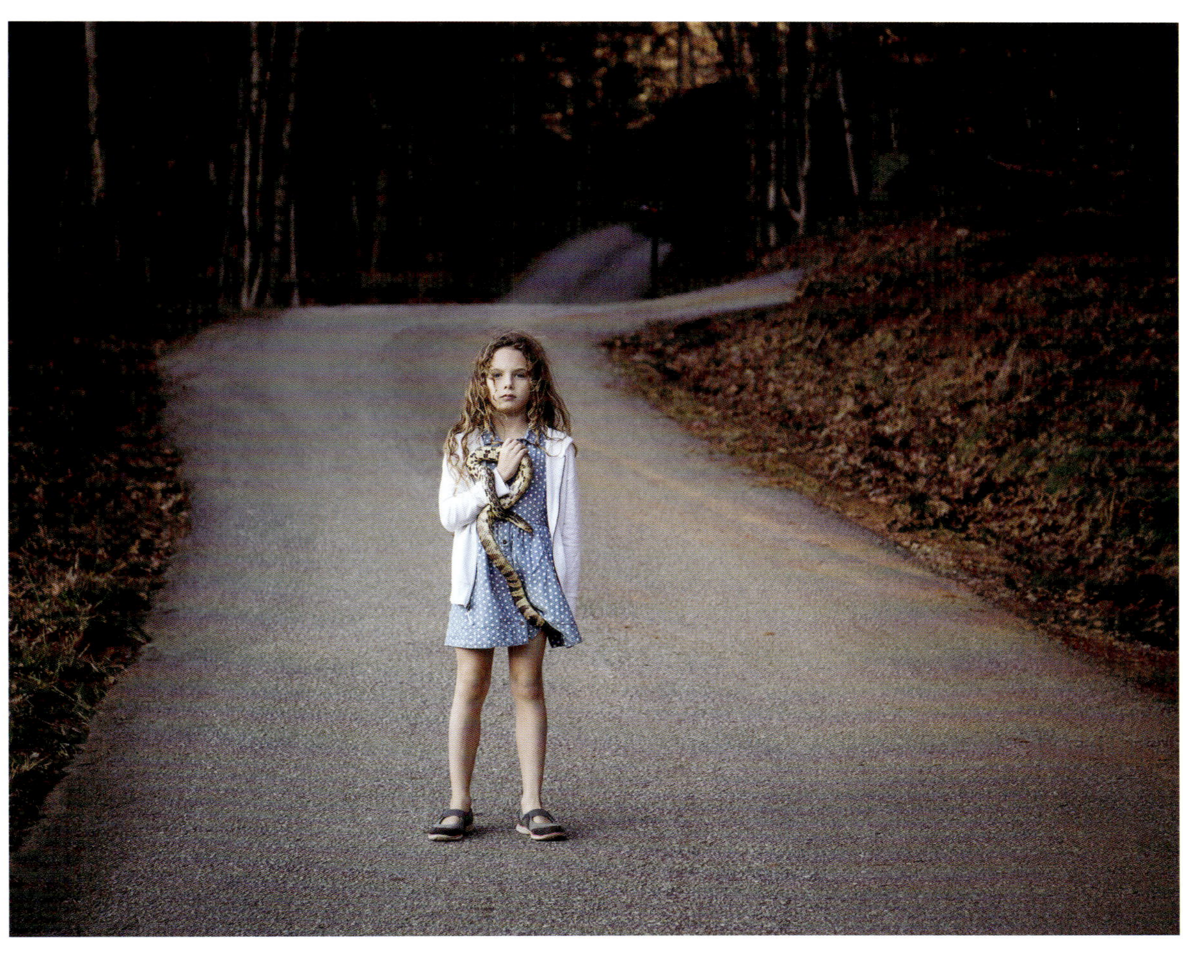

Jennifer Garza-Cuen, *Untitled—Girl with Snake*, n.d.

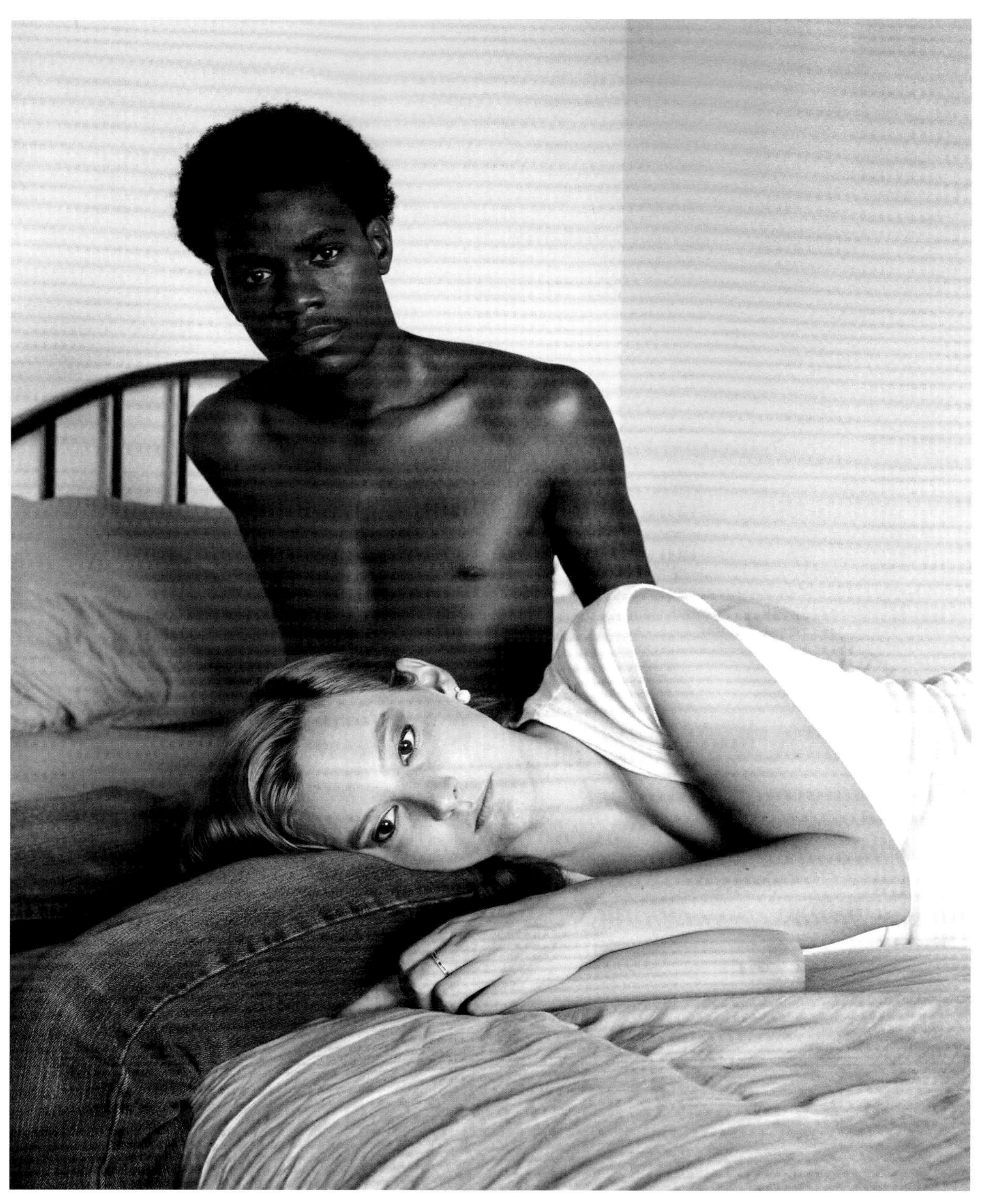

PLATE 44
Andres Gonzalez, *Kim and Josh, Memphis, TN*, 2013

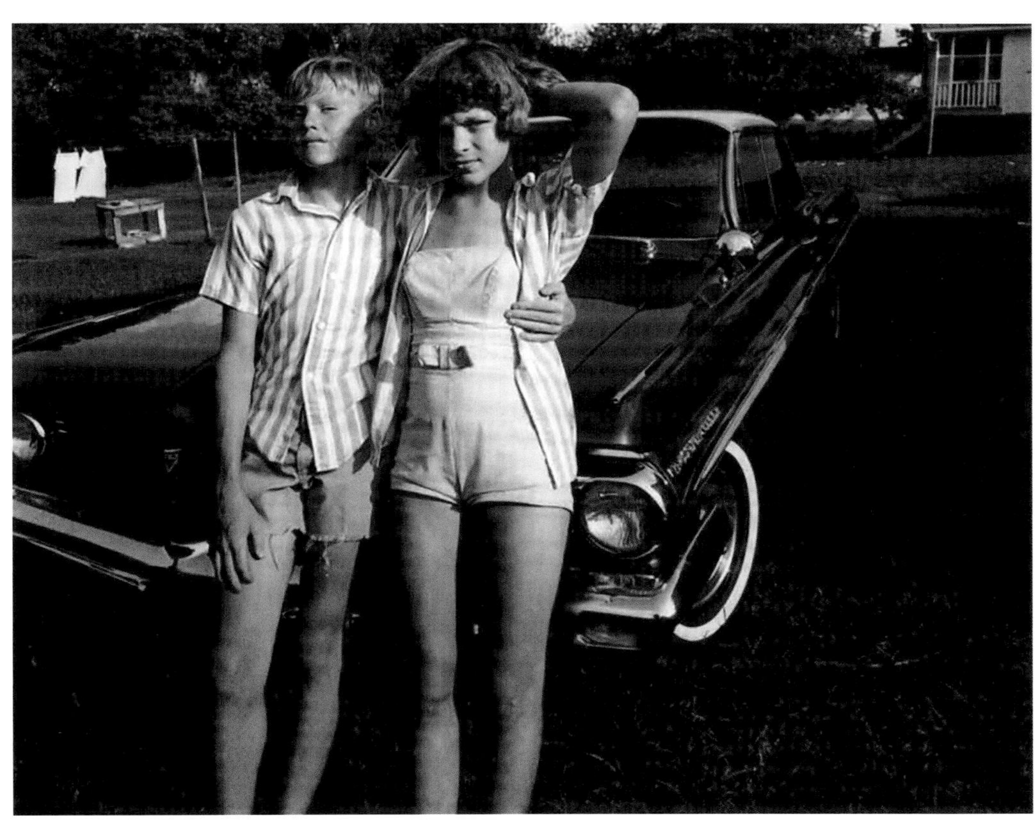

Emmet Gowin, *Danville, Virginia*, 1966

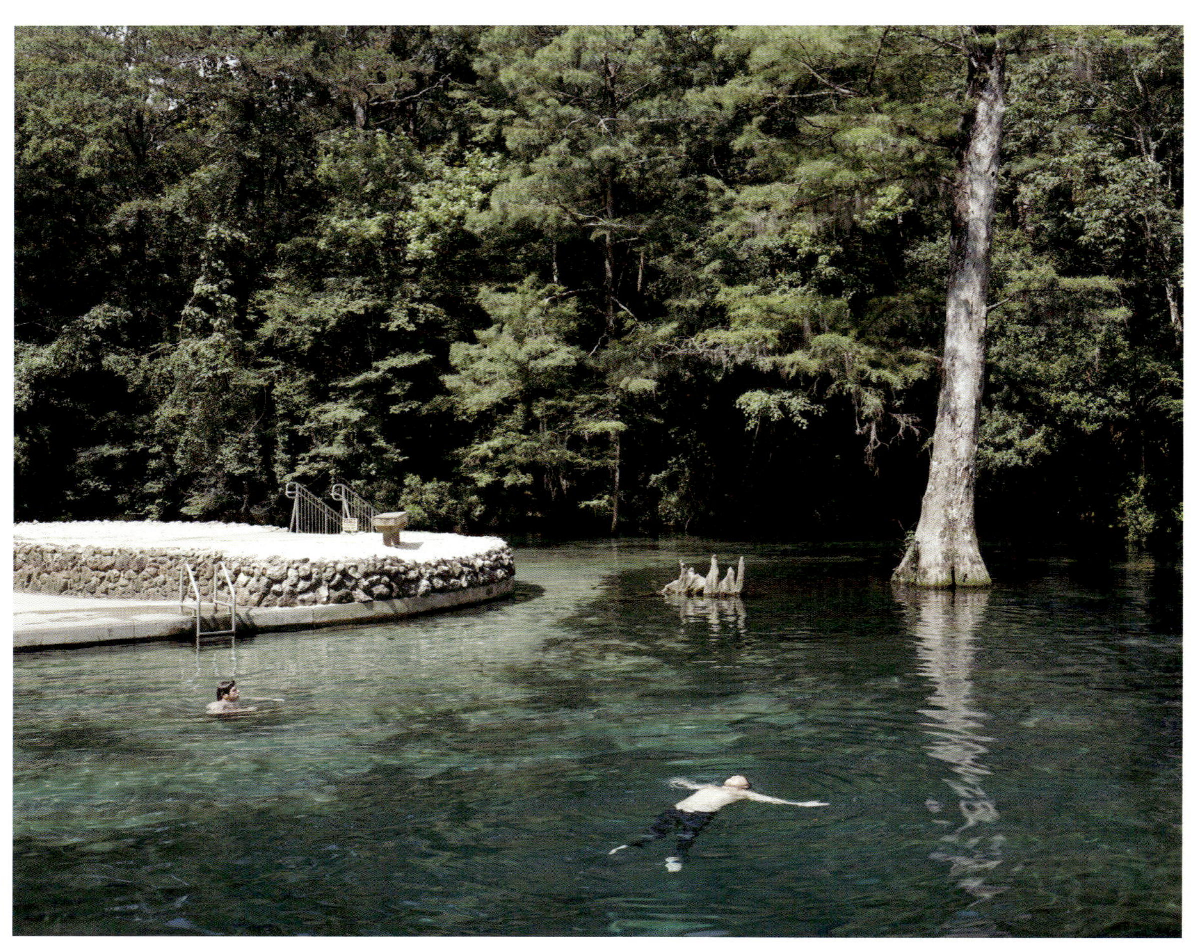

PLATE 46
Joshua Dudley Greer, *Ponce de Leon Springs, Florida*, 2013

I WAS BORN AND RAISED IN NEW ORLEANS, but I fled the city in 2005, after Hurricane Katrina wreaked havoc on my hometown. I moved away fearing further future destruction and storms. But I still go back to visit because New Orleans is a hard city to forget.

These portraits, titled *New Orleans 2017*, were all made on the Mardi Gras day of that year. I was invited to march with a very local parade organization called la Société de Saint Anne. The group, commonly known as the Saint Anne's parade, was founded in 1969 by residents of the French Quarter and adjacent Faubourgs, who recognized the need for a return to the earlier traditions of a walking krewe, devoid of large fancy floats and big marching bands.

Although I was a costumed participant that day, as a photographer, I wanted to document this unique organization. My plan was to be very spontaneous and quick in making the photographs. I did not spend more time than pushing the button on my iPhone before I moved on. So, as the Saint Anne's crew marched through the narrow streets, music blaring, consuming beverages, entertaining those gathered on the sidewalks, I had the added pleasure of making photographs of some beautiful people as they expressed themselves in the City That Care Forgot.

— *William K. Greiner*

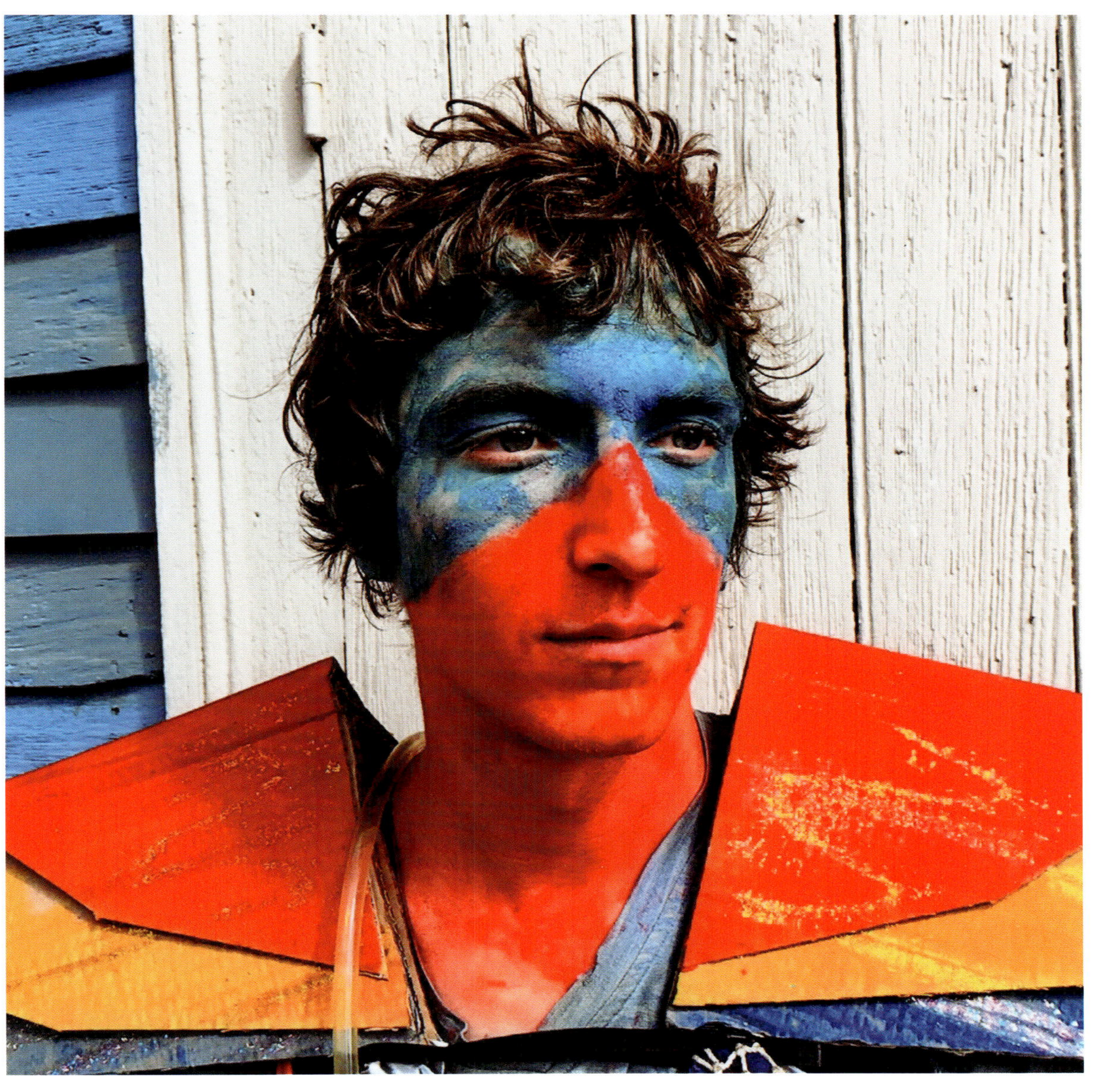

PLATE 47
William K. Greiner, *Mardi Gras P.12—New Orleans, LA*, 2017

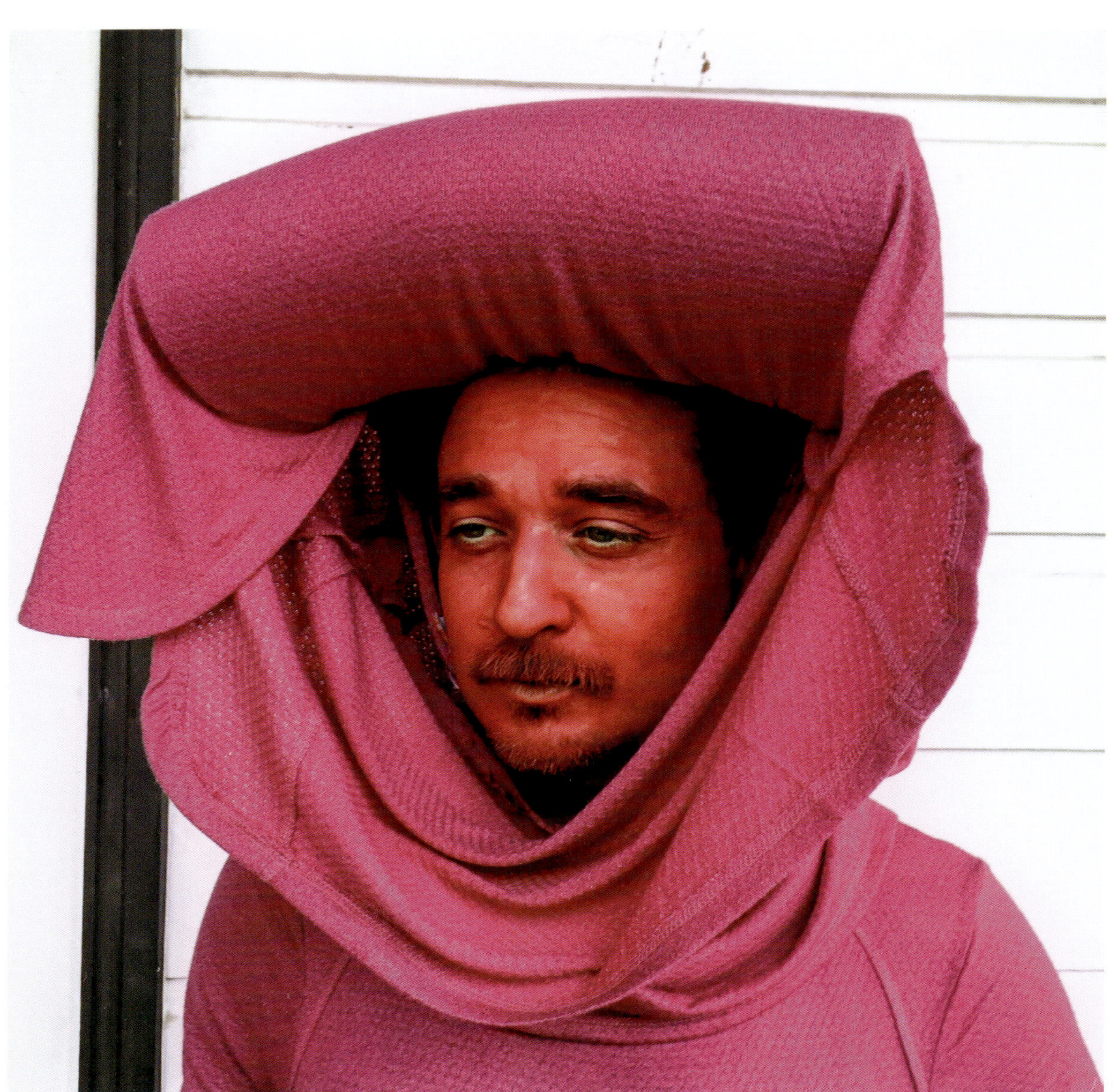

PLATE 48
William K. Greiner, *Mardi Gras P.1—New Orleans, LA*, 2017

I WAS 22, but she couldn't have been more than eighteen years old, nineteen tops. Brown hair, square jaw, clear skin, long daisy-patterned cotton dress, cat-eye glasses, and sandals. She listened to me patiently, holding her toddler boy there on her hip, the youngest of three children, as I explained why I was there. "I'm working on this project, making photographs of the run-down kinds of houses that a lot of people in North Carolina have to live in." While I spoke, she glanced back at her porch where her older son and daughter were playing with the dogs by the wide-open front door. Maybe she was wondering if she actually lived in the sort of house I was describing. But when I paused, she squinted back at me in the midday North Carolina sun. "Okay, if you want to take pictures, just go ahead." So I did. I took five or six shots that went nowhere. At the time I didn't have much experience as a photographer, but I knew when my pictures weren't going to get any better. I thanked the young woman and said goodbye. As she turned, still holding her son to follow her other kids back inside, I lifted my camera and made one more exposure.

This one is like a dream. It's a southern dream that any of us could have. The bare bones of a story we can imagine. A woman of indeterminate age strides toward an open door. She walks with purpose and grace, left foot forward and poised above the floor. Her child hidden from view but there in her tight embrace. She could be all our mothers, perhaps even the Madonna, protecting the child who will one day save us all. But for now, she's walking past a large, spray-painted letter, a dark cursive R. R for reap, rejoice, repent? Below that R, an old brown chair radiates so much personality, its three buttons forming the eyes and nose of a face, with perhaps a dark, smiling mouth in shadow below. She is walking from light into darkness. Three steps beyond is a second door through which I see a dog, a junk car, and part of a tree shading a dazzlingly bright yard. From light to darkness and back into the light.

This is my own moment, perhaps the first time that my camera has pointed me toward possibilities of photography to suggest meanings beyond words. For the last five decades, I've searched for these moments, never anticipating when they will occur, the rare kinds of moments that appear in dreams and sometimes in photographs.

— Alex Harris

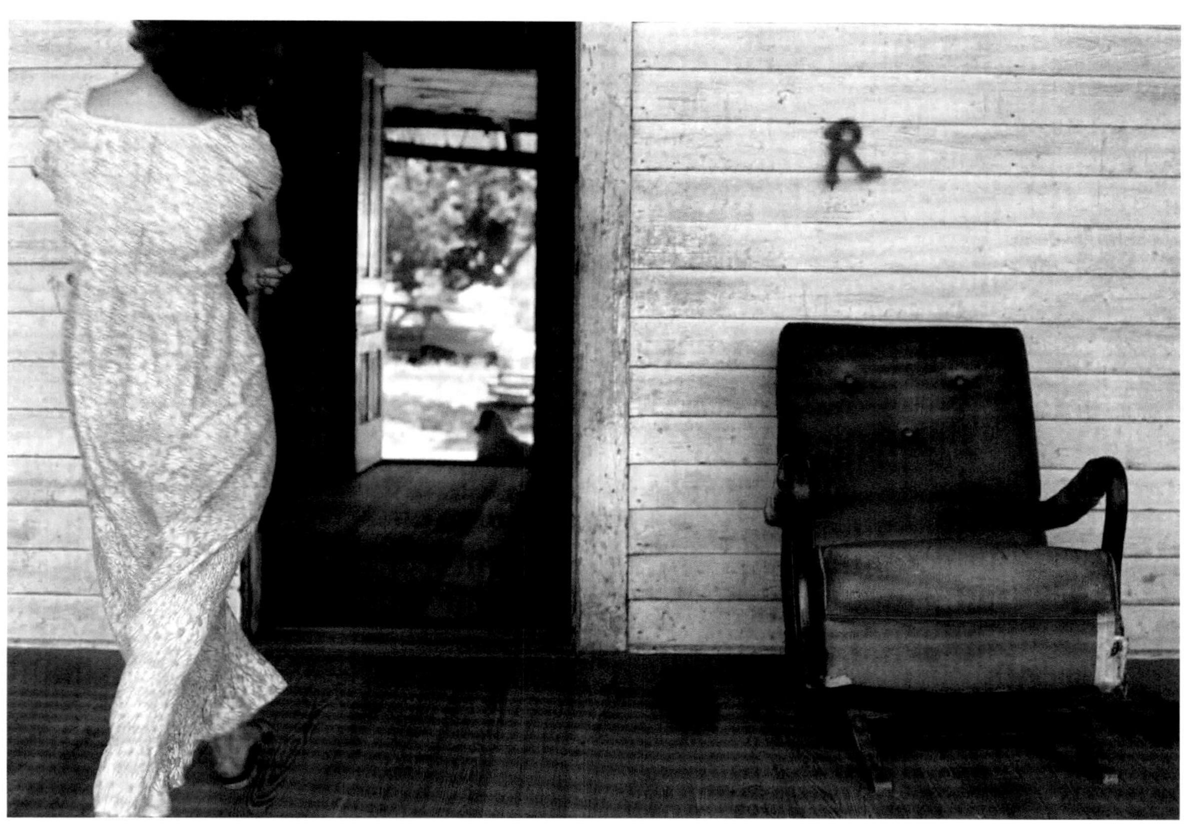

PLATE 49
Alex Harris, *Transylvania County, North Carolina*, 1972

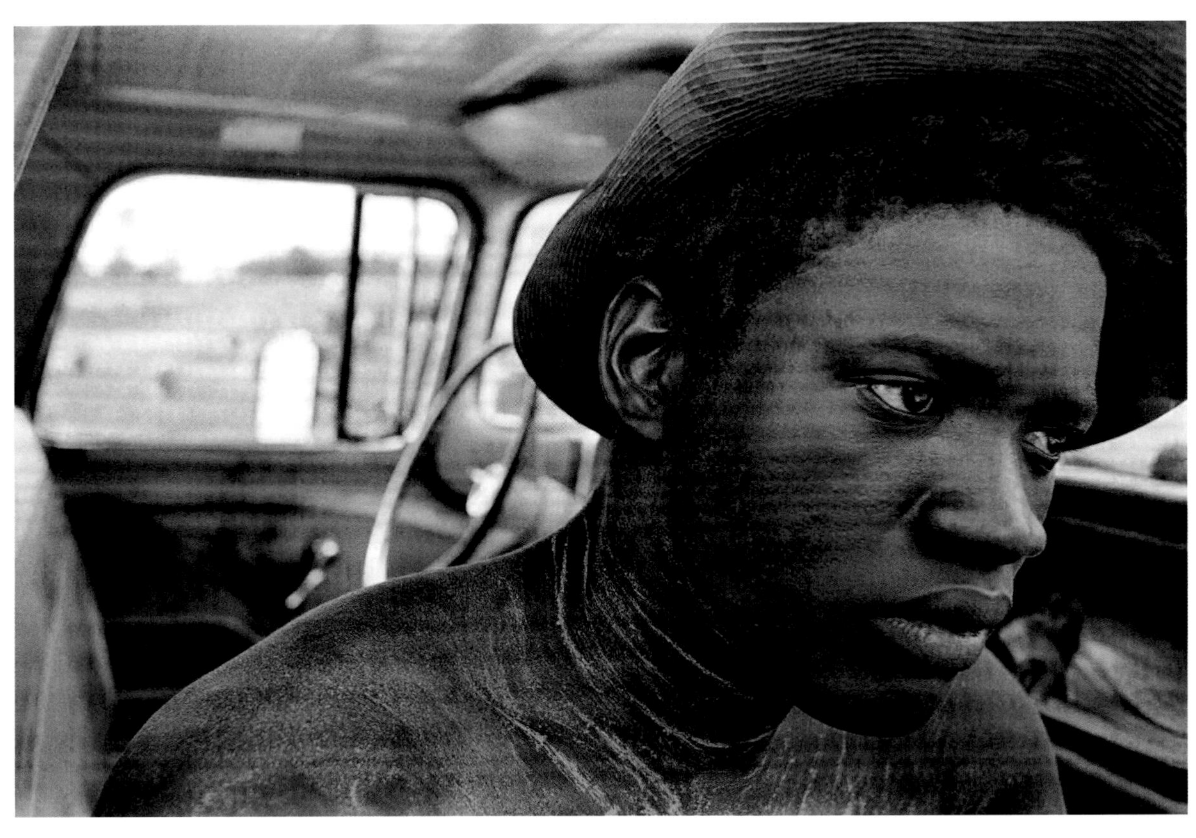

PLATE 50

Alex Harris, *Migrant Worker, Carteret County, North Carolina*, 1972

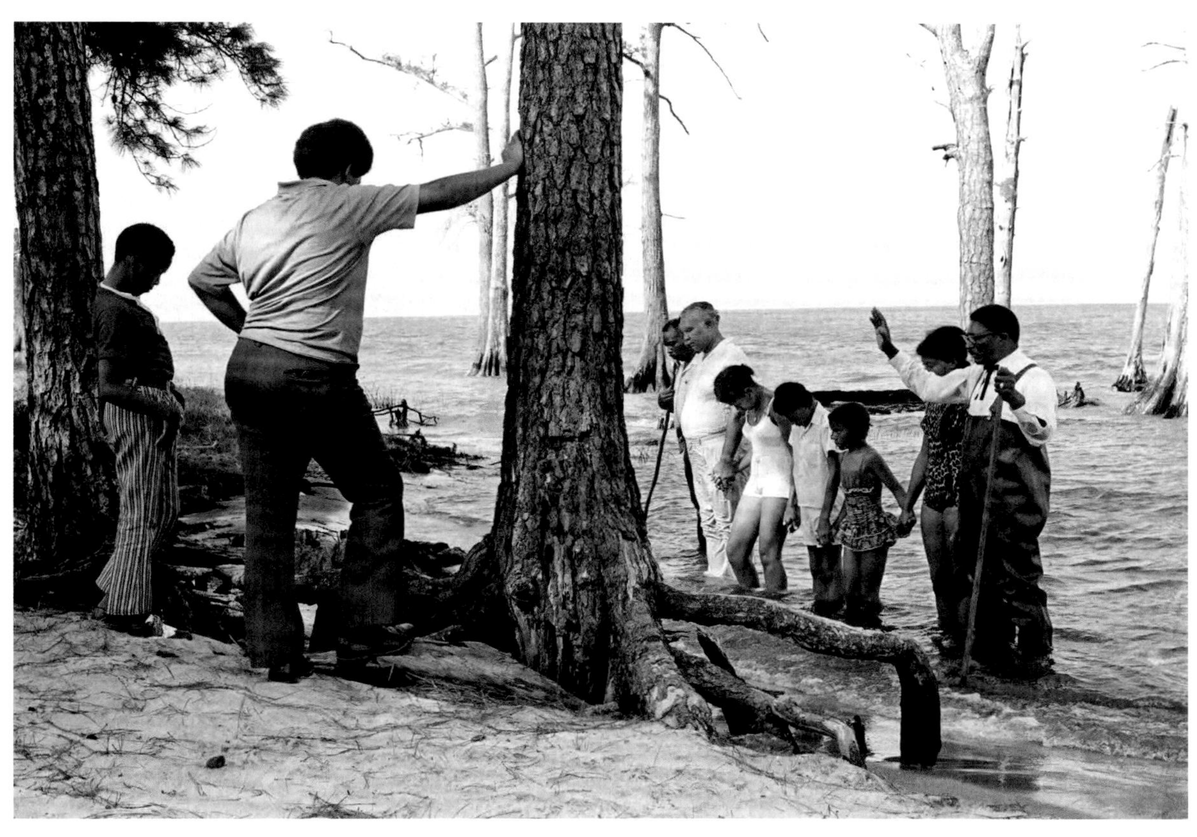

Alex Harris, *Ocean Baptism, Currituck County, North Carolina*, 1972

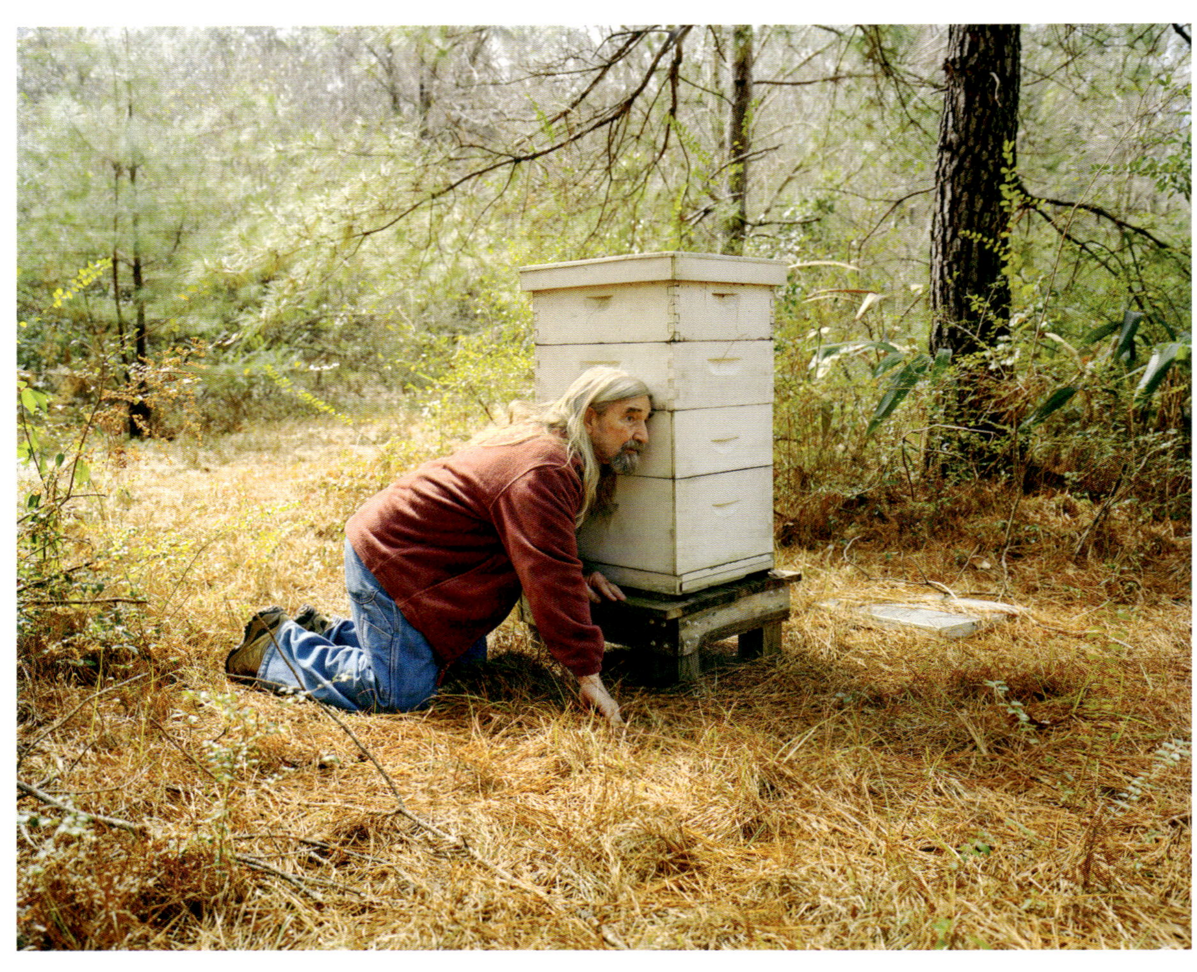

PLATE 52
Alex Harris, *Roy Hyde, Fairhope, Alabama*, 2010

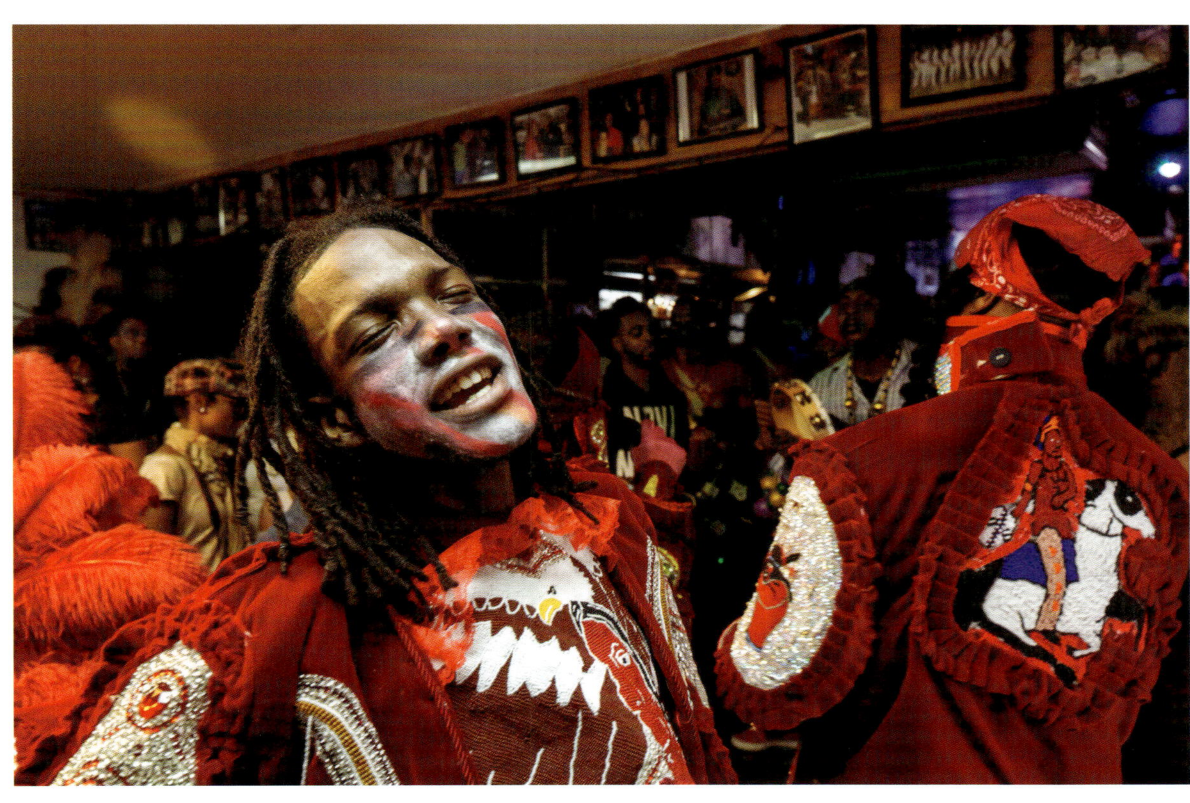

L. Kasimu Harris, *Come Tuesday (Sportsman's Corner)*, 2018

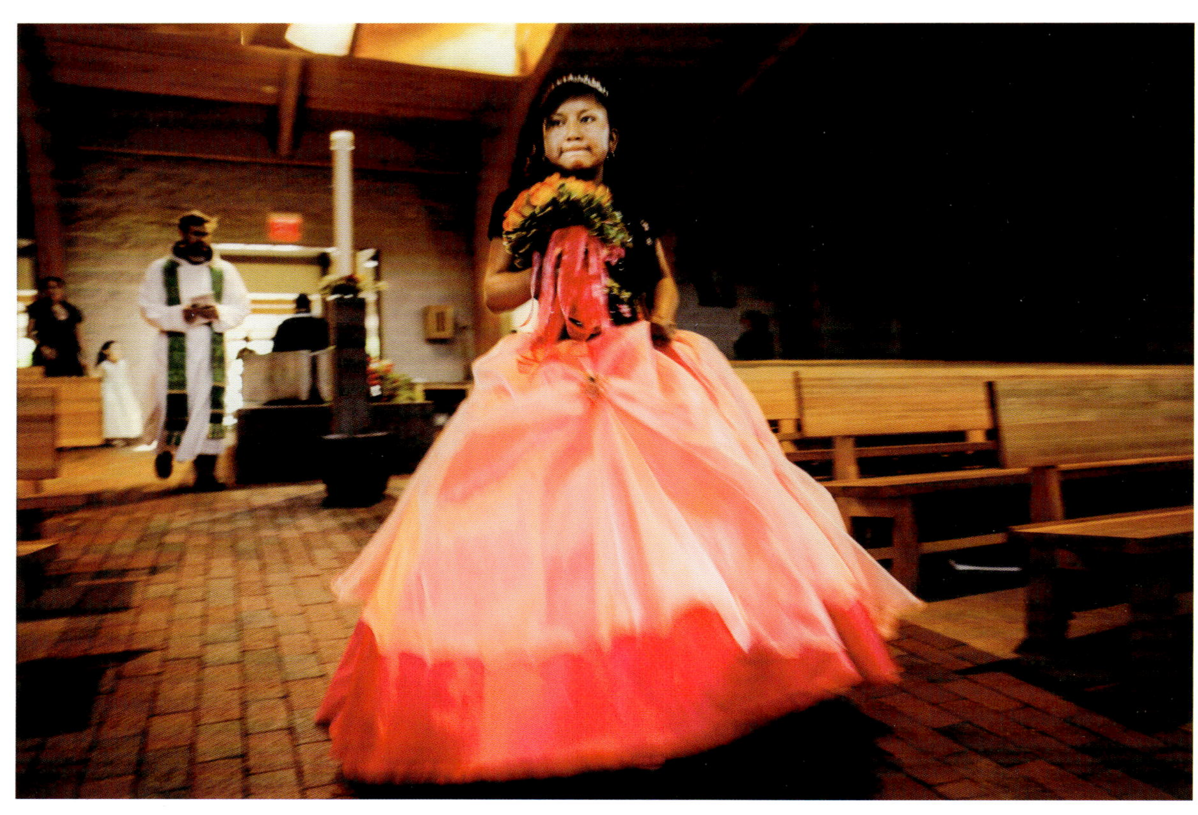

PLATE 54
Titus Brooks Heagins, *Marivi's Quinceañera*, 2008

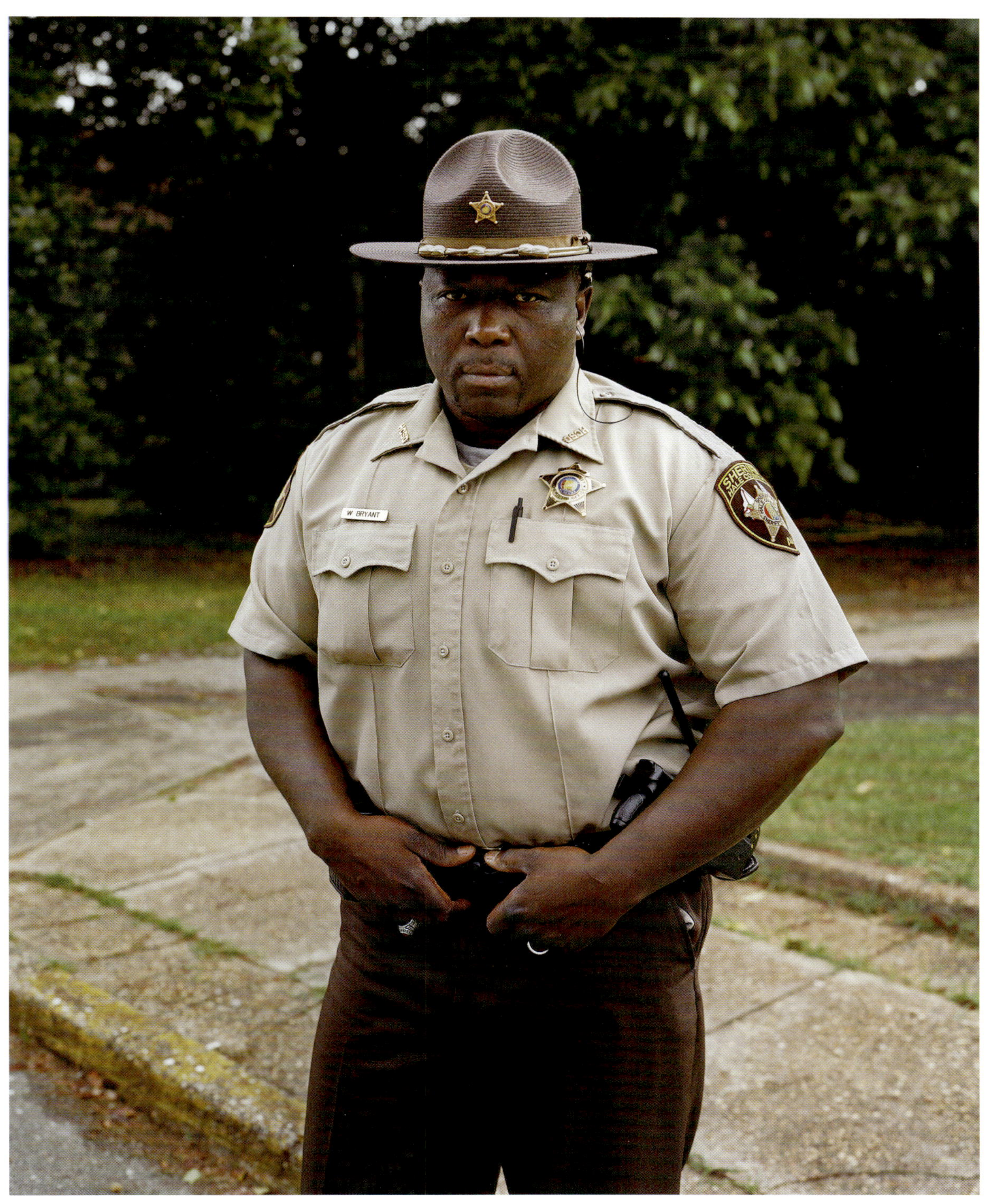

PLATE 55
Lauren Henkin, *Keep this book of the law always on your lips*, 2015

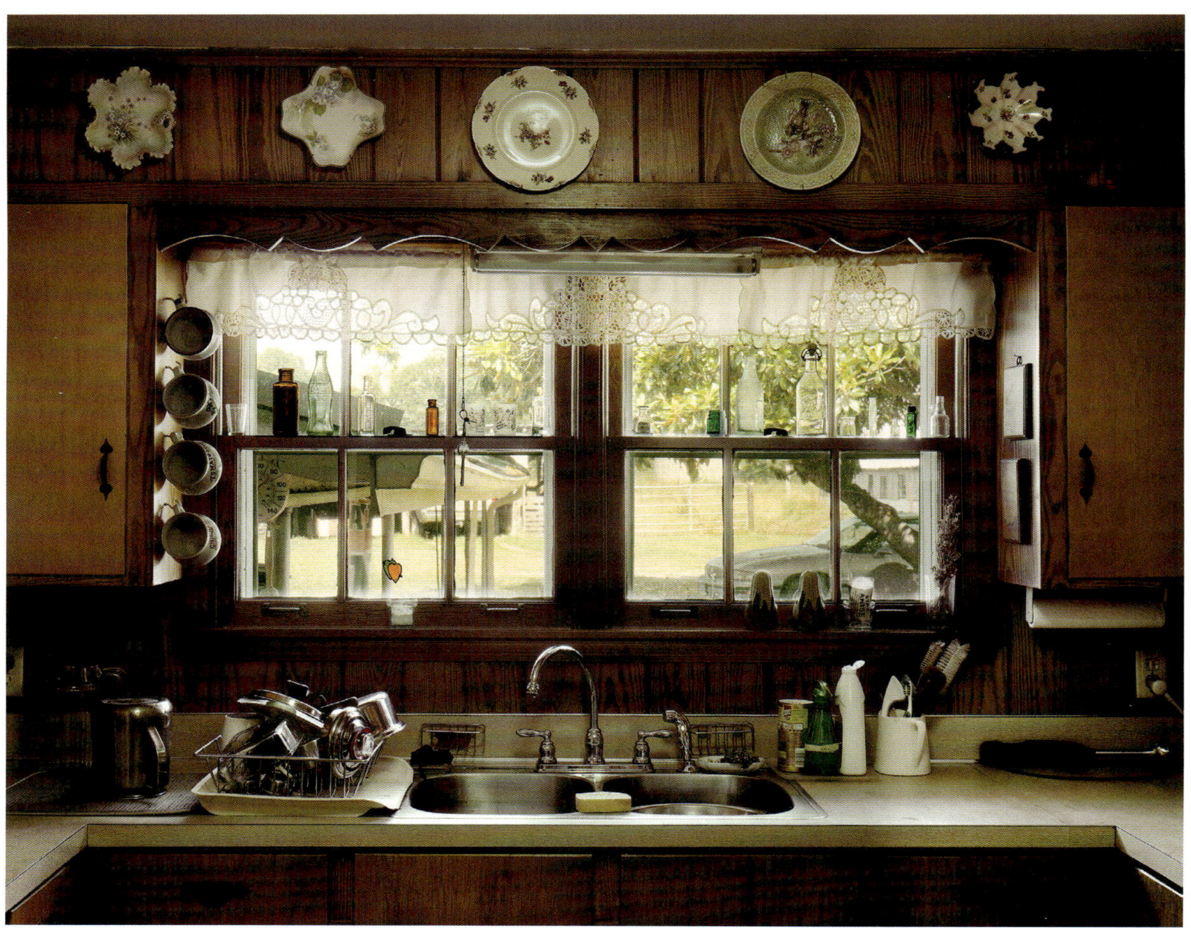

PLATE 56

Lauren Henkin, *Whoever comes to me shall not hunger, and whoever believes in me shall never thirst*, 2015

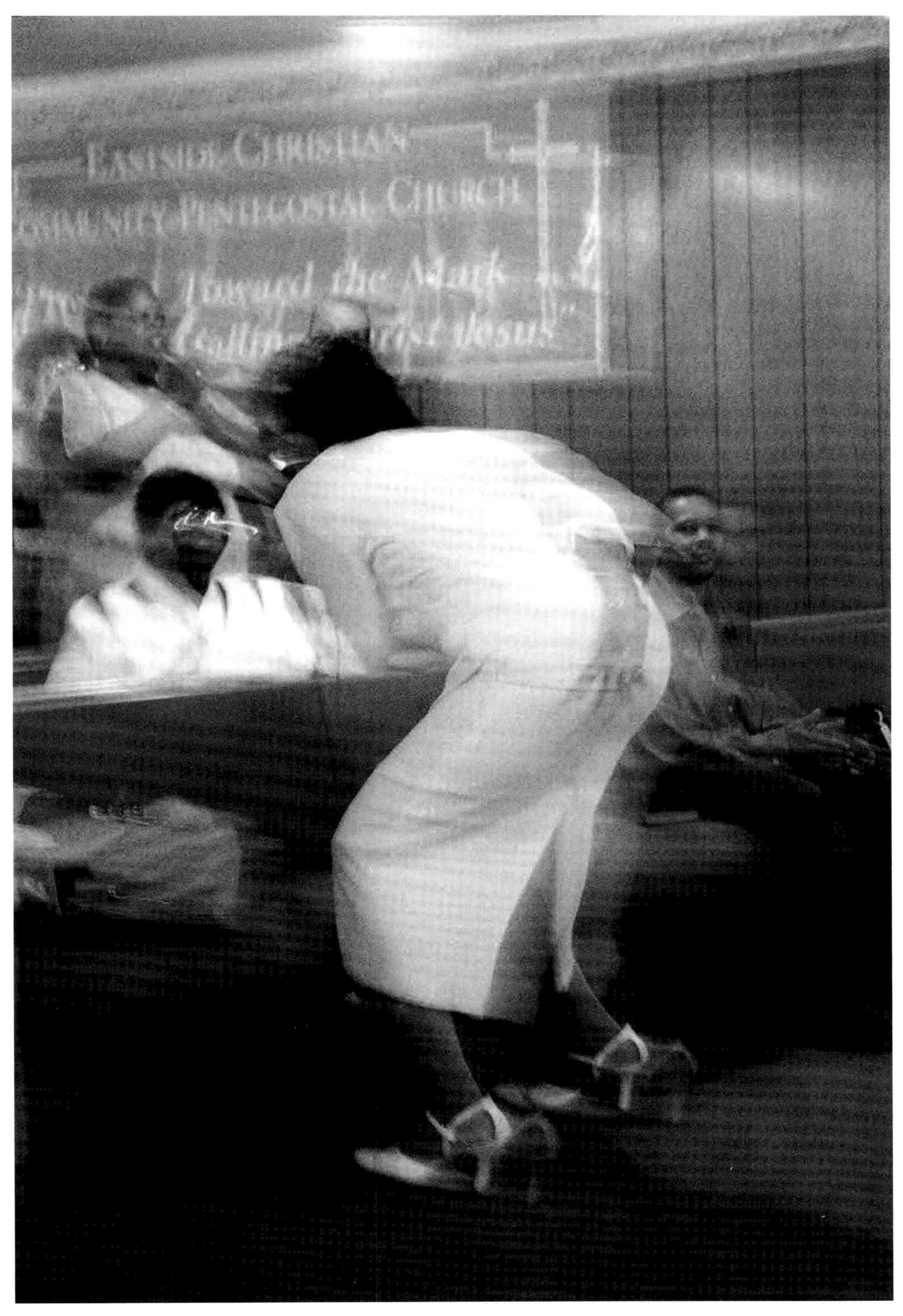

Jane Robbins Kerr, *Hallelujah Lady*, 2006

NEAR MY HOUSE, THERE'S A CORNER STORE where several old-timers hang out. First thing in the morning, they arrive, and mostly they stay there all day. They sit outside gossiping with each other and the neighbors. Some of the guys have their Social Security checks cashed there and keep a running tab for beer, cigarettes, plate lunches. They know everything going on in the neighborhood and they keep an eye on things. This image is of one of those fellows. I'd see him every day. His wife hung out there, too. I'd often find her sitting inside on a stool with a cigarette in one hand and a beer in the other. She took in small sewing jobs to make a little money. When she passed away a few years ago, this man became distraught and his way of dealing with it was to wear women's clothes. It was his way of coping with her death and with his loss. He would even wear her clothes at times. After a year or so, he stopped dressing that way.

— Kevin Kline

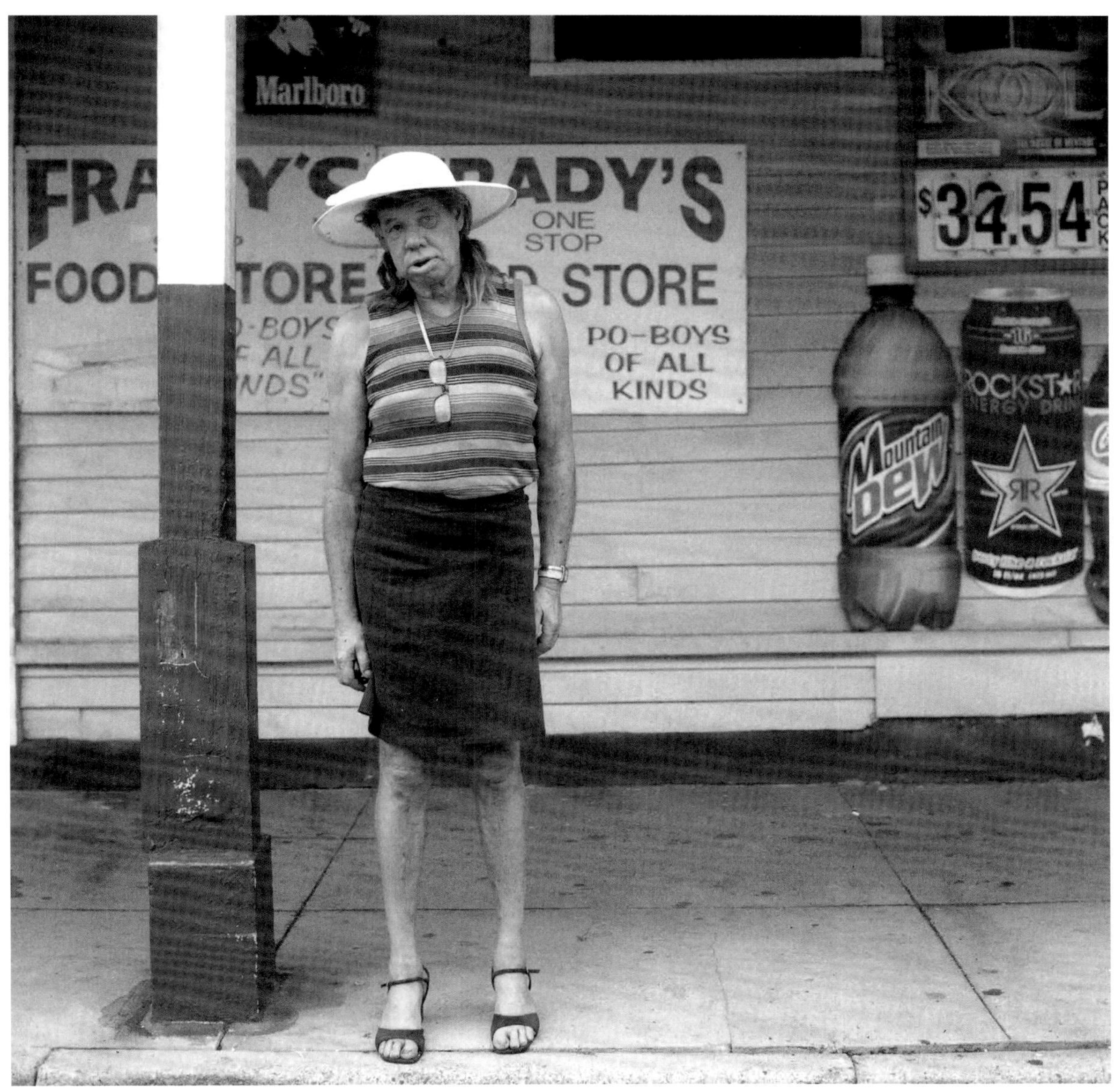

Kevin Kline, *Man at Corner Store, New Orleans*, 2008

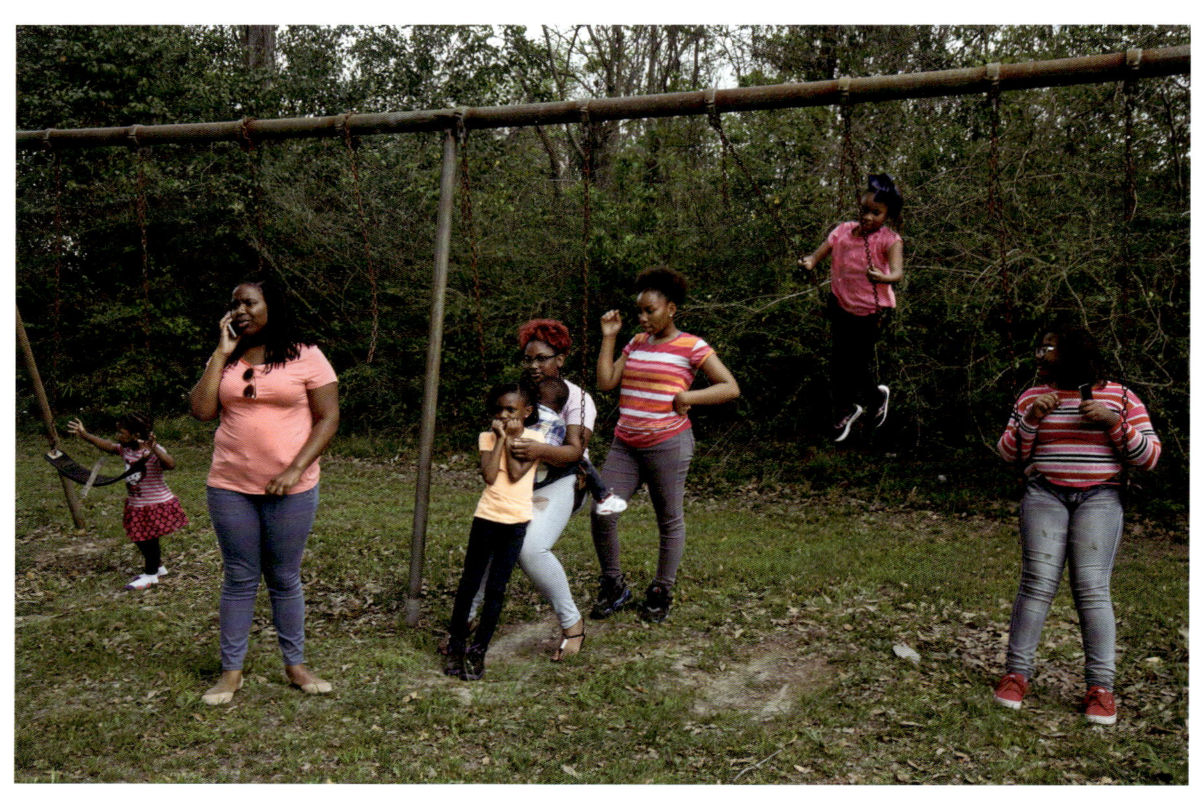

Stacy Kranitz, *Ronaldson Field Debris Landfill, Alsen, LA*, 2017

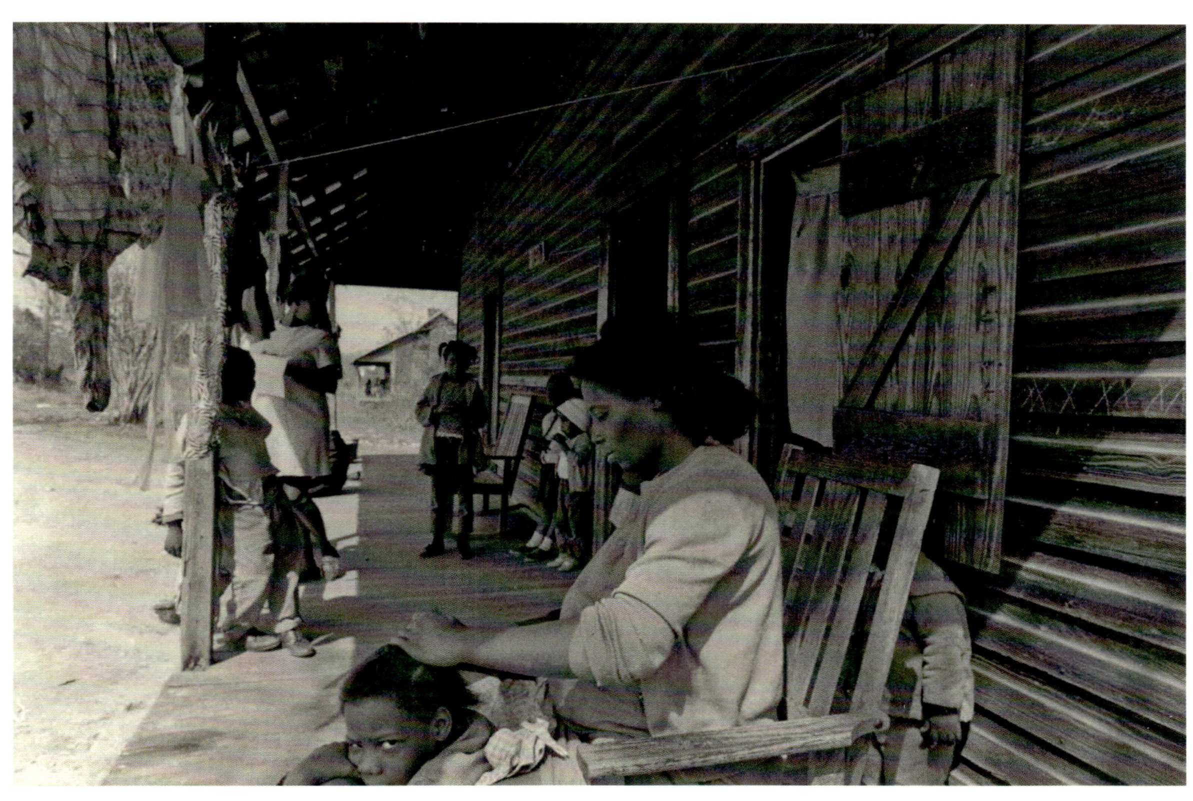

Paul Kwilecki, *Two-family tobacco tenant house*, 1964

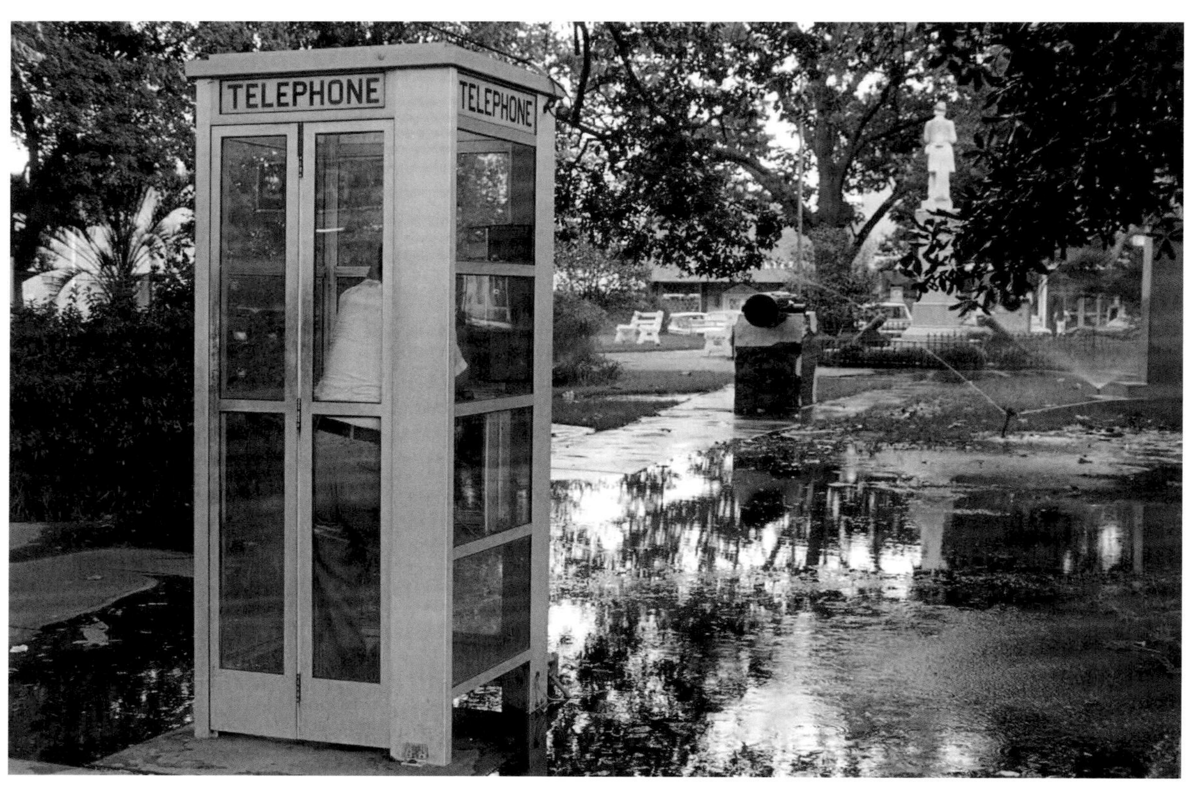

PLATE 61
Paul Kwilecki, *Willis Park*, 1976

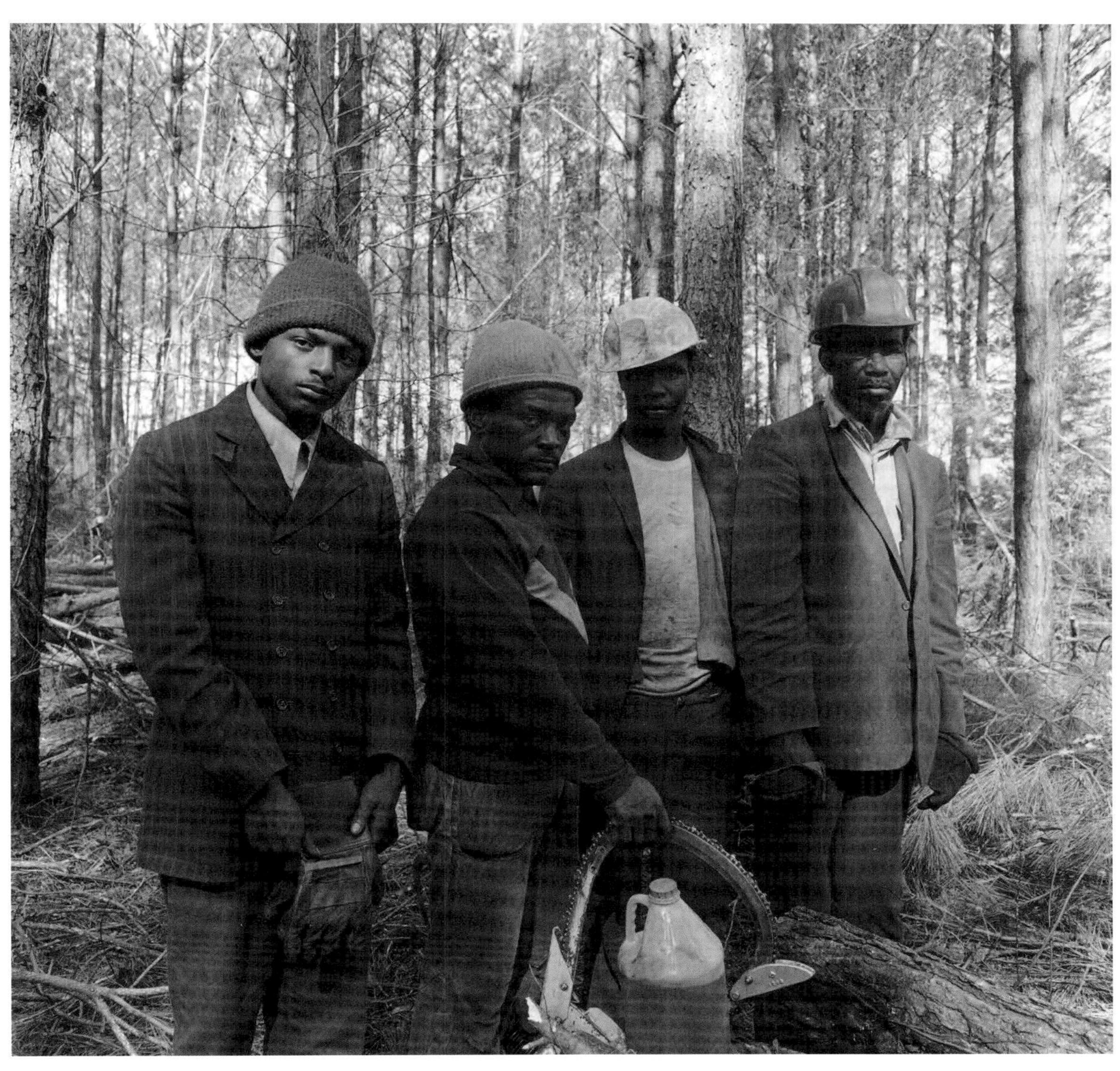

PLATE 62
Paul Kwilecki, *Loggers in the woods, near Attapulgus*, 1978

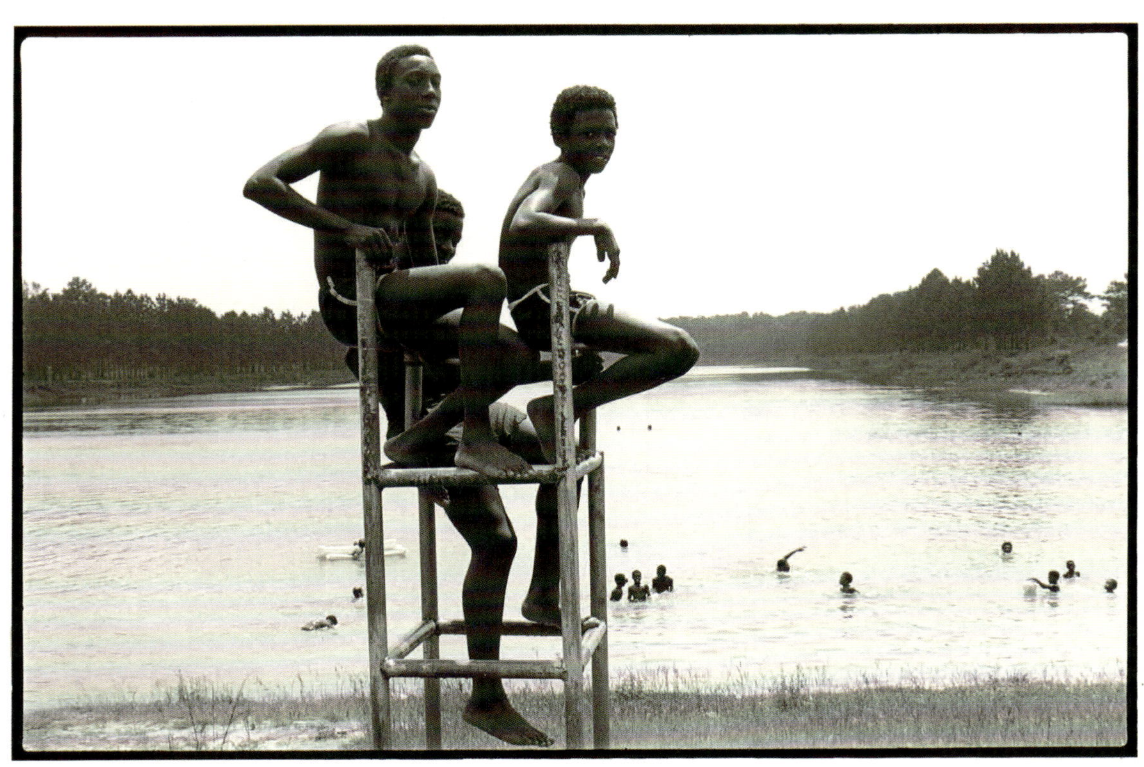

PLATE 63
Paul Kwilecki, *Flint River Boat Basin*, 1979

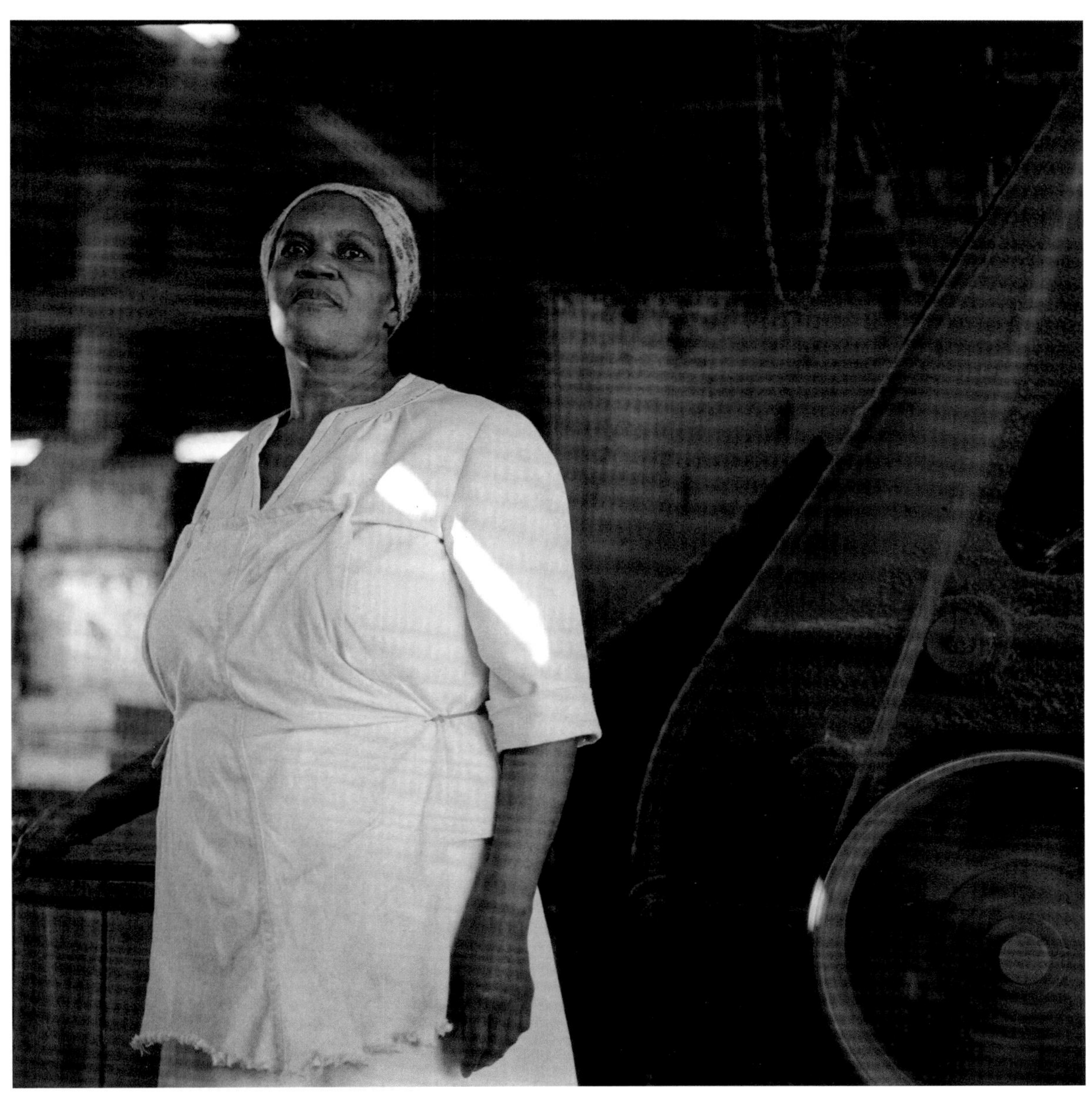

Paul Kwilecki, *Elberta Crate & Box Company*, 1981

I WAS DRAWN TO THE COURTHOUSE as a subject because it is inherently dramatic, and because it is where politics gets down to the individual. No matter how much newsprint and airtime is spent on politicians, it isn't until the laws they enact make contact with you and me that we feel the yoke of government. The building's institutional coldness and its clumsy hulking that dwarfs the human figure, strike at the vulnerability of people, producing an atmosphere of estrangement that can be read on the faces of all who go there. In its most authoritative mode, the courthouse is where one may enter a free man and exit a prisoner. The collective will of society, euphemistically called "justice" can fall like a sledgehammer. . . .

The courthouse was a warren of dark corridors and dirty offices smelling of cigar butts, spittoons, and disinfectants. Only men held elected positions. The women who worked for them as secretaries or clerks were housekeepers. Exposed to the language and intrigues of county politicians, they became irascible and masculine. A black teacher said that twice a month she went to the courthouse for her check. She was made to wait on a bench while white teachers were paid. This was the policy of the Board of Education and the County School Superintendent (elected by an all-white electorate). There was neither excuse nor attempt to hide the humiliation. Even educators, trusted with the minds of our children, thought of African Americans as a race of servants.[1]

— Paul Kwilecki

1   From Paul Kwilecki, *One Place: Paul Kwilecki and Four Decades of Photographs from Decatur County*, ed. Tom Rankin (Durham: University of North Carolina Press, 2013), 115 and 238.

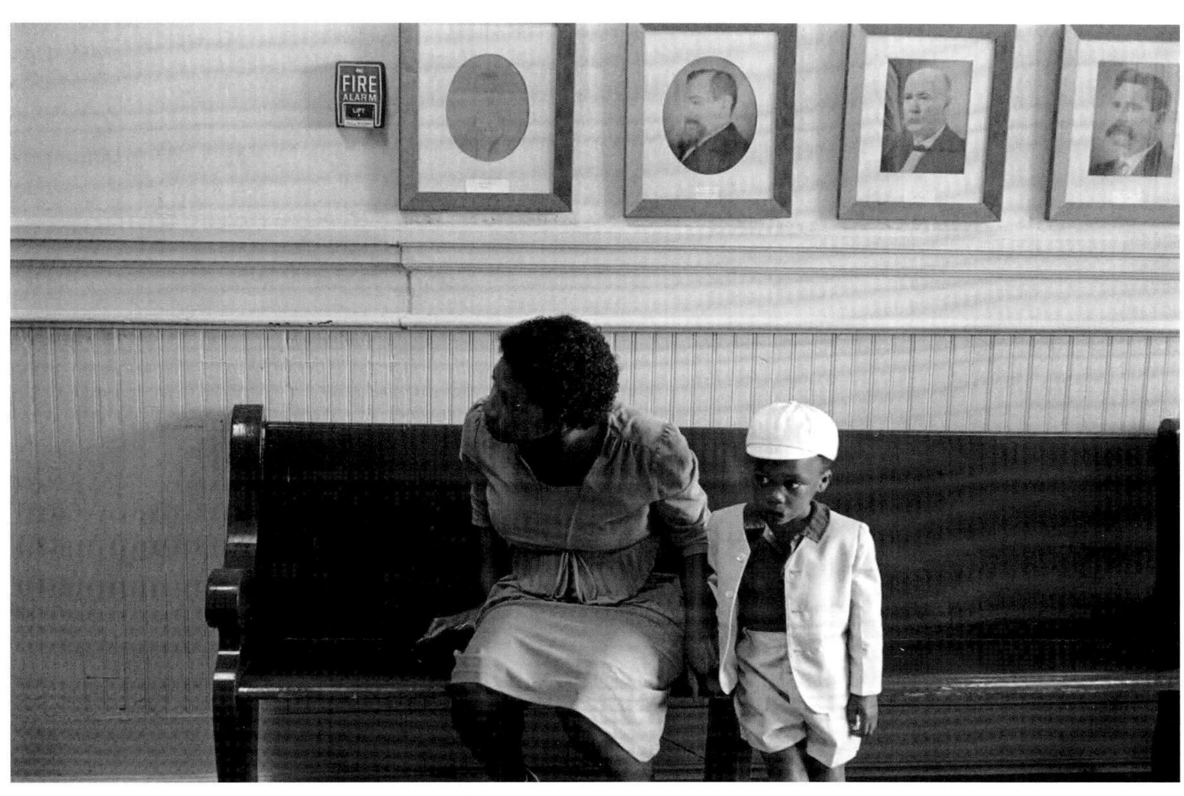

PLATE 65
Paul Kwilecki, *Outside courtroom*, 1982

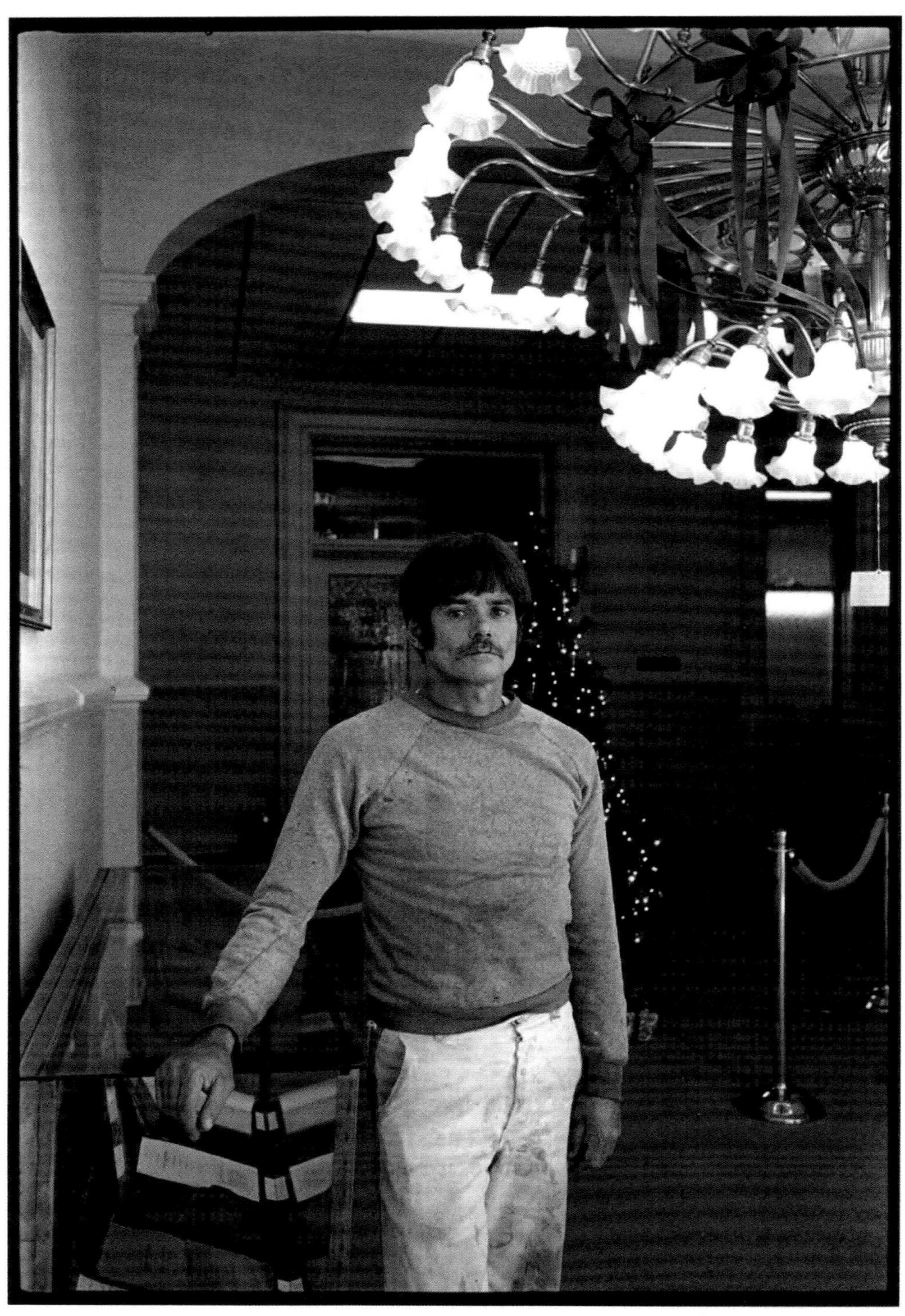

PLATE 66
Paul Kwilecki, *Prisoner with light fixture that he restored*, 1998

IF I LOOKED JUST BEYOND MY FATHER'S SHOULDER when he was sitting across the table from me, I could fall into the view of a mountain range, framed and hanging on the wall. I remember the purples and blues. His other photographs were around, too—storied landscapes whispering to skies, still water cradling cypress trees, lightning, a butterfly. Years after he passed away, my stepmother carefully copied each page of his poetry journal and gave it to me. Although he encouraged my early curiosity about photography and gave me my first camera, I was too young then to realize that he was an artist.

Both photography and writing have always been part of my own creative process. They're continually in conversation, each inspiring the other. I think of a photograph and a poem very similarly and love how they each delicately conjure the tangible from the intangible—the shape of light, the shape of a word, and hopefully, the shape of a story.

The series *Take Care of Your Sister* is a meditation on how the landscape gives shape to the resonance of loss and family history. It meanders through memories of the Mississippi Delta where my father grew up and where my brother and I spent time with our grandparents when we were very young.

When my father was a child, he was asked to take care of his younger sister.

When I was a child, the last words my father said to my brother were "Take care of your sister."

— Molly Lamb

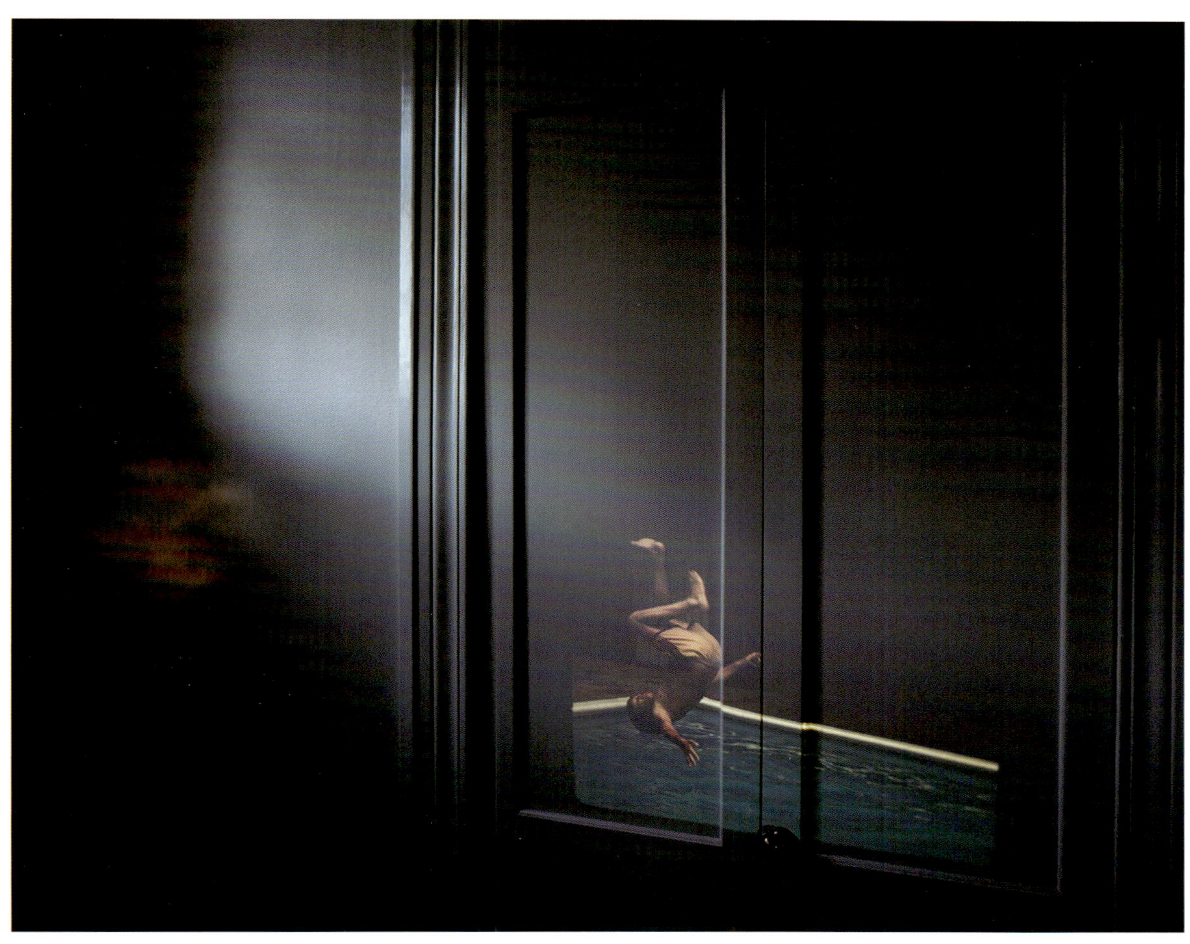

Molly Lamb, *Untitled 9*, 2016

THE WEIGHT OF AIR

Moths
circling and circling
uneasy yellow light
suspended
in speckled black
below the stars
and cicada silence.
Strong wind on the bridge –
dirt in the air, in my hair,
in the shades of darkness
where the light laps against
the water's whirling
solid,
where they caught
moths
when they were young.
That is not cotton.
He is not him.
Fields
rows
divides
dirt
cracks
where there is no rain.
Thick summer
clings to my skin
quietly urging
its way into my bones.
Ghosts in my eye
under the shroud cry
leave me here no more.

— Molly Lamb

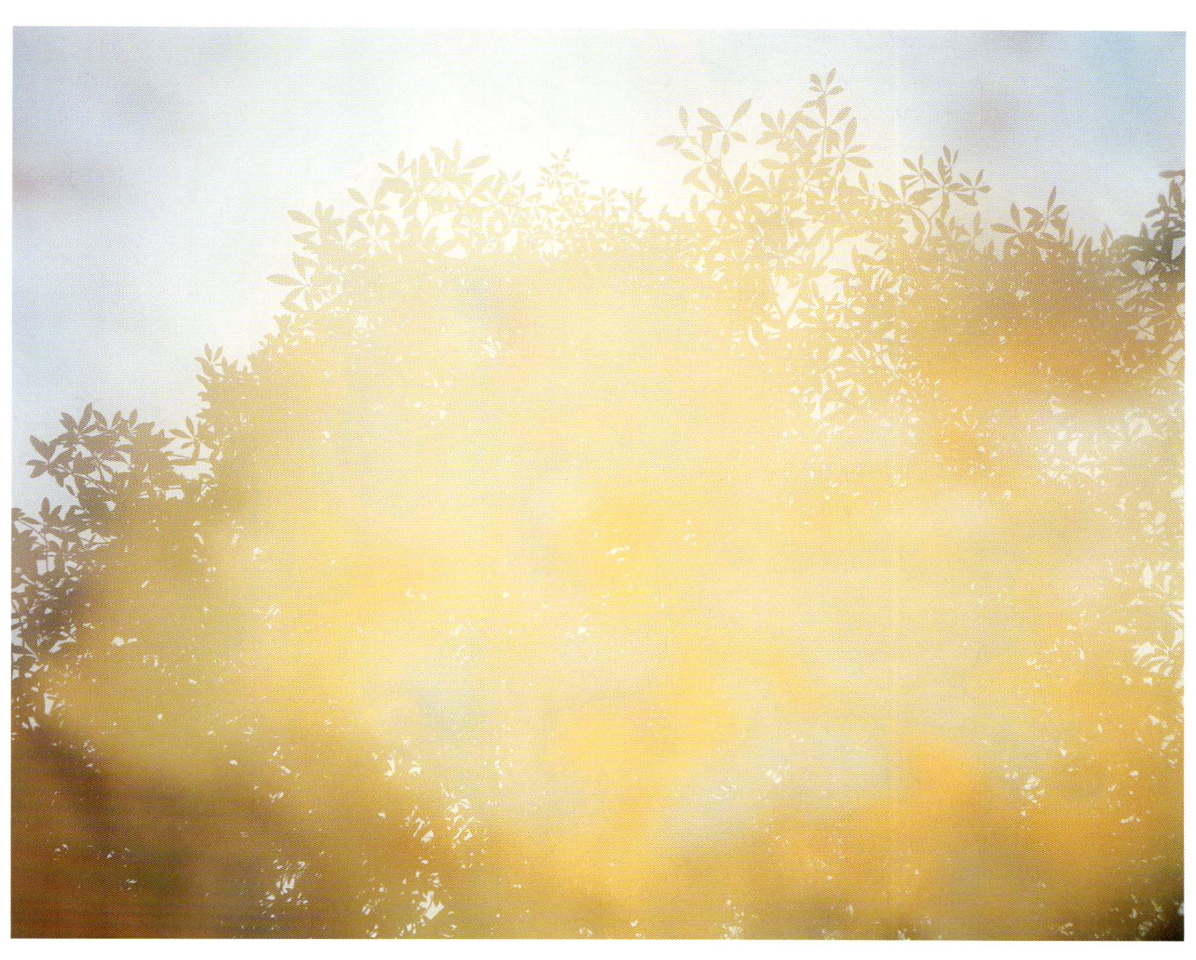

PLATE 68
Molly Lamb, *Untitled 10*, 2016

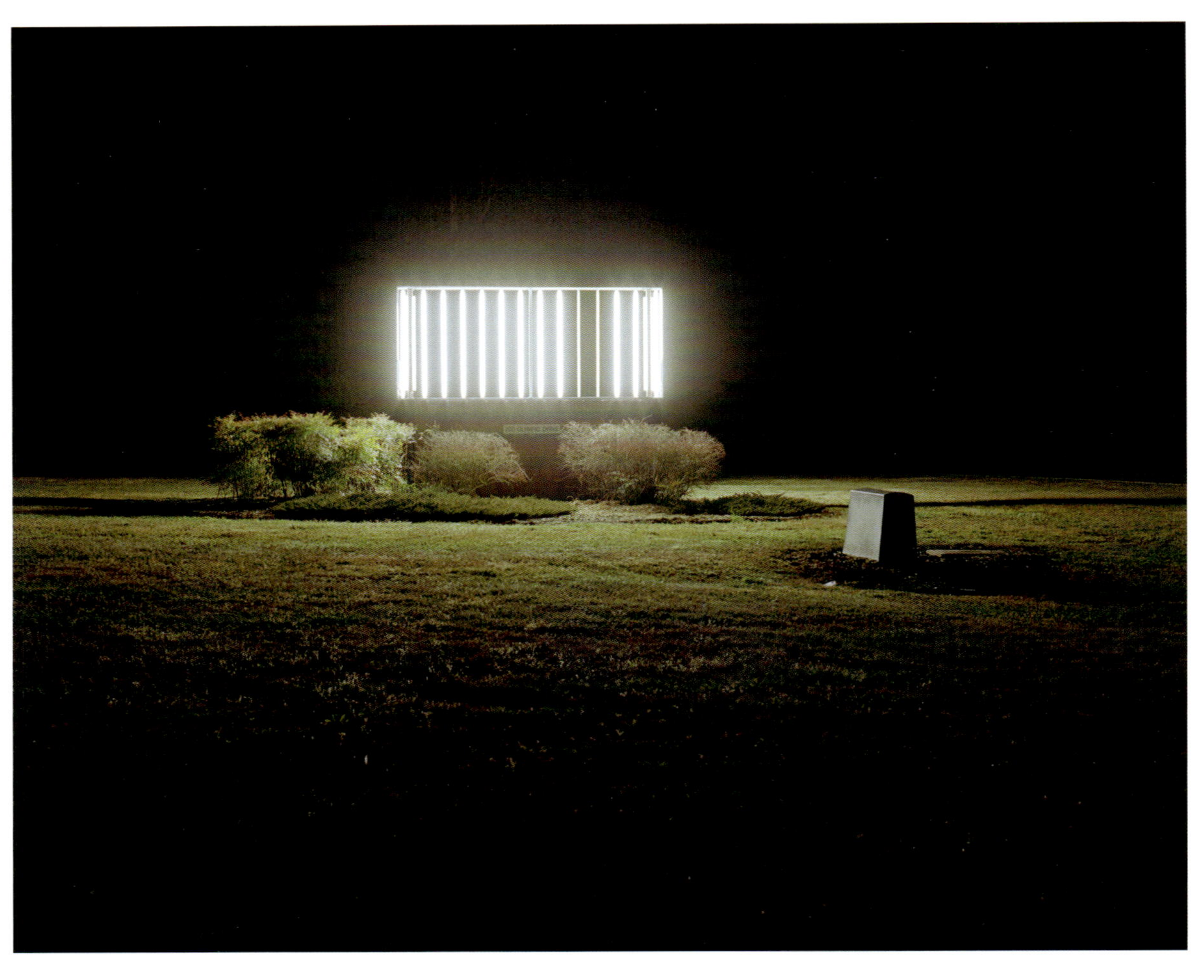

PLATE 69
Brittainy Lauback, *Sign*, 2013

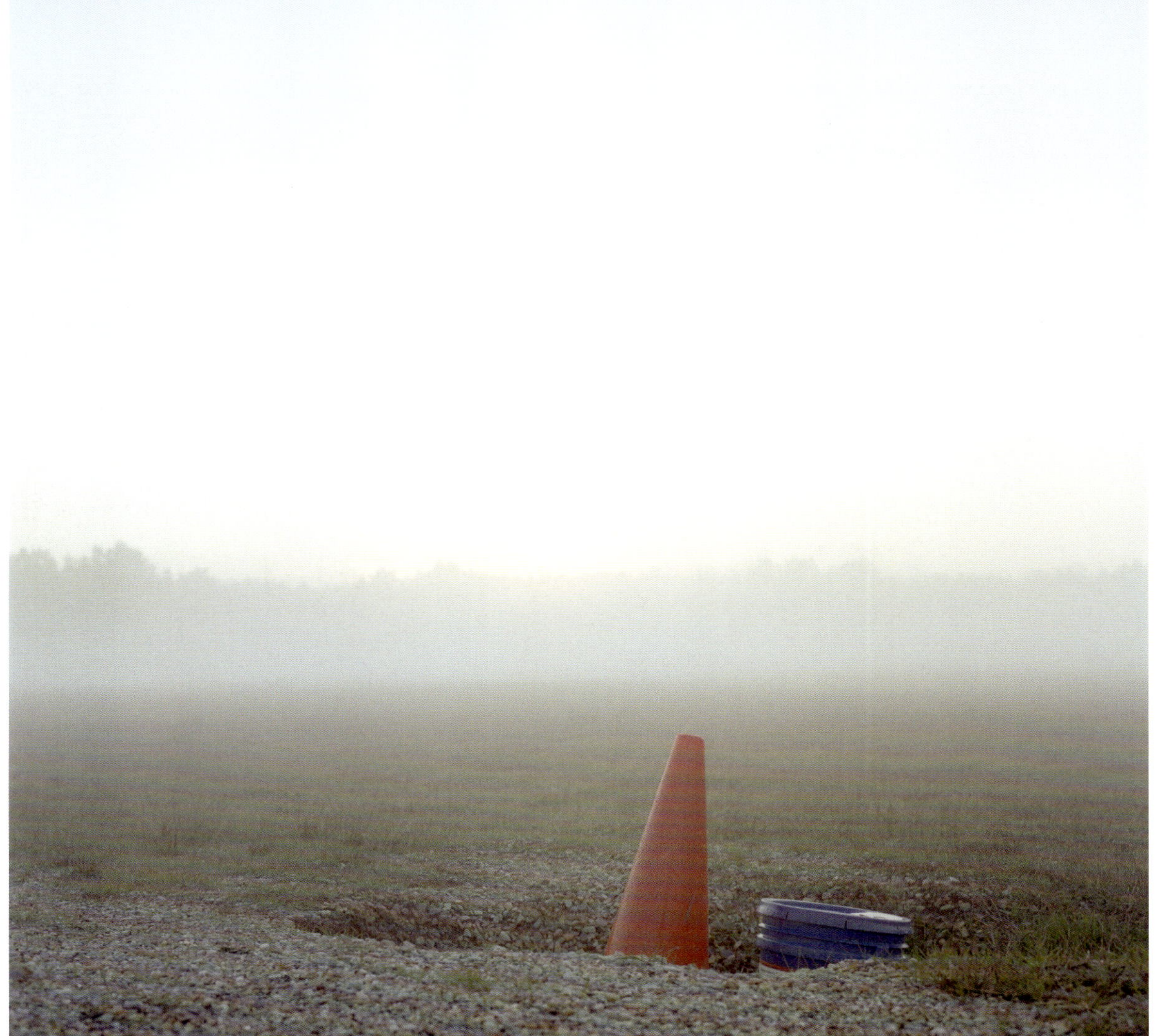

PLATE 70
Brittainy Lauback, *Pylon, Tuskegee, AL*, 2017

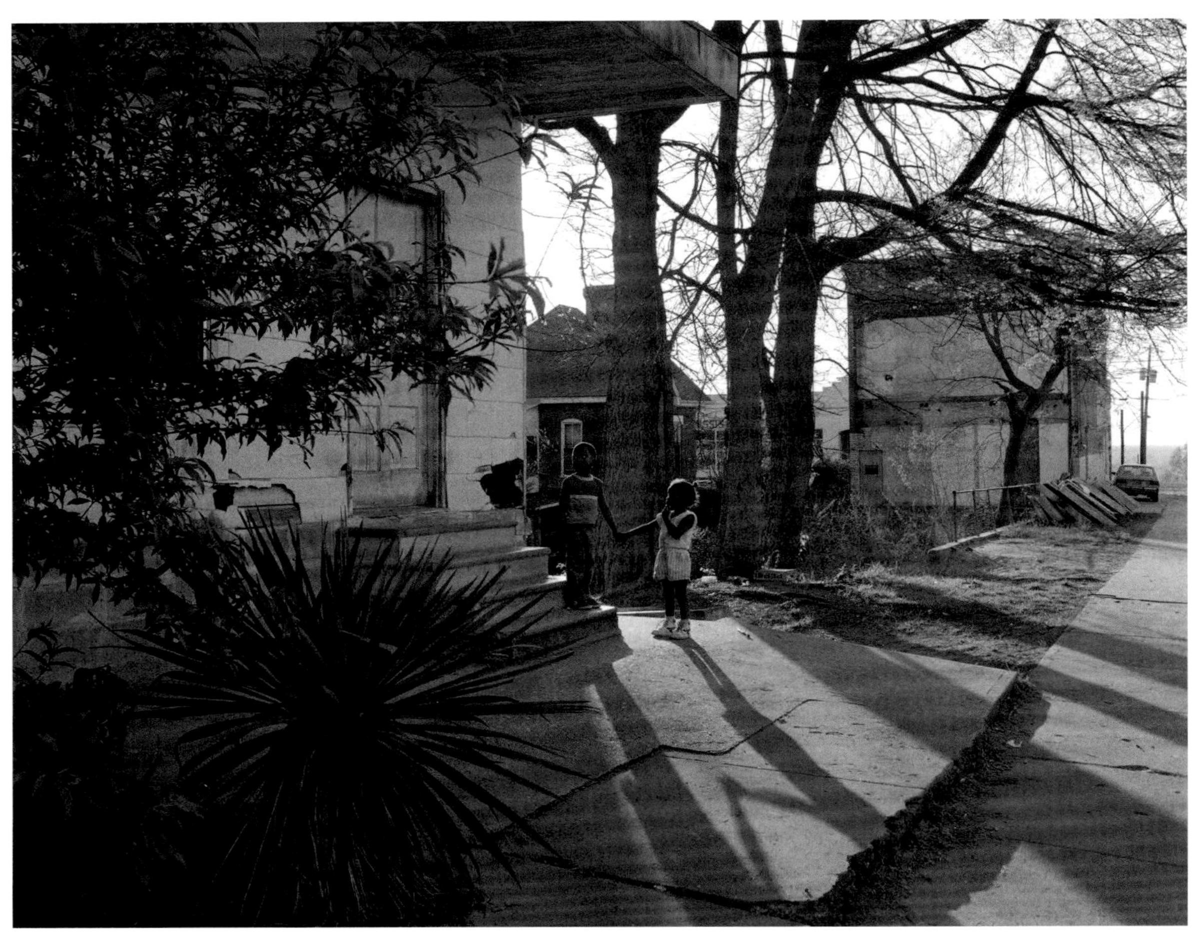

PLATE 71
Baldwin Lee, *Children Holding Hands, Vicksburg, MS*, 1984

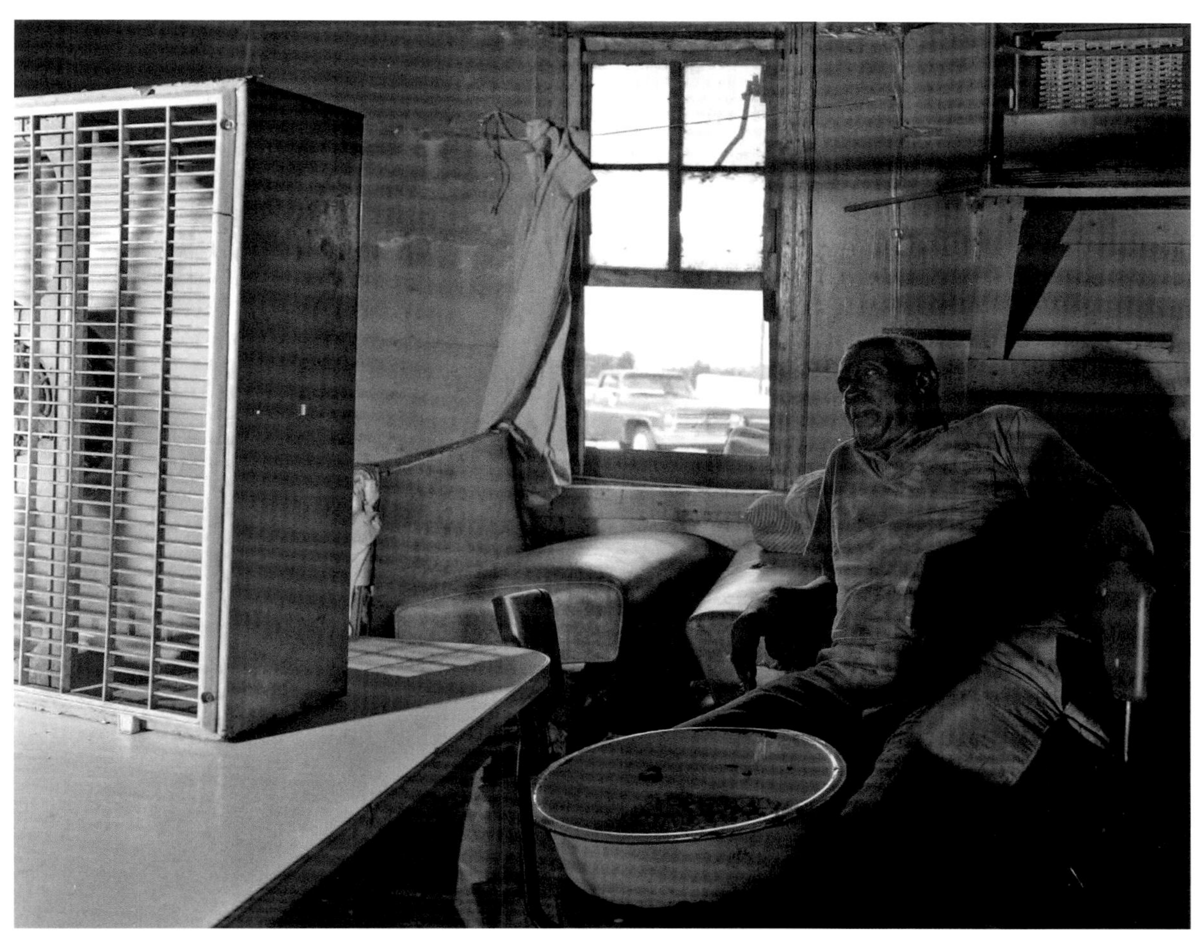

PLATE 72
Baldwin Lee, *Beans, Canton, MS*, 1985

OFTENTIMES AFTER PHOTOGRAPHING ALL DAY, I'm pretty much exhausted. On this day, I was ready to pack it in, to get back to the car, to drive back to the motel for a hot shower and meal, but for some reason I decided to walk a little bit further in this Monroe, Louisiana, neighborhood. As I turned a corner, I saw these young men playing basketball. The man who's leaning up against the post seemed to me to be absolutely wonderful. And I knew that there was a photographic possibility here. In this case, I felt it so strongly that what I did was, I think, really pretty forward. I walked right up to them and I said, "You have to let me take a picture. I have to make a photograph here. You are so great, you are going to make a wonderful photograph." They responded by laughing, looking at each other, and saying, "There's no picture here to be taken." I said, "I assure you, I'm positive of it." They finally agreed, and I went ahead and I posed them the way that you see. The man leaning against the post, I think, is one of the most amazing-looking people I have ever photographed. Better than anything I could have imagined.

Photographers who take pictures of people depend on intuition in selecting subjects. That sense alerts them when they are in the presence of someone who will enter a photograph and become its raison d'être. If the photograph is to show more than one person, this singular individual will take the leading role; the others will become supporting characters. The word "photogenic" does not sufficiently describe this quality. It merely connotes the unremarkable attribute of having a generically flattering appearance in photographs. When a photographer captures a subject with a higher order of distinctiveness, there is an obligation to impart that quality accurately. Such a person is able to metamorphose before the camera into a character whose life is insistent, multifarious, and convincing. Photographers hope to find these extraordinary individuals; they are the ones who can bear the responsibility of being a photograph's linchpin.

— Baldwin Lee

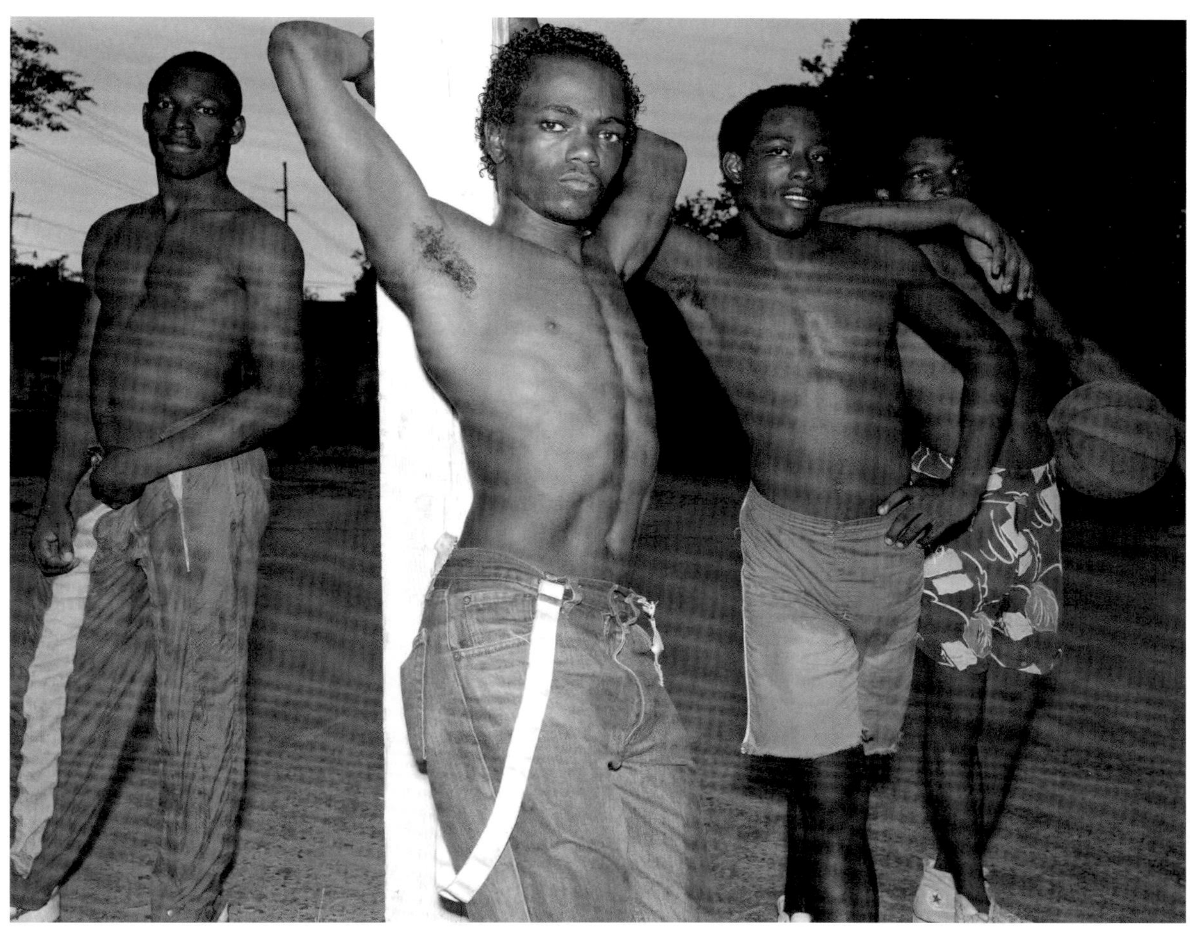

PLATE 73
Baldwin Lee, *Basketball Players at Night, Monroe, LA*, 1985

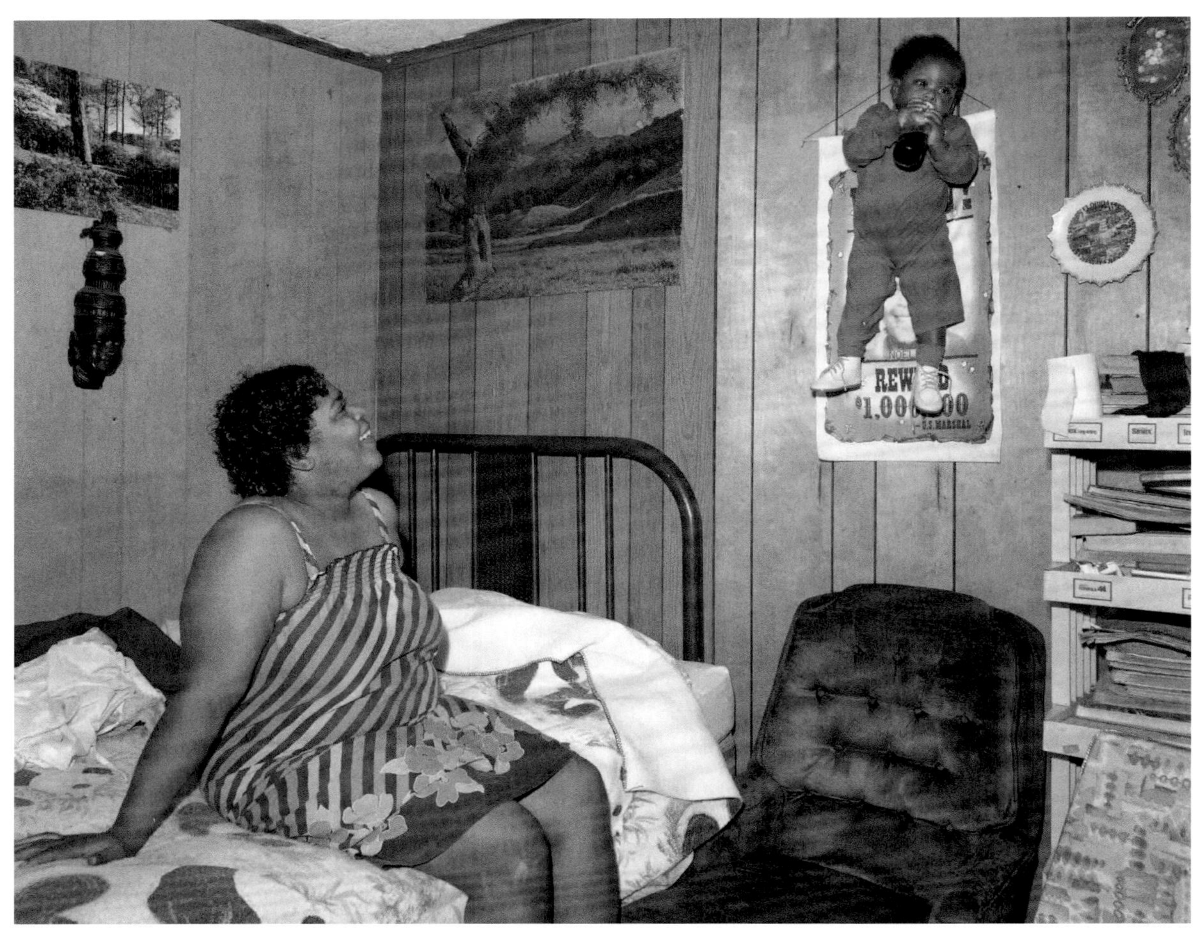

PLATE 74
Baldwin Lee, *Baby on Wall, Rosedale, MS*, 1986

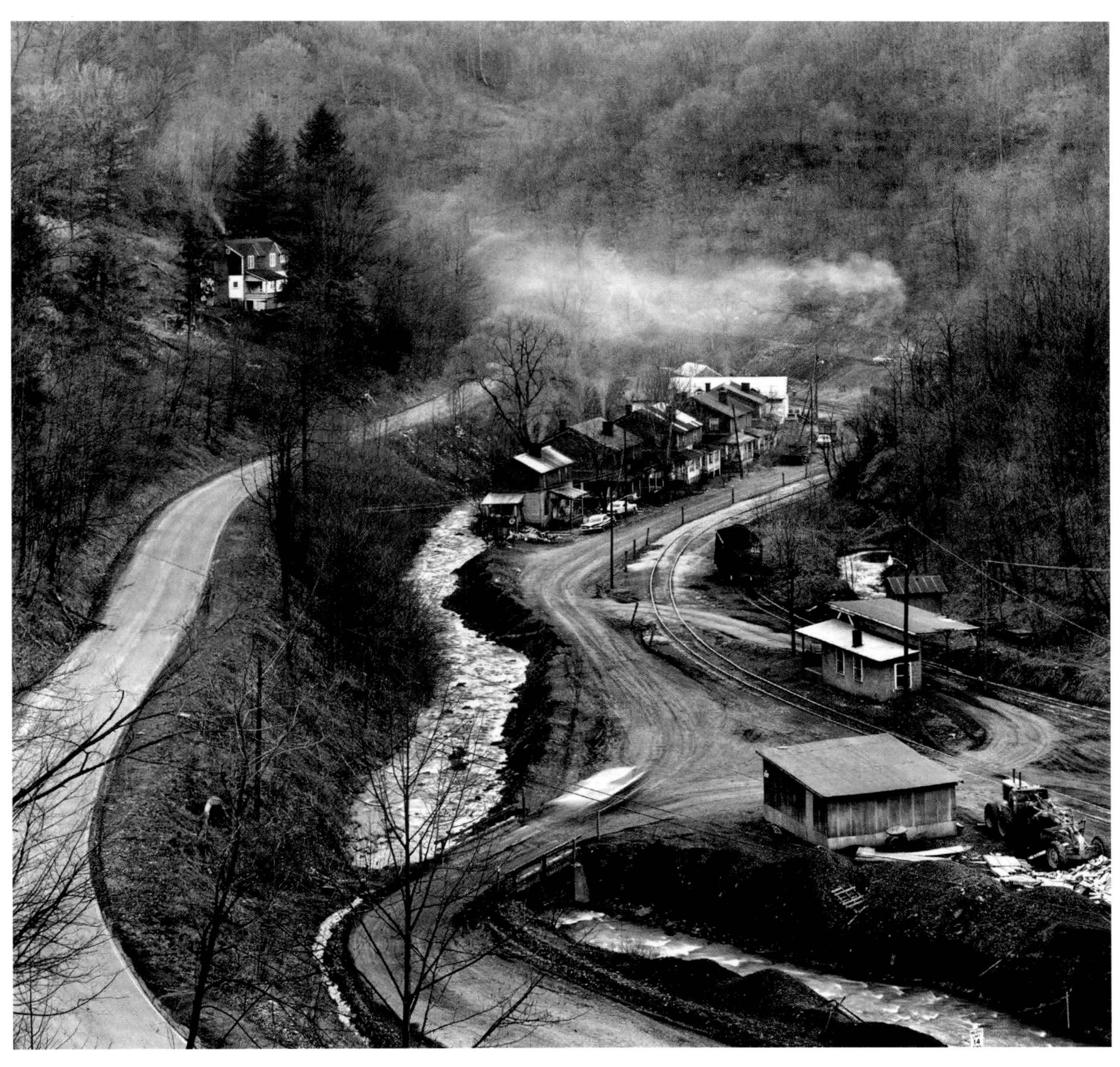

PLATE 75

Builder Levy, *Coal Camp, Near Grundy, Buchanan County, Virginia*, 1970

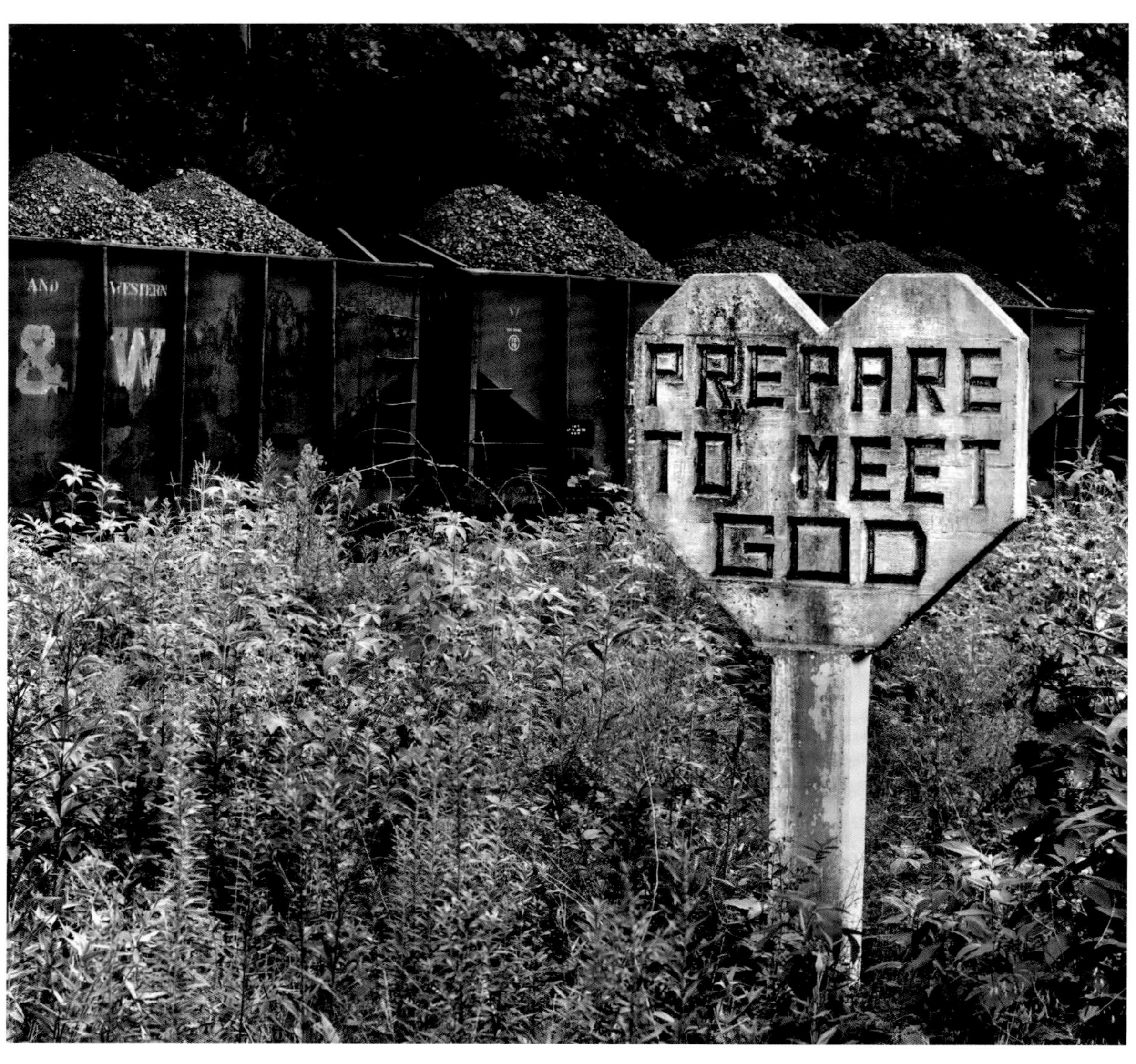

PLATE 76
Builder Levy, *Prepare to Meet God, Williamson, Mingo County, West Virginia*, 1971

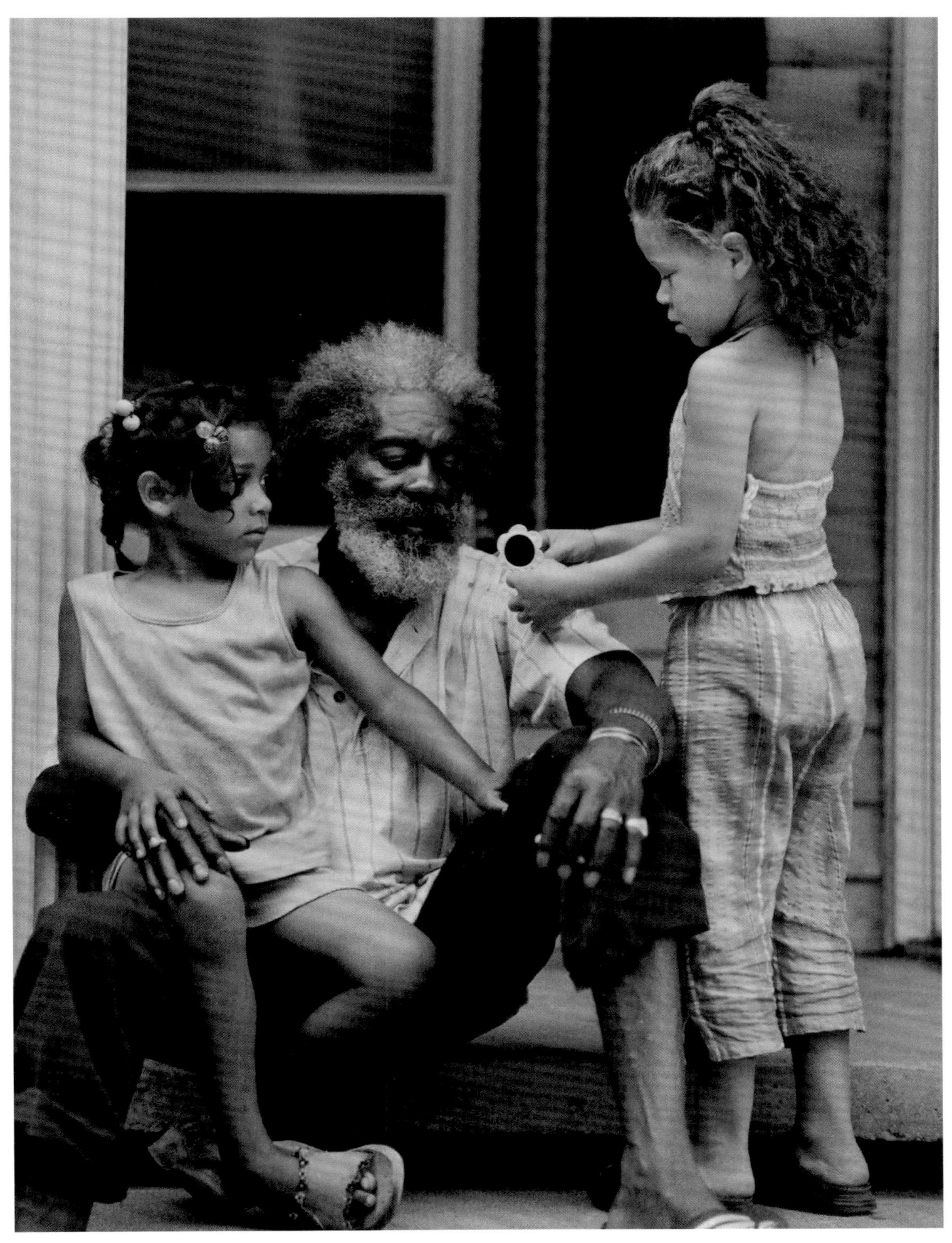

PLATE 77

Builder Levy, *Lucious Thompson with Destiny Clark and Delena Brooks, Tom Biggs Hollow, McRoberts, Letcher County, Kentucky*, 2002

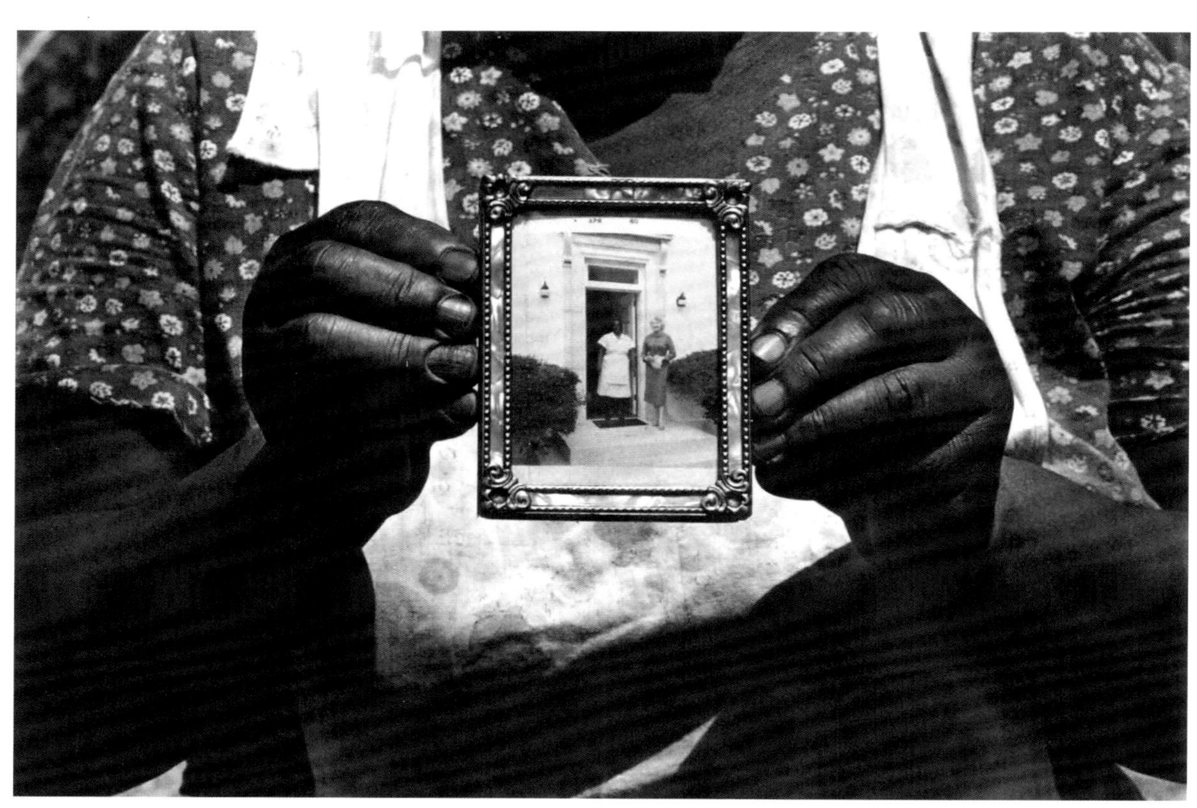

I FIRST PICKED UP A CAMERA following the contract killing of my
mother. Traumatized, I would roam the back roads near my home in coastal
North Carolina, stopping when a place insisted, taking photographs in an
attempt to make contact with the world again.

One afternoon I stepped into an otherworldly cacophony-of-a-compound
just off Silver Dollar Road in the middle of a nowhere place called the
Open Ground. Sandra Calhoun met me and showed me her taxidermy
studio. The plywood walls of her studio were hung with precise specimens
of nearly every critter in the woods. The counter was strewn with glass
eyeballs. Outside, hounds were howling at dark clouds rolling overhead.
Chickens and turkeys ran here and there underfoot. There were purring
cats and kittens, livestock, you name it. Squirrels were chasing each other
around a live oak tree where young Margie sat quietly on a limb reading
a book as lightning flashed close by. And her brother, Michael, a blur of
a boy, was everywhere at once. A Tasmanian devil. He disappeared for
a moment and returned holding a taxidermied fox head. He came whiz-
zing past and paused for a fraction of a second before turning to taunt his
Bluetick bearhound, Blu Gal. A few minutes later, Michael and Margie
came running up carrying a limp puppy and screaming, "Mama, do something!" Sandra performed CPR on the puppy. It was wild, more performance than place.

Sandra and I became friends. She called me Kodak. One day I got a
message: "Kodak, come on out. I shot a bear." She had killed a 620-pound
bear (gutted) with one shot, taken while lying on the ground with a .308
rifle, the stock secured with duct tape. She named the bear Volkswagen.

Today, Sandra spends a lot of time in nature, but no longer hunts or
practices taxidermy.

— Deborah Luster

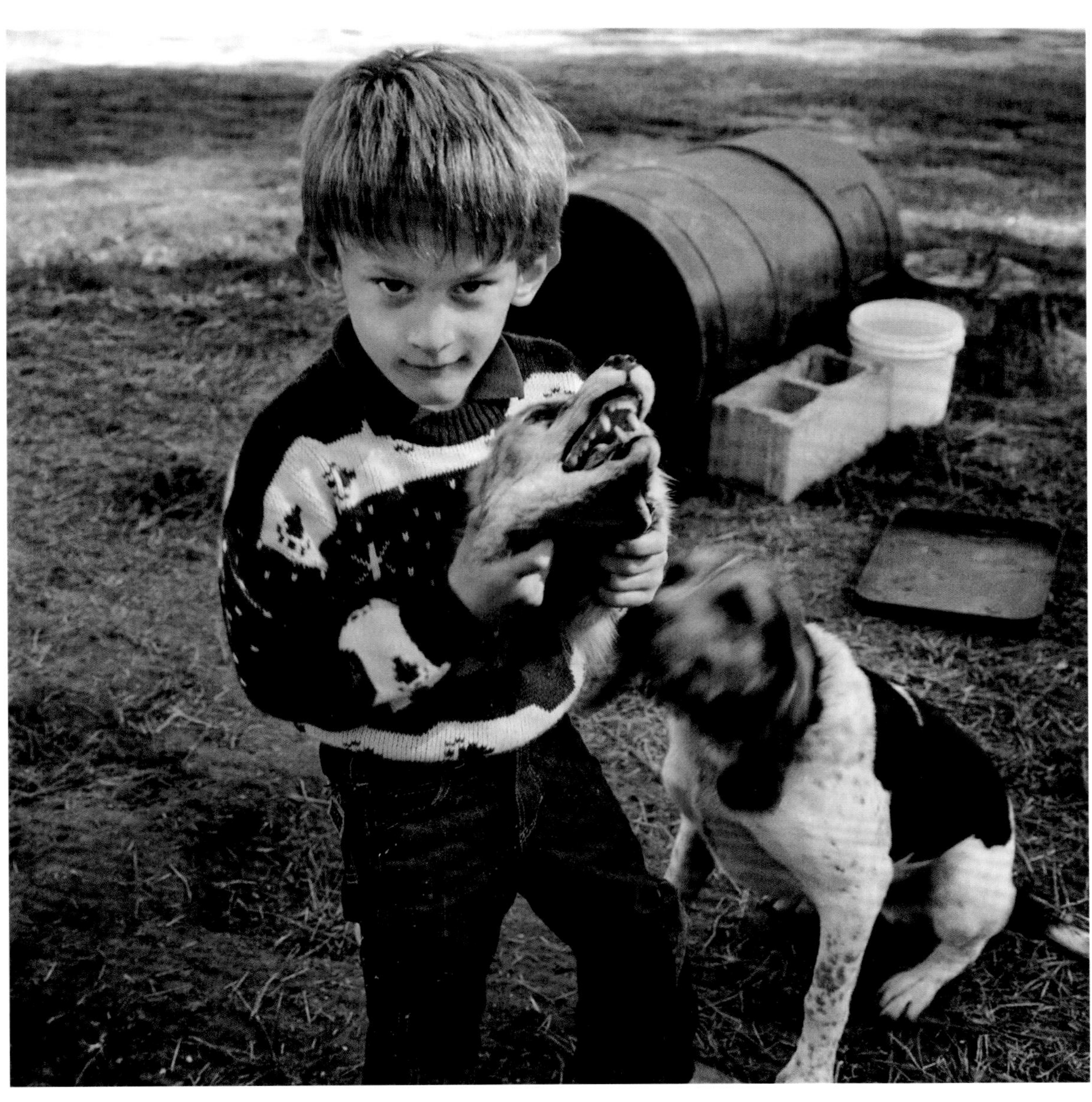

PLATE 79
Deborah Luster, *The Taxidermist's Son*, 1994

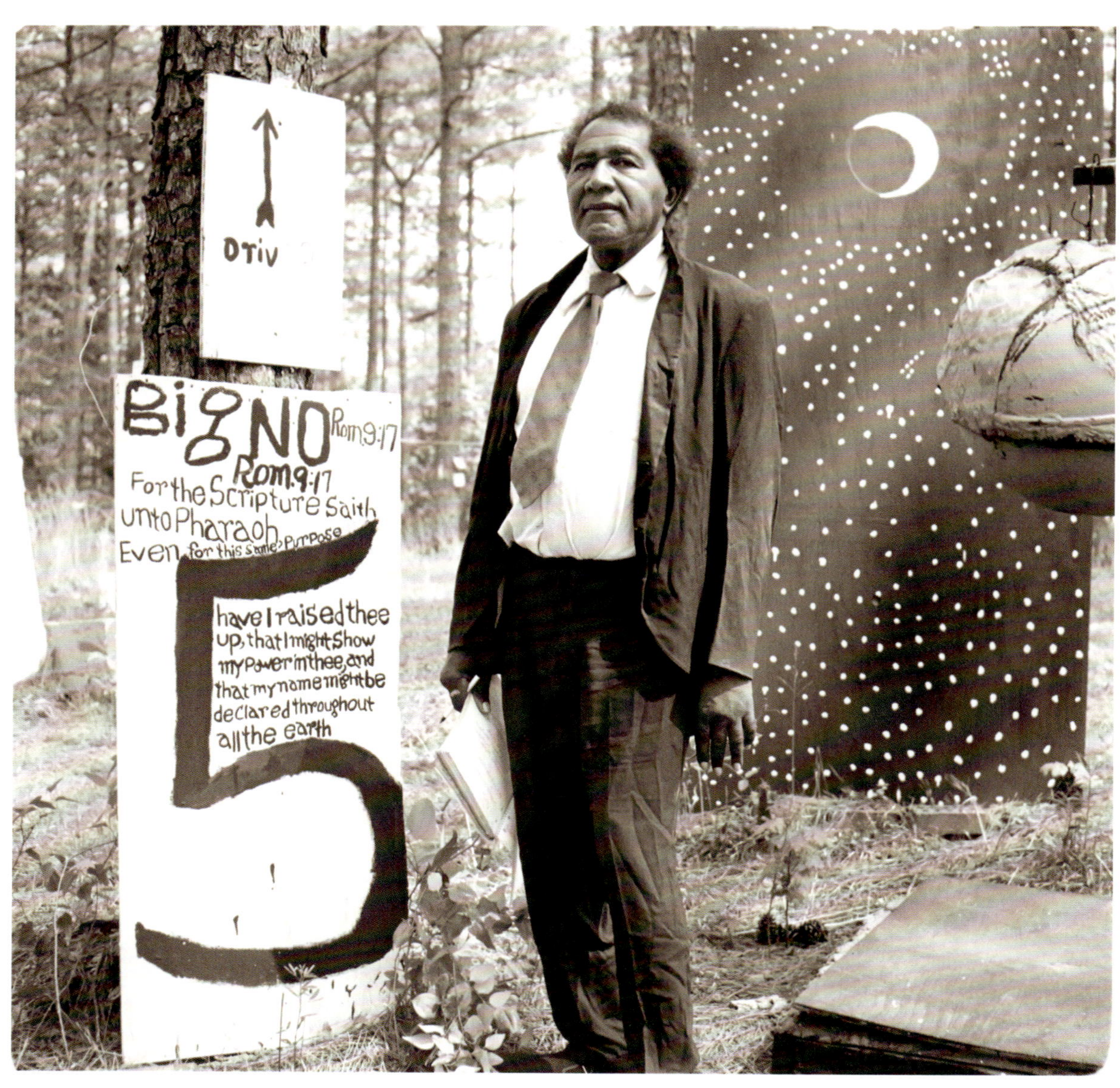

Roger Manley, *Reverend Ruth at Big Number 5, Woodville, GA*, 1985

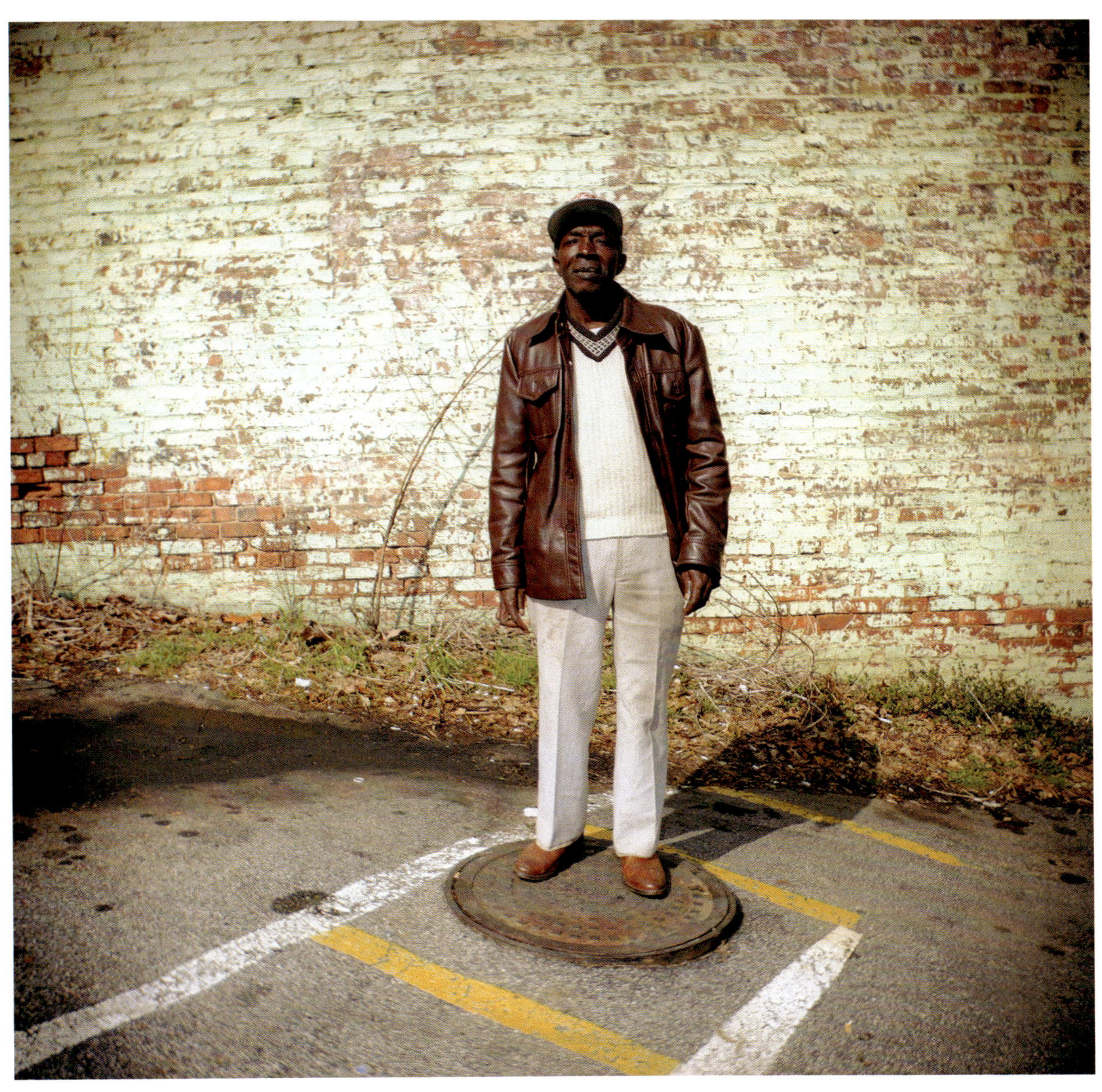

PLATE 81
Carl Martin, *Man on Manhole Cover*, 1996–98

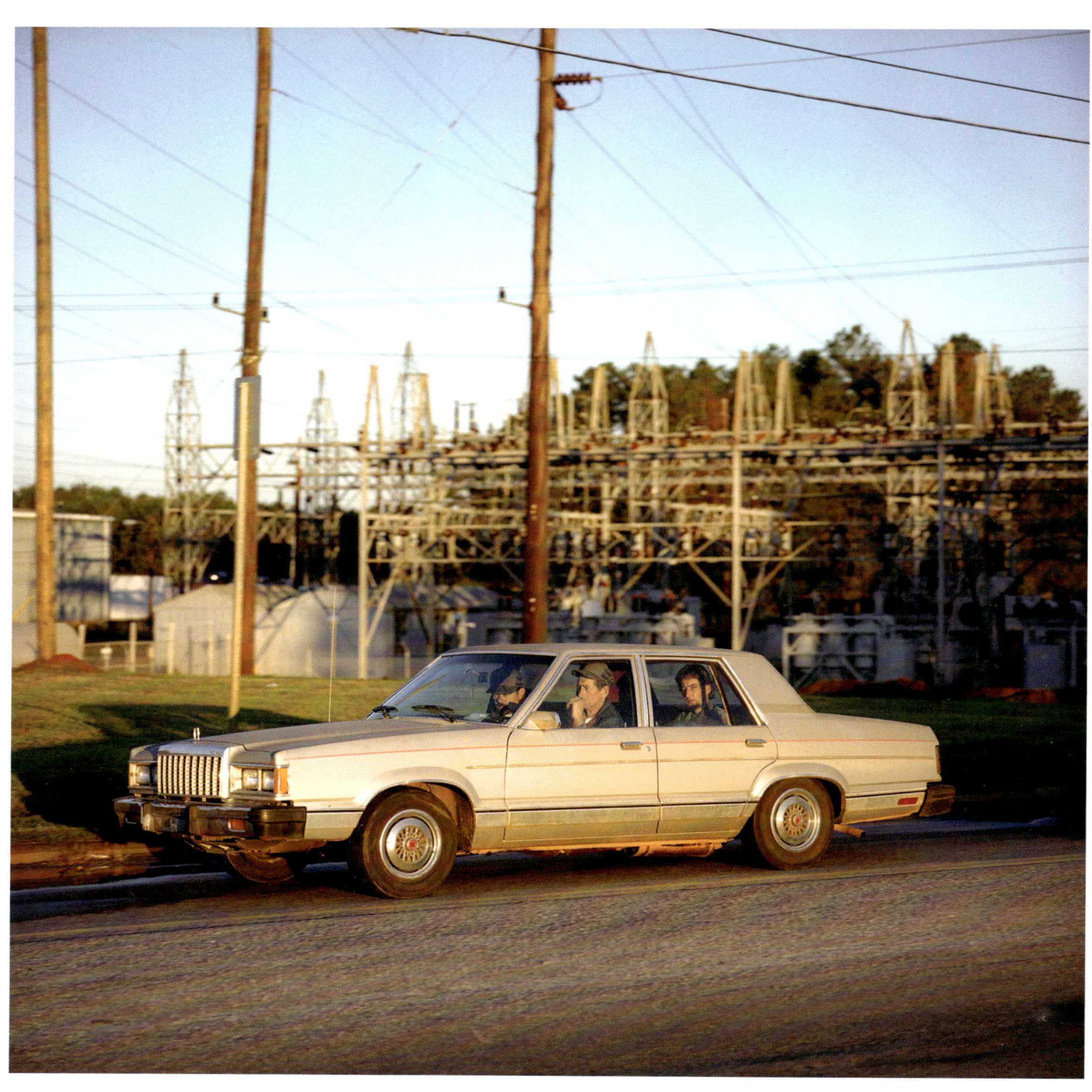

PLATE 82
Carl Martin, *Men in Car*, 1996-98

I ONCE HAD THE SAD AND DAUNTING TASK of dismantling the house where my family had lived for generations. Probably because of this, such old houses have for me a particular charm and resonance. Houses where, over the years, objects accumulate and settle in an organic, unself-conscious muddle, where time slows and ghosts whisper.

This is the interior of one of the four remaining slave cabins at Stagville Plantation just north of Durham, North Carolina. The Bennehan and Cameron families owned 30,000 acres and 900 enslaved people. This house, which had been home to four families, stands in a grove of trees overlooking a majestic barn. When Stagville was first made a state historic site, most of its educational focus was on the story of the owners and on aspects of its historic preservation and research. Now it is almost wholly devoted to teaching about the lives and work of the people who lived in cabins like this one back of the big house.

— *Elizabeth Matheson*

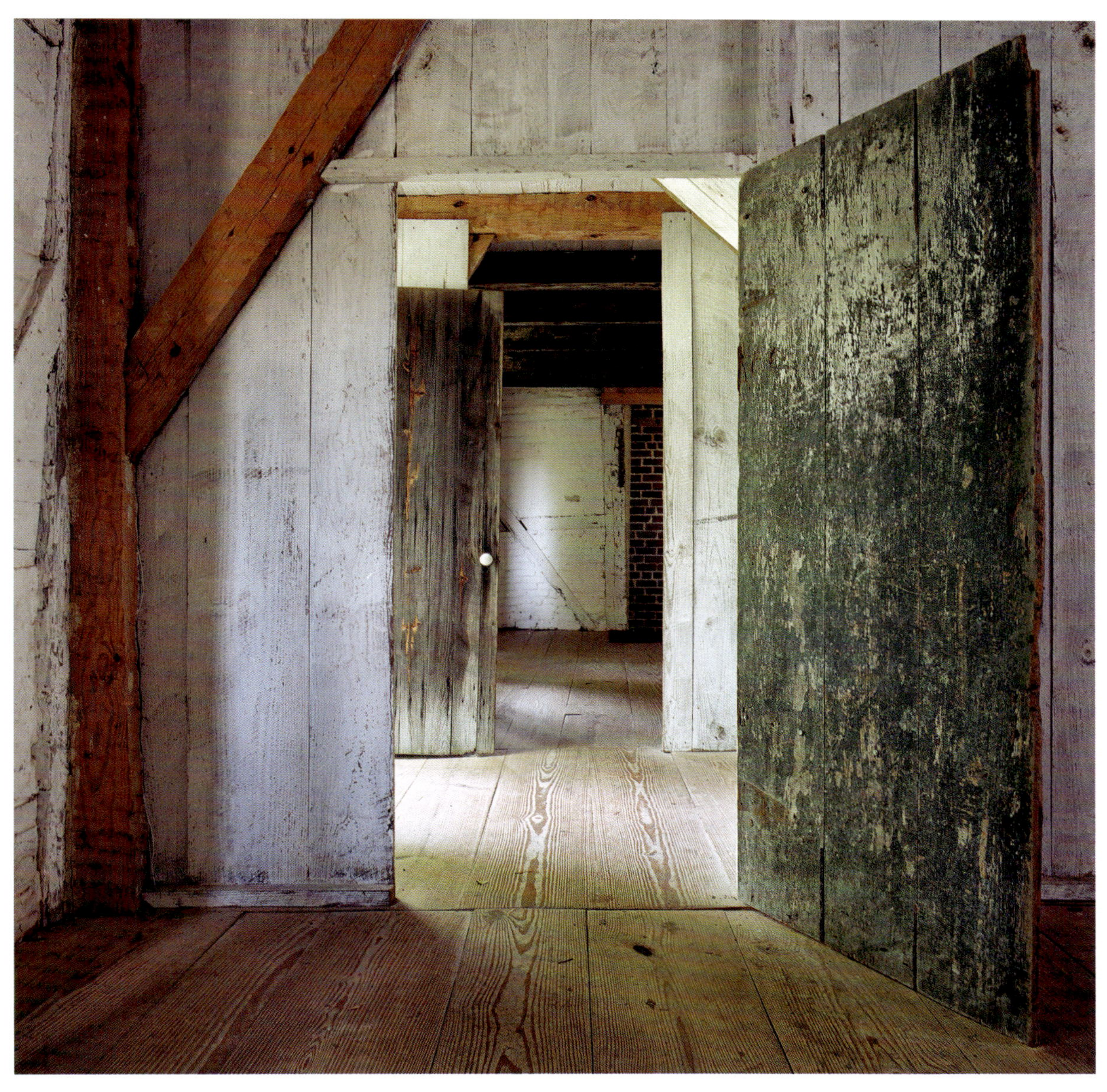

PLATE 83
Elizabeth Matheson, *Slave Quarters, Stagville Plantation, Durham, NC*, n.d.

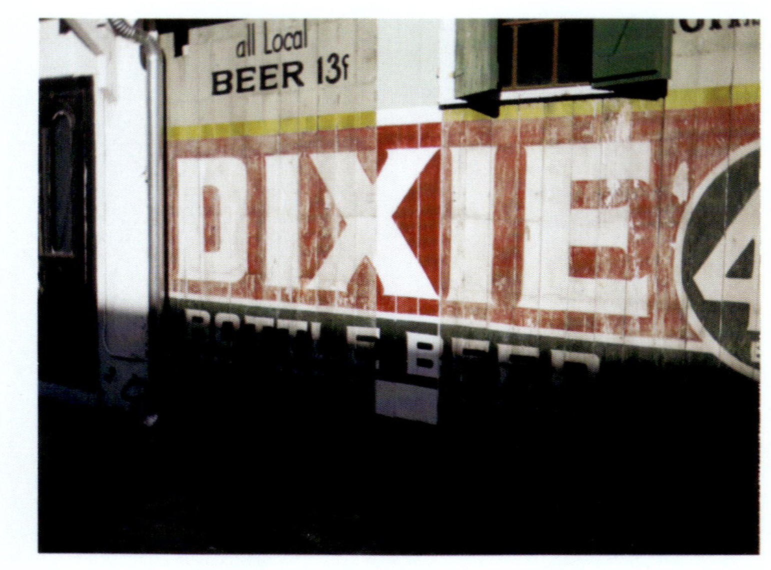

PLATE 84
Richard McCabe, *Dixie, LA*, 2014

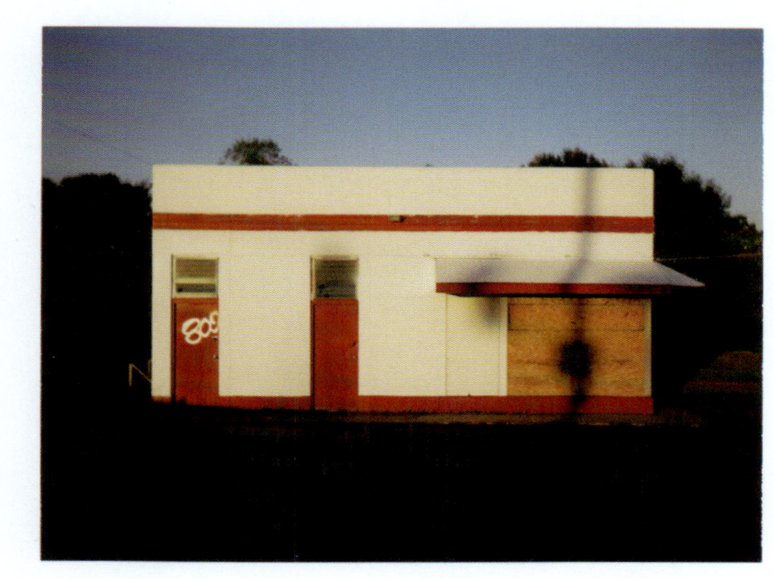

PLATE 85
Richard McCabe, *Jackson, MS (Gas Station)*, 2015

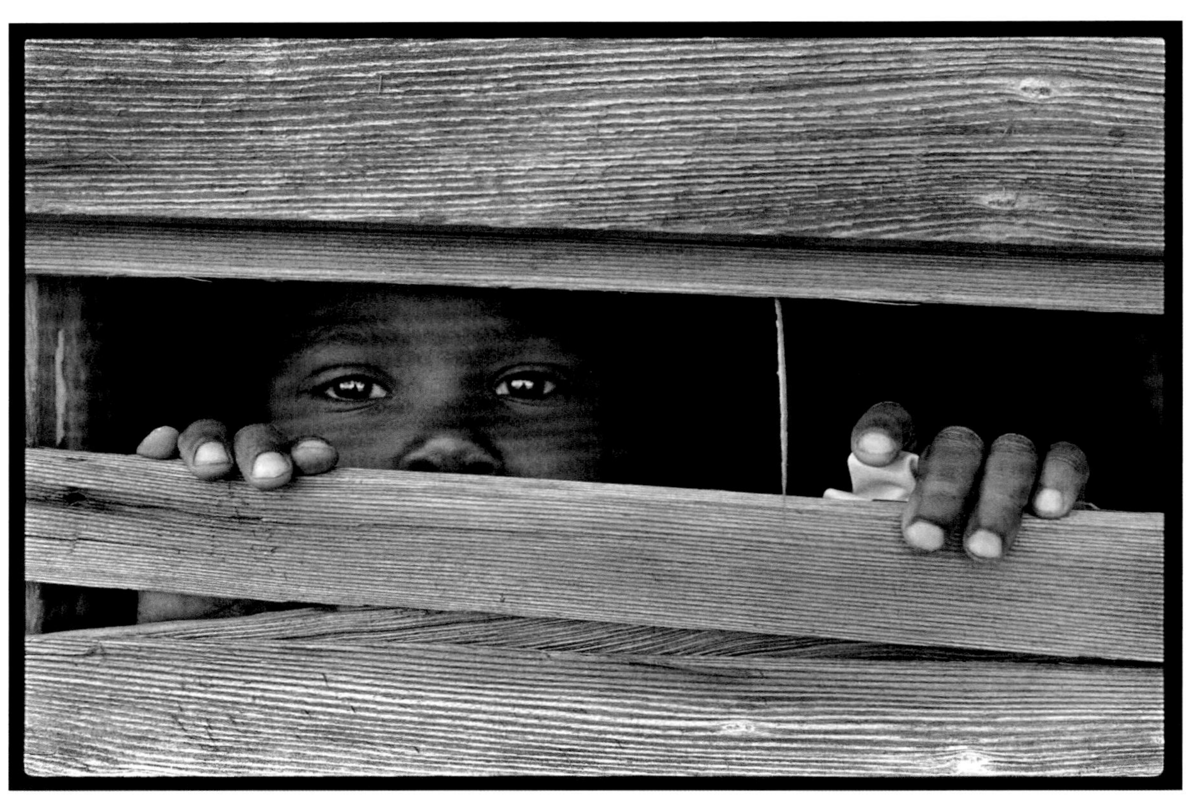

PLATE 86
Chandra McCormick, *La Shonda Morgan, Ashland Plantation, Port Allen, LA*, 1986

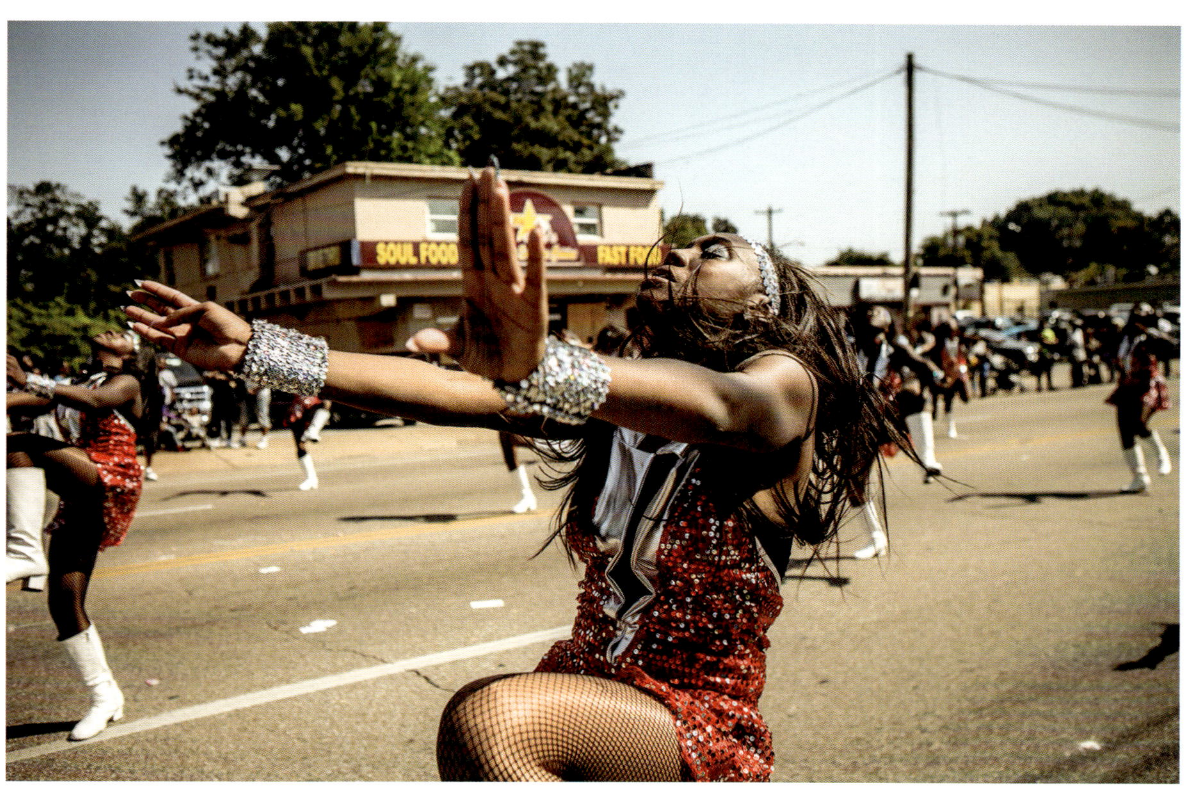

PLATE 87
Andrea Morales, *Southern Heritage Classic Parade*, 2017

WHILE DRIVING DOWN FROM MEMPHIS, TENNESSEE,
to Utica, Mississippi, on a freelance assignment, I started getting calls
relaying the rumors. Rumor soon became triumph: statues to the Confederate generals and the slavers that stood in Memphis, one of this nation's
Blackest cities, were scheduled for removal that night. Nathan Bedford
Forrest and Jefferson Davis both had been memorialized in the heart of
the city and residents had spent much of 2017 fighting, buoyed by successful Confederate monument removals across the country.

For months, I'd documented the local movements calling for removal and
oppression both by the Memphis police and racist Confederate apologists.
It'd been a brutally hot summer with protests stretching into the dog days.
Tami Sawyer, a Black Memphian, and a coalition of other Black leaders led
the movement against the statues with the support of hundreds of everyday
folks. They were met with arrests and harassment.

After finishing my assignment as quickly and carefully as I could, so as
not to let the excitement overtake me, I white knuckled it the nearly four
hours back to Memphis. When I arrived, I was met by police barricades
and officers with the Memphis police's Organized Crime Unit. They asked
me for an "event pass" to grant me access to the park where the removal was
happening. Closing off these public spaces felt like a sublimation against
history. For an excruciating half hour, I negotiated with them about my
validity as a member of the press.

Finally, after a colleague vouched for me, I was able to approach the
perimeter of the park where a small crowd gathered. Many had arrived as
soon as the news had broken and before the barricades went up. Some had
been part of the protests. Others were simply attracted by the spectacle of
a gigantic bronze statue being escorted away on a winter's night. Whatever brought them to that edge of sidewalk along Union Avenue, everyone
seemed to agree that it was important to be a witness.

Shortly after 9 p.m., the statue was lifted off its base. Thousands of pounds
of bronze, fixed for a century with a deliberate and unambiguous defiance, from Jim Crow through the civil rights movement, were now gone.
Tami Sawyer was embraced by a crowd offering hugs and congratulations.
Workers placed the statue on the bed of a rig, covered the image of the
general and his gargantuan horse with a tarp, and escorted it away to storage, out of sight, its message finally disrupted.

— Andrea Morales

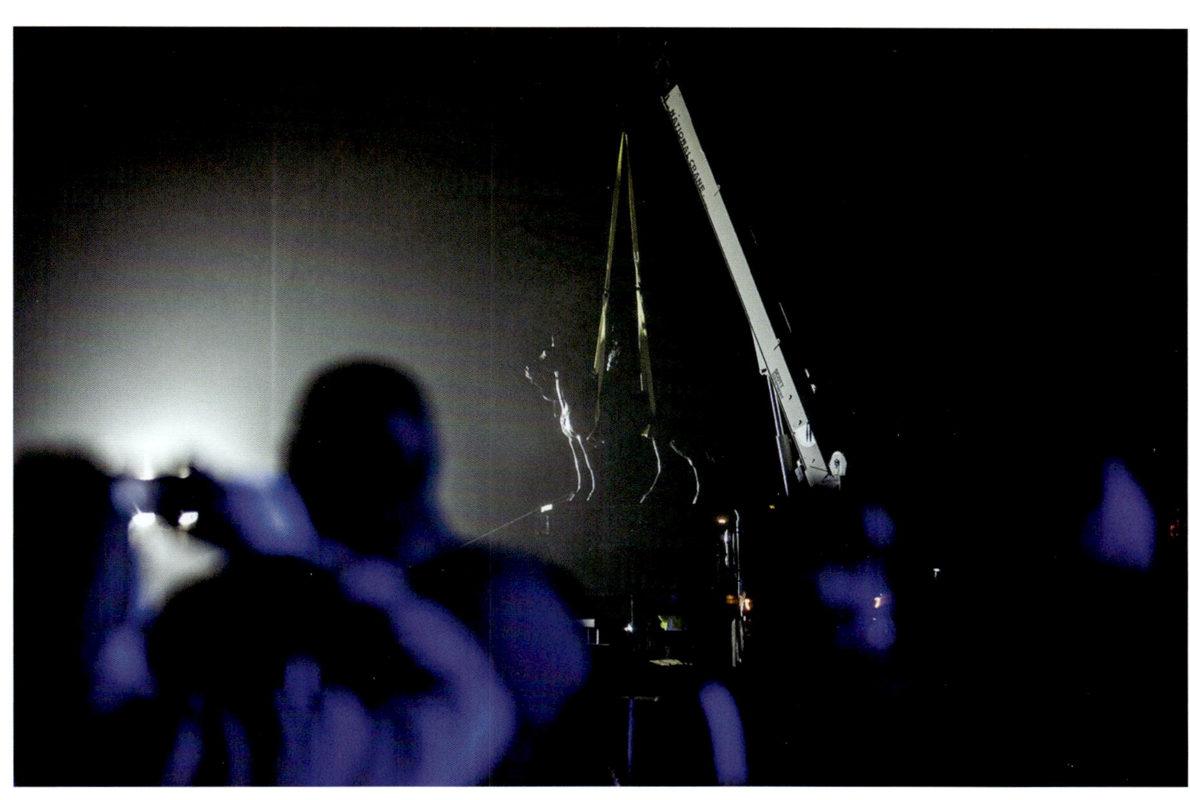

PLATE 88
Andrea Morales, *Monument*, 2017

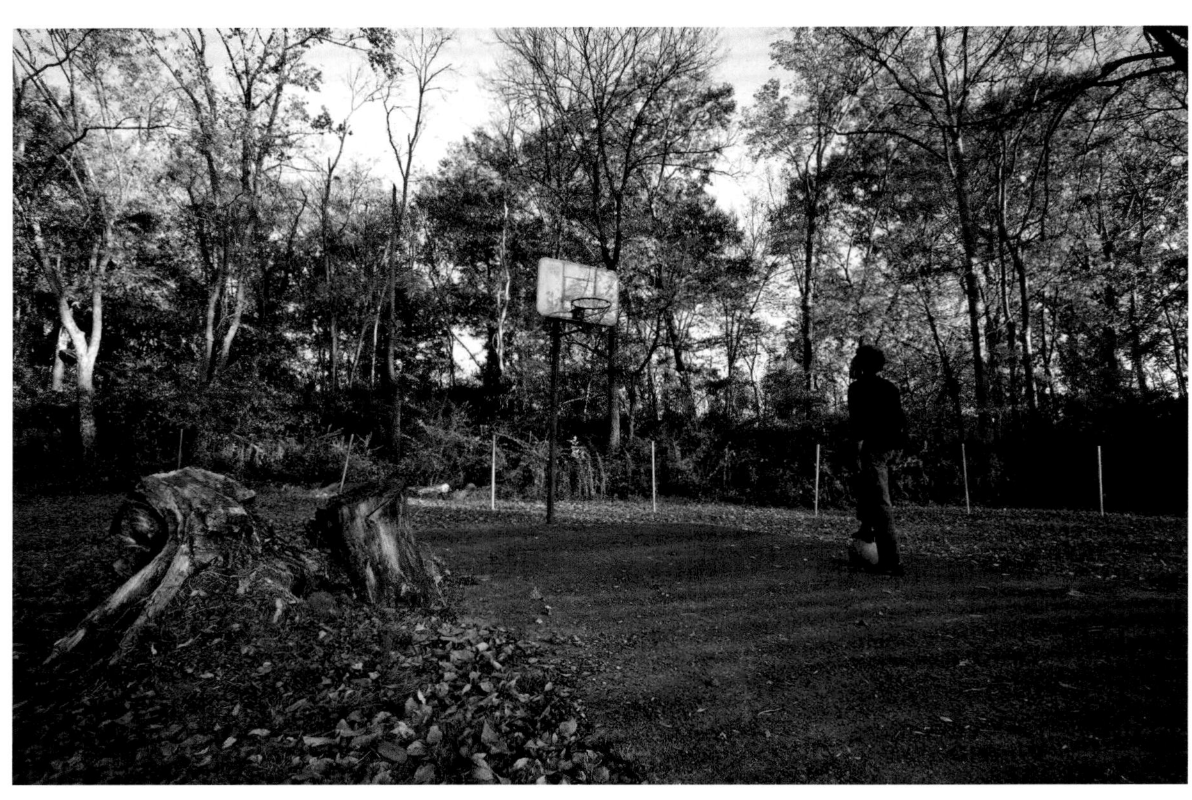

PLATE 89
Celestia Morgan, *My Court*, 2013

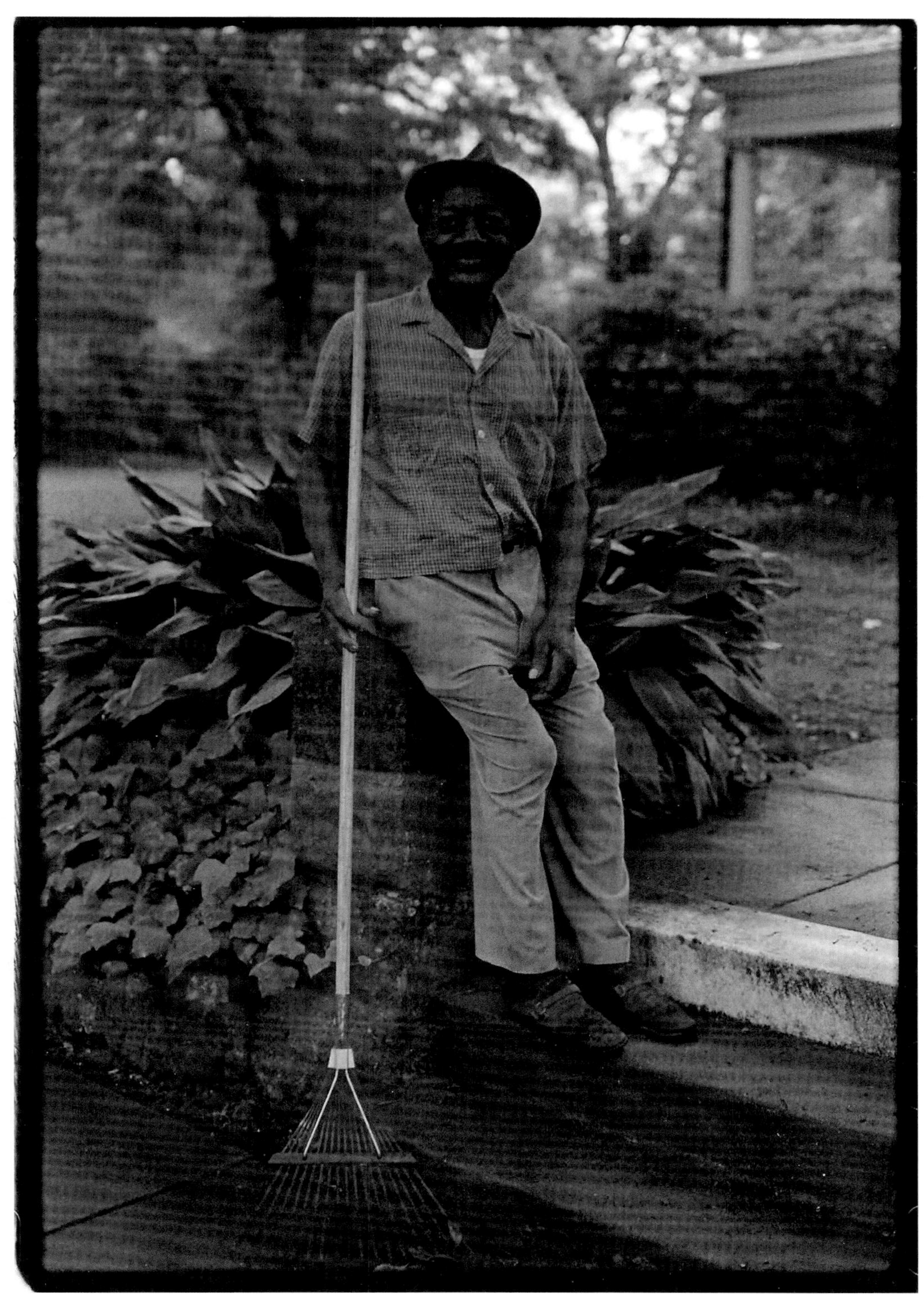

PLATE 90
Jimmy Nicholson, *Mr. Mose Tomlin, 617 Broughton Street, Early Morning, Bainbridge, GA*, 1978

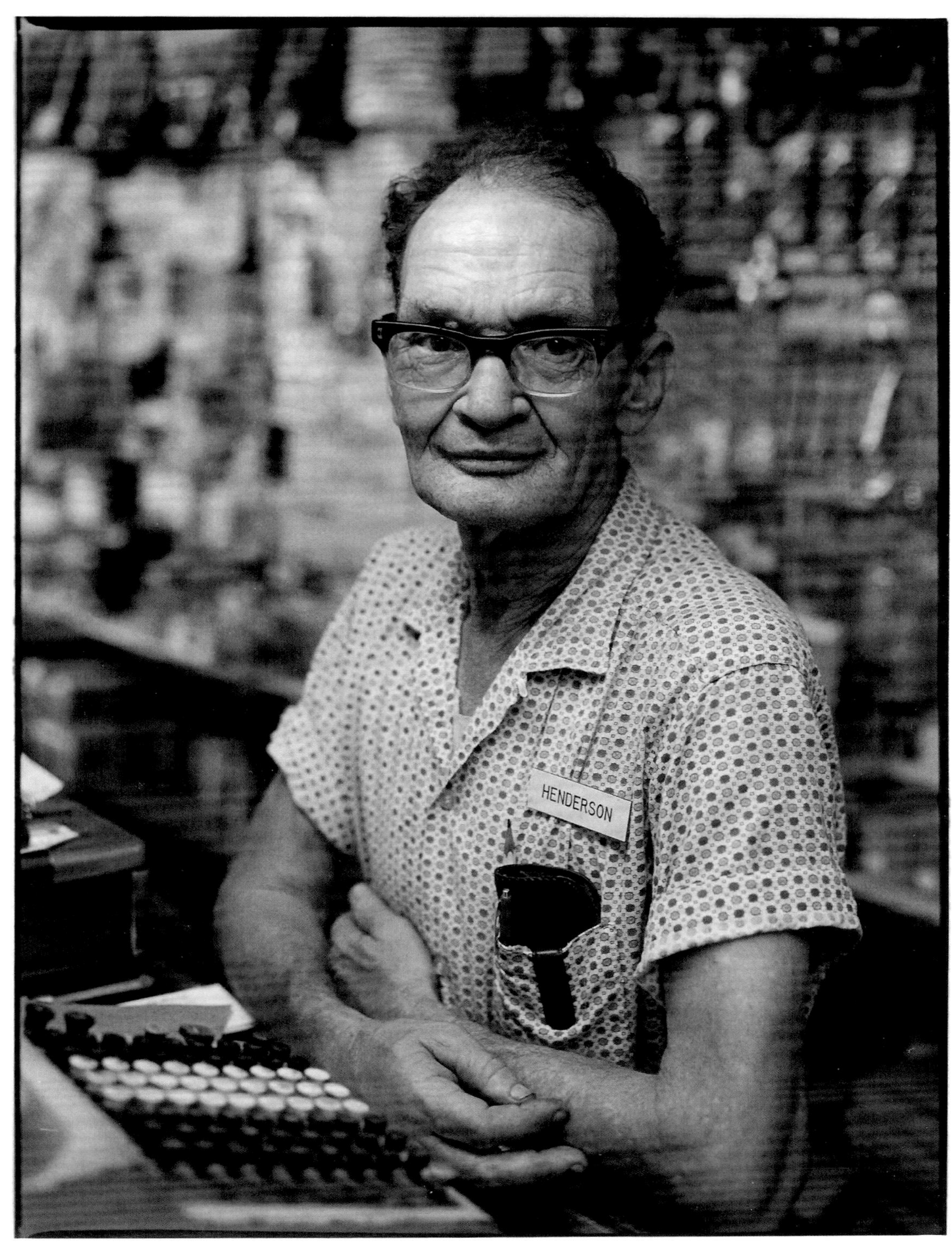

PLATE 91
Jimmy Nicholson, *Mr. Scrap Henderson Inside Red Long's Bait & Tackle Shop, Bainbridge, GA*, 1980

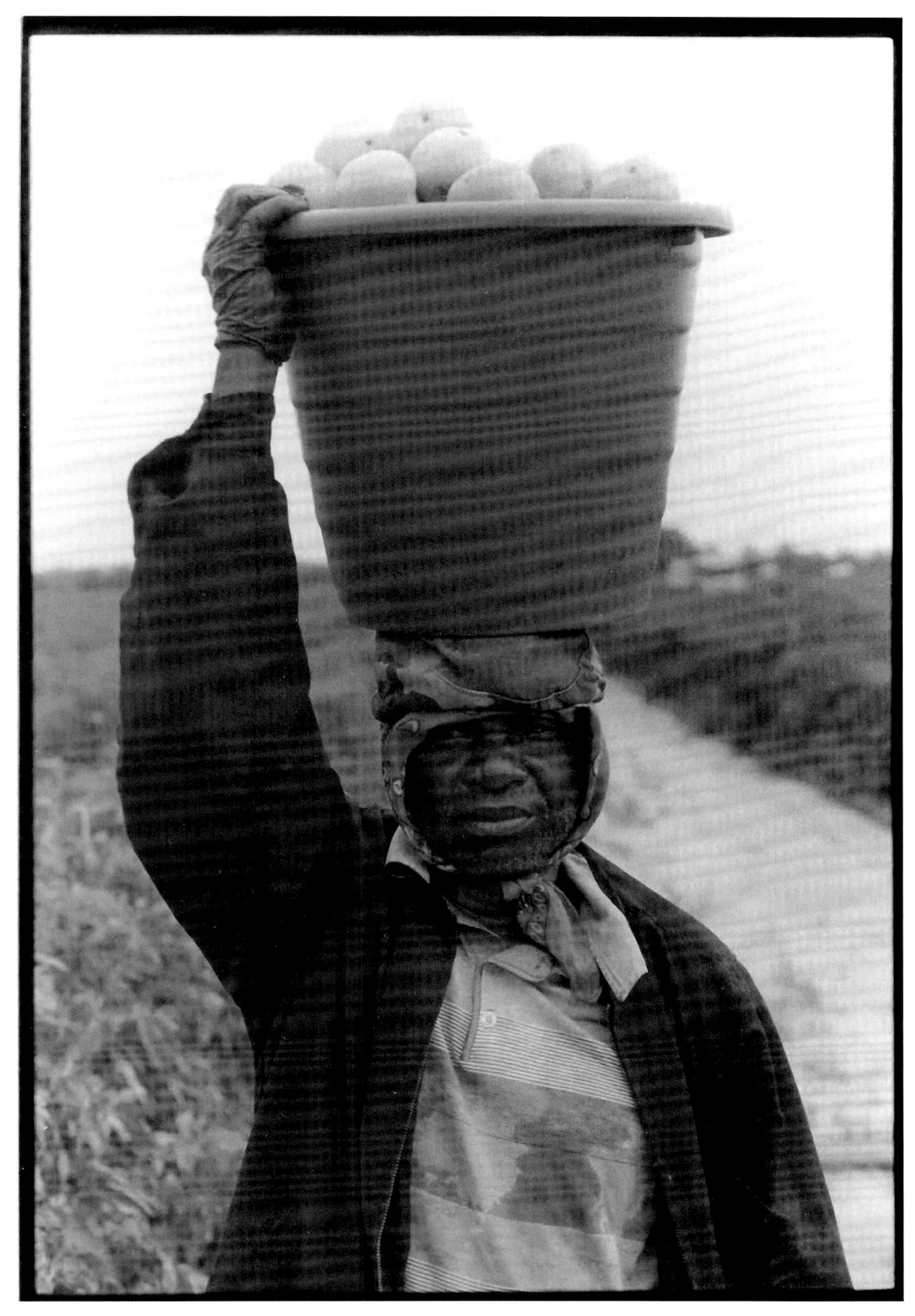

PLATE 92

Jimmy Nicholson, *Migrant Farm Worker Picking Tomatoes, Gadsden County, FL*, 2020

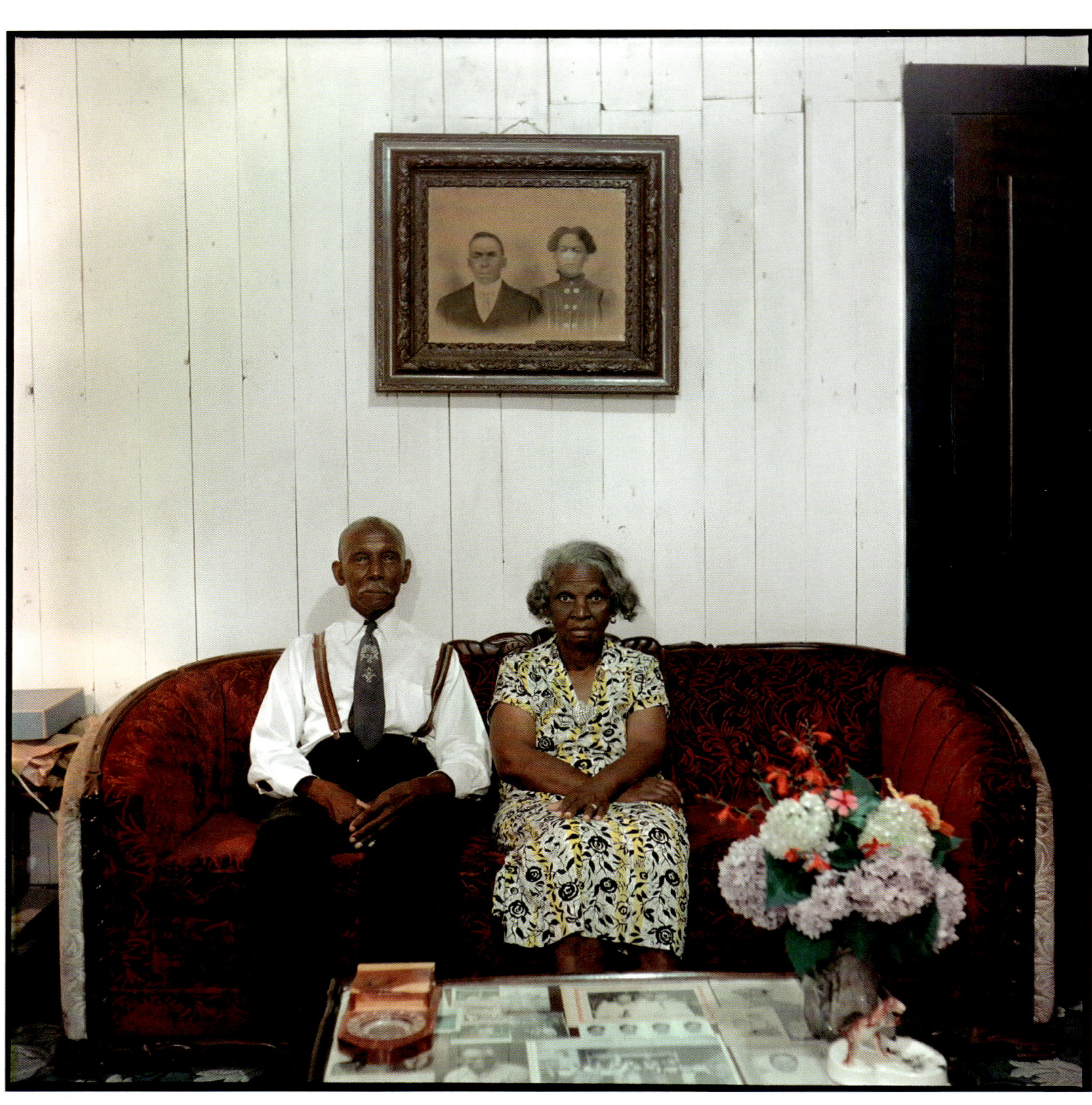

PLATE 93
Gordon Parks, *Mr. and Mrs. Thornton, Mobile, Alabama*, 1956

"A SEPARATE WAY OF LIFE"

One of Mr. and Mrs. Albert Thornton's granddaughters, Virgie Lee Tanner, lives near them in Mobile. At 25 she has four children, having been married for six years to Henry Tanner, 34, a mechanic at Brookley Air Force Base. Discrimination in employment does not affect her family. Her husband's civil service job pays $80 a week. But other restraints do affect them. They must tell their children, for example, that they cannot play in a nearby playground for whites but must use a "separate but equal" one for Negroes. The children do not grasp the logic of this and view the white playground as a special, wonderful place from which they are being deliberately excluded.

The Tanners' house is a two-room, $20-a-month shack with one bedroom, in which all six members of the family sleep. Little else is available for them to rent in the segregated neighborhood in which they live. Mr. Tanner is now taking the only way out of the situation he can see. He is building his own four-bedroom house on a lot he has purchased in another part of town. But he has no illusions about what it will be when it is finished: another small, crowded house in another segregated neighborhood.[1]

— Gordon Parks

1 Robert Wallace and Gordon Parks, "The Restraints: Open and Hidden," *Life,* September 24, 1956, 106–7. The words accompanying Gordon Parks's photographs in this article are credited to Robert Wallace; however, recent scholars have underscored Parks's voice in the text, suggesting that Wallace largely reorganized and rewrote Parks's shooting scripts and field notes for the assignment. See Maurice Berger, "With a Small Camera Tucked in My Pocket," in *Gordon Parks: Segregation Story* (Göttingen, Germany: Steidl; Pleasantville, NY: Gordon Parks Foundation, 2014), 16.

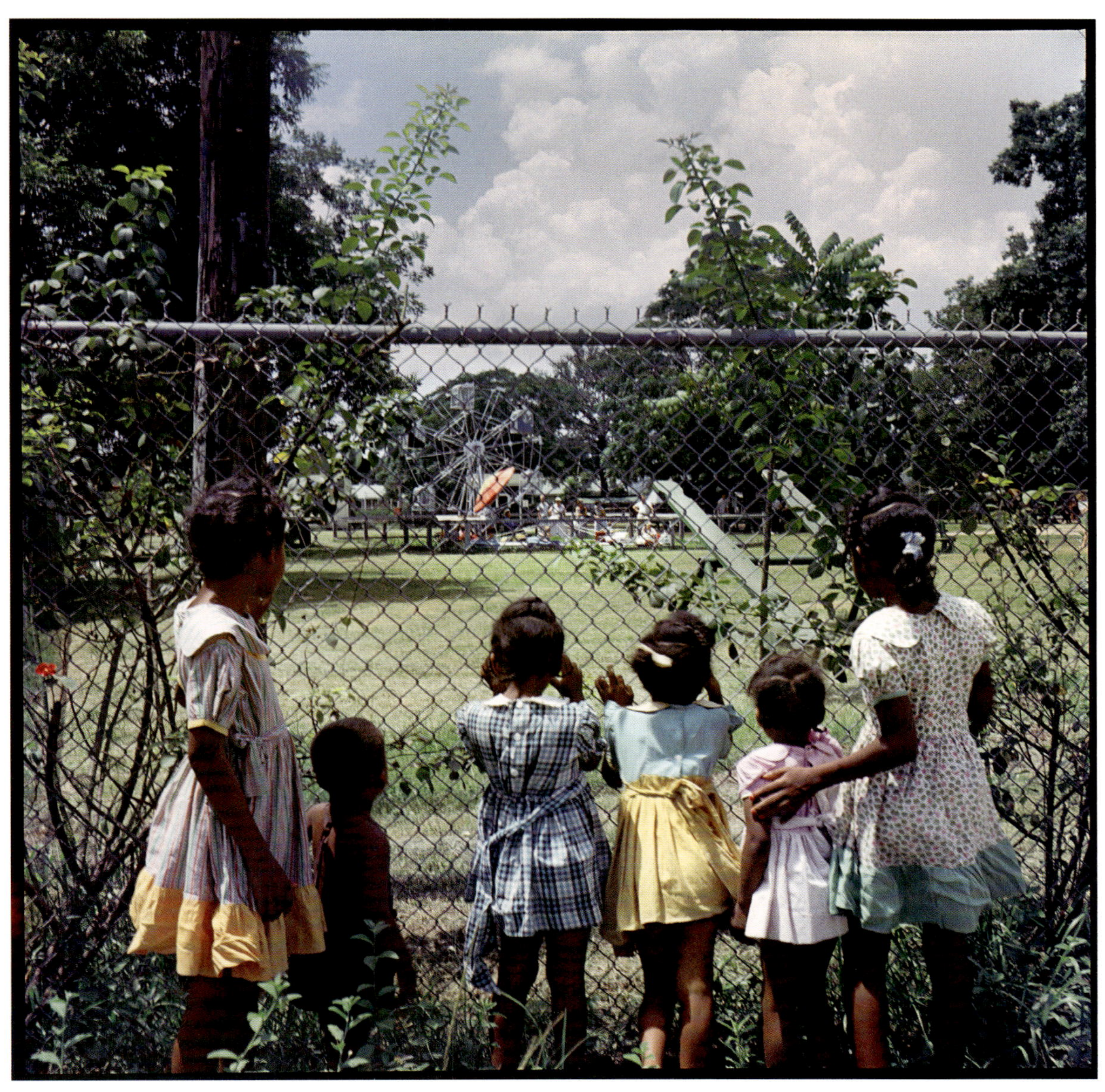

PLATE 94

Gordon Parks, *Outside Looking In, Mobile, Alabama*, 1956

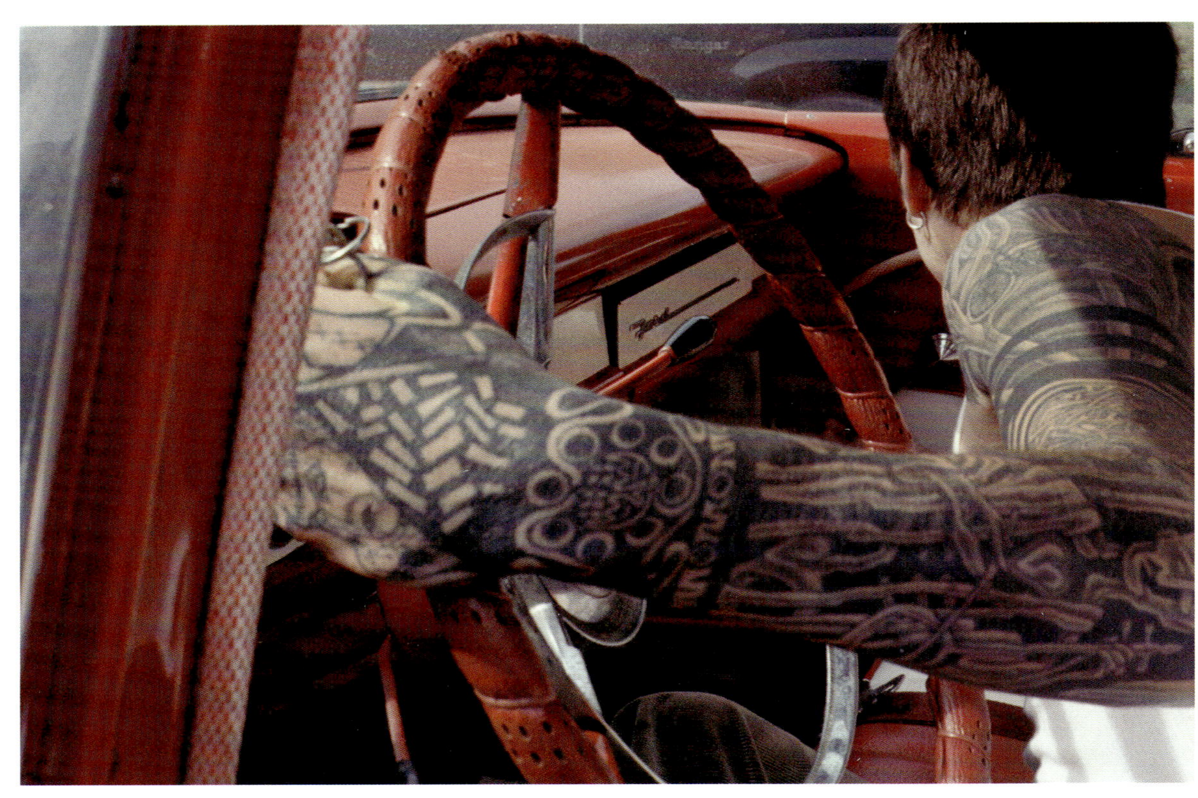

PLATE 95
Pamela Pecchio, *Mitchell's Arm*, 1997

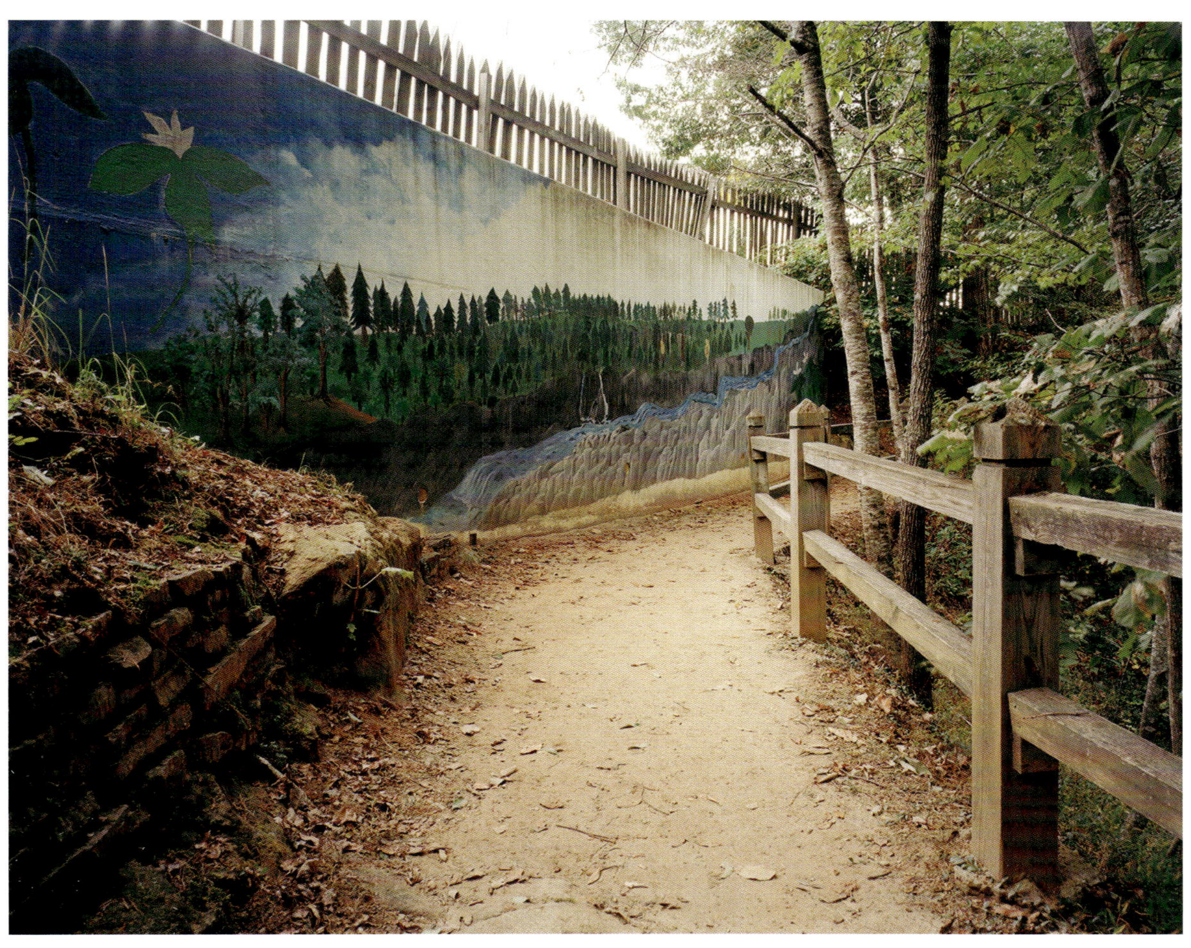

PLATE 96
Caitlin Peterson, *Tallulah Gorge*, 2013

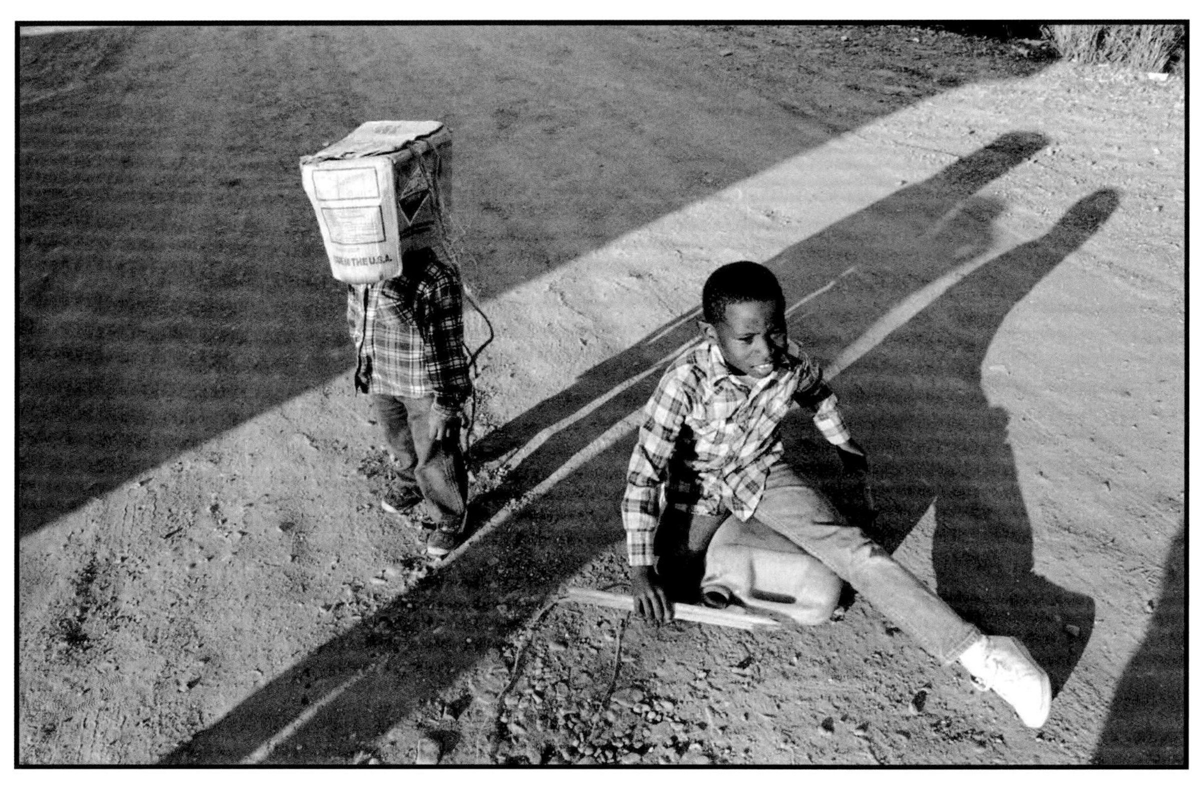

PLATE 97
Eli Reed, *Children at Play, Tunica (Sugar Ditch), Mississippi*, 1986

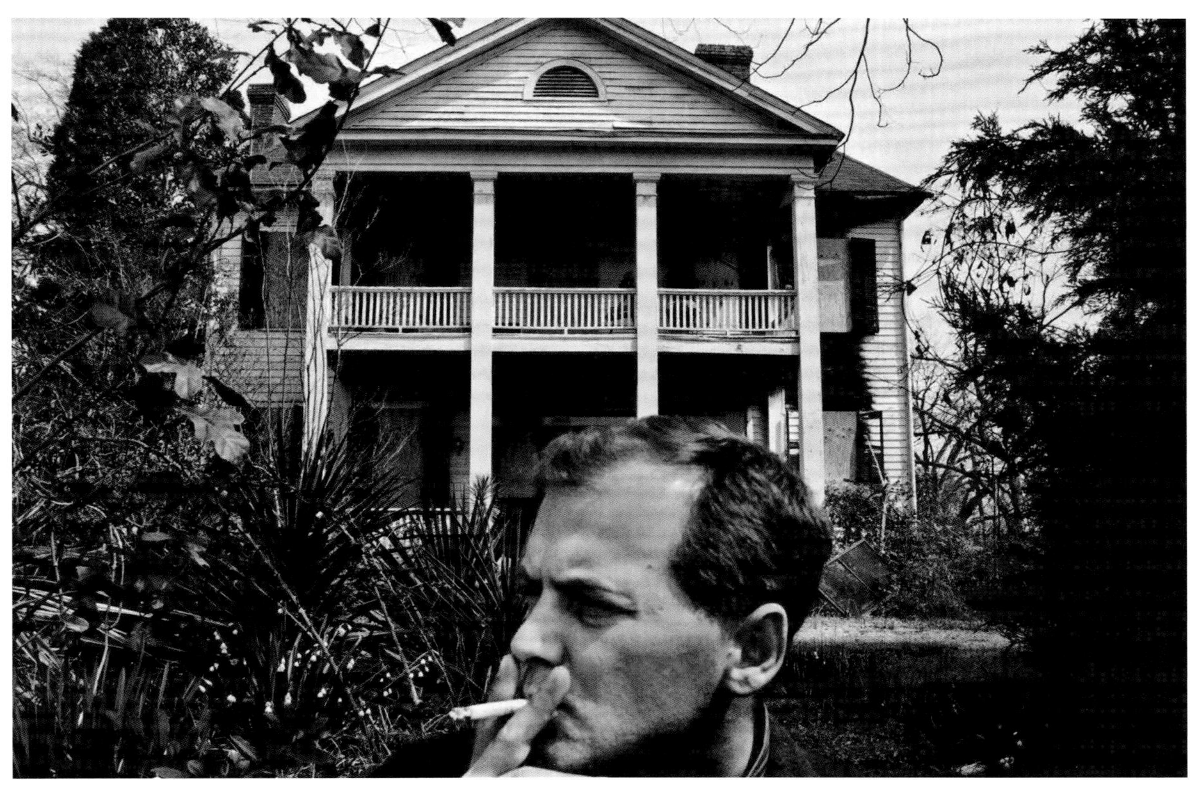

PLATE 98

Eli Reed, *Rhett Anders, Eau Claire Community Council president and real estate agent in front of a historic property, Eau Claire—North Columbia, South Carolina*, 1999

THIS PHOTO OF A YOUNG GIRL, MACY, with her stepfather on the front porch swing, was taken in Kingston, Tennessee—a small town west of Knoxville. I believe the year was 2012.

As I was driving home along Highway 70, I saw her walking through an overgrown, roadside lot. A tabby cat was following her. They were both backlit by the setting sun. She stood out in her well-worn and cherished green Care Bears T-shirt amongst all the wheat-colored brush. How wonderful, I thought. I remember things such as this when I was about her age: similar clothing, free-range nature, pets that tagged along, bare feet. I pulled over, struck up a conversation, and asked to photograph her. She invited me back to her house, so I could introduce myself to her parents. I spent a couple hours talking, exploring, and photographing.

This particular image in the collection says a lot about the relationship between the two of them. She's comfortable with him. He's protective of her. They're regarding me with some skepticism, yet I'm invited onto their small front porch. I like the dichotomy their guardedness and generosity creates.

Macy recently contacted me through social media. She's a mother now, married, and still living in Kingston.

— Tamara Reynolds

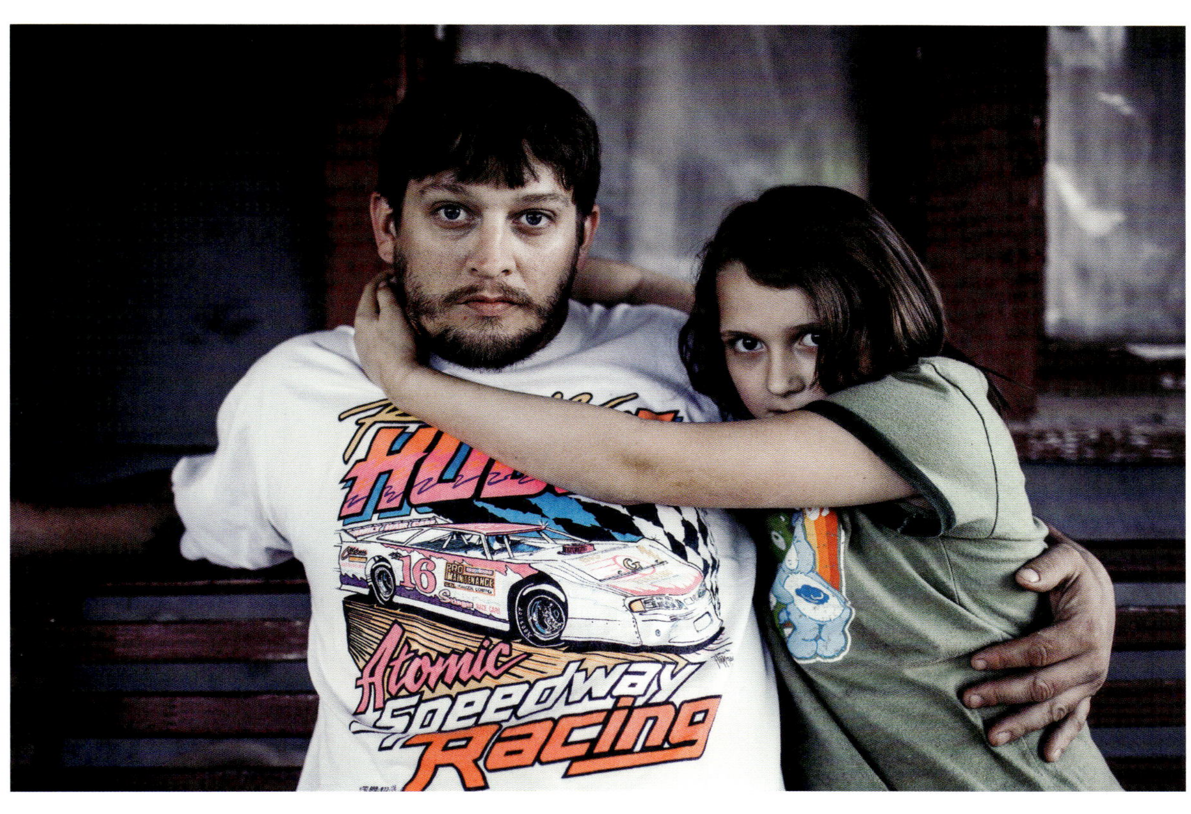

PLATE 99
Tamara Reynolds, *Untitled (Kingston, TN, Macy with Stepfather)*, 2012

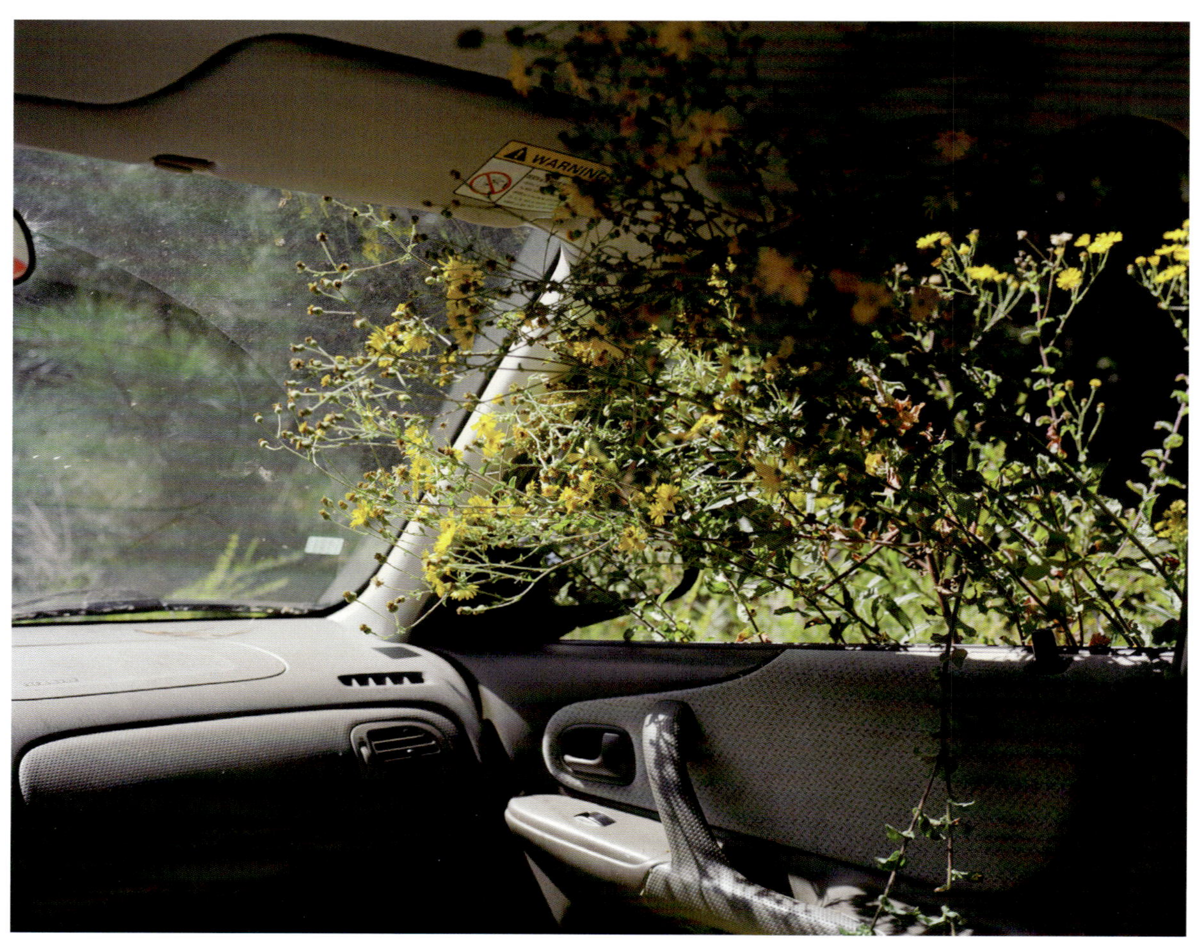

PLATE 100
Georgia Rhodes, *Roadtrip*, 2014

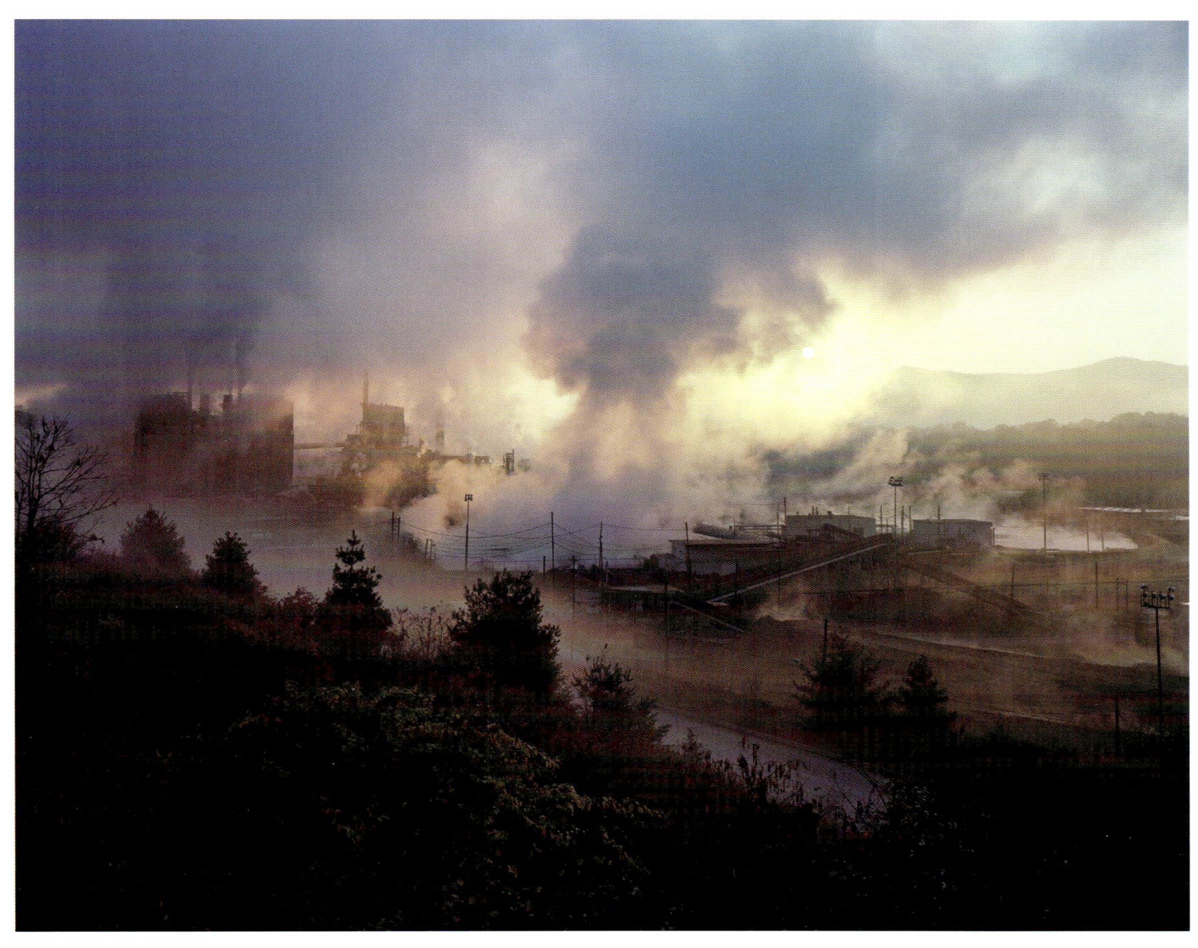

Jeff Rich, *Blue Ridge Paper Mill, The Pigeon River, Canton, North Carolina*, 2008

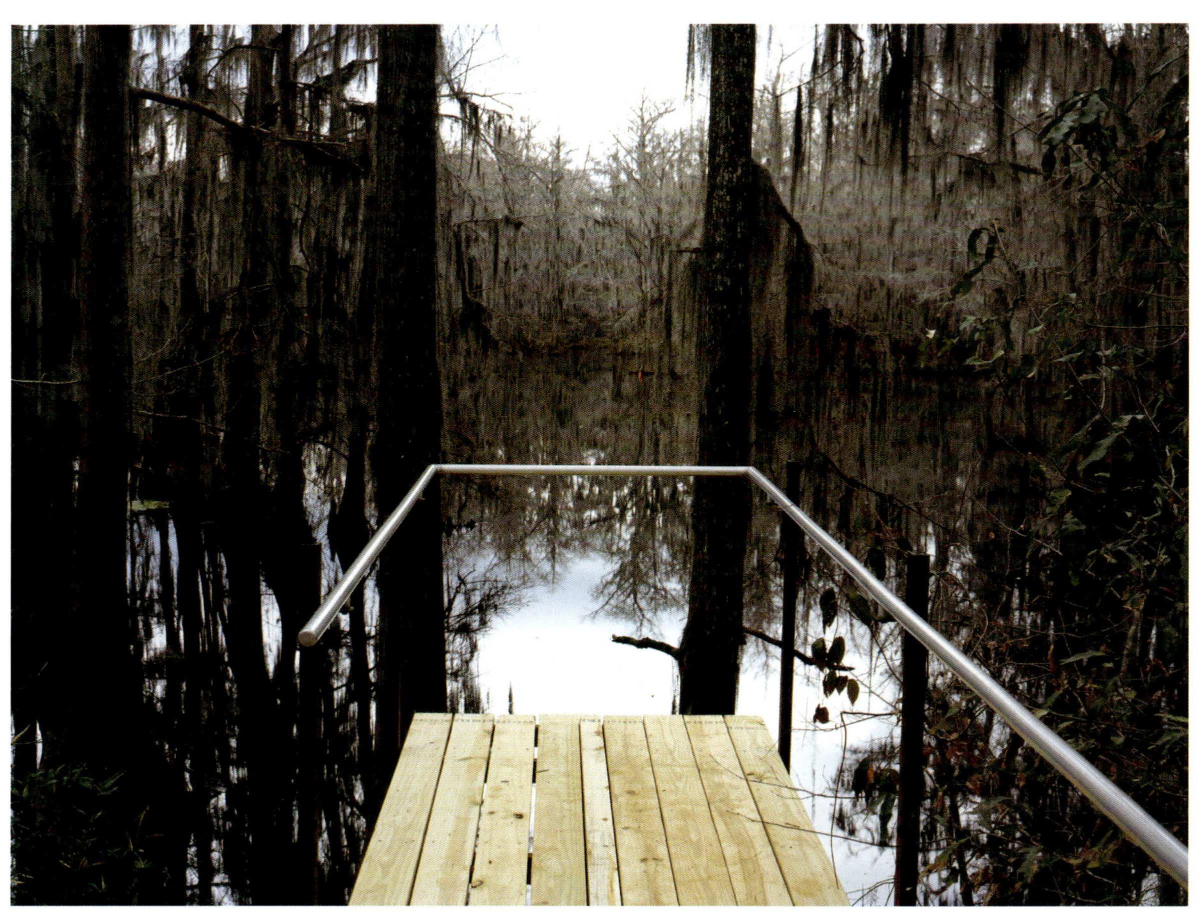

PLATE 102
RaMell Ross, *Interface*, 2012

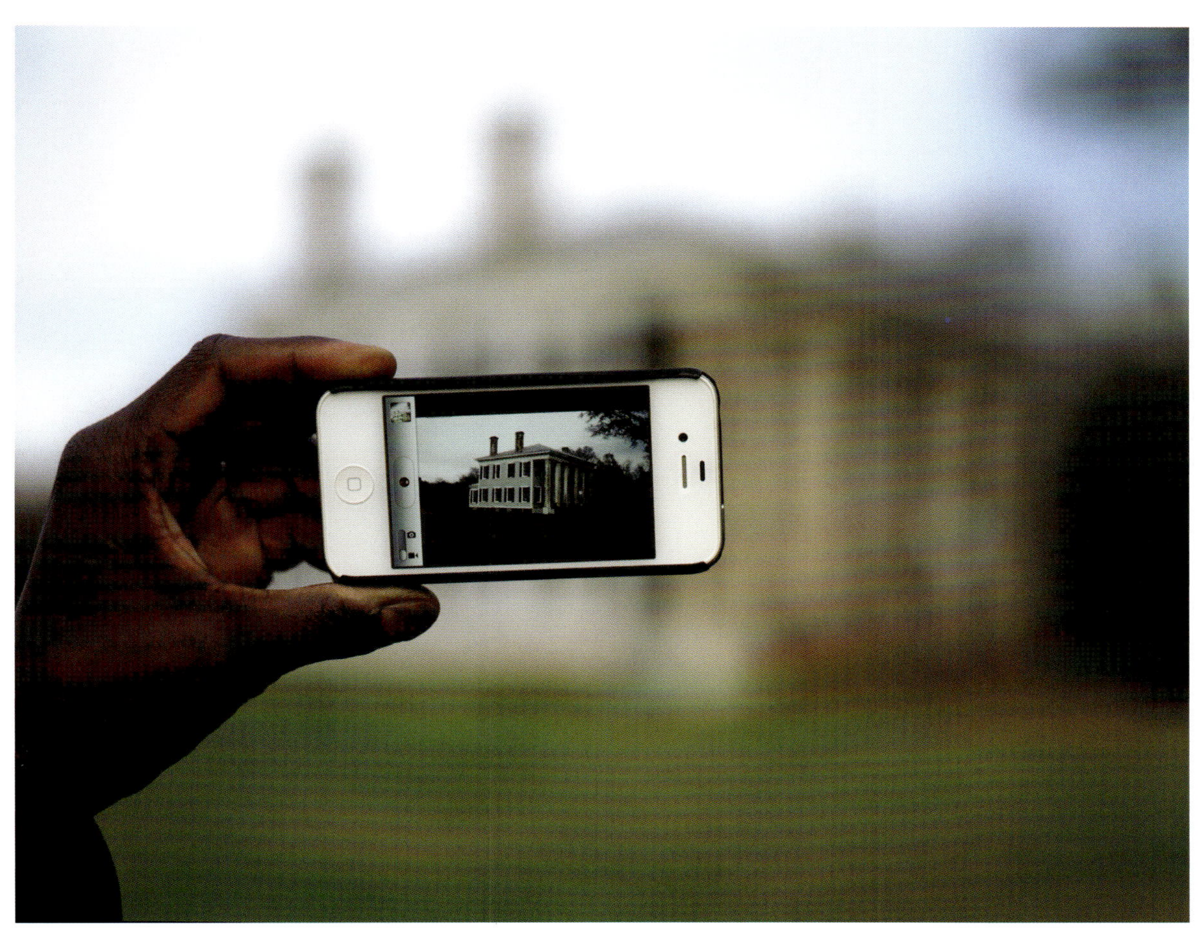

PLATE 103
RaMell Ross, *iHome*, 2012

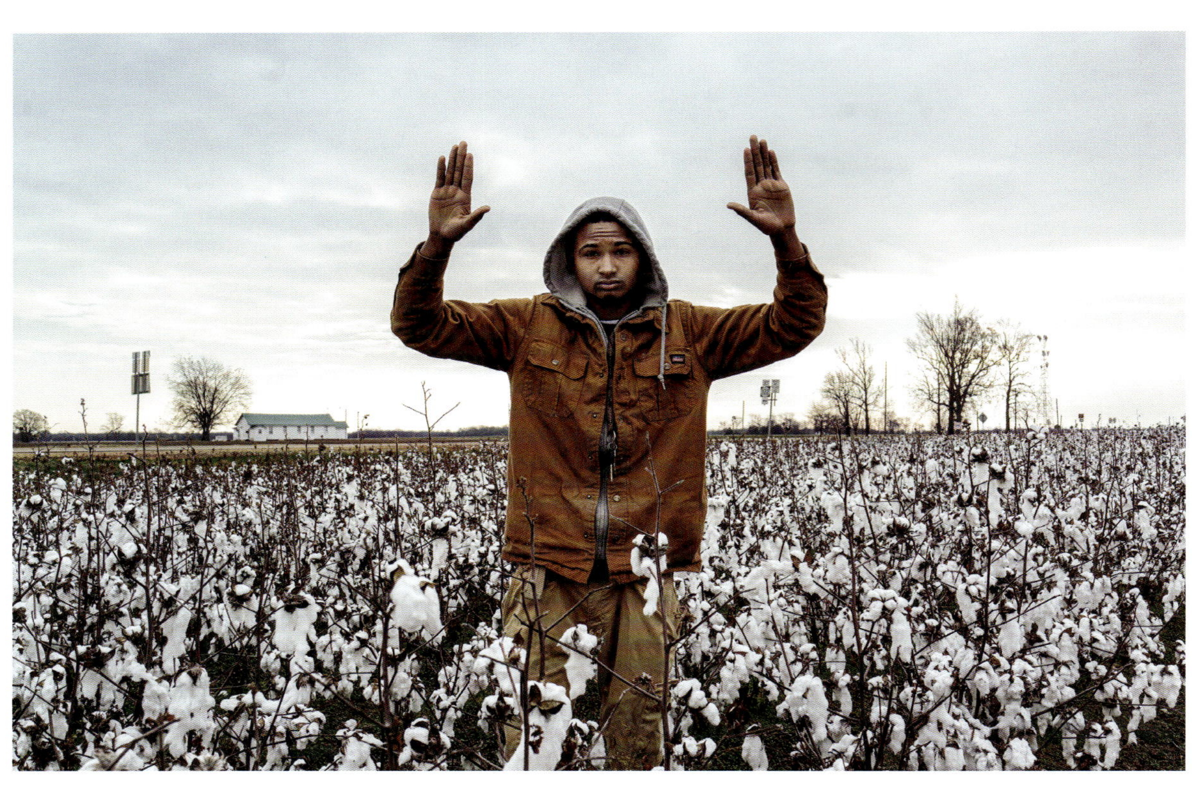

PLATE 104
Ruddy Roye, *Shack Up Inn*, 2014

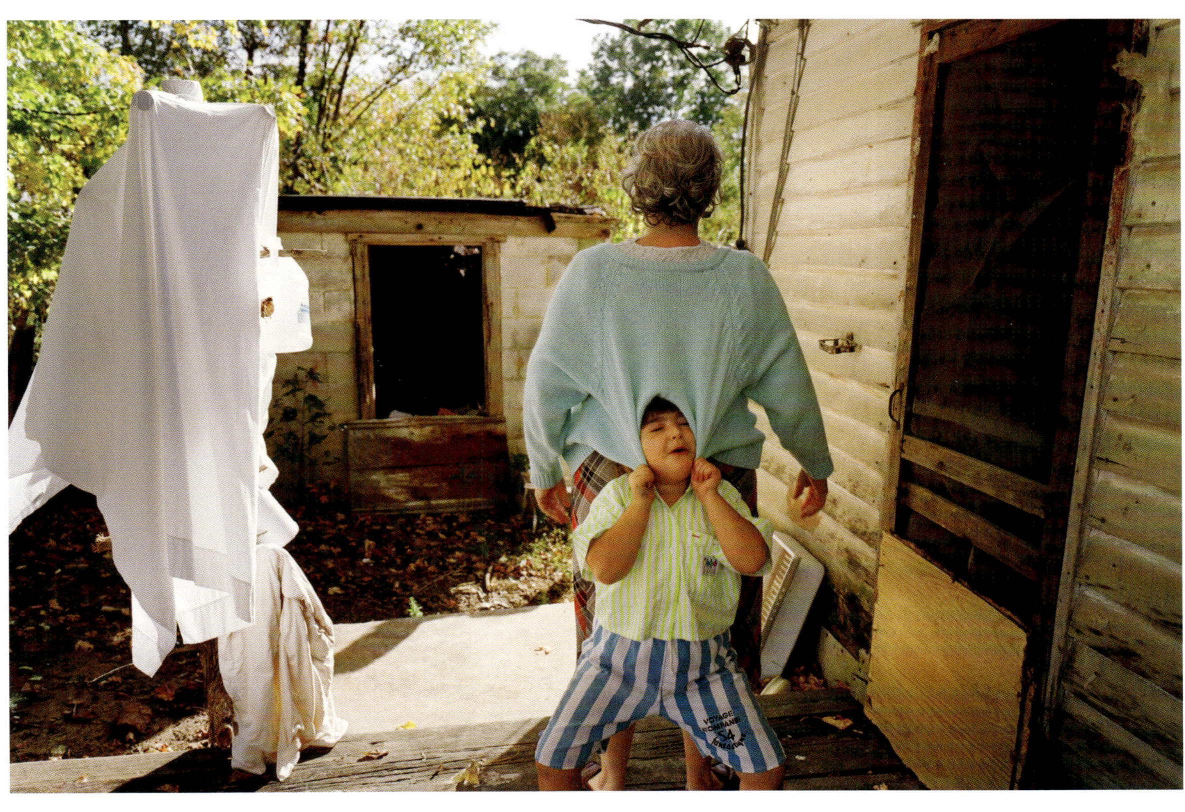

PLATE 105
Sheron Rupp, *Lucille and LaTosha, Moss, Tennessee*, 1990

WE FIRST MET ONE AFTERNOON IN 1988 IN SELMA at the
gallery of my uncle, the other Jerry Siegel. Mary Ward Brown was an
award-winning writer of short stories. She asked me if I would shoot a
new author's portrait for her, which I was thrilled to do. We became great
friends. We would get together and talk about life, art, music, and whatever was going on in our lives. She was my best friend and she loved to ride
around with me as I shot photos in the area. On most days we would go to
the handful of local options for lunch. On this particular day, she said, "Let's
go over to J&R's." It was my first time there. She said, "They have the best
burgers and barbecue and great soft-serve ice cream." It sounded perfect to
me. We drove over to Highway 5 and pulled up to the front of the small,
fast-food burger joint next to the Liberty gas station and went in to eat.
Everyone knew Mary and wanted to say hello.

As they were all catching up on the local buzz, I turned around and saw all
the deer heads mounted above the bright red booths. As always, I had my
camera with me. I grabbed my Fuji panorama camera and framed the image
of the booths and deer heads. Even with a high ISO film, I knew the exposure would require a slow shutter speed. I took a deep breath to settle myself
and made a few exposures. I have pretty quiet hands and was able to hold
still long enough to get a good sharp negative. We went back multiple times
for lunch and took the owner a print. Unfortunately, J&R's went through
several changes and last time I went by, it was closed down. The image of
J&R's deer heads has always been a favorite image of mine not just because
of the image itself, but as a reminder of the great day with Mary.

— Jerry Siegel

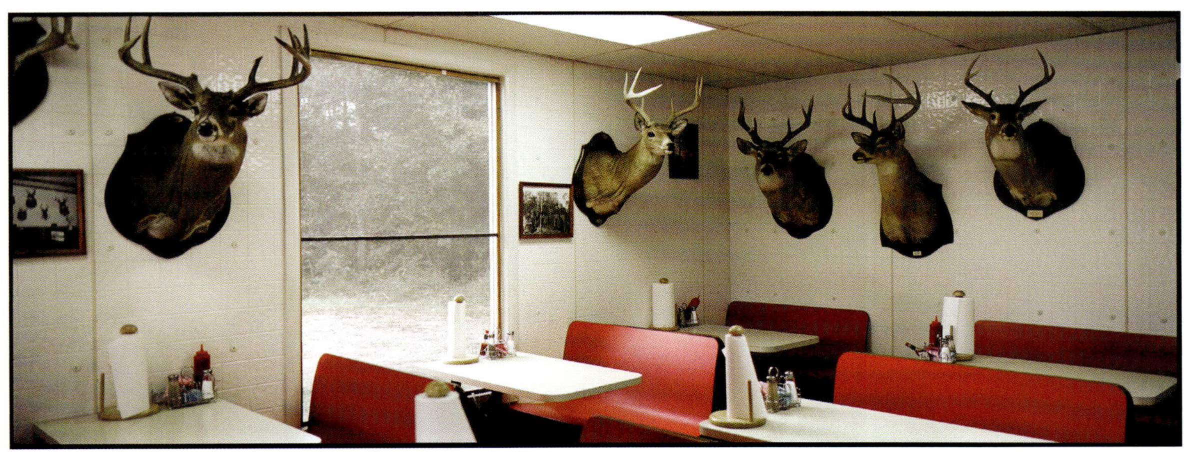

PLATE 106
Jerry Siegel, *J&R's, Deer Heads, Perry County, AL*, 2002

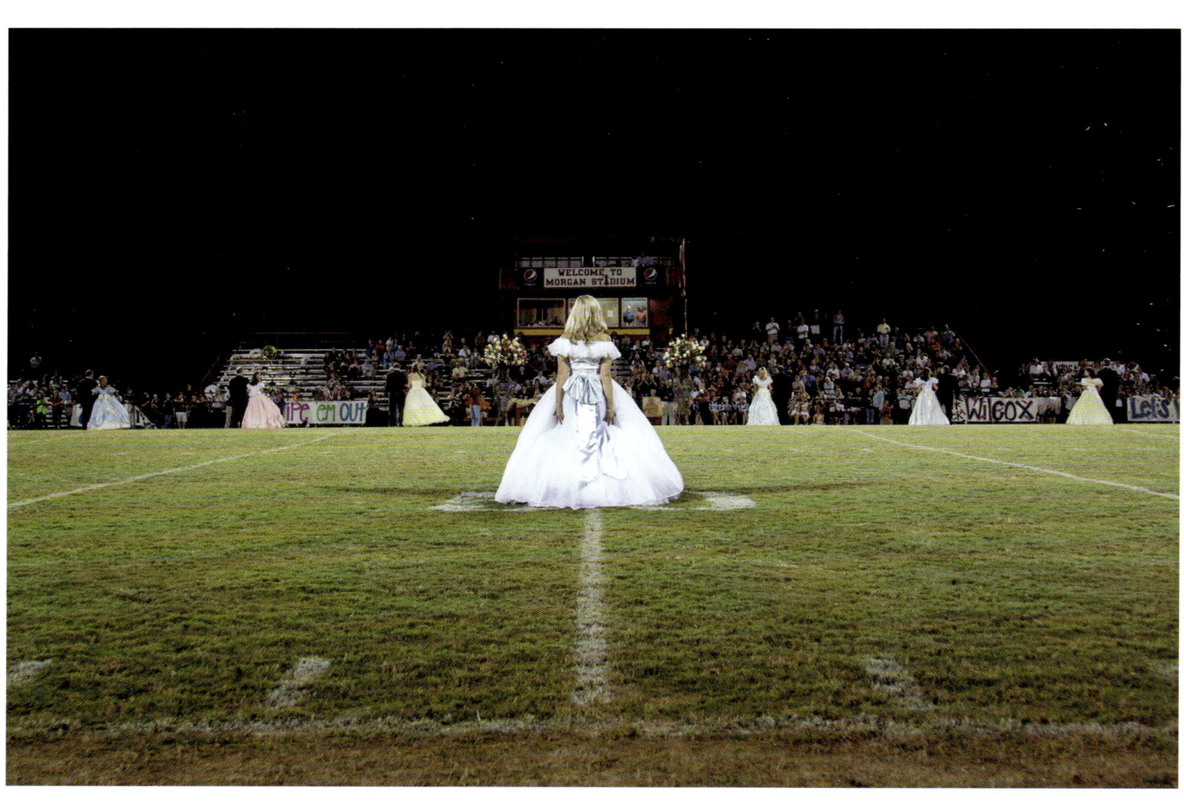

PLATE 107
Jerry Siegel, *Homecoming, Selma, AL*, 2009

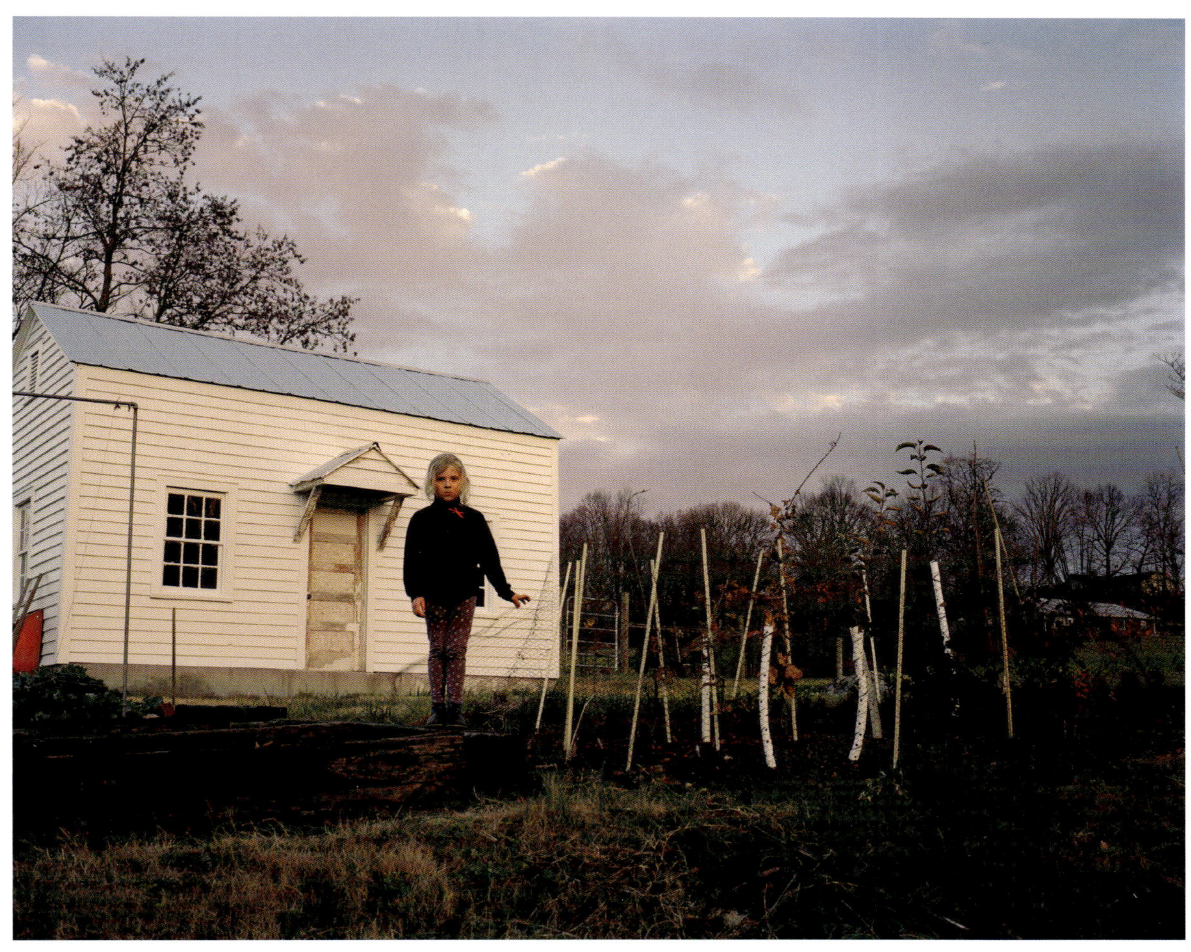

PLATE 108
Mike Smith, *Piney Flats, TN*, 1999

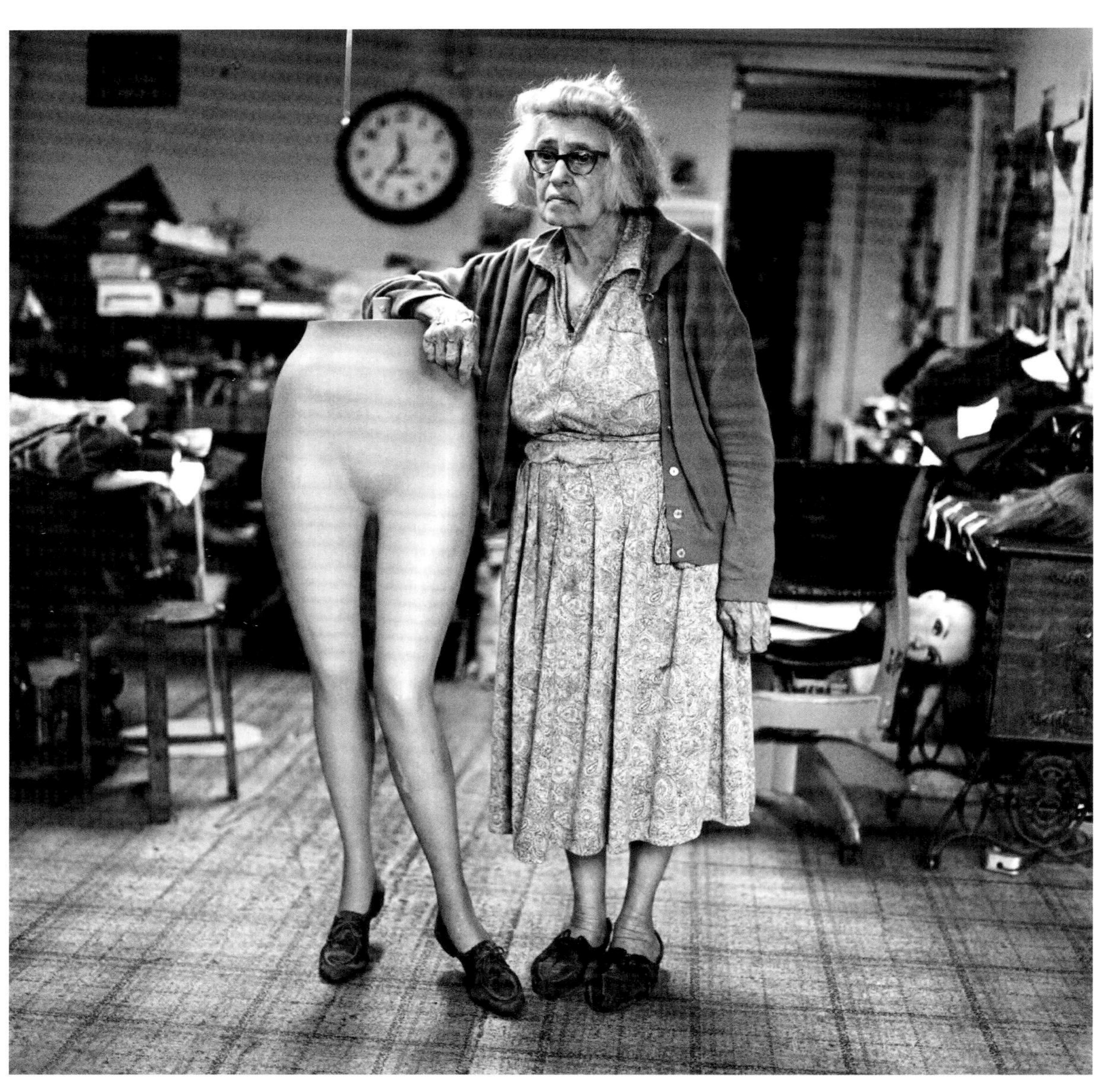

PLATE 109
Rosalind Fox Solomon, *Mrs. Ova Heggi and Her Mannequin, Chattanooga, TN*, 1974

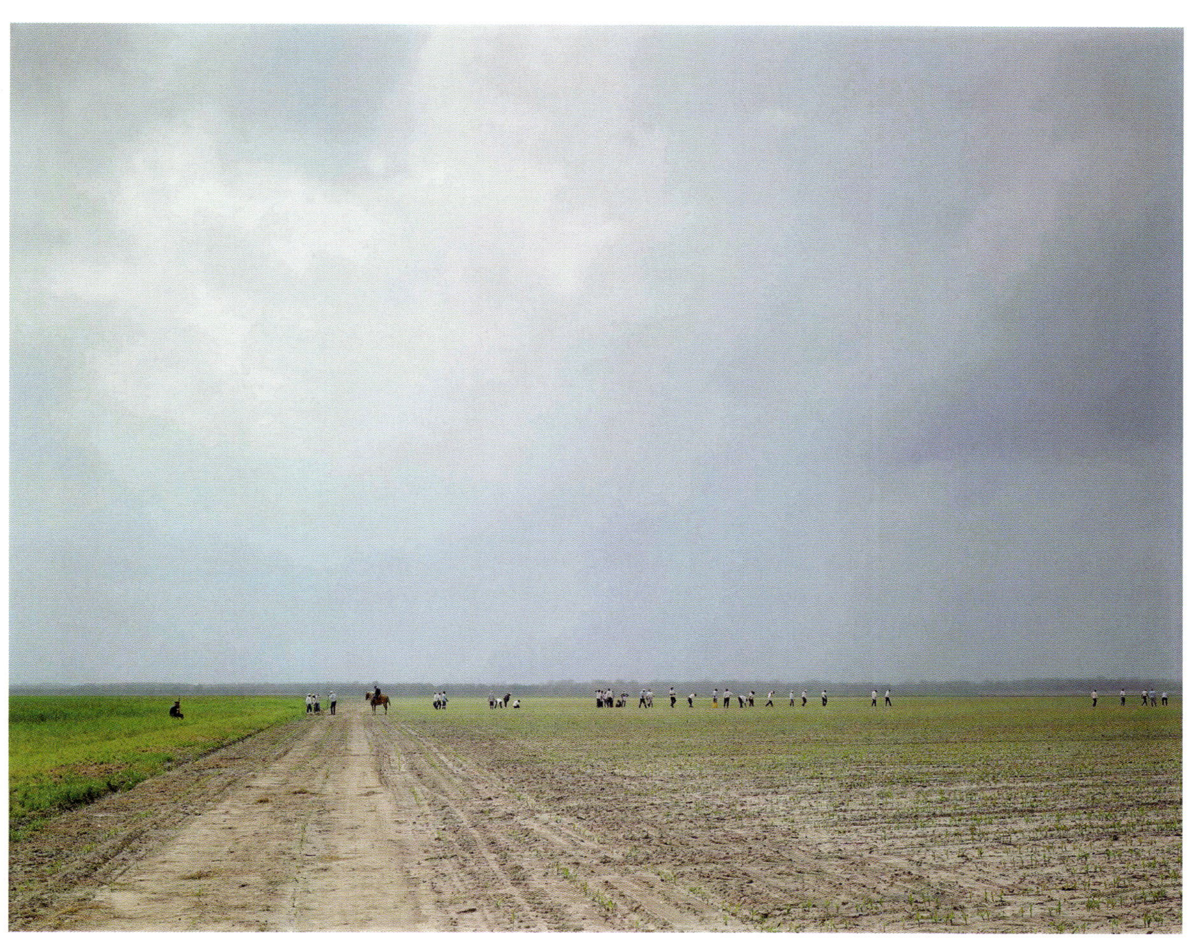

PLATE 110
Alec Soth, *The Farm, Angola State Prison, Angola, Louisiana*, 2002

AVE MARIA WAS BUILT IN THE WETLANDS of south Florida, east of Naples and south of Immokalee. The photographs in this series, which I created using a large-format camera, explore the changing landscape and utopian vision of this Catholic-inspired master-planned community.

The planners who laid out Ave Maria designed the entire community around a towering oratory. Early one spring morning, I was driving around looking for a way to see the oratory in the background beyond the neighborhood's homes. The houses in the foreground were among the first built in the new community, but Ave Maria struggled through the 2008 recession and continued to build very slowly. As I walked the neighborhood that day, I noticed a basketball in the center of the small alleyway that runs behind these houses. The details of the photograph—the palm trees, the architecture, the color of the light—became symbols that related Ave Maria to other newly built communities, especially those in the fast-growing regions of rural and suburban Florida. During the five years I photographed there, I continually searched for a way to capture the process of creating a community that was both physically and philosophically isolated from so much of the population. The basketball that had been left abandoned all night became a way to represent the quiet, safety, and isolation that I experienced throughout my time in Ave Maria.

— Rylan Steele

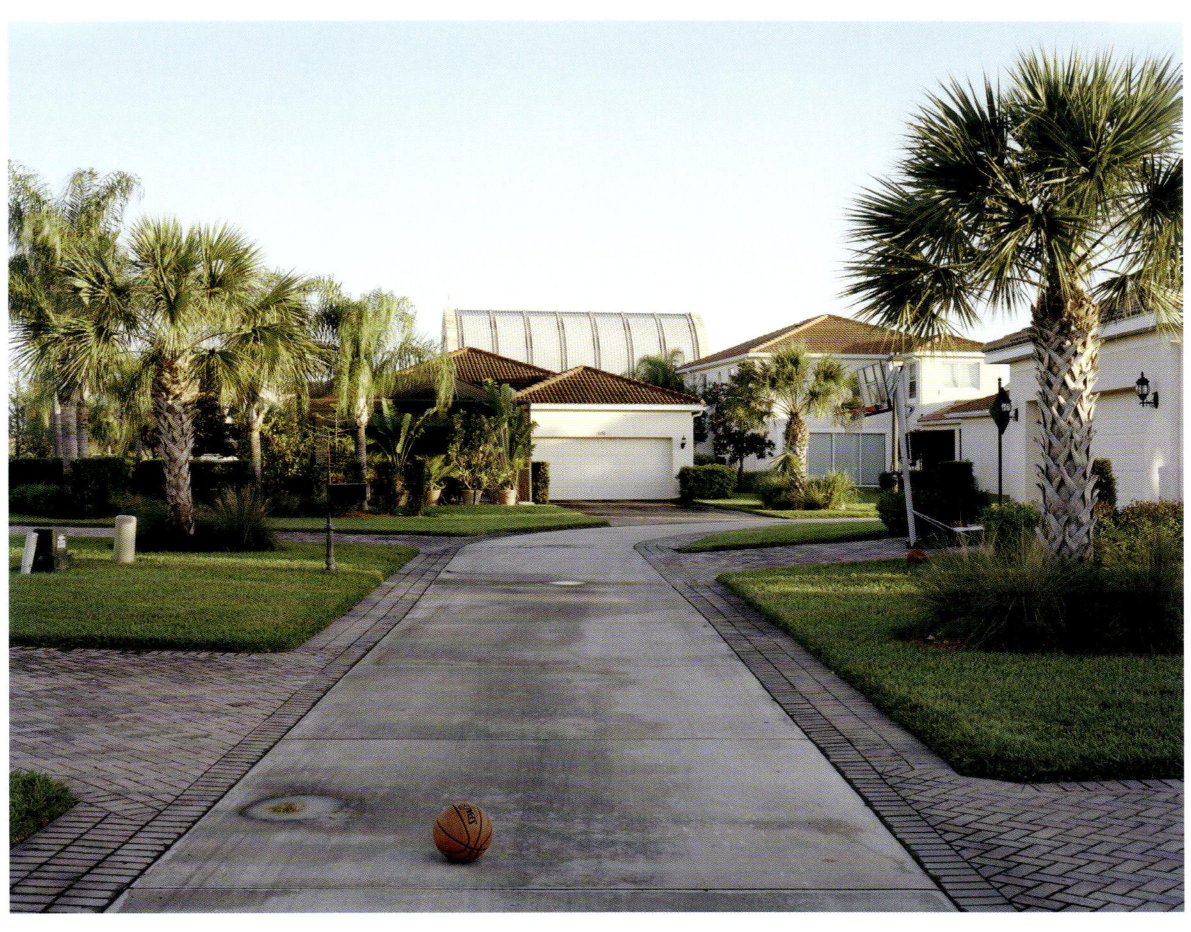

PLATE 111
Rylan Steele, *Alcott Avenue, Ave Maria, Florida*, 2016

THIS PHOTOGRAPH APPEARED ON THE COVER of *Greater Atlanta* (2010), which was the final book in a trilogy on the American South. *Greater Atlanta* takes a look at our contemporary civilization and in some ways questions notions of progress. In the book, there are several images of roads and gas stations, big box stores and fast-food chains—all features of our car-centric society. Some images capture rampant development and deforestation.

I made this photograph in March; the spring night must have been warm. I find that people are more open to being photographed when the temperature starts to rise, and when sweaters and coats can be shed. In winter, people tend to be more guarded. The bright fluorescent lighting from the canopy over the gas pumps was bright enough so that I could hold my bulky camera steady to make a sharp picture. The young woman pumping gas may have been wearing some kind of uniform. Perhaps she had just gotten off her shift or was on her way to work.

The way her head is turning over her shoulder, her slightly parted lips, and the oval shape of her face reminds me of the famous painting by Vermeer, *Girl with a Pearl Earring*. The circumstances are very different of course. Instead of a seventeenth-century Dutch interior, we are at a gas station in Georgia; instead of an exotic turban, this young woman has long shiny ribbons of curled hair. Both women look confidently and comfortably toward the viewer; the whites of their eyes stand out and also the light in their eyes.

— Mark Steinmetz

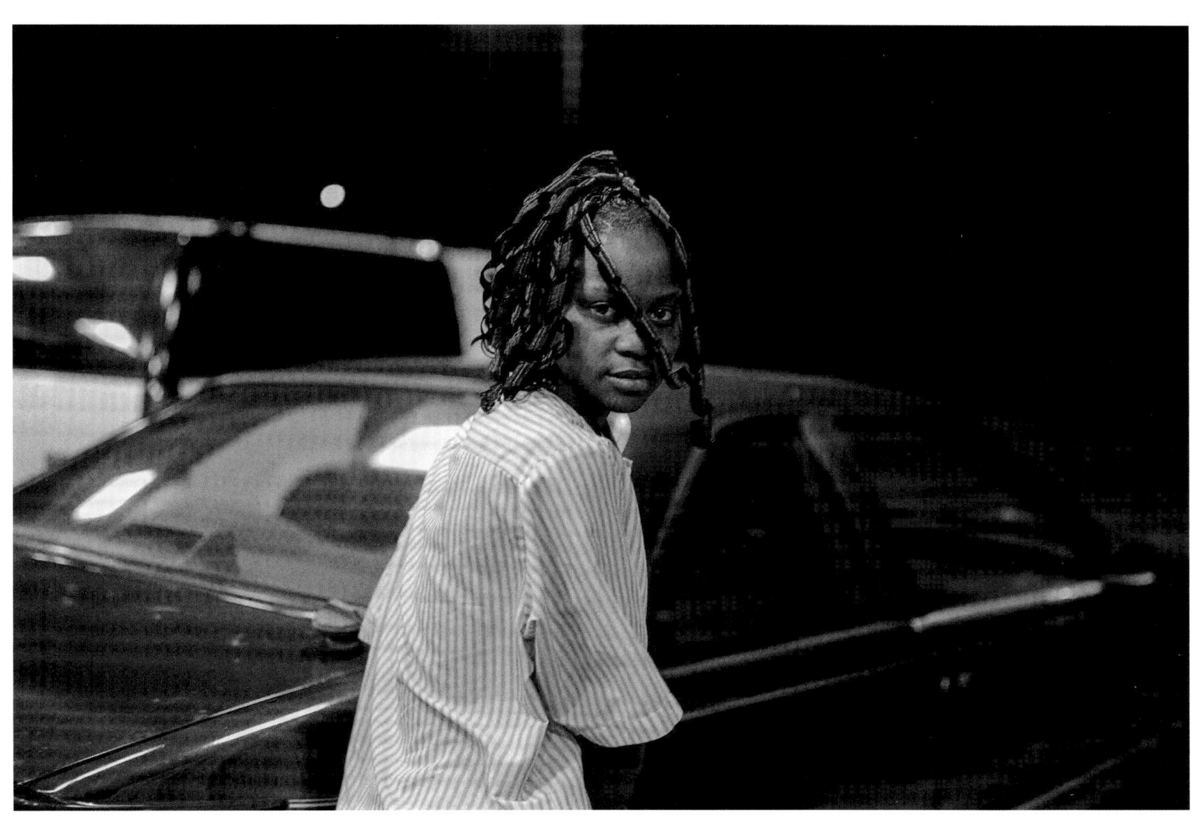

PLATE 112
Mark Steinmetz, *Off Route 316, Barrow County, Georgia*, 1994

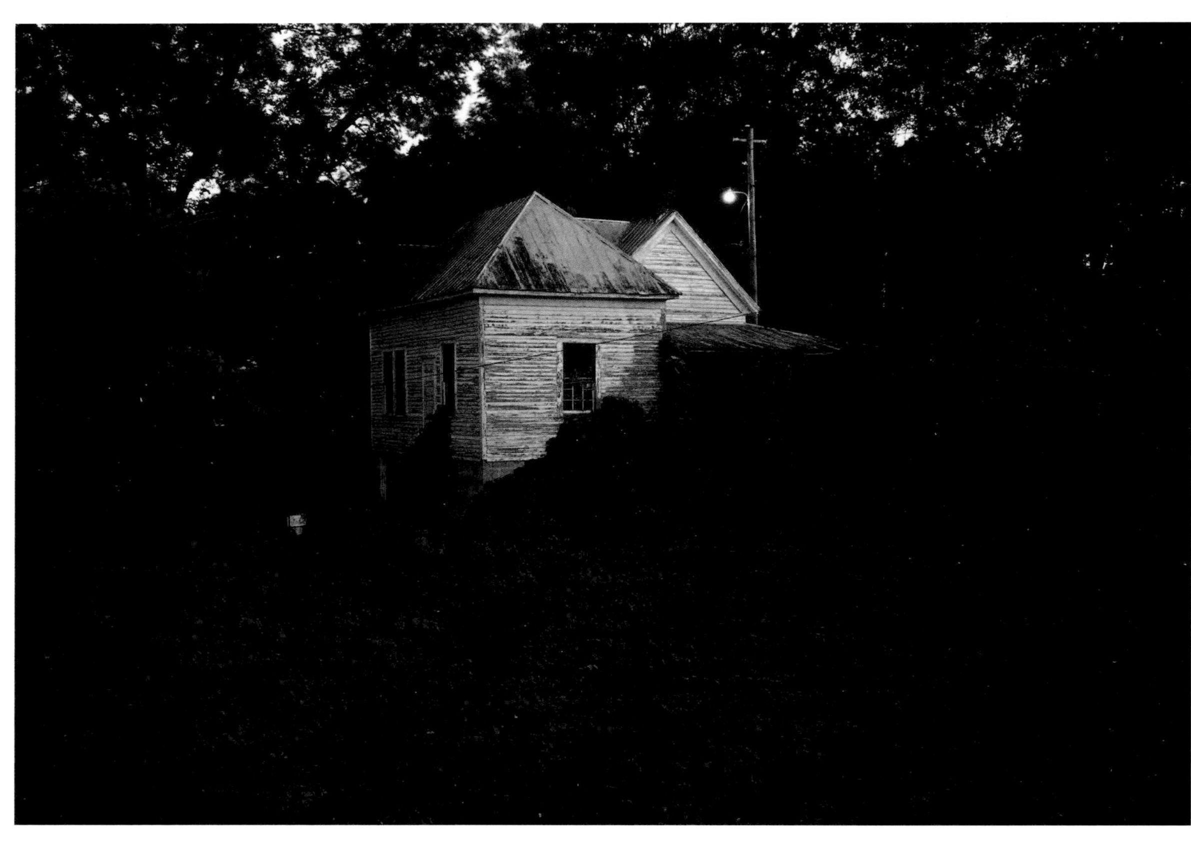

PLATE 113
Mark Steinmetz, *Athens, Georgia*, 1995

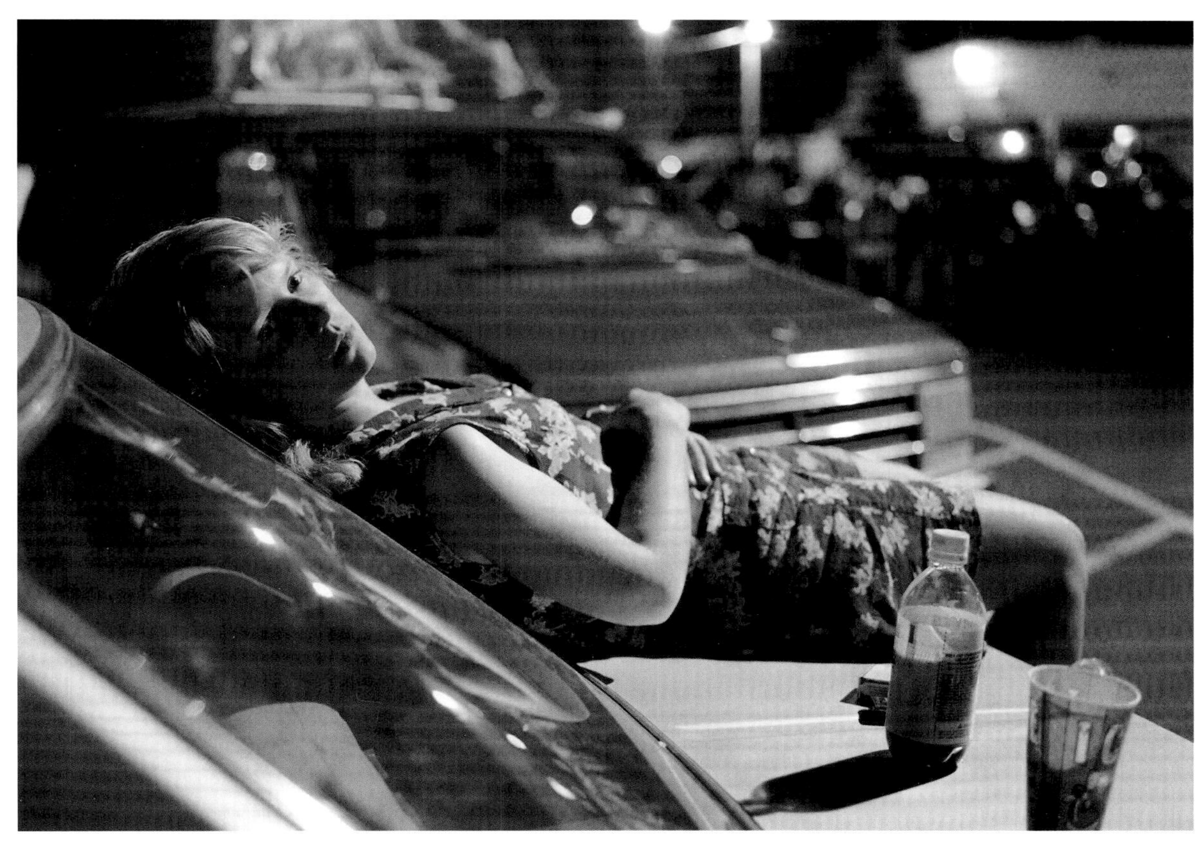

PLATE 114
Mark Steinmetz, *Athens, GA*, 1996

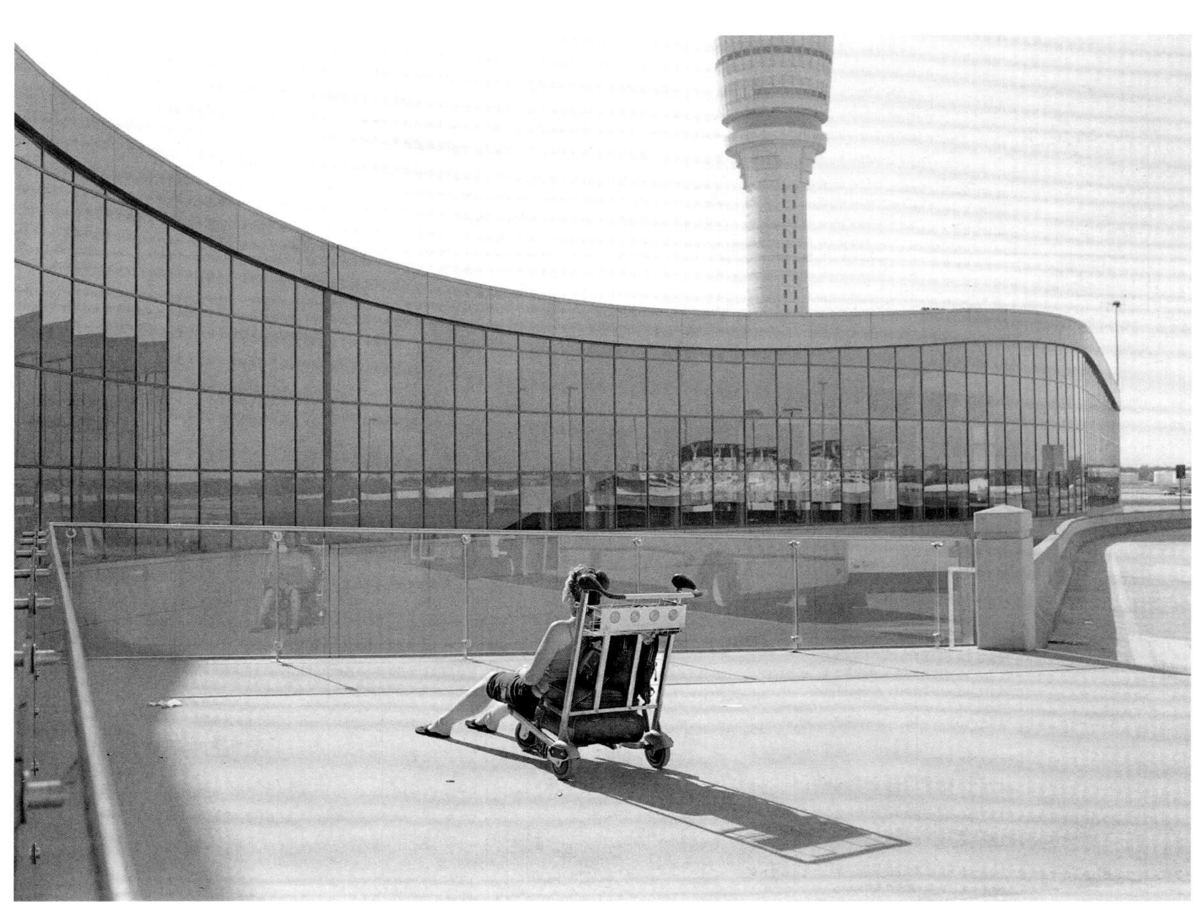

PLATE 115
Mark Steinmetz, *Atlanta Airport*, 2016

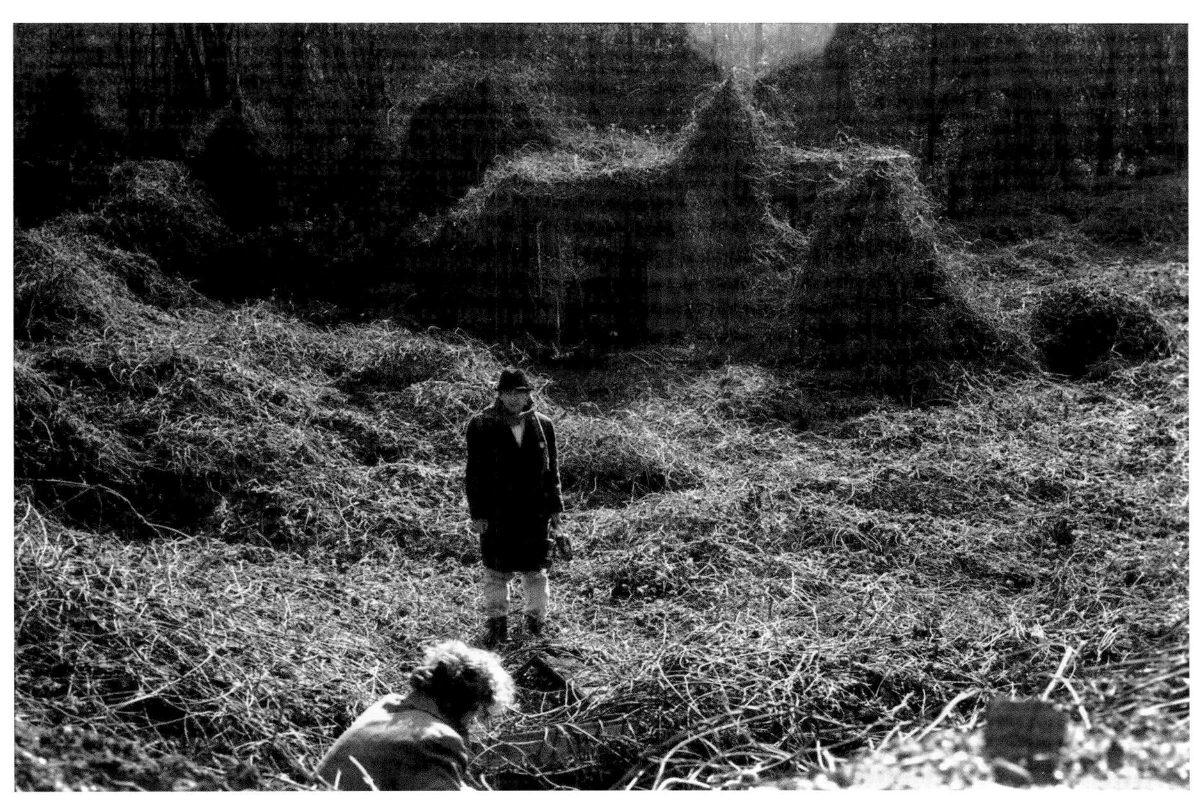

PLATE 116
Michael Stipe, *Lynda, Jeremy, kudzu field, Athens*, 1982

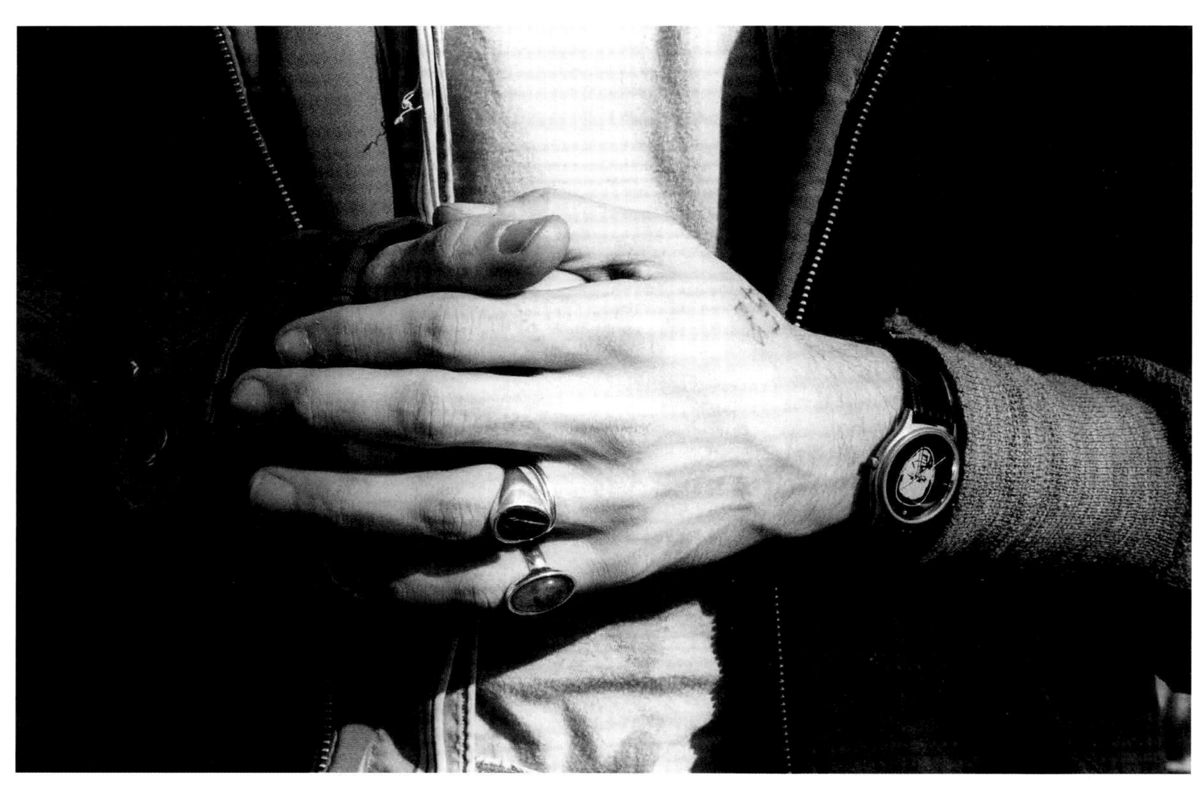

PLATE 117
Michael Stipe, *Kurt Cobain's hands, Grady Avenue, Athens*, 1993

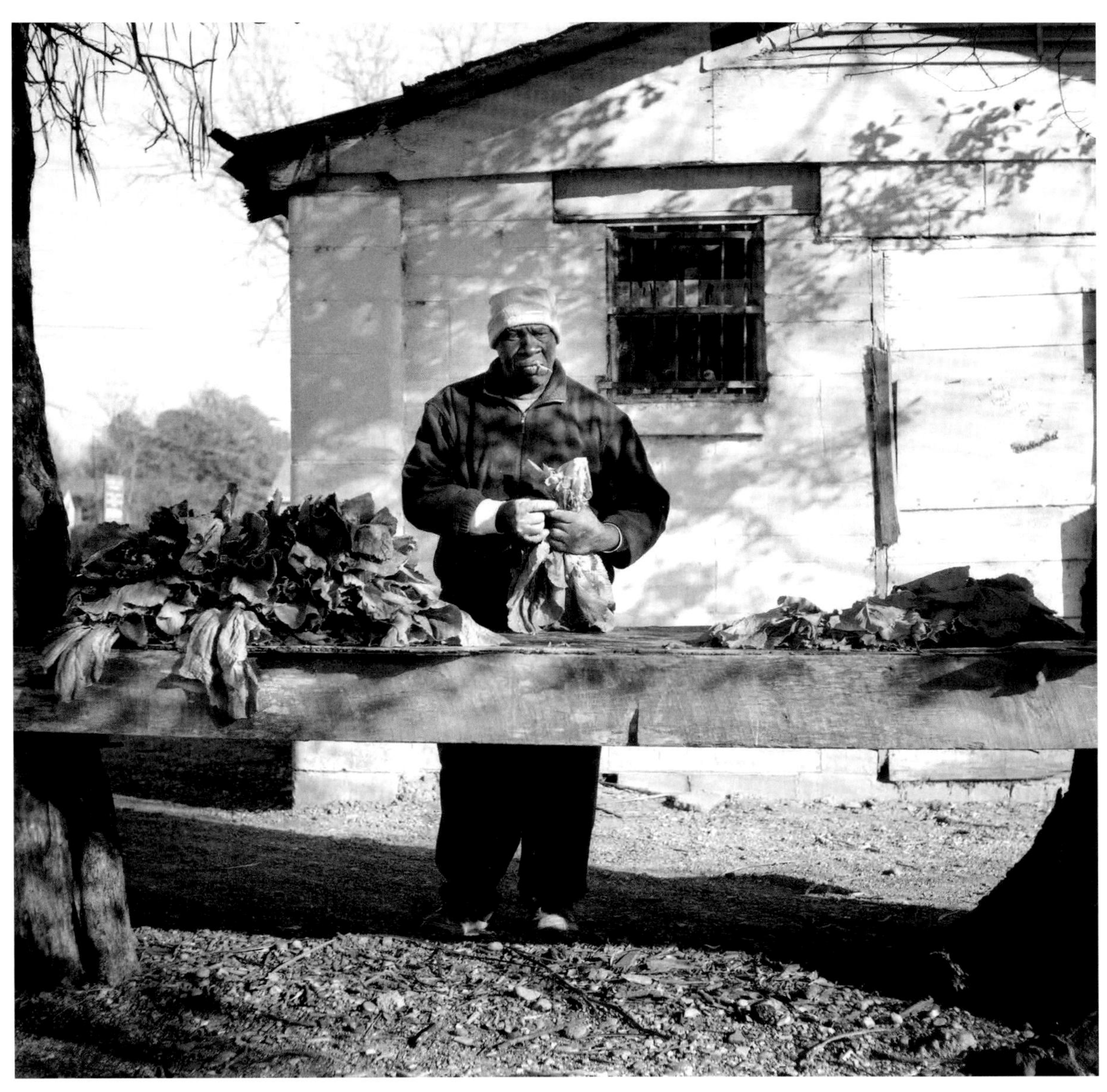

PLATE 118
Brandon Thibodeaux, *Harry Hope; Mound Bayou, MS*, 2010

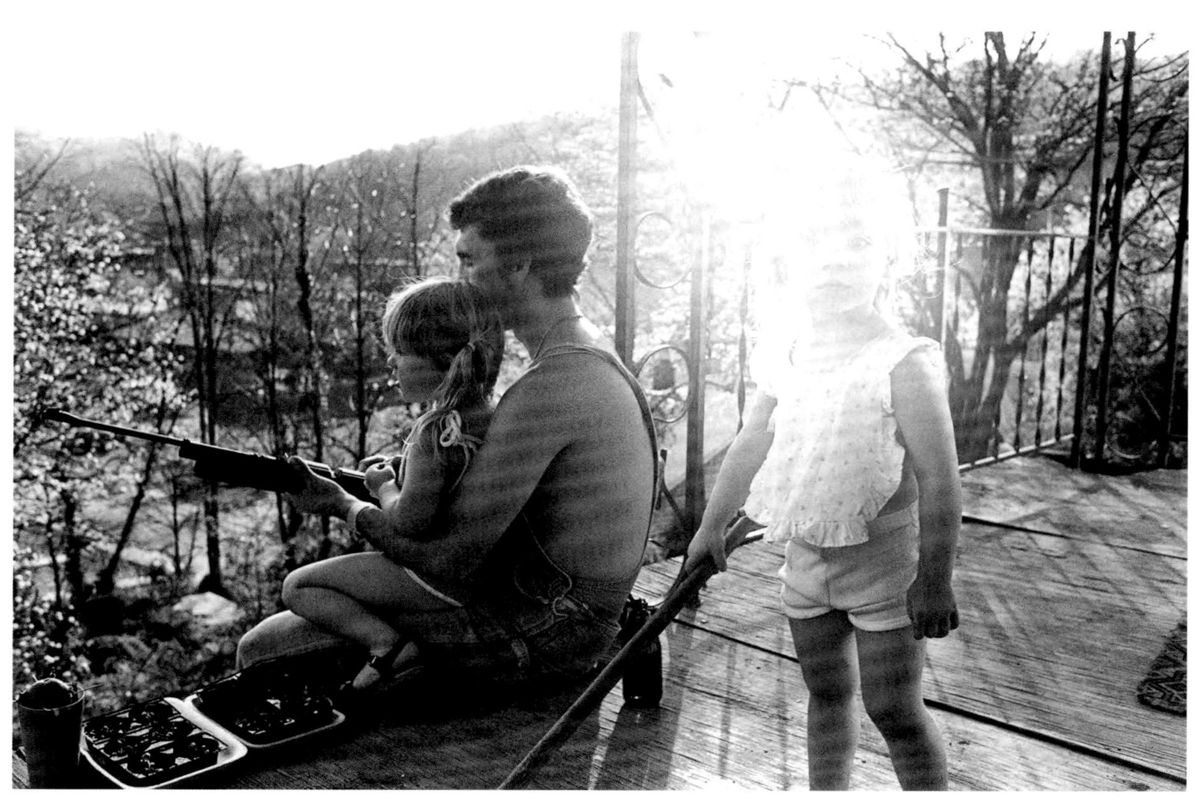

PLATE 119

Bertien van Manen, *Amanda, Bobby, Magi on porch, Cumberland, KY*, 1987

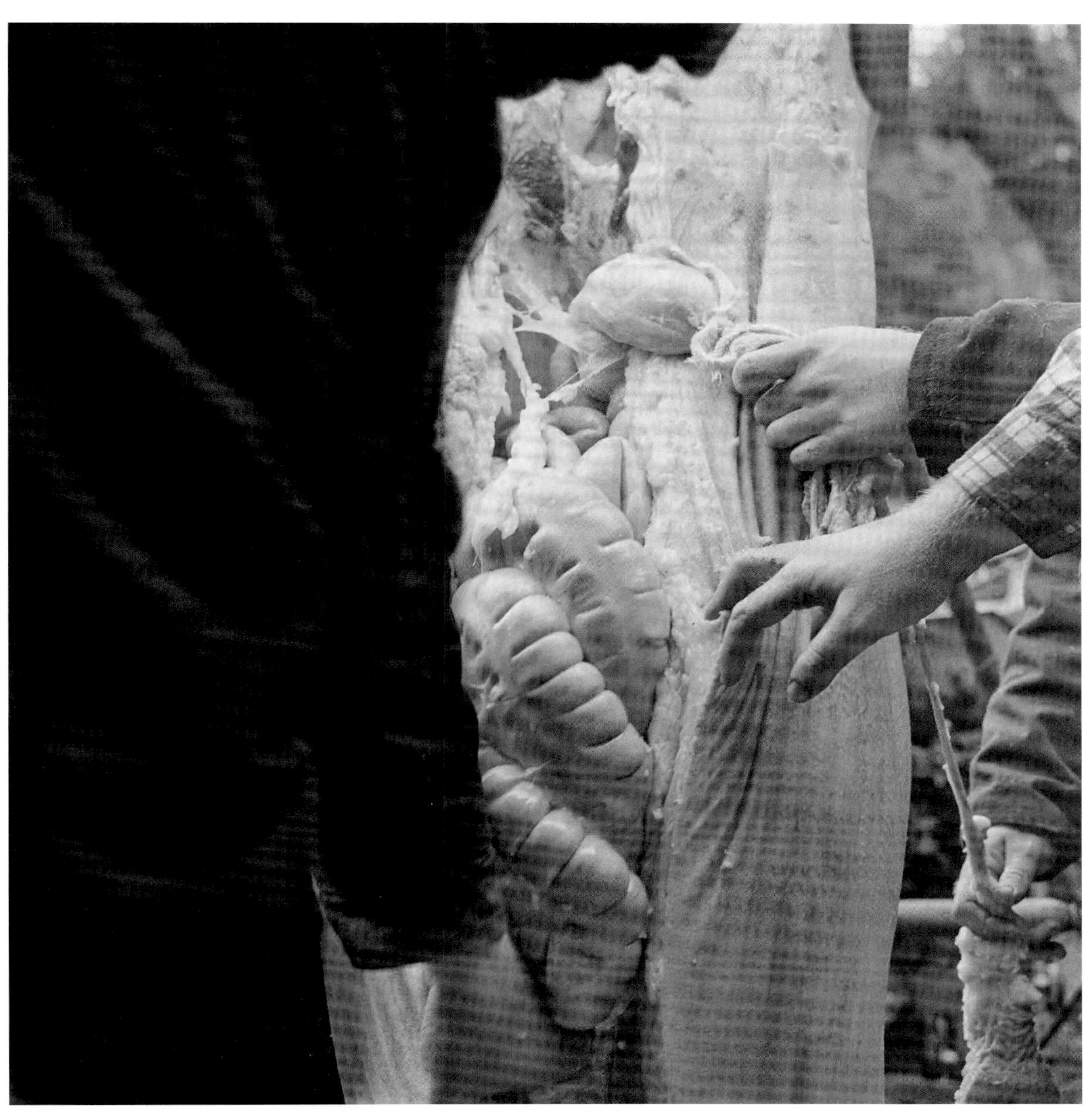

PLATE 120
Jeff Whetstone, *Hog Kill, Oscaloosa, Kentucky*, 1994

BEGINNING IN 2004, I MOVED TO THE DEEP SOUTH for my
first teaching job, and I mention this because it's critical to the development of my work and also my intense focus on the land. Prior to moving
to Oxford, I hadn't been much farther south than Virginia and one of the
first things that struck me about the landscape here was the rural nature
of the South, which mimicked areas of the Northeast where I grew up. As
a photographer, I have always made work about the landscape, ever since I
started making art. And as my practice evolved, I've become more interested in the ways that the politics of place, memory, and identity are evident
in the landscapes that surround us.

The images in the Do Good Fund collection are part of an ongoing project
that investigates the ever-changing landscapes of the rural South. Images like *Kudzu Car* and *Sardis Lake* show the remnants and traces that
are left behind in the landscape. I'm fascinated by elements like these
because of what they reveal to us about the people who inhabit the region
and, in turn, how this affects our relationship to place. Images like *Dollar
Tree Store* show the shifting landscapes that are a result of global markets
infringing on rural life. All these images are also purposefully devoid of
human beings, but their presence is very much felt. It is my hope that, by
making these traces in the land more visible, we are able to see ourselves in
these constantly evolving landscapes.

— Brooke C. White

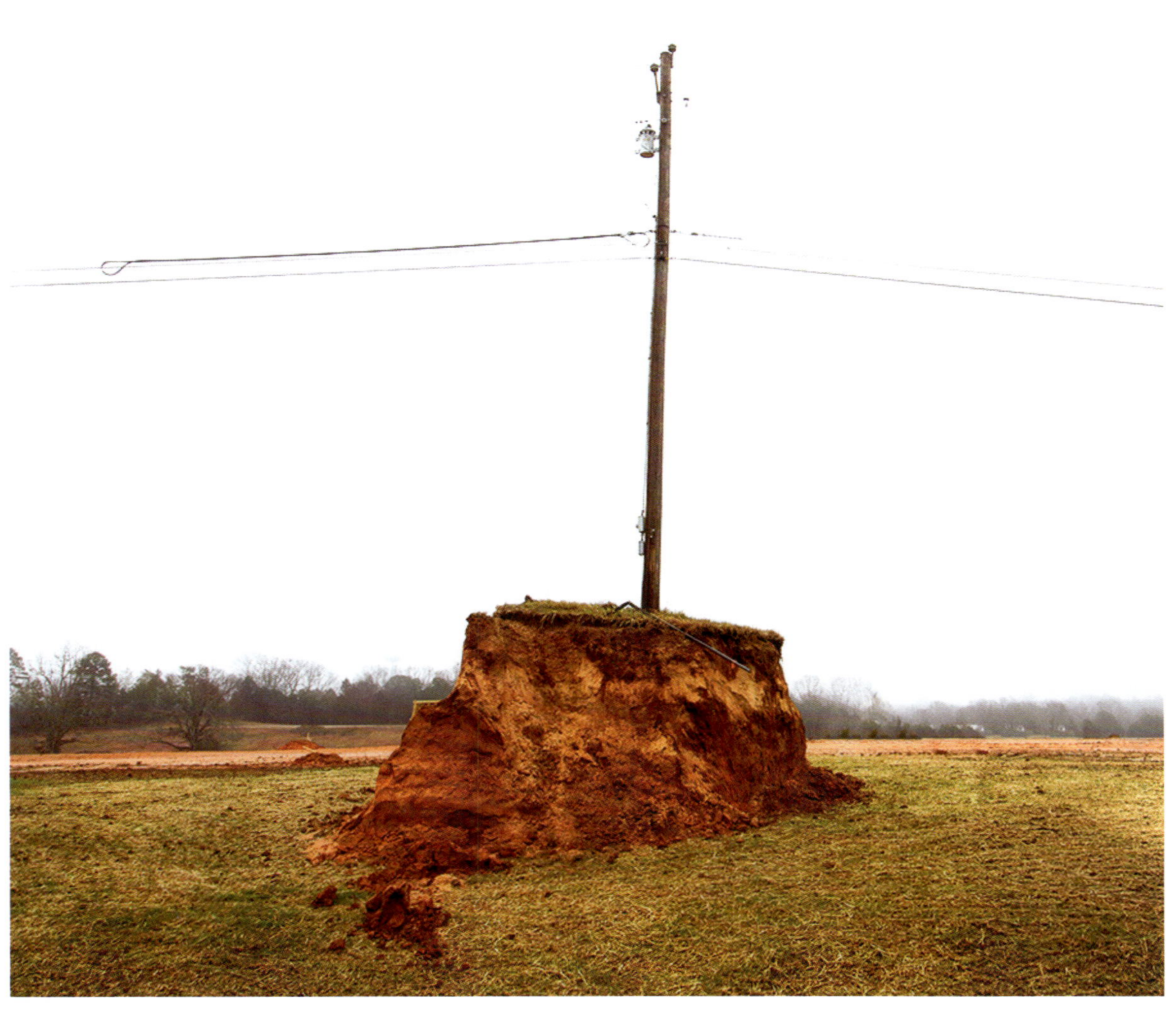

PLATE 121
Brooke C. White, *Dollar Tree Store, Abbeville, MS*, 2013

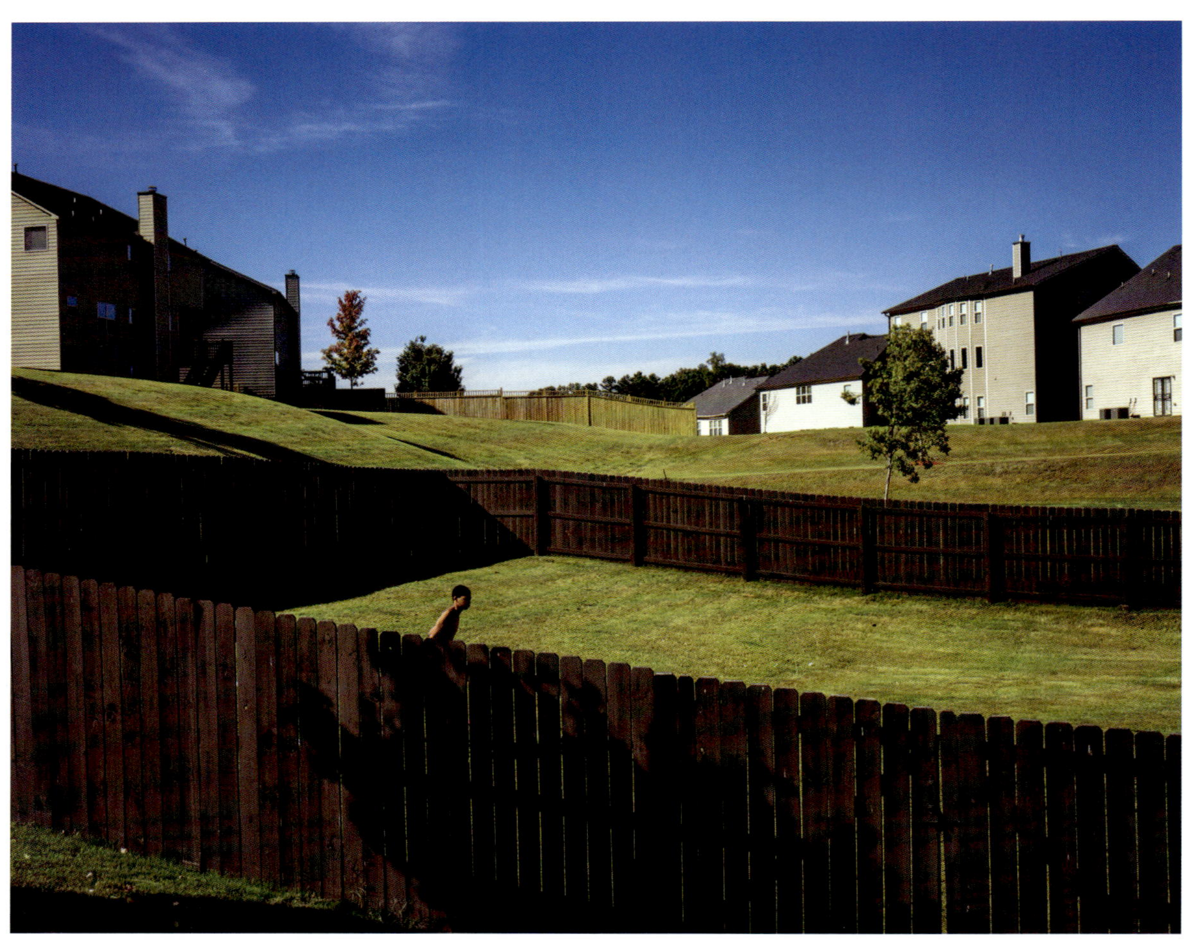

PLATE 122
Alex Christopher Williams, *Untitled*, 2016

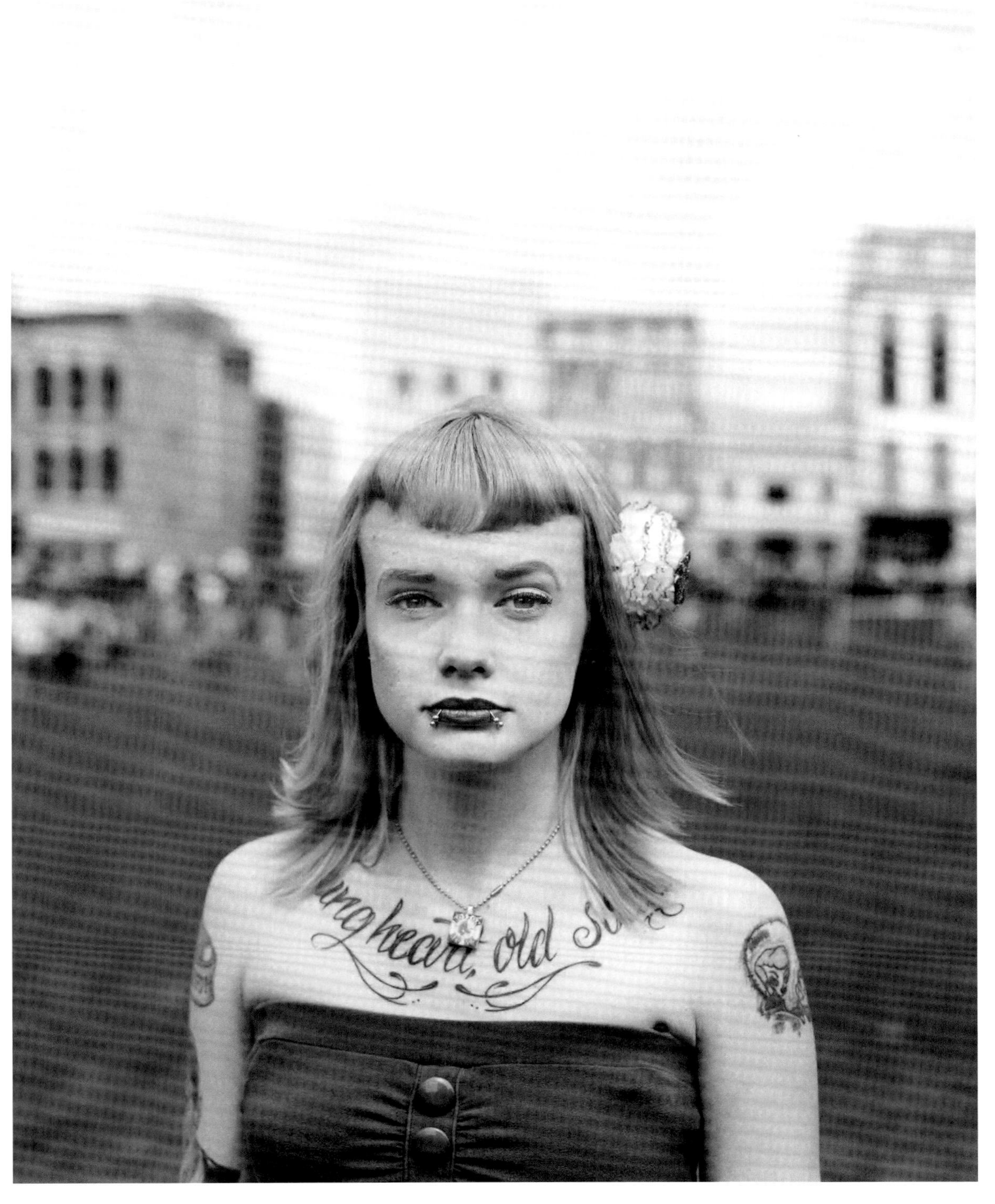

PLATE 123

Vanessa Winship, *Colleen, March 17th, 2012, Lexington, Kentucky, USA*, 2012

RHUBARB, COLLECTED LIKE BONES, stretches out in a long pink taffy pull, with plums, black and not golden.

Fruit has become a metaphor in my work, a lesson that returns season after season mimicking the loss of the land every winter and its growth in spring.

I photograph my oldest neighbor Margaret, whose hand and wedding ring are pictured here. She was the last person to see my brother alive.

My brother was paralyzed in a motorcycle accident and on his first visit home Margaret made him her homemade bread, buttered a slice, and took it up to him. As my mother and Margaret took a walk down the lane Russell finished the whole loaf and then shot himself.

She told me this story as I was under the dark cloth focusing my camera on her face during our first portrait sitting.

I would return again and again to make photographs, and eventually record her voice and stories on a small handheld audio recorder. When I press play, I can hear Margaret's voice telling me that she and my father would buy flowers together and plant them on the lane. She bought pink azaleas and he bought white, along with a camellia tree he planted for my mother.

My family has all passed, but the camellias and azaleas still return every year like a remembrance.

— Susan Worsham

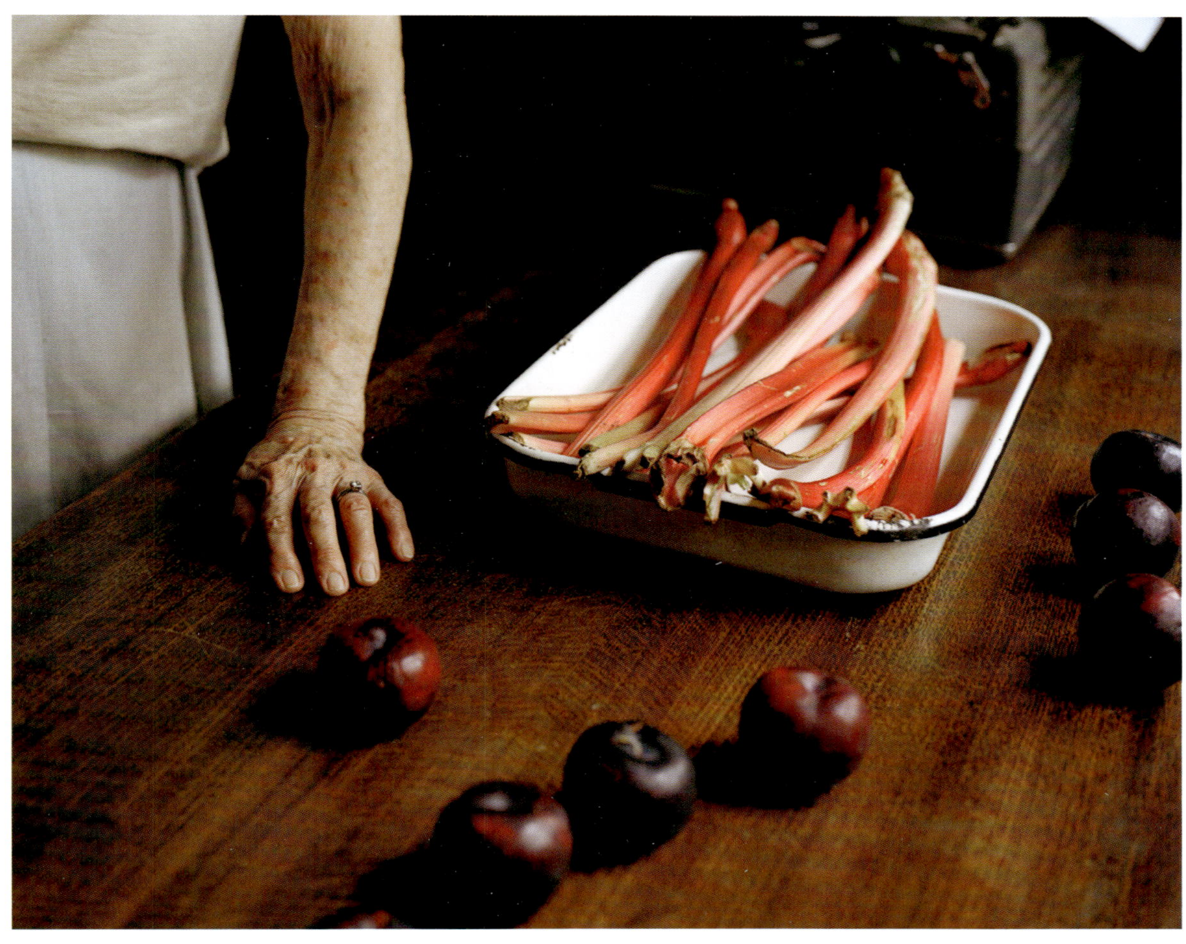

PLATE 124
Susan Worsham, *Margaret's Rhubarb*, 2010

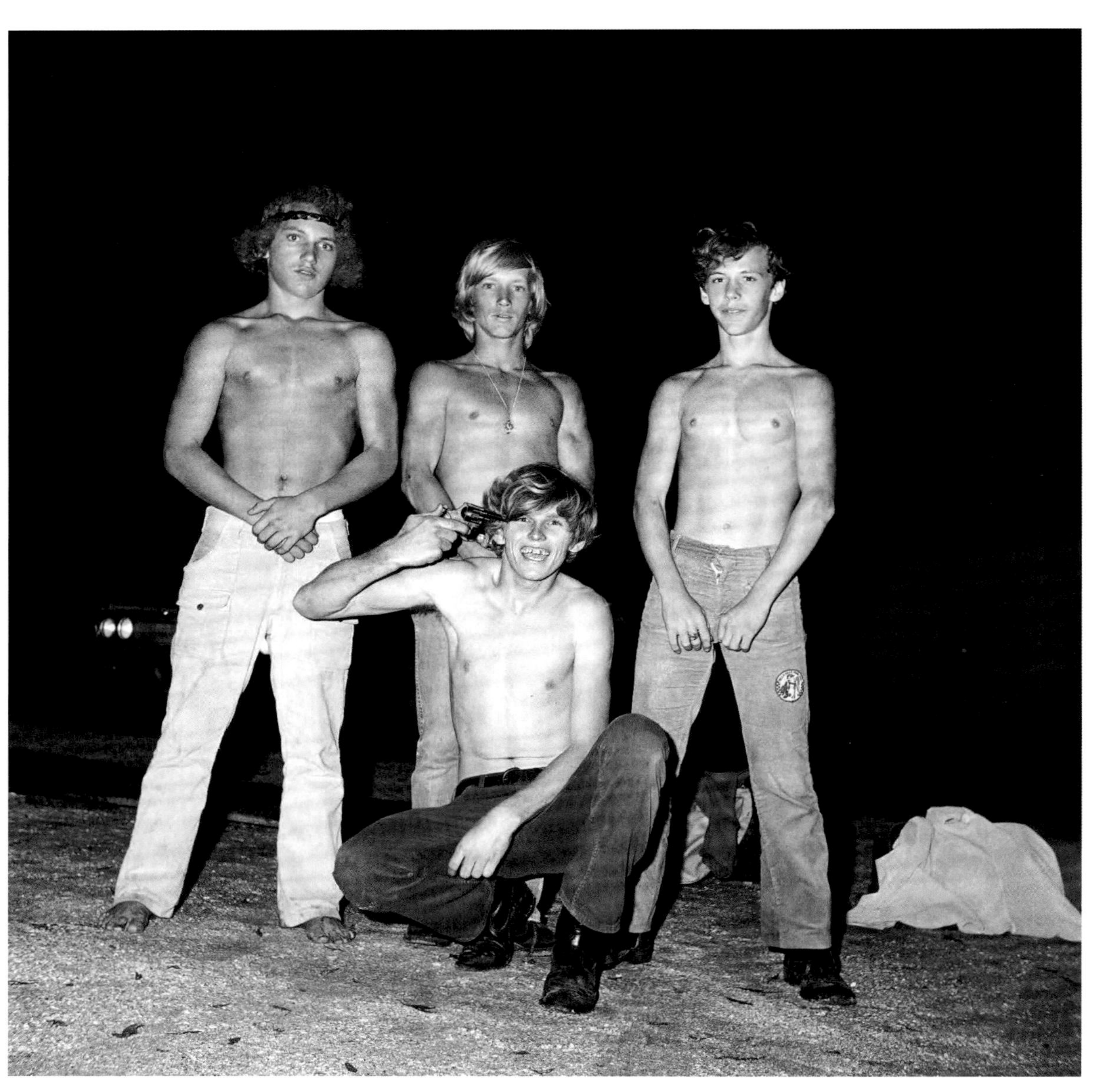

PLATE 125
Bill Yates, *Untitled 34–3*, 1973

LIST OF PLATES

PLATE 1
Shelby Lee Adams (b. 1950)
Lee Hall, Coal Miner, Thorton, Kentucky, 1983
Toned silver gelatin print
12 ¼ × 9 ½ inches
The Do Good Fund, Inc.
2017–95

PLATE 2
Shelby Lee Adams (b. 1950)
Blind Serpent Handler, 1987
Toned silver gelatin print
14 ½ × 18 inches
The Do Good Fund, Inc.
2017–93

PLATE 3
Rob Amberg (b. 1947)
Vicky Ray on Prom Night, Sodom, Madison County, NC, 1977
Archival pigment print
8 ½ × 13 inches
The Do Good Fund, Inc.
2016–35

PLATE 4
Rob Amberg (b. 1947)
Angie and Juanita Shelton Unloading Tobacco, Hopewell, Madison County, NC, 1983
Archival pigment print
8 ½ × 13 inches
The Do Good Fund, Inc.
2016–36

PLATE 5
Rob Amberg (b. 1947)
Estate Auction, Bishopville, SC, 1987
Archival pigment print
8 ½ × 13 inches
The Do Good Fund, Inc.
2016–33

PLATE 6
Dave Anderson (b. 1970)
Toolbelt, 2007
Archival inkjet print
30 × 30 inches
The Do Good Fund, Inc.
2014–22

PLATE 7
Dave Anderson (b. 1970)
Breeze, 2004
Gelatin silver print
15 × 15 inches
The Do Good Fund, Inc.
2013–6

PLATE 8
Dave Anderson (b. 1970)
Jug Riding, 2004
Gelatin silver print
15 × 15 inches
The Do Good Fund, Inc.
2013–5

PLATE 9
Rachel Boillot (b. 1987)
28464, Marty's Place, Teachey, NC, 2014
Archival pigment print
20 × 25 inches
The Do Good Fund, Inc.
2017–145
© Rachel Boillot

PLATE 10
Rachel Boillot (b. 1987)
Postmistress Ida, Sherard, MS, 2013
Chromogenic print
19 ½ × 24 ¼ inches
The Do Good Fund, Inc.
2015–42
© Rachel Boillot

PLATE 11
Sheila Pree Bright (b. 1967)
#SayHerName, from *#1960Now* series, 2016
Archival pigment print
30 × 30 inches
The Do Good Fund, Inc.
2019–25

PLATE 12
Sheila Pree Bright (b. 1967)
#ATLisReady, from *#1960Now* series, 2016
Archival pigment print
30 × 30 inches
The Do Good Fund, Inc.
2019–23

PLATE 13
Rosie Brock (b. 1995)
Woman at Fair, 2017
Archival inkjet print
12 × 12 inches
The Do Good Fund, Inc.
2020–25
© Rosie Brock

PLATE 14
Rosie Brock (b. 1995)
Rose Bush Portrait, 2019
Archival inkjet print
12 × 12 inches
The Do Good Fund, Inc.
2020–24
© Rosie Brock

PLATE 15
Lucinda Bunnen (1930–2022)
Herman Russell and Coretta Scott King, at Spelman College, 1977
Digital print
7 ⅞ × 7 ½ inches
The Do Good Fund, Inc.
2015–90

PLATE 16
Debbie Fleming Caffery (b. 1948)
Harry's Hands, 1984
Gelatin silver print
18 ¾ × 18 ¾ inches
The Do Good Fund, Inc.
2014–7
© Debbie Fleming Caffery

PLATE 17
Keith Calhoun (b. 1955)
I'm the One They Talk About, Big Chief Darryl Montana, the Yellow Pocahontas, 2016
Archival pigment print
23 ⅞ × 15 ⅞ inches
The Do Good Fund, Inc.
2019–29

PLATE 18
Michael Carlebach (b. 1945)
Key West, 1971
Gelatin silver print
13 ⅛ × 8 ⅞ inches
The Do Good Fund, Inc.
2021-7
© Michael Carlebach, 1971

PLATE 19
Michael Carlebach (b. 1945)
Mosquito spray plane, North Key Largo, Florida, 1980
Gelatin silver print
8 ¹¹⁄₁₆ × 13 inches
The Do Good Fund, Inc.
2021–10
© Michael Carlebach, 1980

PLATE 20
Keith Carter (b. 1948)
Garlic, 1991
Gelatin silver print
15 ⅜ × 15 ⅜ inches
The Do Good Fund, Inc.
2013–1
Image courtesy of the Museum of Contemporary Photography at Columbia College Chicago.

PLATE 21
William Christenberry (1936–2016)
Abandoned House in Field (View III), Near Montgomery, Alabama, 1971
Dye coupler color print
3 ¼ × 5 inches
The Do Good Fund, Inc.
2016–121

PLATE 22

William Christenberry (1936–2016)
China Grove Church, Hale County, Alabama, 1979
Archival pigment print
18 ¼ × 23 inches
The Do Good Fund, Inc.
2014–23

PLATE 23

Maude Schuyler Clay (b. 1953)
Delta Hunters, 1984
Color archival print
14 × 14 inches
The Do Good Fund, Inc.
2016–7
© Maude Schuyler Clay

PLATE 24

Maude Schuyler Clay (b. 1953)
Sophie with Kittens, Sumner, Mississippi, 2002
Chromogenic print
14 × 14 inches
The Do Good Fund, Inc.
2014–26
© Maude Schuyler Clay

PLATE 25

Dennis Darling (b. 1946)
Family at Klan Rally, South Carolina, 1974
Archival pigment print
10 ½ × 15 ½ inches
The Do Good Fund, Inc.
2013–22
© Dennis Carlyle Darling

PLATE 26

Colby Deal (b. 1988)
Ethereal, 2017
Lightjet print
18 ¾ × 15 ¾ inches
The Do Good Fund, Inc.
2021–11
© Colby Deal

PLATE 27

Colby Deal (b. 1988)
Pressure Chess, 2017
Lightjet print
15 ⅞ × 19 inches
The Do Good Fund, Inc.
2021–13
© Colby Deal

PLATE 28

Carolyn Drake (b. 1971)
Mexican Grocery, Albertville, AL, 2013
Archival pigment print
20 × 30 inches
The Do Good Fund, Inc.
2016–73

PLATE 29

Carolyn Drake (b. 1971)
Deviled Eggs, 2017
Archival inkjet print
15 × 20 inches
The Do Good Fund, Inc.
2019–11

PLATE 30

Carolyn Drake (b. 1971)
Megan and Hazel Sue, 2018
Archival inkjet print
15 × 20 inches
The Do Good Fund, Inc.
2019–12

PLATE 31

Carolyn Drake (b. 1971)
Elise with Snake, 2019
Archival inkjet print
15 × 20 inches
The Do Good Fund, Inc.
2019–18

PLATE 32

Matt Eich (b. 1986)
Double-Tap, Shell Island, Louisiana, 2009
Archival pigment print
16 × 24 inches
The Do Good Fund, Inc.
2020–3
© Matt Eich

PLATE 33

Matt Eich (b. 1986)
Firehose baptism, Newport News, Virginia
(from the series *The Invisible Yoke, Volume III:
The Seven Cities*), 2013
Archival pigment print
16 × 24 inches
The Do Good Fund, Inc.
2020–5
© Matt Eich

PLATE 34

William Ferris (b. 1942)
*Rose Hill Church, Fisher Ferry Road, Warren County
Mississippi*, 1975
Archival pigment print
13 × 20 inches
The Do Good Fund, Inc.
2016–156
Photograph by William Ferris. Image supplied by
William R. Ferris Collection, Southern Folklife
Collection, The Wilson Library, University of North
Carolina at Chapel Hill.

PLATE 35

William Ferris (b. 1942)
*Rose Hill Church, Fisher Ferry Road, Warren County
Mississippi*, 1975
Archival pigment print
13 × 20 inches
The Do Good Fund, Inc.
2016–154
Photograph by William Ferris. Image supplied by
William R. Ferris Collection, Southern Folklife
Collection, The Wilson Library, University of North
Carolina at Chapel Hill.

PLATE 36

William Ferris (b. 1942)
*Unidentified rider and pony, Yazoo City,
Mississippi*, 1975
Archival pigment print
13 × 20 inches
The Do Good Fund, Inc.
2016–149
Photograph by William Ferris. Image supplied by
William R. Ferris Collection, Southern Folklife
Collection, The Wilson Library, University of North
Carolina at Chapel Hill.

PLATE 37

Jill Frank (b. 1978)
Couple on dock, 2013
Archival inkjet print
30 × 24 inches
The Do Good Fund, Inc.
2016–66
© Jill Frank

PLATE 38

Jill Frank (b. 1978)
everyone who woke up at the yellow house 1, 2016
Archival inkjet print
18 × 15 inches
The Do Good Fund, Inc.
2019–5
© Jill Frank

PLATE 39

Jill Frank (b. 1978)
everyone who woke up at the yellow house 3, 2016
Archival inkjet print
18 × 15 inches
The Do Good Fund, Inc.
2019–7
© Jill Frank

PLATE 40

Peyton Fulford (b. 1994)
Becoming One (Annie and Trevor), 2016
Archival pigment print
19 × 23 ¼ inches
The Do Good Fund, Inc.
2017–138

PLATE 41

Preston Gannaway (b. 1977)
Watermelons (from the series *Between the Devil
and the Deep Blue Sea*), 2013
Archival pigment print
12 ½ × 17 ¾ inches
The Do Good Fund, Inc.
2017–108

PLATE 42

Preston Gannaway (b. 1977)
Sledding (from the series *Between the Devil
and the Deep Blue Sea*), 2010
Archival pigment print
20 × 30 inches
The Do Good Fund, Inc.
2017–110

PLATE 43
Jennifer Garza-Cuen (b. 1972)
Untitled—Girl with Snake, n.d.
Archival pigment print
20 ¼ × 25 ¼ inches
The Do Good Fund, Inc.
2017–124
© Jennifer Garza-Cuen

PLATE 44
Andres Gonzalez (b. 1977)
Kim and Josh, Memphis, TN, 2013
Piezography selenium ink print
15 × 12 inches
The Do Good Fund, Inc.
2016–55
Copyright the artist

PLATE 45
Emmet Gowin (b. 1941)
Danville, Virginia, 1966
Gelatin silver print
4 ½ × 5 ½ inches
The Do Good Fund, Inc.
2016–90
© Emmet Gowin, courtesy Pace Gallery

PLATE 46
Joshua Dudley Greer (b. 1980)
Ponce de Leon Springs, Florida, 2013
Archival pigment print
19 × 24 inches
The Do Good Fund, Inc.
2013–13
© Joshua Dudley Greer

PLATE 47
William K. Greiner (b. 1957)
Mardi Gras P.12– New Orleans, LA, 2017
Inkjet print
7 × 7 inches
The Do Good Fund, Inc.
2018–10
© William Greiner

PLATE 48
William K. Greiner (b. 1957)
Mardi Gras P.1– New Orleans, LA, 2017
Inkjet print
7 × 7 inches
The Do Good Fund, Inc.
2018–18
© William Greiner

PLATE 49
Alex Harris (b. 1949)
Transylvania County, North Carolina, 1972
Archival pigment print
16 ½ × 24 inches
The Do Good Fund, Inc.
2017–23
© Alex Harris

PLATE 50
Alex Harris (b. 1949)
Migrant Worker, Carteret County, North Carolina, 1972
Archival pigment print
16 ½ × 24 inches
The Do Good Fund, Inc.
2017–24
© Alex Harris

PLATE 51
Alex Harris (b. 1949)
Ocean Baptism, Currituck County, North Carolina, 1972
Archival pigment print
16 ½ × 24 inches
The Do Good Fund, Inc.
2017–25
© Alex Harris

PLATE 52
Alex Harris (b. 1949)
Roy Hyde, Fairhope, Alabama, 2010
Archival pigment print
22 × 27 inches
The Do Good Fund, Inc.
2018–70
© Alex Harris

PLATE 53
L. Kasimu Harris (b. 1978)
Come Tuesday (Sportsman's Corner), 2018
Inkjet print
24 × 36 inches
The Do Good Fund, Inc.
2020–18

PLATE 54
Titus Brooks Heagins (b. 1950)
Marivi's Quinceañera, 2008
Archival pigment print
13 × 19 inches
The Do Good Fund, Inc.
2017–129

PLATE 55
Lauren Henkin (b. 1974)
Keep this book of the law always on your lips, 2015
Pigment print
16 × 12 ¾ inches
The Do Good Fund, Inc.
2016–52
© Lauren Henkin

PLATE 56
Lauren Henkin (b. 1974)
Whoever comes to me shall not hunger, and whoever believes in me shall never thirst, 2015
Pigment print
12 ¾ × 16 inches
The Do Good Fund, Inc.
2016–47
© Lauren Henkin

PLATE 57
Jane Robbins Kerr (b. 1933)
Hallelujah Lady, 2006
Gelatin silver print
12 × 8 inches
The Do Good Fund, Inc.
2014–52
Copyright the artist

PLATE 58
Kevin Kline (b. 1965)
Man at Corner Store, New Orleans, 2008
Gelatin silver print
10 ¾ × 10 ¾ inches
The Do Good Fund, Inc.
2015–52
© Kevin Kline

PLATE 59
Stacy Kranitz (b. 1976)
Ronaldson Field Debris Landfill, Alsen, LA, 2017
Archival pigment print
16 ¼ × 24 ¼ inches
The Do Good Fund, Inc.
2018–66

PLATE 60
Paul Kwilecki (1928–2009)
Two-family tobacco tenant house, 1964
Gelatin silver print
4 ¾ × 7 ¼ inches
The Do Good Fund, Inc.
2017–44
© The Paul Kwilecki Family

PLATE 61
Paul Kwilecki (1928–2009)
Willis Park, 1976
Gelatin silver print
6 ¼ × 9 ½ inches
The Do Good Fund, Inc.
2017–68
© The Paul Kwilecki Family

PLATE 62
Paul Kwilecki (1928–2009)
Loggers in the woods, near Attapulgus, 1978
Gelatin silver print
10 ¼ × 10 ½ inches
The Do Good Fund, Inc.
2017–38
© The Paul Kwilecki Family

PLATE 63
Paul Kwilecki (1928–2009)
Flint River Boat Basin, 1979
Gelatin silver print
8 ¼ × 12 ⅜ inches
The Do Good Fund, Inc.
2015–60
© The Paul Kwilecki Family

PLATE 64
Paul Kwilecki (1928–2009)
Elberta Crate & Box Company, 1981
Gelatin silver print
9 ½ × 9 ½ inches
The Do Good Fund, Inc.
2017–65
© The Paul Kwilecki Family

PLATE 65
Paul Kwilecki (1928–2009)
Outside courtroom, 1982
Gelatin silver print
8 ½ × 12 ½ inches
The Do Good Fund, Inc.
2017–61
© The Paul Kwilecki Family

PLATE 66
Paul Kwilecki (1928–2009)
Prisoner with light fixture that he restored, 1998
Gelatin silver print
12 ½ × 8 ¼ inches
The Do Good Fund, Inc.
2017–70
© The Paul Kwilecki Family

PLATE 67

Molly Lamb (b. 1975)

Untitled 9 (from the series *Take Care of Your Sister*), 2016

Archival pigment print

15 × 18 ¾ inches

The Do Good Fund, Inc.

2016–80

© Molly Lamb

PLATE 68

Molly Lamb (b. 1975)

Untitled 10 (from the series *Take Care of Your Sister*), 2016

Archival pigment print

15 × 18 ¾ inches

The Do Good Fund, Inc.

2016–79

© Molly Lamb

PLATE 69

Brittainy Lauback (b. 1978)

Sign, 2013

Archival inkjet print

20 × 16 inches

The Do Good Fund, Inc.

2020–28

© Brittainy Lauback

PLATE 70

Brittainy Lauback (b. 1978)

Pylon, Tuskegee, AL, 2017

Archival inkjet print

20 × 20 inches

The Do Good Fund, Inc.

2020–27

© Brittainy Lauback

PLATE 71

Baldwin Lee (b. 1951)

Children Holding Hands, Vicksburg, MS, 1984

Archival pigment print

15 × 19 inches

The Do Good Fund, Inc.

2016–26

PLATE 72

Baldwin Lee (b. 1951)

Beans, Canton, MS, 1985

Archival pigment print

15 × 19 inches

The Do Good Fund, Inc.

2016–22

PLATE 73

Baldwin Lee (b. 1951)

Basketball Players at Night, Monroe, LA, 1985

Archival pigment print

15 × 19 inches

The Do Good Fund, Inc.

2016–18

PLATE 74

Baldwin Lee (b. 1951)

Baby on Wall, Rosedale, MS, 1986

Archival pigment print

15 × 19 inches

The Do Good Fund, Inc.

2016–31

PLATE 75

Builder Levy (b. 1942)

Coal Camp, Near Grundy, Buchanan County, Virginia, 1970

Gold-tone silver gelatin print

10 × 10 ½ inches

The Do Good Fund, Inc.

2016–108

PLATE 76

Builder Levy (b. 1942)

Prepare to Meet God, Williamson, Mingo County, West Virginia, 1971

Gold-tone silver gelatin print

13 × 12 inches

The Do Good Fund, Inc.

2015–83

PLATE 77

Builder Levy (b. 1942)

Lucious Thompson with Destiny Clark and Delena Brooks, Tom Biggs Hollow, McRoberts, Letcher County, Kentucky, 2002

Gold-tone silver gelatin print

13 × 9 ¾ inches

The Do Good Fund, Inc.

2016–82

PLATE 78

Lawson Little (b. 1945)

Georgia, 1969

Gelatin silver print

4 ½ × 6 ½ inches

The Do Good Fund, Inc.

2016–91

PLATE 79

Deborah Luster (b. 1951)

The Taxidermist's Son, 1994

Gelatin silver print

20 × 20 inches

The Do Good Fund, Inc.

2014–64

PLATE 80

Roger Manley (b. 1952)

Reverend Ruth at Big Number 5, Woodville, GA, 1985

Gelatin silver print

14 × 14 ½ inches

The Do Good Fund, Inc.

2016–2

Copyright the artist

PLATE 81

Carl Martin (b. 1958)

Man on Manhole Cover, 1996–98

Archival pigment print (from digital film scan)

14 × 14 inches

The Do Good Fund, Inc.

2016–11

© Carl Martin

PLATE 82

Carl Martin (b. 1958)

Men in Car (from the series *Downtowners* and *Toward Salvage*), 1996–98

Archival pigment print (from digital film scan)

19 ½ × 19 ½ inches

The Do Good Fund, Inc.

2020–2

© Carl Martin

PLATE 83

Elizabeth Matheson (b. 1942)

Slave Quarters, Stagville Plantation, Durham, NC, n.d.

Archival digital print

16 × 16 inches

The Do Good Fund, Inc.

2017–13

Copyright of the artist

PLATE 84

Richard McCabe (b. 1961)

Dixie, LA, 2014

Fuji-FP100C print

3 × 3 ¾ inches

The Do Good Fund, Inc.

2015–44

PLATE 85

Richard McCabe (b. 1961)

Jackson, MS (Gas Station), 2015

Fuji-FP100C print

3 × 3 ¾ inches

The Do Good Fund, Inc.

2017–118

PLATE 86

Chandra McCormick (b. 1957)

La Shonda Morgan, Ashland Plantation, Port Allen, LA, 1986

Inkjet print

20 ⅞ × 26 ⅞ inches

The Do Good Fund, Inc.

2019–30

PLATE 87

Andrea Morales (b. 1984)

Southern Heritage Classic Parade, 2017

Inkjet print

14 ½ × 21 ¾ inches

The Do Good Fund, Inc.

2020–34

© Andrea Morales

PLATE 88

Andrea Morales (b. 1984)

Monument, 2017

Inkjet print

14 ½ × 22 inches

The Do Good Fund, Inc.

2020–33

© Andrea Morales

PLATE 89

Celestia Morgan (b. 1981)

My Court, 2013

Archival pigment print

11 ½ × 17 inches

The Do Good Fund, Inc.

2016–97

© Celestia Morgan, 2013

PLATE 90

Jimmy Nicholson (b. 1954)

Mr. Mose Tomlin, 617 Broughton Street, Early Morning, Bainbridge, GA, 1978

Gelatin silver print

8 × 5 ½ inches

The Do Good Fund, Inc.

2020–53

© 1978 Jimmy Nicholson All Rights Reserved

PLATE 91
Jimmy Nicholson (b. 1954)
*Mr. Scrap Henderson Inside Red Long's
Bait & Tackle Shop, Bainbridge, GA*, 1980
Gelatin silver print
9 ½ × 7 ⅛ inches
The Do Good Fund, Inc.
2020–54
© 1980 Jimmy Nicholson All Rights Reserved

PLATE 92
Jimmy Nicholson (b. 1954)
*Migrant Farm Worker Picking Tomatoes,
Gadsden County, FL*, 2020
Gelatin silver print
8 ¼ × 5 ½ inches
The Do Good Fund, Inc.
2020–50
© 2020 Jimmy Nicholson All Rights Reserved

PLATE 93
Gordon Parks (1912–2006)
Mr. and Mrs. Thornton, Mobile, Alabama, 1956
Archival pigment print
14 × 14 inches
The Do Good Fund, Inc.
2015–2
Courtesy of and copyright The Gordon Parks
Foundation

PLATE 94
Gordon Parks (1912–2006)
Outside Looking In, Mobile, Alabama, 1956
Archival pigment print
14 × 14 inches
The Do Good Fund, Inc.
2015–4
Courtesy of and copyright The Gordon Parks
Foundation

PLATE 95
Pamela Pecchio (b. 1974)
Mitchell's Arm, 1997
Fiber pigment print
11 × 16 inches
The Do Good Fund, Inc.
2014–60
© Pamela Pecchio

PLATE 96
Caitlin Peterson (b. 1991)
Tallulah Gorge, 2013
Digital chromogenic print
23 ½ × 29 ½ inches
The Do Good Fund, Inc.
2014–63
© Caitlin Peterson

PLATE 97
Eli Reed (b. 1946)
*Children at Play, Tunica (Sugar Ditch),
Mississippi*, 1986
Archival pigment print
11 ⅝ × 17 ⅝ inches
The Do Good Fund, Inc.
2018–2
© Eli Reed/Magnum Photos

PLATE 98
Eli Reed (b. 1946)
*Rhett Anders, Eau Claire Community Council president and real estate agent in front of a historic property,
Eau Claire—North Columbia, South Carolina*, 1999
Archival pigment print
12 × 17 ¹⁵⁄₁₆ inches
The Do Good Fund, Inc.
2018–5
© Eli Reed/Magnum Photos

PLATE 99
Tamara Reynolds (b. 1960)
*Untitled (Kingston, TN, Macy with
Stepfather)*, 2012
Archival pigment print
20 × 26 inches
The Do Good Fund, Inc.
2013–17
© Tamara Reynolds

PLATE 100
Georgia Rhodes (b. 1988)
Roadtrip, 2014
Archival inkjet print
on Canson Platine Fibre rag paper
16 × 20
The Do Good Fund, Inc.
2016–45
© Georgia Rhodes

PLATE 101
Jeff Rich (b. 1977)
*Blue Ridge Paper Mill, The Pigeon
River, Canton, North Carolina*, 2008
Archival inkjet print
28 × 35 inches
The Do Good Fund, Inc.
2014–21
© Jeff Rich

PLATE 102
RaMell Ross (b. 1982)
Interface, 2012
Archival pigment print
19 × 24 inches
The Do Good Fund, Inc.
2016–88

PLATE 103
RaMell Ross (b. 1982)
iHome, 2012
Archival pigment print
19 × 24 inches
The Do Good Fund, Inc.
2016–89

PLATE 104
Ruddy Roye (b. 1969)
Shack Up Inn, 2014
Inkjet print
24 × 36 inches
The Do Good Fund, Inc.
2020–40
Copyright Ruddy Roye

PLATE 105
Sheron Rupp (b. 1943)
Lucille and LaTosha, Moss, Tennessee, 1990
Inkjet print
18 × 26 ½ inches
The Do Good Fund, Inc.
2021–17
© Sheron Rupp

PLATE 106
Jerry Siegel (b. 1958)
J&R's, Deer Heads, Perry County, AL, 2002
Archival pigment print
15 ¼ × 40 inches
The Do Good Fund, Inc.
2014–27
© Jerry Siegel, jerrysiegel.com

PLATE 107
Jerry Siegel (b. 1958)
Homecoming, Selma, AL, 2009
Archival pigment print
11 ⁵⁄₁₆ × 17
The Do Good Fund, Inc.
2014–28
© Jerry Siegel, jerrysiegel.com

PLATE 108
Mike Smith (b. 1951)
Piney Flats, TN, 1999
Archival pigment print
16 ¾ × 21 inches
The Do Good Fund, Inc.
2014–34
Copyright the artist

PLATE 109
Rosalind Fox Solomon (b. 1930)
*Mrs. Ova Heggi and Her Mannequin,
Chattanooga, TN*, 1974
Gelatin silver print
20 × 16 inches
The Do Good Fund, Inc.
2015–13
© Rosalind Fox Solomon,
www.rosalindfoxsolomon.com

PLATE 110
Alec Soth (b. 1969)
The Farm, Angola State Prison, Angola, Louisiana,
2002
Chromogenic print
15 ½ × 19 ½ inches
The Do Good Fund, Inc.
2019–1
Copyright the artist

PLATE 111
Rylan Steele (b. 1980)
Alcott Avenue, Ave Maria, Florida, 2016
Archival pigment print
15 × 19 ½ inches
The Do Good Fund, Inc.
2018–1
Copyright the artist

PLATE 112

Mark Steinmetz (b. 1961)
Off Route 316, Barrow County, Georgia, 1994
Gelatin silver print
12 ⅝ × 17 ⅝ inches
The Do Good Fund, Inc.
2018–49
© Mark Steinmetz

PLATE 113

Mark Steinmetz (b. 1961)
Athens, Georgia, 1995
Gelatin silver print
12 ⅛ × 17 ⅛ inches
The Do Good Fund, Inc.
2018–35
© Mark Steinmetz

PLATE 114

Mark Steinmetz (b. 1961)
Athens, Georgia, 1996
Gelatin silver print
16 × 20 inches
The Do Good Fund, Inc.
2013–7
© Mark Steinmetz

PLATE 115

Mark Steinmetz (b. 1961)
Atlanta Airport, 2016
Gelatin silver print
15 ⅛ × 20 ⅞ inches
The Do Good Fund, Inc.
2018–52
© Mark Steinmetz

PLATE 116

Michael Stipe (b. 1960)
Lynda, Jeremy, kudzu field, Athens, 1982
Archival inkjet print
14 × 21 ¾ inches
The Do Good Fund, Inc.
2020–31

PLATE 117

Michael Stipe (b. 1960)
Kurt Cobain's hands, Grady Avenue, Athens, 1993
Archival pigment print
14 ½ × 21 ¾ inches
The Do Good Fund, Inc.
2020–30

PLATE 118

Brandon Thibodeaux (b. 1981)
Harry Hope; Mound Bayou, MS, 2010
Gelatin silver print
14 × 14 inches
The Do Good Fund, Inc.
2014–2
© Brandon Thibodeaux

PLATE 119

Bertien van Manen (b. 1942)
Amanda, Bobby, Magi on porch, Cumberland, KY, 1987
Archival pigment print
11 ½ × 17 ¼ inches
The Do Good Fund, Inc.
2017–114

PLATE 120

Jeff Whetstone (b. 1968)
Hog Kill, Oscaloosa, Kentucky, 1994
Gelatin silver print
15 × 15 inches
The Do Good Fund, Inc.
2014–44
© Jeff Whetstone

PLATE 121

Brooke C. White (b. 1975)
Dollar Tree Store, Abbeville, MS, 2013
Archival pigment print
20 × 20 inches
The Do Good Fund, Inc.
2017–99
© Brooke C. White

PLATE 122

Alex Christopher Williams (b. 1989)
Untitled from *Black, like Paul* series, 2016
Archival pigment print
16 × 20 inches
The Do Good Fund, Inc.
2020–36
© Alex Christopher Williams

PLATE 123

Vanessa Winship (b. 1960)
Colleen, March 17th, 2012, Lexington, Kentucky, USA, 2012
Archival pigment print
20 × 16 inches
The Do Good Fund, Inc.
2017–115
Copyright the artist

PLATE 124

Susan Worsham (b. 1969)
Margaret's Rhubarb, 2010
Archival pigment print
20 × 25 inches
The Do Good Fund, Inc.
2014–9
© Susan Worsham

PLATE 125

Bill Yates (b. 1946)
Untitled 34-3, 1973
Gelatin silver print
14 × 14 inches
The Do Good Fund, Inc.
2015–79
Copyright the artist

AUTHOR BIOGRAPHIES

JASMINE AMUSSEN is a writer and editor living in Atlanta, Georgia. She is a master of fine arts degree candidate at Bard College.

ROSALIND BENTLEY is the interim director of the narrative nonfiction master of fine arts program in the Grady College of Journalism and Mass Communication at the University of Georgia. She is also deputy editor at the Southern Foodways Alliance's journal, *Gravy*, and editor-at-large for the *Oxford American*. She is a Pulitzer Prize finalist and two-time James Beard Award finalist. Bentley received her bachelor of science in journalism from Florida A&M University. Her work has been anthologized in the *Best American Newspaper Narratives* series and named as a notable essay in *Best American Essays 2021*. Her essay "Iron and Brass" appears in September 2022 in the anthology *Bigger Than Bravery: Black Resilience and Reclamation in a Time of Pandemic* (Lookout Books).

W. RALPH EUBANKS is a visiting professor of English and southern studies at the University of Mississippi. He is the author of *A Place Like Mississippi: A Journey Through a Real and Imagined Literary Landscape* as well as two other works of nonfiction, *Ever Is a Long Time* and *The House at the End of the Road*. His work focuses on race, identity, and the American South, and his writing has appeared in *Vanity Fair*, the *American Scholar*, the *Georgia Review*, and the *New Yorker*. He is a 2007 Guggenheim fellow and a 2021–22 Harvard Radcliffe Institute fellow.

GRACE ELIZABETH HALE is the Commonwealth Professor of American Studies and History at the University of Virginia and a 2018 Carnegie Fellow. She is the author of the award-winning *Making Whiteness: The Culture of Segregation in the South, 1890–1940*; *A Nation of Outsiders: How the White Middle Class Fell in Love with Rebellion in Postwar America*; and, most recently, the award-winning *Cool Town: How Athens, Georgia, Launched Alternative Music and Changed American Culture*, listed as a best book of 2020 by National Public Radio, Slate, *Rolling Stone*, *Kirkus Reviews*, and *Publisher's Weekly*. She has written for the *New York Times*, the *Washington Post*, and Slate and produces a regular column called Shutter that reviews art exhibitions and examines the work of artists making photography in and about the South for *Southern Cultures*. Forthcoming in early 2024 from Little, Brown, her new book *The Lyncher in the Family* explores the history and legacy of racial violence through the story of her white grandfather and the Black man he killed when he served as a Mississippi sheriff.

Born in Washington, DC, artist **LAUREN HENKIN** graduated with a bachelor of arts in architecture from Washington University in St. Louis and now resides in Maine. Her work for the last two decades has focused on how we occupy and relate to space, the built and constructed form, and our surrounding landscape. Her work resides in over twenty institutional collections including the Cleveland Museum of Art, Amon Carter Museum of American Art, Portland Art Museum, and High Museum of Art. Yale University has the largest collection of her work at over 160 works.

JEFFREY RICHMOND-MOLL is curator of American art at the Georgia Museum of Art. He received his bachelor's degree from Princeton University and his master's and doctoral degrees from the University of Delaware. Essays on early American still-life painting, portraiture, neoclassical sculpture, ecocriticism, modernism in the Southwest, magic realism, and wartime material culture have appeared in numerous journals and anthologies. His most recent project, *Extra Ordinary: Magic, Mystery, and Imagination in American Realism*, won the 2021 SECAC Award for Outstanding Exhibition and Catalogue of Historical Materials. He is chair emeritus of the Association of Historians of American Art.

RAMELL ROSS is an artist, filmmaker, writer, and liberated documentarian. His work has appeared in places like Aperture; the Hammer Museum; the Institute of Contemporary Arts, London; the Museum of Modern Art, New York; the National Gallery of Art, Washington, DC; and the Walker Art Center. He has been awarded an Aaron Siskind Foundation Individual Photographer's Fellowship and was a 2020 USA Artist Fellow and a 2022 Solomon Fellow at Harvard University. He holds degrees in sociology and English from Georgetown University and is an associate professor in Brown University's visual art department. His work is in various public and private collections.

JEFF WHETSTONE's photographs and films imagine America through lenses of anthropology and mythology. Trained as a biologist, Whetstone portrays the natural world in a political context and the built environment within the web of nature. His work is in the collections of the Metropolitan Museum of Art, Whitney Museum of American Art, Yale University Art Gallery, and New York Public Library, among others. Whetstone is a professor of photography and the director of the program for visual art at Princeton University.